ADDITIONAL PRAISE

"*Reenvisioning Peacebuilding and Conflict Resolution in Islam* is a tour de force. Qamar-ul Huda challenges established narratives and offers a comprehensive exploration of the multifaceted dimensions of Islamic peacebuilding."
—**Zainab Al-Suiwaj**, president, American Islamic Congress

"Huda's insightful work provides a nuanced and comprehensive understanding of Islamic peacebuilding principles and practices in the modern world. This book outlines a practical vision for fostering inner and communal peace amidst global conflict, highlighting real-world applications of peace education and conflict resolution strategies. This book is essential reading for both scholars and practitioners." —**Tahir Abbas**, professor, Institute of Security and Global Affairs, Leiden University

"Huda's work is a must-read for the international affairs and donor community. There is often a mismatch between peacebuilding and conflict resolution educational endeavors and the reality on the ground in Muslim-majority societies. This engaging and astute analysis unpacks this conundrum and provides an alternate conceptual and practical framework." —**Peter Weinberger**, senior advisor, World Learning Institute

"This is a significant contribution to peace and methods of conflict resolution as recorded in the classical sources of Islam. Huda's work explores the relevance of these Islamic methods and approaches to peacebuilding in contemporary circumstances where there are many misperceptions. This work is a bold vision to help readers understand peacebuilding from the perspectives of Islam." —**Muhammad zia Rehman**, President of International Islamic Research University, Pakistan

"Huda, a master of the art of peace and diplomacy, skillfully blends scholarship, passion, and practicality to offer fresh perspectives on conflict resolution and peacebuilding, as demonstrated in this timely and captivating book." —**Flamur Vehapi**, author, *The Alchemy of Mind* and *Kosovo: A Short History*

"This book fills a crucial and needed gap in understanding the varieties of and complex dynamics of peacebuilding in Muslim countries. Huda successfully demonstrates the wide misconceptions often raised by Western scholars about the compatibility of religious diplomacy and peacebuilding with a paradigm of liberal objectivism toward creating equitable societies." —**Rashad Bukhari**, director, International Research Council for Religious Affairs

"In the face of relentless terrorism and propaganda from radical groups in Muslim-majority communities and unfettered headlines regularly portraying Islam as a violent tradition, this book examines diverse ways in which local Muslim peacebuilders design and implement programs based on nonviolence, reconciliation, community healing, and forging acceptance of others through peace education and their creative moral imagination." —**Qibla Ayaz**, director, Institute of Islamic and Arabic Studies, University of Peshawar

"This book is a comprehensive and insightful exploration of the role of religion in peacebuilding, with a focus on Islam and its diverse traditions. It combines rigorous scholarship with inspiring vision and deserves to be widely read and discussed by all who care about the constructive role of religion in the future of humanity." —**Ammar Khan Nasir**, director of Islamic studies, Gujranwala Institute of Future Technologies University

"Huda makes a forceful case that an understanding of Islamic peacebuilding strategies must be a central part of the international peacebuilding field. His analysis offers fresh perspectives and innovative tools for reconciliation, peace processes, national dialogues on the past. This is a very welcome addition to the growing literature on the role of religion in peacebuilding."
—**Christine Schliesser**, senior lecturer of systematic theology and ethics, Zurich University

Reenvisioning Peacebuilding and Conflict Resolution in Islam

Reenvisioning Peacebuilding and Conflict Resolution in Islam

Qamar-ul Huda

ROWMAN & LITTLEFIELD
Lanham • Boulder • New York • London

Published by Rowman & Littlefield
An imprint of The Rowman & Littlefield Publishing Group, Inc.
4501 Forbes Boulevard, Suite 200, Lanham, Maryland 20706
www.rowman.com

86-90 Paul Street, London EC2A 4NE

Copyright © 2024 by The Rowman & Littlefield Publishing Group, Inc.

All rights reserved. No part of this book may be reproduced in any form or by any electronic or mechanical means, including information storage and retrieval systems, without written permission from the publisher, except by a reviewer who may quote passages in a review.

British Library Cataloguing in Publication Information Available

Library of Congress Cataloging-in-Publication Data

Names: Huda, Qamar-ul, 1968– author.
Title: Reenvisioning peacebuilding and conflict resolution in Islam / Qamar-ul Huda.
Description: Lanham : Rowman & Littlefield Publishers, 2024. | Includes bibliographical references and index.
Identifiers: LCCN 2023057639 (print) | LCCN 2023057640 (ebook) | ISBN 9781538192238 (cloth) | ISBN 9781538192245 (paperback) | ISBN 9781538192252 (ebook)
Subjects: LCSH: Peace—Religious aspects—Islam. | Conflict management—Religious aspects—Islam. | Islam and world politics.
Classification: LCC BP190.5.P34 H835 2024 (print) | LCC BP190.5.P34 (ebook) | DDC 297.2/727172—dc23/eng/20240126
LC record available at https://lccn.loc.gov/2023057639
LC ebook record available at https://lccn.loc.gov/2023057640

∞™ The paper used in this publication meets the minimum requirements of American National Standard for Information Sciences—Permanence of Paper for Printed Library Materials, ANSI/NISO Z39.48-1992.

DEDICATED TO:

Mahsa Amini, whose young life was brutally taken away but gave life to the Women, Life, Freedom Movement in Iran

Dekha Ibrahim Abdi, who is the founder of the Wajir Peace and Development Committee and the Coalition for Peace in Africa

Sayed Ali Shah Geelani, who tirelessly worked for the dignity and human rights of the Jammu and Kashmir people

Contents

Acknowledgments · xi

A Note on Transliteration, Spelling, and Other Conventions · xiii

Introduction · 1

SECTION I. PEACEBUILDING, CONFLICT RESOLUTION, AND VIOLENCE

1. Integrated Peace and Human Security Paradigms · 13
2. Peacebuilding in a Globalized World · 45
3. Rethinking Violence and Countering Violent Extremism · 67

SECTION II. RELIGION AS AN INFLUENTIAL FORCE

4. Religion and Civil Society · 103
5. The Discourse of Islam and Peacebuilding · 120
6. Living in Peace · 145
7. Intrafaith and Interfaith Dialogue and the Challenges of Pluralism · 161

SECTION III. PEACEBUILDING WITH PEACE EDUCATION

8. Peace Education · 187
9. Islamic Peace Education · 207

SECTION IV. ETHICS, MUSIC, AND THE SACRED

10 Modern Islamic Ethics in a Global World — 227

11 The Sacred, Memory, Music, and Peacebuilding — 248

Conclusion — 273

Epilogue — 279

Glossary of Terms — 283

Bibliography — 293

Index — 305

About the Author — 311

Acknowledgments

This work could not have been possible without the generous people who made time to listen to my research work and endless questions on seeking sources. I am grateful to Peter Weinberger, Asma Afsaruddin, Ayse Kadayifci-Orellana, Russel Cogar, and Azza Karam. In tackling sensitive issues of countering violent extremism and rehabilitation, I appreciate my many conversations with Tahir Abbas, Arif Ansar, Hassan Abbas, Ivo Veenkamp, Naureen Chowdhry Fink, Michael Williams, Ahmed Al-Qasimi, Lilah ElSayed, John Horgan, and Hisham H. Hellyer.

At the US Naval Academy, there is no substitute for the collegial support and friendship of Ernie Tucker, Kurtis Swope, Dave Richardson, Gary Espinas, Guilnard Moufarrej, Murhaf Jouejati, Michael Styskal, Stephen Wrage, Lorne Teitelbaum, Deborah Wheeler, Chris Costello, and Samara Firebaugh. So many friends were instrumental in helping me in many ways to navigate peacebuilding organizations and fieldwork research. I am grateful to Ahmed Abbadi, Qibla Ayaz, Maria Saifuddin, Asma Amin Koul, Rashad Bukhari, and Sameena Imtiaz. Learning directly from Sufi and religious leaders was an enlightening experience; for these conversations, I am grateful to Khawaja Kaleem Koreja, Makhdoom Nadeem Hashmi, Syed Mehdi Shah Subzwari, Muhammad Khalid Masud, Moeen Nizami, Shaykh Dr. Tahir ul-Qadri, Suhayl Umar, Iqbal Mujaddidi, Hanif Jalandhari, Maulana Tariq Jameel, Shaykh Mubarak sahib, Mufti Muhammad Taqi Usmani, Shah Awais Sohrwardi, Hakim Muhammad Musa sahib, Shaykh Sibghatullah Mojaddedi, Abdul Sami Al-Ghaznawi, Ahmed Toufiq, Shaykh Nuh Ha Mim Keller, Skaykh Habib Umar bin Hafiz, and Shaykh Izz al-Din al-Khatib.

There are outstanding practitioners in the field of peacebuilding whose work I deeply admire; they have helped me understand the complexities of their work on the ground. I appreciate the kind support of Yasmine Sarhrouny, Houda Abbadi, Abdullah Ahmadi, Noufal Abboud, Jean-Louis Romanet Perroux, Nader Nadery, Raz Mohammad Dalili, Azhar Hussein, Najiba Ayubi, Ahmad Idress Rahmani, Mossarat Qadeem, and Mackey Abogrean.

While my father passed away a decade ago, I am very grateful to my parents, Anwarul and Shafia Huda, who prepared me with many years of support to do this work and use my curiosity to share and teach the knowledge I've acquired. My blessings are too numerous to count for having marvelous family members, Rizwan Huda, Yasmin Huda, Faiza Wahid, and Diane Abrahms, who express their keen interest in my work and support me more than they know. I appreciate the hard work of my editor, Michael Tan, and the brilliant team at Rowman & Littlefield Publishing.

I am grateful to my two sons, Zain and Noah, who supplied impressive technical help with the manuscript and watched me labor over this book project over joining them on movie nights. Finally, this work could not have been possible without my phenomenally patient wife, Rena, who has been a steady source of support and astonishing inspiration.

A Note on Transliteration, Spelling, and Other Conventions

Since this book consists of Urdu, Pashto, Arabic, Persian, Turkish and Bahasa pronouns and terms, it is difficult to comply with one single system of transliteration. In order for the non-specialist to appreciate the terms and broader ideas, diacritics are not used. The two exceptions are in the use of the Arabic letter *'ayn*, as in the word *shari'a*, and to represent the *hamza*, as in the word *Qur'an*. With an exception, I used the *hamza* when in occurs within a word but not when it occurs at the end of the word, for example, *'ulama* is used rather than *'ulama'*. The plural forms are usually indicated by adding an "s" to the word in the singular, as in *hadiths* rather *ahadith*. Non-English terms that occur repeatedly in the book, such as imam or Qur'an, are not italicized.

The translated passages from the Qur'an follow M.A.S. Abdel Haleem, *The Qur'an: A New Translation* (Oxford, UK: Oxford University Press, 2004) or translated by me.

LIST OF TABLES AND CHARTS

2022 Global Terrorism Index	54
UN Report on Preventing Violent Extremism	57
Markers of Radicalization	59
Civil Society Influence	107
Peacebuilding Competency Domains	192
Peace Education Textbook Benefits	195
Data Collection and Monitoring Process	199

Introduction

Traveling through the hills of the Khyber Pakhtunkhwa province or the saintly city of Multan in Pakistan, I recall sitting for days speaking with Shaykh Mubarak sahib and Hakim Muhammad Musa sahib, both Naqshbandi Sufi masters, on topics of envy, humility, justice, reconciliation, and how the modern person needs to escape being a prisoner of their ego. Their ideas were built upon thousands of years of spiritual tradition and a language aimed at being free from the material world by practicing an unwavering commitment to the discipline of *tasawwuf* or Sufism. The unique role of spiritual masters of the Naqshbandi order served as consummate mediators in society and were able to integrate their diverse experiences into a cohesive religious experience throughout the South Asian continent, Central Asia, Eastern European states, the Middle East, and the African continent. These two spiritual Sufi guides mediate between the inner and outer worlds, transforming an understanding of the earthly world and supporting disciples of a spiritual journey. Since those days of intense conversations, I wondered why spiritual practice and spiritual lives were ignored and neglected fields in peacebuilding, conflict resolution, history, and the actual practice of peacebuilding.

This book examines the variety and diversity of strategic peacebuilding activities conducted by Muslim practitioners and Muslim nongovernmental organizations (NGOs). In the past three decades, there has been a surge in interest in ways Muslim scholars and civil society members interpret violence and nonviolence, peacebuilding, conflict resolution, conflict mitigation, peace processes, and frameworks in designing reconciliation and restorative justice platforms. The secular paradigm of analysis is tied to global affairs, and liberal strategies, methods, and approaches to peacebuilding and conflict resolution. The field of peacebuilding and conflict resolution evolved within a liberal objectivism philosophy claiming that religion is inherently irrational, divisive, anti-science, and opposed to the secularization paradigm's mission of creating an equitable society. During the past twenty-five years, religious peacebuilding has proven to be a legitimate field of research and practice in active conflicts but remains siloed and broadly viewed with suspicion by researchers and international organizations. The bias of the secularization paradigm is pervasive not only in academia and research but also in the execution of peacebuilding programs funded by the United Nations, the European Union, the World Bank, and other leading international philanthropic foundations and peacebuilding organizations.

This book contends that one of the key problems with the field of religious peacebuilding, a subset in conflict resolution, is that it is dominated by Catholic, Mennonite, Lutheran, Presbyterian, Methodist, and other Christian scholars who have streamlined, systematized, and normalized these denominations' theories of peacebuilding while occasionally including Hindu, Islamic, Buddhist, Sikh, and other traditions to appear inclusive. However, a careful examination of religious peacebuilding studies reveals that scholars use these very denomination affiliations and denomination sectarianism to define or redefine "true and authentic" perspectives of Christian peacebuilding while proposing universal perspectives onto the field of peacebuilding. In this process of competing with other Christian denominations to illustrate their specific peacebuilding approaches and frameworks, these scholars sought to champion their religious tradition as the source for mediation, peacebuilding, and conflict prevention, but these scholars fundamentally use their concepts of fairness, justice, peace, inclusiveness, and forgiveness based upon some iteration of their church's teachings. On top of this layer of Christian hermeneutics in religious peacebuilding is their context of competition with other denominations to show either authentic tradition or a tradition capable of remaining relevant with postmodernity's grappling of diversity, acceptance, inclusiveness, and institutional importance in relation to the other. Recognizing the research gaps and religious denominational competition manifesting in the field, this book contributes by investigating the application of strategic peacebuilding in Muslim-majority communities and highlighting the distinguishing markers of Islamic peacebuilding and conflict resolution.

This book follows the use of "peacebuilding" in conflict resolution, an overarching concept and practice involving activities in resolving violent conflict to bring the parties to long-term sustained peace. These peacebuilding activities may include training on violence prevention and mitigation, designing and implementing interventions, peace negotiations, peace agreements, creating neutral spaces for dialogue, restorative justice or reconciliation, and trauma healing programs. Building upon this is the term "religious peacebuilding," which involves members of a religion or religious community who rely on their religious tradition as the source of inspiration, identity, and guidance to find ways and practical solutions that are aligned with their values, ethics, principles, and understanding of religious law. The term "faith-based peacebuilding" has been used to include not only the diversity of faith traditions within a particular religion, in this case, the religion of Islam; many researchers and activists use the term to indicate the distinguishing markers of gender dynamics of religious peacebuilding.

SIGNIFICANCE

The uniqueness of religious peacebuilding versus secular approaches is that the former involves spiritual dimensions to frame the problems and spiritual answers to establish peace. This means an understanding of the variety of spiritual realities that transcends the material world and, most importantly, the ways in which the person understands the self in relation to the divine, prophetic history, and how rituals, discipline, language, contemplative tradition, and law binds these universes together. These dimensions take into account that the participants involved in religious peacebuilding often, not always, stress the personal requirements needed for transformation to move away from conflict. Advocating for serious personal contemplation for personal growth, religious peacebuilders view this work as tied to preserving the sacred—life, sites, geography, narratives, rituals, and histories.

This work focuses on peacebuilding and conflict resolution methods and practices by Muslim peacebuilders in an Islamic context. It investigates methods, approaches, and outcomes of Islamic peacebuilding within the conflict resolution field. The fundamental principle is that a faith-based commitment retains the capacity to empower effective social, political, and intellectual action that results in meaningful change. The research presented in this book examines how Muslim peacebuilders use or rely upon their faith to identify values and practices that will motivate individuals and groups to engage in reconciliation. It analyzes case studies on Islamic peace education, mediation, peace negotiations in Libya, and case studies on approaches to preventing violent extremism and countering violent extremism with civil society members. There are astonishing examples of Islamic peacebuilding strategies that enhance local capacity with long-term strategies to engage and empower local actors with critical peacemaking skills. These cases are studied within a vital context: Who are the actors involved in peacebuilding? Who is financing the peacebuilding activities? How do these peacebuilding activities affect identity, ethnicity, religion, culture, gender, and educational levels?

The data collected for this research has short-term and long-term implications for the peacebuilding trends. Collecting data regularly across different geographic regions and cultures allowed me to observe changes and continuity over time. Also, in addition to being a research analyst, I have been directly involved in Islamic peacebuilding and conflict resolution over multiple years as an instructor, consultant, and project director, positions which have yielded invaluable insights into the long-term patterns of civil society organizations (CSOs) and NGOs that provide a better understanding of underlying dynamics at work.

This work studies divergent theories, methods, practices, and approaches to Islamic peacebuilding and conflict resolution in an evolving globalized world. With a grounding in Islamic peacebuilding and the field of peacebuilding, this book raises broader stakes of research for global affairs and on the role of Muslim-majority communities in an interconnected globalized age. In international relations, the cardinal rule of the state to extend its influence is effectively utilizing a combination of hard and soft power in global diplomacy as states rely upon the success of soft power. In contrast, CSOs and NGOs maximize their vast social networks to engage in peace and resolve conflicts. It is essential to position an understanding of peacebuilding activities of CSOs within this soft power geopolitics that aims to provide concrete benefits and persuade others to mitigate conflict and transform their societies. This correlation to the broader field of international affairs and geopolitics sheds essential information on the role of civil society in soft power politics and how some peacebuilding organizations are drastically out of step with local Muslim cultures and religious customs.

METHODOLOGY

The first section, "Peacebuilding, Conflict Resolution, and Violence," analyzes current trends and critical themes in the field of peace, peacebuilding, and conflict resolution theories and practices. Chapter 1 explores tensions between "secular" versus religious approaches to peacebuilding and the variety of biases, limitations, and opportunities in each direction. It proceeds to examine the complex reasons for the appeal to the growing field of Islamic peacebuilding in Muslim-majority communities as a new generation of peacebuilders struggle with modern state-religion alliances, inherited narratives of Islamism, and the exploitation of the religion by local and national institutions. Chapter 2, "Peacebuilding in a Globalized World," explores ways Muslim peacebuilders are structuring their activities to integrate human security paradigms with their value systems and ethics of social change. There is a desire to work beyond individual transformation and interpersonal reconciliation because there is a powerful advocacy dimension for transforming unjust systems to alter structures that contribute to conflict, ethnic sectarianism, and violence.

Chapter 3, "Rethinking Violence and Countering Violent Extremism," examines how the younger generation of Muslim peacebuilders have a distant memory of the September 11 attacks on the United States, and their memories are fundamentally tied to the US wars in Afghanistan and Iraq which intertwined with their analysis of civil wars in Yemen, Libya, Syria, and the failure of the Arab Spring nonviolent protests and the Green Movement self-determination protests in Iran. Contemporary scholars like Tahir Abbas, Arun Kundnani, Sahar Aziz, Chris Allen, Khaled Beydoun, and James Carr have argued that the wars in Afghanistan and Iraq are directly linked to the calamitous rise of violent extremism and religious radicalism, which spurred an intense global reaction against Islam and fueling Islamophobia by right-wing movements. Within this context, I argue that Muslim peacebuilders recalibrated, reconfigured, and redefined a new locally driven vision to support their community's peacebuilding efforts.

Section II, "Religion as an Influential Force," consists of four chapters, beginning with chapter 4, "Religion and Civil Society," which examines the broader impact of prominent twentieth-century thinkers like Albert Camus, Ayn Rand, and John Rawls's ideas promoting pursuing human values in a secular context. To create a conscious citizen interested in participatory liberal principles, they needed to use individual reason and self-interest rationality as a basis for critical thinking. The philosophy of objectivism became the fundamental idea for a true liberal democracy, which meant a rejection of religion. The assumption was unambiguous: Religious beliefs are lessened when analytical thinking rises in liberal democracies. More recently, works by Richard Dawkins (*The God Delusion*), Sam Harris (*The End of Faith*), and Christopher Hitchens (*God Is Not Great: How Religion Poisons Everything*), among others, continue the intellectual genre of minimizing the importance of religion in modernity. The chapter analyzes these anti-religious values in peacebuilding and conflict resolution and how they continue to negate the importance of engaging with religion and faith traditions worldwide.

After analyzing religious peacebuilding in the context of the dominant secular peacebuilding approaches, chapter 5, "The Discourse of Islam and Peacebuilding," addresses the challenges thinkers and practitioners face with Islamic peacebuilding within the field and their communities. Against the backdrop of viewing religion as irrational, nonobjective, unreasonable, and even poisonous, this chapter, "The Discourse of Islam and Peacebuilding," examines the variety of Islamic religious actors and with whom to engage. Men dominate the Islamic religious scholarly class (*'ulama*); how have Western international organizations attempted to work with the *'ulama* or exclude them? Aside from *'ulama*, who have enormous authority with the government and with the public, this chapter explores female Muslim peacebuilders and the challenges they face in operating within conflict zones and male-dominated systems.

Chapter 6, "Living in Peace," discusses how prominent Muslim theologians, philosophers, and Sufi masters have defined essential elements of peace within the tradition. Building upon sources of al-Ghazali's (d.1111) *Kitab Dhamm al Kibr wa-l-'Ujb* ("On Condemnation of Pride and Self-Admiration"), Abu Hafs Umar al-Suhrwardi's *'Awarif al-Ma'rif* ("Knowledge for Divine Encounters") and other scholars of the Chishti, Naqshbandi, Suhrawardi, Shadhili, and Qadiri orders, this chapter examines the way peace is understood and practiced in relation to humility, character, etiquette, commitment, prayers, supplications, sacrifice, fasting, obedience, and surrender. Turning to prominent spiritual masters like Shaykh Ahmad Zarruq and Ibn 'Ata Allah examines how the spiritual tradition of Islam has resources that can contribute toward healing from traumatized experiences of war, conflict, displacement, and other horrendous experiences.

Chapter 7, "Intrafaith and Interfaith Dialogue and the Challenges of Pluralism," assesses and critiques current Islamic scholars, activists, jurists, and peacebuilding practitioners' coexistence, diversity, and pluralism concepts. As identity politics, sectarianism, and ethnic divisions contribute to the fragmentation of societies, this chapter uses a peacebuilding perspective to analyze current Muslim thinkers' understanding of challenges that impact social cohesion, inequality, and the promotion of tolerance.

Section III, entitled "Peacebuilding with Peace Education," consists of two chapters studying peacebuilding efforts through peace education programs and utilizing peace messaging educational campaigns in Muslim-majority communities. It begins with chapter 8, "Peace Education," which examines the purpose and function of peace education programs and a case study of a peace education project in Libya. There is a common consensus among scholars, practitioners, and international development organizations that peace education is the antidote to existing conflict because it brings interactive transformative education to communities experiencing conflict. The field of peace education is approximately seventy-five years old; it has evolved with interdisciplinary contributions and perspectives on pedagogy, teaching content, monitoring and evaluation, and other areas of effectiveness. This chapter challenges the discourses on the purpose and accepted outcomes of peace education in Muslim-majority communities by affirming that without consultation with local CSOs and experts, these curricula lack fundamental cultural, ethical, ethnic, and religious principles in the frameworks of the peace curricula.

After examining the complexities of a peace education curriculum, chapter 9, "Islamic Peace Education," explores case studies from Pakistan, the Philippines, Indonesia, Afghanistan, and Bangladesh on designing, structuring, and implementing Islamic and "secular" peace education curricula in public and private schools. The divergent thinking and formulation of curricula, and ultimately the implementation of a peace curriculum, is dependent on complex relationships with the international donor organizations, philanthropies who have their institutional priorities on effective peacebuilding, and the internal dynamics of the local CSOs and the relentless interference of local government ministries with bureaucratic obstacles. The data collected from these case studies were based on interviews with focus groups with religious scholars, CSOs, and NGOs, illustrating the complex way the final educational product was implemented in schools.

Finally, section IV, entitled "Ethics, Music, and the Sacred," examines an often-missing dimension of cultural and social approaches to peacebuilding: an integrative and interdisciplinary approach to understanding ethics, aesthetics, music, memory, language, rituals, and the role of the arts. Muslim-majority communities not only inherited a living civilization but a tortuous complex modernization process that fragmented, compartmentalized, and lessened the integrative nature of these cultural experiences. Chapter 10, "Modern Islamic Ethics in a Global World," explores shared values that foster harmony, inclusivity, tolerance, the desire to know the "other," and enhance social cohesion. Building upon a convergence between Western and Islamic approaches toward cultivating peace, it examines some critical issues within Islamic ethics and ways to reconcile them to pursue peacebuilding efforts—a perennial study of critical ethical questions facing Muslim peacemakers and the broader Muslim-majority questions. Critiques of the Islamic peacebuilding field claim that it is insular and inward-facing and does not engage with the global struggles of postmodernity, environmental change, and issues relating to fairness and justice. In response to these questionable claims, this chapter builds upon Paul Lederach's *Moral Imagination: Art and Soul of Building Peace* and Tariq Ramadan's *Radical Reform: Islamic Ethics and Liberation*. In a world that emphasizes scholarship and programming activities tied to "disrupting discourse narratives," this chapter analyzes the varied but compelling issues of "non-disruptive discourses" within Islamic ethics of pluralism, ethics of responsibility to self and others, service ethics, the ethics of being an agent of positive change, ethics of active citizenship, and applied ethics of contributing to the betterment of all communities.

Chapter 11, "The Sacred, Memory, Music, and Peacebuilding," expands upon how beliefs, practices, and rituals associated with the spiritual tradition of Islam foster a transcendental connection with the divine. The inner peace approach within the Islamic peacebuilding field enables practitioners to emphasize the power of using the memory of the past, specifically how the recollection of sacred events of the prophetic and saintly periods opens oneself to a more profound knowledge of the divine. Spiritual performance music, poetry, and powerful pilgrimages to saint shrines are believed to create a pristine encounter with the sacred, opening the door for self-examination, reconciliation with shortcomings, and a path toward inner peace. It shows how Muslim peacebuilders capitalize on memory, music, aesthetics, and the arts in their peacebuilding activities.

The epilogue was written during the heart-wrenching time of October 7, 2023, when Hamas attacked Israeli civilians and are still holding hostages, and the Israeli invasion and relentless bombardment upon the Gazan civilian population killed over fourteen thousand civilians. With close friends on both sides of the war, I am sensitive to the quest for human security of both Palestinians and Israelis and have observed how the past three decades of violence have further polarized their societies. The polarization of Israeli and Palestinian societies has reached global proportions, with most Western governments supporting the Israeli invasion of Gaza, whereas most global CSOs and NGOs, including the Secretary General of the United Nations, have advocated for a unilateral ceasefire to deliver humanitarian aid to Gaza and address the roots of the conflict. I share my thoughts on a broken Western conflict resolution model, which has made it vividly clear that peacebuilding and conflict mitigation are only applied for a particular place, time, or region and when political actors are aligned with specific agendas. Despite the seven and half decades of this particular conflict, I believe this book's contribution to highlighting the role of religious peacebuilding offers a real commitment by civil society members, scholars, spiritual guides, and networks, and tradition provides precise answers to prevent conflict and create peaceful societies.

Section I

PEACEBUILDING, CONFLICT RESOLUTION, AND VIOLENCE

Chapter One

Integrated Peace and Human Security Paradigms

In 2022, I traveled to Afghanistan and met Zabiullah Mujahid, the Islamic Emirate of Afghanistan's deputy minister of information and culture, for an extensive interview. While passing the shopping mall, customers hustled for sales support at wedding shops, tailor shops, and mobile phone shops; there were lines of customers outside these stores waiting their turn to enter the stores. Mujahid told me, "You cannot drink chai without Afghanistan's classic sheer pira," a milk fudge dessert. He only took a few sips of his chai, but he was attentive to my questions about Taliban governance and the global community's isolation of Afghanistan. "Listen," he firmly said, "this country has a long way before a renaissance [occurs], but it will happen in front of the whole world. You'll see."

Mujahid's optimism is not an anomaly; Taliban government officials I interviewed had well-choreographed responses claiming that the Islamic Emirate is seeding better times. Outside of the Taliban's estranged bubble, teachers, lawyers, college students, and a few fledging civil society groups couldn't feel differently about Afghanistan's future. "There are no jobs; we have no money," said a lawyer recently fired from the Ministry of Education. Men, women, and children beg on the street, stating they haven't eaten for days. A close friend of mine, a researcher with a conflict and peace institute based in Kabul, said the Taliban shut down his organization because they knew it was supported by the US Agency for International Development and the US Institute of Peace, believing their work portrayed a negative image of Afghanistan.

In retrospect, the winter of 2022 was considered one of the worst humanitarian crises in Afghanistan's history, with access to food, clean water, and human security at an all-time low. For twenty years, American diplomats were a major presence in Afghanistan as US Special Representative for Afghanistan Tom West reminded the global community: "The United States has been the largest donor of aid to Afghanistan to avoid a famine and a shortage of food to civilians."[1] However, in my discussions, merchants said emphatically that they have no food supplies, and meat merchants said their supplies are down significantly. But, since the capture of Kabul by Taliban forces in August 2021, American policy experts have tried to understand the strategic mistakes made in Afghanistan. The Afghanistan War Commission was formed in 2022 to identify lessons from America's war in Afghanistan, seeking to understand the tensions between civilian and military efforts, how the deep-seated corruption sowed by nation-building activities contributed to corruption cycles and the exit strategy's mishandling. Over two years later, the problem remains the same: Washington cannot shift from the past to the present. On multiple occasions, I met with State Department officials and Afghan experts about the human security problem by focusing on the internal power dynamics of the Taliban: what governs their mentalities, which internal factions are struggling for power, the divergent roles of the Taliban's religious Deobandism, and, importantly, how to use this information to be informed about them and remain engaged to shape the Taliban's development in the region.

I have argued that increasing our knowledge of the Emirate's internal dynamics, divisions, and the complex factors that impact decision-making will not lessen the American commitment to freedom of speech or undermine advocacy for women's rights and human rights. Rather, the United States and its allies would be better positioned to influence, shape, and pressure the Taliban by bringing them closer to respecting and perhaps implementing fundamental principles of democracy. The Taliban's internal disputes over inclusivity, governance, multilateral engagement with Western states, and human rights are all heavily split by the different branches of thought of Deobandism, particularly the nuanced understandings formed during the war. A faction of "global-minded" thinkers believes funds from the global community should be invested in the economy and infrastructure, which is ultimately tied to engaging in global diplomacy. Among the fighters within the Haqqani clan, there is intense pressure to implement the ideals they fought for in the public sphere. The Haqqani Taliban are used to making their own decisions on the battlefield, but they have recently expressed fatigue with the slow pace of decision-making at the *Shura* Council in Kandahar. The balancing act for the Emirate is to appease all the factions at the table while not losing trust in global diplomacy.

DEOBANDISM DIVIDED

The Emirate of Afghanistan's primary leader is a scholar of Islamic jurisprudence named Mawlawi Haibatullah Akhundzada. Akhundzada was trained in Sunni Deobandi Islam, which was initially a reform theological movement in British India to counter imperialism, counteract forced conversions to Hinduism, and sustain Muslim educational institutions. However, it has evolved into a modern movement with Salafi influences—political aspirations to redesign society according to narrow interpretations of Islamic principles of law. Akhundzada's acting defense minister is Mullah Mohammad Yaqoob, who is Mullah Omar's son.[2] The acting deputy prime minister and public face of the Emirate is Abdul Ghani Baradar, who was the key negotiator with the Americans during the Qatar peace process. Sirajuddin Haqqani is the interior minister, and his uncle, Khalil Haqqani, is the minister of refugees; the United States wants both for terrorism charges. Haqqani fighters protect the outskirts of Kabul and major ministries and hotel buildings. In addition, the Haqqani clan has a tight network of loyal fighters across the provinces.

Baradar and Sher Muhammad Abbas Stanikzai, the deputy minister of foreign affairs, represent the more politically minded who wanted to create a more global-thinking state. Among the top leaders is the acting prime minister, Mullah Mohammad Hassan Akhund, who was formally the Taliban's foreign minister in the 1990s. To illustrate their sense of inclusivity, the Taliban said they appointed numerous Tajik and Uzbek ministers from Panjshir, Baghlan, and Sar-e Pol provinces. Although they made room for Tajiks, Uzbeks, and Turkmen, there are still no Shias, Hazaras, or any other minorities in the government.

The real power is the *Shura* Council of key elder Taliban leaders in Kandahar—the advisory body for political affairs, where the current chief, Hibutallah Akhunzada, is based. These decision-makers in Kandahar are primarily Pashtun but have members from northern, central, and western provinces. In the backdrop of the decision-makers are Hamid Karzai, who served as president from 2004 to 2014, and Dr. Abdullah Abdullah, the former chief executive of Afghanistan—both of whom meet regularly with the Emirate's leadership in Kabul and the *Shura* Council. Baradar, Din Mohammad Hanif, Prime Minister Hasan Akhund, Minister of the Economy Din Mohammad Hanif, and Minister of Finance Hedayatullah Badri represent a branch of the Talibs that is practical, is interested in global relationships, hopes to foster economic ties, and sees multilateral relations as key to ending Afghanistan's isolation. These Taliban members have lived in Qatar; their practical worldview is connected to their experience traveling the world, leading them to believe that Afghanistan should be integrated into world affairs and global markets.

However, within the cabinet are Yaqoob Haqqani and Acting Deputy Minister of Defense Abdul Qayyum Zakir, who prioritize consolidation of military power domestically and stress the importance of protecting Afghanistan's borders and identifying loyalists of the previous regime, whom they believe directly operated with the resistance movement. Other key figures, such as Ministry of Technology and Defense official Maulvi Attallah Omri and Ministry of Justice official Maulvi Abdul Karim, advocate for immediate reforms by instituting "*shari'a* at all levels of society" to lay the foundations of a conservative, theocratic state. Omri tells me, "Technology will make the difference to our defensive abilities and [ensure] we have a holistic Islamic society."[3]

These former fighters believe their sacrifices during the fight against "foreign intervention" and "Western puppet regimes" were tied to establishing an emirate that implements Islamic idealism. Concurrently, the Haqqani and Zakir factions in the western and southwestern provinces are in the field fighting the nascent National Resistance Front, and former Taliban fighters in the western provinces are getting exhausted with promises from the *Shura* Council elders and the verbose Taliban bureaucrats in Kabul.

"GLOBAL-MINDED" TALIBAN ON THE MOVE

Perhaps overlooked by most Afghanistan experts and State Department officials was the savvy effectiveness of the "global-minded" Taliban in two instances: a bilateral meeting with Norway in January and the Tashkent Conference over six months later. In January 2022, Norway hosted a bilateral meeting with the Taliban in Oslo aimed at salvaging its two decades of work in Afghanistan's healthcare, education, and civil society sectors. Many in the West criticized Norway's dialogue with the Taliban for legitimizing their human rights violations and repression of women's access to education and employment. However, priding itself as an international mediator, Norway viewed this meeting as a critical step toward bilateral dialogue. In addition to facilitating discussions on humanitarian relief to save Afghan civilians from famine, Norway's first move was to test its leadership in post-conflict development and mediation. Notably, the Taliban delegation reported to the Kandahar *Shura* that the meeting produced positive first steps toward building bilateral relations.

The Oslo meeting was an internal victory for Baradar and Akhund because it undeniably signaled to the internal factions and to the *Shura* that their team was able to rebuild bilateral relationships, cooperate with Western leaders, move Afghanistan out of isolation without rattling ultra-conservative elements within the Taliban, and, most importantly, solidify investment from China, Russia, and Uzbekistan. Afghanistan experts dismissed the Oslo meeting as a publicity stunt for the Taliban to gain international legitimacy and seek funds. However, skeptics miss Norway's ability to gain trust to permit its hospitals, clinics, private schools, nongovernmental organizations (NGOs), and specific vocational programs for girls to operate throughout Afghanistan. Under the radar, without interference from Taliban fighters, Norwegian all-girls schools and educational NGOs are working in the northwest and northeast of Afghanistan with Taliban support.

TALIBAN ENGAGEMENT

With support from non-Western allies like Turkey, Russia, and China, Uzbekistan hosted the Tashkent Conference in July 2022 to address Afghanistan's security and economic development. With over thirty countries and 125 delegates in attendance, Uzbek President Shavkat Mirziyoyev said, "The international isolation of Afghanistan shall inevitably lead to further deterioration of the humanitarian situation. It is important not to allow this since the fate of millions is at stake."[4] Mirziyoyev's economic deputy outlined several ongoing bilateral projects, including a proposed trans-Afghan railway running from Termez at the Uzbekistan-Afghanistan border through Mazar-e-Sharif and Kabul to Peshawar in Pakistan, and an energy power transmission line running from Uzbekistan to Afghanistan.

The globally thinking Taliban factions have strong support from the Kandahar *Shura* to build infrastructure projects with Central Asian, Russian,

Chinese, Iranian, Pakistani, and Indian private and public investment. Hanif and Badri were instructed to connect Afghanistan with Central Asia, Iran, Pakistan, and India, which will inevitably transform markets, open trade opportunities, and invest in the agriculture and energy sectors, radically diversifying the economy. Hanif, Badri, and Baradar are taking the lead in driving Chinese interest in expanding the China-Pakistan Economic Corridor (CPEC) into Afghanistan and developing Afghanistan's three trillion dollar mineral industry.[5] At the Tashkent Conference, Chinese Foreign Minister Wang Yi pledged humanitarian aid and technical and financial support for Afghan farmers. US envoys Tom West and Rina Amiri attended the Tashkent Conference and pressed for girls' education, the return of women to work, and the peace and security of Afghanistan. The Oslo and Tashkent meetings illustrate how more than thirty countries are moving ahead in identifying specific economic, security, and infrastructure projects to expand their influence while the United States lags in engaging with the Emirate. Two and half years after the US withdrawal, Washington still lacks the appetite for strategic engagement with the Emirate, regrettably limiting opportunities for the United States to demonstrate leadership influence and steering the Taliban's second return with judicious decisions.

Concerning Afghanistan, the seismic shift of a religious scholar and Deobandi leader like Maulawi Akhundzada to ascend to a prominent public role demonstrates a nexus between faith and political actors. The United States must define a diplomatic strategy to work with leaders like Akhundzada and Yaqoob. Indeed, Washington's decision to withdraw from Afghanistan was because the American policymakers knew the nation-building costs were enabling corruption, poor governance, insecurity, codependency on international aid, and the global industry of civil society organization (CSO) operations. The Afghan political leadership from 2001–2021 was effectively using the fears of Western and regional allies to pump in more funds into a botched maladministered crooked elite class interfacing with the allies. However, while Afghanistan's political elite class was profiteering in shady deals with no accountability, the departure of the US and Western allies opened the power vacuum for regional players like Iran, Turkey, Pakistan, and China. To move beyond the unscrupulous exploitation of the global powers by Afghanistan's elite malfeasance, the United States should concentrate on a strategic relationship, such as diminishing global terrorist threats of Al Qaeda and the Islamic State–Khorasan Province. A well-defined partnership with the Emirate will empower them to make progress in promoting common values such as the rule of law, freedom of expression, the rights of minorities, women's rights, girls' education, and establishing an independent judiciary. The combination of being disengaged and lacking religious experts is handicapping American diplomacy and political leverage in Afghanistan and beyond.

LOSS OF RELIGION EXPERTISE

Since August 15, 2021, when the Americans left Kabul, there has been no functioning American embassy in Kabul, and there is an incohesive "don't ask" approach to Afghanistan. Unfortunately, DC policymakers have not defined a strategic, meaningful diplomatic relationship with leading Taliban officials. The United States can leverage its diplomatic relationship with the Emirate by rapidly increasing its religion and foreign affairs expertise. For example, in 2012, Secretary of State John Kerry established the Office of Religion and Global Affairs, which supported American diplomats in understanding the complex, fluid dynamics of religious communities and institutions. Kerry recognized that diplomats needed to factor in these important stakeholders to foster long-term political relationships and security.[6] The office of thirty-eight foreign service and religion experts supported National Security Council directors, the secretary of state's office, regional bureaus, and other functional areas at the State Department. As a result, the State Department had diverse expertise in the Sunni Islam of Afghanistan and South Asia, the Shi'i Islam of Iraq and Iran, Buddhism in Myanmar, African traditional religions, various dharma traditions worldwide, and the orthodox churches in Ukraine and Russia. The de facto termination of the Office of Religion and Global Affairs by former Secretary of State Rex Tillerson[7] created an enormous vacuum at the State Department because currently there is a significant lack of religion expertise and strategists available to counsel senior leadership and simultaneously work with religious leaders in the context of fluctuating internal religious, political, and social dynamics.

Instead, under Secretary of State Mike Pompeo, the State Department shifted its focus to promoting international religious freedom, thereby losing religion experts who knew intricate details of transregional networks and how complex internal divisions of religious thought and practice contributed to factionalism or sustained economic interests. Office of Religion and Global Affairs experts moved beyond trite categories of "moderate," "liberal," "conservative," and "traditional" religious actors, which were meaningless because they do not supply detailed information to help diplomats navigate the complicated landscape of religion, especially in Afghanistan. It was neither the office of religion and conflict nor the office of exploiting religion for security and stability. That is, during the US cooperation with the UN Assistance Mission in Afghanistan, the UN Assistance Mission for Iraq, the UN Investigative Team to Promote Accountability for Crimes Committed by ISIL, and the civil wars in Yemen, Libya, and Syria, the Office of Religion and Global Affairs remained faithful to policy priorities to engage with religious leaders and build diplomatic relationships with a variety of religious communities.

Currently, in 2023, appointed by Secretary Blinken, the Ambassador-at-Large for International Religious Freedom is Rashad Hussain—the head of the Office of International Religious Freedom (IRF)—has a team of twenty-four, with only three experts on religion and international affairs.[8] Moreover, IRF staff members mainly do programming activities, plan for the ambassador's speaking engagements, and position him with high-level meetings. Without the religion and global affairs expertise at the US State Department, they are prevented from directly engaging with diverse religious stakeholders to advance US policy priorities and work with their counterparts in other ministry of foreign affairs. Within the State Department, the IRF office is viewed as the home of "all things religious." If an American embassy official needs a detailed strategic engagement policy for Deobandis in the broader Central and South Asia region, they are directed to the IRF office. Suppose an American diplomat in Cairo needs to understand why the local Egyptian Coptic Orthodox Church does not align with Russian Orthodox demands to isolate Ukrainian churches. In that case, they must turn to the IRF. The absurdity in eviscerating expertise in religion and global affairs at a time when it is desperately needed exemplifies how American diplomats, policymakers, and strategists are out of step with current foreign policy needs and understanding the role of religion in international affairs.[9] Ministries of foreign affairs of Western countries, including the US Department of State, did not retain or recruit dedicated religion and international affairs experts. Without expertise, state actors are not acknowledging the diversity of religious political actors on the world political stage, like the Taliban, and how they are acutely aware of their political value in regional and international politics. Religious leaders understand that local governments and global coalitions are seeking them out to counterbalance the weight of China or Russia or key policy priorities such as preventing the spread of violent extremism. Instead of finding common ground to build multilateral ties for stability and economic benefits, the state infrastructure lacks a key dimension in analyzing and engaging with Muslim religious-political actors. Ultimately, the key issue with Afghanistan is whether the Emirate can deliver stability, a working economy for the nonelite class, and prevent further conflict with the former regime resistance fighters—all while improving conditions for the Afghanistan population. The Taliban has numerous challenges transforming from militia-minded fighters to nation-building technocrats; however, the power dynamics within the Taliban are enabling the global-minded Taliban actors to move ahead with forging multilateral engagements.

In public forums, I have vociferously pointed out that the State Department is crippled without religion and foreign affairs experts to provide thoughtful sensible policy guidance on religious, political activism and insights into how the Taliban maneuver within social hierarchies. Reinstating experts who can analyze divergent interpretations of Sunni Hanafi Islam within Taliban power structures will improve the State Department's analysis, especially regarding how the Emirate thinks of governance, finance, law enforcement, global engagement, and policymaking dynamics.

PEACEBUILDING AND HUMAN SECURITY

In retrospect, the COVID-19 pandemic from 2020 to 2022 was a fortuitous time to reflect on our lives and work-life balance and rethink what is important to us and our communities. Within the human security field, there were reflections on thinking for creativity to identify new frameworks and approaches for transforming protracted conflicts into tomorrow's sustainable peace. Despite some common thinking during a global pandemic and in unpredictable and uncertain times—it was an excruciating time of suffering and loss of loved ones, which elicited thoughts tied to frenetic insecurity, ambiguity, and relentless confusing messages—the public health and political leadership resulted in depressing thoughts or a more extraordinary heightened imagination. During these painful times of trying to forget loss, suffering, and unanticipated isolation from social and professional circles, there were emerging thoughts from and for practitioners on rethinking the infrastructure of the peacebuilding field—from the role of the global donor industry to ways CSOs could create cluster networks to share best practices, from more inclusive activities to center gender and youth activities to thinking about using technology effectively to monitor and evaluate the complex on-the-ground work.

During the COVID-19 pandemic, in 2020, the World Health Organization and the UN Children's Fund claimed that twenty-three million children globally missed basic vaccinations.[10] Even with robust government efforts to minimize the spread of the pandemic, health experts, policymakers, and researchers needed to rethink new strategic ways to manage many moving parts. The pandemic illustrated that health security is no less essential than a personal health issue but rather a human security issue. There were arguments by economists stressing that for any real economic growth to return, governments must work with industry leaders for an astute aggressive pandemic policy. Again, we were reminded of the dependency on technology and how it is inexorably important for work, the economy, and saving the lives of those who are struggling within conflict zones and fragile states. We realized that digital technology allowed us to modestly continue our lives, with several modifications, in areas of education, governance, banking, and professional work. But reliant on digital technology meant rethinking new ways to manage personal lives and business affairs, and from conducting global diplomacy to adjusting practices to mitigate conflict.

But how do we rethink human security and integrated peace in a post-pandemic era? Should we just continue the status quo of international donors connecting with local CSOs to implement peacebuilding and conflict resolution programs? How do we develop new thinking about strategies of peacebuilding considering the lessons we learned from our ill-preparedness during and post-pandemic? Do scholars, practitioners, international donor organizations, CSOs, NGOs, and industry leaders adjust or pivot toward new frameworks of peacebuilding? I pose these questions for this study to think more deeply about these issues and to factor in more nuanced analytical thinking and practice in peacebuilding. There is no shortage of books dedicated to thinking better, thinking for progress, efficient thinking for results, and strategic thinking. The field ranges from self-help, psychology, behavioral sciences, education, management, business, philosophy, religion, new age, meditation, finances, and other related fields. It is outside this study to navigate through these books, but the key concern here is: what do we really mean with rethinking? Can the field of "thinking" provide new perspectives and approaches, as well as point out gaps in human security and integrated peacebuilding field.

I will examine several key works in the field of thinking, purposely outside of peace and conflict studies, to illustrate why these ideas are relevant to peacebuilding. For instance, an expert in biological anthropologist, Helen Fisher, focuses on thinking and understanding personality and temperament as the essential building blocks of the self. Fisher asserts that personality is composed of two fundamentally different types of traits: those of "character" and those of "temperament." Our character traits stem from our culminative experiences: our childhood games, your family's interests and values, how people in your community express love and hate, what relatives and friends regard as courteous or perilous, how those around us worship, what they sing, when they laugh, how they make a living—innumerable cultural experiences build your unique set of character traits. Simultaneously, the balance of your personality is your temperament, all the biologically based tendencies that contribute to your consistent patterns of feeling, thinking, and behaving. Self-knowledge is by thinking about how personality and temperament conflict or complement each other.

Martin Seligman of the University of Pennsylvania, the father of positive psychology, speaks of the five pillars of well-being: positive emotion, engagement, positive relationships, meaning and purpose, and accomplishment, or PERMA. Seligman's popular work suggests that reducing disabling conditions like isolation, poverty, disease, depression, aggression, negative thoughts, and ignorance is only part of the work on recuperating or healing. Seligman thinks modern scientists and public policy practitioners are solely remediating the disabling conditions, but Seligman's PERMA framework suggests that this is insufficient. According to Seligman, if you wish to flourish personally by getting rid of depression, anxiety, anger, loneliness, and pain, one needs to focus on positive thinking and the discipline of exercising PERMA. I have yet to find Seligman's work in peacebuilding activities or presented as a framework to use in the area of integrated peacebuilding.

Kathryn Schulz, an expert in the field of "Wrongology" highlights the importance of regret, commonly referred to as the psychology of regret, where individuals might find optimism in the pessimistic meta-induction from the history of science. She thinks that since we now know scientific theories of the past have often been wrong, it's safe to assume our own present-day theories are quite possibly wrong as well. By being wrong on topics, one can uncover mistakes to revise and improve our understanding of the world. The idea is that error, failure, misunderstanding, and uncertainty are not only common to both the scientific method and the human condition but also essential to refine thinking. Failure, or more accurately failed thinking, is not something to be avoided but rather something to be embraced. This is not only part of the scientific method that benefits laboratory research, but for these scholars, the same approach can be applied to design, arts, information technology, sports, engineering, entrepreneurship, and even daily life itself. All creative avenues can yield maximum insights when failures are embraced and not ignored.

The key question is: what scientific concept will improve everybody's cognitive toolkit? A group of influential scientists, authors, and thought architects believe there is a toolkit to think in *This Will Make You Smarter: New Scientific Concepts to Improve Your Thinking*. It is an impressive anthology of essays by 151 major thinkers on subjects as diverse as the power of networks, cognitive humility, the thinking paradoxes of daydreaming, information flow of thinking, collective intelligence, and a wide range in between. Together, they construct a powerful toolbox of thinking called metacognition, a new way to think about thinking itself. Editor of the anthology John Brockman states the "scientific" term is to be understood in a broad sense. For him, the scientific method is the most reliable way of gaining knowledge about anything, whether it be human behavior, corporate behavior, curing illnesses, the fate of the planet, or understanding the universe. Scientific thinking is the rigorous tool for thinking and understanding the world.

Adam Grant, a psychology professor at The Wharton College of Business at the University of Pennsylvania and the author of *Think Again*, *Originals*, and *Give and Take*, urges us to constantly rethink our beliefs about politics, science, work, and relationships. Like Kathryn Schultz, Grant believes we can be earnest in our ability to seek the truth while acknowledging we may be wrong at the present time with certain ideas. In this process of uncovering, it is important to share our uncertainties and information gaps with others to achieve "confidence humility." This is achieved by seeking out information that goes against our views and resisting the temptation to preach, prosecute, or politick. In this way, Grant thinks our thinking will mirror a scientist. Big ideas, original ideas that are pioneering, come from seeking out new thinking patterns.

The psychological behavioral sciences, and management sciences, are influential within the wider field of thinking. There is an advocacy element to use the "scientific method" of thinking and rethinking to reach truth. Behavioral scientists, anthropologists, biologists, humanists, and cognitive psychologists are defining the thinking field with a strong emphasis of neurology and brain activity. For example, Shankar Vedantam and Bill Mesler's *Useful Delusions: The Power and Paradox of the Self-Deceiving Brain* emphasizes consequences and effective outcomes. It is not veracity, virtue, or real truth in thinking models, nor even a belief that makes thinking principled or ethical, but rather it is whether the thinking process puts out the desired results. Here ethics, character, or even evolution is not the issue, but whether we can trick our brain into thinking how to work for us. "Delusional decision-making" can in effect redirect the brain to perform the needed outcomes. Vedantam and Mesler's approach to thinking is utilitarian: what works is what matters to the brain because thinking is essentially tied to manipulating brain activity to reach desired results. If one wants to lose weight, trick the brain; if you want to overcome depression or aim for the heights of your profession, then trick the brain.

Reading these scholars in the field of thinking made me reflect on the global infrastructure for peacebuilding, its institutions and networks working on peacebuilding research, policy, and practice. As the United States withdrew from Afghanistan and Iraq to refocus on global superpower competition—containing Russia and China—global military spending surpassed resources for international development, peacebuilding, conflict mitigation, and supporting forced displaced persons or refugees. Reflecting on these challenges, perhaps we are deceiving ourselves into thinking that humanitarian relief, peacebuilding, development, and post-conflict reconstruction fields would collaborate more. Vedantam's approach of tricking the brain is useful in understanding how psychology and neuroscience could have an important role in rethinking the field of peacebuilding. The field has ample evidence illustrating that development work cannot advance without addressing the fundamental underlying dynamics of conflict and violence. Peacebuilding scholars have shown that arriving at a peace process or an agreement by warring factions is flawed unless there is economic justice, access to public health, employment opportunities for the youth, an examination of landownership, institutional violence, and a legal system that is meant for the entire population.

Grant's assertion that our uncertainties and information gaps may indeed force the peacebuilding field to a sense of "confidence humility," but there remains a massive gap in integrative approaches to peacebuilding or conflict resolution. With all the exhilarating propositions on how technology was going to be a panacea for coordination issues, for increased collaboration, and for ensuring that international donor organizations would increase their impact with local CSOs, technology would bring laser-focused solutions to all atrocities before it happened. Integrative peace approaches would usher in a new era in human security; an era of efficiency, cross-cultural communications, policymakers and CSOs on the same page, and the forging of new linkages never seen before.

It is, perhaps, essential to consider Schulz's "Wrongology" thinking where being wrong on topics, on past assumptions, and an entire peacebuilding industry built on conflict resolution theories has exposed our mistakes, in theory and practice. By learning and admitting these mistakes, we can revise and improve our understanding of the peacebuilding world seriously. Our errors, failures, and misunderstandings in integrating and applying technology to the peacebuilding and development sectors will allow us to take stock of incorrect thinking and refine our thinking. If the scientific method fundamentally acknowledges uncertainty and areas to build upon, then it would be wise to think that the grandiose integrative peacebuilding systems were going to work. In 1975, Johan Galtung was a founder of the peace studies field where he outlined three broad approaches to conflict intervention that correlate with the stages of conflict: peacekeeping, peacemaking, and peacebuilding. Since the early days of these concepts, a fourth stage of conflict prevention was added. Since the 1960s, conflict resolution emerged as a discipline and the term "conflict resolution" was used to generalize the broader field. However, since the mid-1990s, peacebuilding as a term replaced conflict resolution to capture various stages of conflict and post-conflict. Conflict resolution became more closely aligned with mediation, negotiations, conflict analysis, communication skills, facilitation, and conflict scenario planning. Peacebuilding evolved to reflect broader stages, such as conflict mitigation, crisis prevention, conflict management, conflict transformation, and stabilization.

What does integrative peacebuilding really mean? Former professor of the Conflict Resolution Graduate Studies program at Georgetown University, Craig Zelizer, editor of *Integrative Peacebuilding: Innovative Approaches to Transforming Conflict*, states, "Integrative peace is a set of processes and tools used by civil society and government actors to transform the relationships, culture, and institutions of society to prevent, end, and transform conflicts."[11] The 2010 Report of the United Nations Working Group on Lessons Learned of the Peacebuilding Commission stated, "Peacebuilding is a long-term investment by all relevant actors and requires a shared vision and long-term strategy to address the root causes of conflict."[12] Contributors to Zelizer's book recognize that building peace, reducing conflicts, and bringing warring parties to the table for dialogue is a process that requires sustained effort, meaningful activity, funding, and political will. Ingrained in the peacebuilding process are expected setbacks when personalities clash, conflicts escalate, agreements fail, violence does not cease, conflicting parties become more entrenched, or local, regional, or international spoilers calculate to prolong the conflict. There is a consensus that ending a conflict and identifying an adequate peace deal can take a generation or more for sustainable peace.

If reaching a sustainable peace will take at least two generations, the interim work is for the international aid community to donate to peacebuilding work to ensure support continues in the areas of education, relief aid, access to public health, opportunities in vocational and nonvocational training, and institutional development. Many in the peacebuilding field contest these international donors are more concerned about limiting the escalation of conflict and less about confronting to end the power imbalances within institutions. Donor agencies from Western countries, the World Bank, the European Union, foundations, philanthropies, and multilateral organizations have been heavily criticized for their funding mechanisms, narrow funding of projects, and operating with local-only known CSOs. Seasoned peacebuilding practitioner Diana Frances said, "We are not only reluctant to compromise our impartiality but also properly wary of action to confront structural violence and bring hidden violence conflict into the open. We know most donors will be unwilling to support interventions that lift the lid off conflict rather than turn the heat down."[13]

Some peacebuilding scholars and practitioners lament that governments, foundations, and multilateral organizations fund peacebuilding work and participate in three main areas: national security, commercial interests, and humanitarian concerns. In the twenty-two years after 9/11, scholars believe there has been an obvious move toward the "securitization" of aid by some donors as international assistance is increasingly connected to broader security and military objectives. During the 2001–2021 Global War on Terror, development experts who oversee projects on the ground cautioned about redirecting the use of development funds for counterinsurgency and countering violent extremism programs. Mark Moyer of the Organisation for Economic Co-operation and Development wrote in *Development in Afghanistan's Counterinsurgency: A New Guide* that, "The primary purpose of development aid in counterinsurgency should be to improve local security and governance because development is less important than security and governance."[14] The issue for many in the peacebuilding field is that during the years of the Iraq and Afghanistan wars, foreign assistance became reassigned and repurposed to fulfill the priorities of stability and security, countering violent extremism, and utilizing peace messaging as a counter-narrative to local radicalism. The field of peacebuilding—local and international practitioners and affiliated peacebuilding institutions—felt that these funds would inherently align them with the security sector.

One way peacebuilding scholars and advocates responded to the "securitization" of the field was to think of a hybrid framework of security and peacebuilding. By early 2000, peacebuilding scholars were using the term "human security" to situate the place of individual security over a state-centered focus. There were indecisive dichotomies in defining human security; the first is "freedom from fear" which included repression, chronic disease, famine, and natural disaster relief. Second, human security included "freedom from want," which consists of social and economic disruptions at home and in communities.[15] By 2009, the UN Trust for Human Security stated that the practice of human security involved people-centered, context-specific, comprehensive, multisectoral approaches, and focused on preventative efforts. With this approach, there were three main phases of implementation: (1) analysis, mapping, landscaping of all stakeholders, and planning; (2) a practical implementation plan; and (3) assessment, evaluation, and impact analysis of the executed programs. These phases were further tiered into distinct stages of conflict, de-escalation of conflict, and post-conflict reconstruction.[16] Nevertheless, some scholars were skeptical about these UN guidelines, such as MacFarlane and Khong, who criticized these definitions stating that it would be difficult to operationalize human security on-the-ground programs.[17]

An example cited in integrating a human security and security-based kinetic approach is the rapid area of security sector reform (SSR). A key assumption is that the security sector—police, intelligence, etc.—consisting of civilian institutions would flourish if it was transparent, accountable, and rewarded, and had respectable ties with the broader civilian population. Focusing on SSR was designed to protect civilians against coercion, abductions, and violence. During a conflict, in which a state is no longer upholding democratic principles, lacking basic government institutions, failing social infrastructure, and failing to protect citizens, SSR was thought to be the beginning point for immediate protection. This was the case in Afghanistan where the United Nations, United States, and the international coalition agreed that the SSR would enhance the protection of civilians from Taliban forces and other insurgents. Afghanistan's army, police, and defense ministry would be the implementing partners for SSR efforts; however, there was a lack of coordination, inconsistent funding, or fleecing of funds from SSR programs; erratic reporting of training of police officers; SSR training was not catered to local cultures; and SSR training in that was not consistent and not aligned with other training programs across the provinces.

SSR in Afghanistan was one experimental area of peacebuilding actions that proved imprudent in design and even more absurd in execution. However, SSR was to be synchronized with another human security peacebuilding approach: Provincial Reconstruction Teams (PRTs) and Human Terrain Systems (HTSs). Now a distant memory from our lexicon, but during the wars in Iraq and Afghanistan (2006–2019), Western diplomats, NATO's International Security Assistance Forces, and international donor agencies in complete cooperation with international and local peacebuilding CSOs participated in the efforts of eliminating terrorists, using intelligence against insurgency groups with PRT and HTS units. The failure of the military (hard power) to squash the spread of radicalism and insurgent attacks against military and civilian outfits prompted military strategists to use soft power resources to uproot terrorism from the local level. Sergeant Major Robert D. Bouley's "Winning Hearts and Minds: The Key to Defeating an Insurgency" used lessons learned from the Vietnam War and insurgents in the Philippines to underscore the important need to focus on local communities who can resist the influence of the enemy. Knowing the local language, the region's history, the people's grievances, and the power dynamics of ethnic rivalries would empower the military to work with locals. The hearts and minds strategy assumes that any insurgency's lifeblood is its access to the population, who provide it with fighters, resources, and intelligence: everything the insurgency needs to thrive. Combating an insurgency, therefore, requires convincing the population, the majority of whom are believed to be neutral or at least passive, away from the insurgency's influence and over to the government side, often by providing political and economic incentives. Military strategists and civilian counterparts in the US State Department linked the development, security, peacebuilding, and other CSOs to develop effective ways to win "hearts and minds." One approach was to infuse local populations with jobs, access to education, vocational training, provide funds for the agriculture sector, cultivate relationships with the local tribal elders, and identify ways to re-engineer social conditions away from insurgency influence. Simultaneously, they worked closely with local religious community leaders and imams to establish contact to gather information on Taliban penetration in communities. These approaches used funds and resources to collaborate with Afghan personnel to support PRT and HTS activities to win over minds and hearts.

In 2015, the Department of Defense quietly shut down the HTS, which embedded social scientists with the military in Afghanistan, Iraq, and other sites. Co-founders Montgomery McFate and Steve Fondacaro were the key architects of this eight hundred million dollar venture where they thought improving ties with academia would bring deeper intelligence gathering and mapping of the human terrain in Iraq and Afghanistan. Primarily targeting anthropologists, sociologists, linguists, ethnographers, cultural experts, and international area studies scholars, McFate and Fondacaro could forge ties with academic scholars and researchers to gather intelligence on locals. The masquerade was to develop ties to bridge the "academic-military divide," but it was an opportunistic project to exploit the knowledge of scholars for the purpose of supplying information to the counterinsurgency strategy. In the absence of linguistic, cultural, and religious expertise in the military, McFate, as a trained anthropologist, developed the Field Manual 3-24 on counterinsurgency, forcing the American Anthropological Association to state, "an unacceptable application of anthropological expertise and a violation of [American Anthropological Association] code of ethics."[18] The HTS program provided anthropologists with temporary security clearance as contractors, military uniforms, access to travel with the military, and access to classified information to share their fieldwork intelligence gathering. Embedding civilian academic researchers in a conflict zone with little or no cultural sensitivity or exposure to the multidimensional contexts exposed the HTS as inadequately conceived, with poor screening of candidates, and raised controversial issues within the academic community and their relationship with military training.[19]

PEACEBUILDING DURING "WHAT WENT WRONG IN THE MUSLIM WORLD?" ERA

For students of peacebuilding, the September 11 attacks were a defining moment for the United States, and these attacks had implications for international relations, but the event was a generation ago. Younger scholars and peacebuilding practitioners do not recall infamous books attempting to explain extremism in the Islamic world because of the so-called decline of the Islamic religion or civilization, nor is there a memory of how these narratives ushered a new world of Islamophobia and new caricatures of the Islamic world. These attacks on the United States established the rationale to defeat terrorism in Muslim-majority lands and the argument that the fight against the enemies will be overseas and not at home became an accepted way of engagement with the Muslim world. In this fight against global terrorism, there was a not-so-subtle system of identifying moderate Muslims to work with and utilize in the fields of counterterrorism, countering violent extremism, and peacebuilding.

At the heart of these formative national and policy debates were the works of Bernard Lewis's *What Went Wrong? Western Impact and Middle Eastern Response*. While positioning the Islamic civilization at its apex as the "Golden Age" with scientific, mathematical, cultural, and intellectual discovery, the decline of Islam was because of the lack of curiosity, political fragmentation, conservative religious reform movements, and the forced subordination of Muslim dynasties from Western imperialism. As a trained historian of the Middle East, Lewis argued that stagnation in the Muslim world, particularly the Middle East, was because of post-independent states seeking to modernize with an emphasis on the sciences, not the social science or the humanities. For international aid agencies and peacebuilding organizations operating in Muslim-majority communities, the What Went Wrong? thesis permeated in the thinking, designing, and implementing of on-the-ground programs. With popular radical ideologies and inadequate educational systems, there was a desperate need to cultivate critical thinking in conflict zones in Muslim-majority communities. The burden to not only mitigate conflict and support local CSOs in peacebuilding now encompassed countering ineffective schools with teacher and student training and seeding the field of peacebuilding in schools.

It is important to recall that it is within this international military, the changing nature of international aid agencies, ways in which peacebuilding organizations are responding to funding, and the questionable criteria in identifying local partners and the diplomatic community pressing forward a public diplomacy policy of winning "Muslim hearts and minds." It was not just enough to defeat insurgents, "inoculate communities" from the penetration of radical ideologies, or fund and pump an entire civil society industry in Iraq or Afghanistan with funds tied to security, but rather the real fear was, after all, if these efforts in the Islamic world would turn against Western military operations and no longer view the West as a model for liberal democratic principles. Abdelwahab El-Affendi,[20] former resident scholar at the Brookings Institution's Saban Center for Middle East Policy and The Brookings Project on US Policy Towards the Islamic World, wrote what was considered an essential policy paper, "The Conquest of Muslim Hearts and Minds? Perspectives on U.S. Reform and Public Diplomacy Strategies." Within the US Policy Towards the Islamic World Program, commonly referred to as the Brookings-Islamic World Project, the conversations were rooted in how the United States will continue to prosecute the war on global terrorism and radicalism while still promoting positive relations with Muslim states and communities. El-Affendi suggested that the US government embarked on a political warfare campaign unmatched since the height of the Cold War, opening a new era in public diplomacy to Muslim audiences who were deeply suspicious of American motives. Understanding former Defense Secretary Rumsfeld's comments on winning hearts and minds as a metaphor for a "war of ideas," El-Affendi suggested that the war context matters to the interpretation. El-Affendi believed public diplomacy to the Muslim world was a "dialogue based on conditions of inequality, leading, inevitably to the establishment of hegemonic or repressive discourse rather than a consensual agreement."[21] Like many of his colleagues from academia, the US engagement with the Muslim world exemplified a paradox of neo-colonialism; discrepancies with power and authority; massive ignorance of cultural, ethnic, tribal, and religious diversity; and the inability of the United States to connect with the local population.

One of El-Affendi's contentions was that the American dialogue with the Islamic world must engage with "genuine representatives" of the target communities. According to him, the problem with US policy is its predilection to talk to the wrong people, mainly entrenched dictators, who were out of touch with their people or an isolated fringe of the pro-Western, secular elites—either in exile or not in power. He believes this serious policy flaw needs to be corrected with a policy change: do not support oppressive regimes and heavily invest in democratic reform in the Middle East and the Islamic world.[22] As a scholar of politics, development, and religion, El-Affendi was more fixated on unraveling US foreign policies and policy assumptions on despotism, terrorism, religious extremism, and reform. For him, winning hearts and minds was a poorly designed public diplomacy policy because it lacked the vision to promote genuine democratic movements for authentic reform in the Islamic world. However, stating that the critical problem with US public diplomacy with the Muslim world was the engagement with dictators and repressive regimes does not recognize the political dynamics in which diplomacy operates, nor does it realize that if a Western country sponsors and funds local democracy movements in the Middle East, it is essentially subverting and sabotaging the sovereignty of that nation.

Conversely, French political Islam analyst Gilles Kepel wrote *The War for Muslim Minds: Islam and the West*,[23] which outlined so-called ideological battles within the Muslim world and how the West will need to navigate with identity issues between conservative, moderate, religious radicals, and existing secular elites. His problematic categories reinforced ideas that any confrontation with the Islamic world would be with the "religious radicals" who have intellectual and spiritual roots with Islamist ideologues like Egyptian Sayyed Qutb or Pakistani Maulana Abu 'Ala Maududi and who are primarily inspired to establish an Islamic state. The problem with Gilles and other Orientalists in political Islam studies is their inability to truly interpret trends in the Muslim world outside of their exotic choices of Islamism, radicalism, and non-Islamism. In the end, because of identity shifts and the need to dominate identity, Kepel asserted that the modern Muslim is a divided schizophrenic who chooses radicalism versus living as an outcast secular anomaly. Engaging with Muslims required an understanding of "what went wrong" with the Islamic religion and civilization. How can Westerners not only understand the Muslim mind but, more importantly, how to correct their minds, hearts, and ill-fated condition. For example, published works focused on Islamist political parties—which were called fundamentalist Islam in the 1990s—demonstrated how the mental structures of Muslims enable and empower radicalization. The What Went Wrong? thesis opened new arguments on why the Muslim mind is incapable of modernity and rational thought, and of fostering scientific, cultural, and artistic achievements; ultimately, they are stuck in a medieval era. Note that when commentators wanted to insult a group of people, they used to explicitly say they were in the medieval period to insinuate stagnation or backward thinking. However, in the Islamic world, the medieval period is viewed as a high civilization period filled with scientific, mathematical, medical, social, spiritual, and cultural discoveries. Nevertheless, some works dominating the field were Robert Reilly's *The Closing of the Muslim Mind: How Intellectual Suicide Created the Modern Islamist*, Edward Hoskins's *A Muslim's Mind*, Gandhi Rajmohan's *Under-*

standing *The Muslim Mind*, and again, Gilles Kepel's *Allah in the West: Islamic Movements in America and Europe*.

Within this period there was a parallel booming industry for Christian evangelical books using interfaith dialogues to bring Muslims to Christianity. Engaging the Islamic world launched more practical books in converting Muslims with study guides, lessons, and links to videos online to evangelize properly. For instance, many Christian evangelical books were published to offer real-life examples of using practical tips with biblical foundations to build relationships to evangelize Muslims in the West and the Islamic world. For example, some of the major books were John Klaasen's *Engaging with Muslims*, Craig A. Evans's *Jesus and the Jihadis: Confronting the Rage of ISIS*, Erwin W. Lutzer's *The Cross in the Shadow of the Crescent: An Informed Response to Islam's War with Christianity*, Norman L. Geisler and Abdul Saleeb's *Answering Islam: The Crescent in Light of the Cross*, Phil Parshall's *Muslim Evangelism: Contemporary Approaches to Contextualization*, David Garrison's *A Wind in the House of Islam: How God is Drawing Muslims Around the World to Faith in Jesus Christ*, William Saal's *Reaching Muslims for Christ*, and George Houssney and Chad Roedel's *Reaching Muslims: A One-Stop Guide for Christians*.

CONSTRUCTING PEACEBUILDING ACTIVITIES WITH WESTERN INCLUSIVENESS AND CORRECTNESS

As Western societies attempt to reconcile the past discrimination and prejudices by bringing greater inclusiveness to include, integrate, and embrace diversity, different cultures, ethnicities, social identities, these notions are permeating into the field of peacebuilding. In the context of institutional violence, marginalization of groups, and systemic intolerance, peacebuilding researchers and practitioners believe it is a responsibility to adopt and enforce inclusive approaches and frameworks. A brief glance at program priorities, staff hiring, changing organization charts, and grant priorities offered to CSOs at the UN Foundation, the UN Development Programme, Humanity United (HU), and the US Institute of Peace reveal changes toward inclusiveness, the very practice of peacebuilding.

It is crucial to examine one philanthropic organization based in the United States to illustrate how the trend of Western inclusiveness complicates, if not exacerbates, problems for peacebuilding work in Muslim-majority communities. HU is a philanthropic organization consisting of a peacebuilding program led by Melanie Greenberg, former president of The Alliance for Peace, who outlined the organization's strategy and vision for change as "an honest broker within the system, to help it heal."[24] The 2023 Peacebuilding Strategy states, "It is interested in transforming human exploitation and violent conflict into enduring peace and freedom. HU's work is anchored in five strategic pillars: building relationships and networks; practicing a philosophy of accompaniment; being learning-focused, systems enabled and people-centered; being expansive in our efforts; and investing internally so we can grow together with our partners."[25] Instead of using the term local communities or local partners, HU uses "proximate peacebuilders" to illustrate those working for peace in the Global South, people of color, youth, women, and marginalized groups. Acknowledging that HU is part of a philanthropy sector with "historic and ongoing inequities and imbalances designed in white, North American and European cultures,"[26] HU is moving away from models of impact philanthropy and committing itself to a practice of accompaniment and trust-based philanthropy.

What does this really mean? HU peacebuilding is interested in tackling the power structures that sustain inequity, inequality, discrimination, and violence against its own population. In a world with heightened Cold War thinking with the Russian invasion of Ukraine and a securitized landscape in peacebuilding and conflict resolution, the HU Strategy Report argues that it is centering its efforts on civilian protection and harm mitigation. Greenberg is a product of the Iraq and Afghanistan war securitization of the peacebuilding field; she is interested in re-engineering to a time focused on nonviolent movements, "marginalized voices," civilian resistance, transitional justice, funding, and fostering inclusive dialogues. HU's Peacebuilding Department's four focus themes are (1) inclusive peace processes, (2) agency for collective action, (3) innovative pathways for peace, and (4) healing and well-being. HU states that "political transitions and peace processes are too often controlled by elite powerholders, who craft narrow processes that leave marginalized communities without voice or agency to build sustainable peace." In light of their work toward dismantling elite powerholders, HU's efforts toward a "healthy system" based on "collective action for marginalized communities proactively build shared norms, values, and institutions that meet their needs."[27]

As much as these focus areas appear strategic in nature by targeting specific sectors, supporting their capacities, and empowering these actors with tools for leadership, negotiation, networking, and increased information sharing, the desire to support groups not involved in official peace processes will raise more undesired attention to the proximate peacebuilders. HU is interested in ensuring there is a robust curriculum and research on civil resistance and coaching to activists will not level the playing field. Instead, HU's direct interventions in their priority countries—Colombia and Sudan—will raise concern for local law enforcement, authorities monitoring the transfer of international funds, and send alerts to those monitoring the activities of civil society groups. Since HU's Strategy Report does not explicitly state who the marginalized communities are and what it means to be inclusive in conflict zones in the Global South, these ambiguities will not contest elite powers or "redistribute the power to create change"[28]; instead, these activities bring greater unfavorable attention to their local partners and their networks.

Drafting a strategy peacebuilding plan for a board of advisors is one exercise; however, implementing a program to redistribute power structures, create transformative changes in social structures, and explicitly affirm that they are funding local partners to work against patriarchy, colonialism, and exploitative economic practices will most likely endanger the lives on the ground. Western peacebuilding organizations imagining their vision and commitment to diversity, equity, inclusion, and justice reflects an idealism they want to see implemented in Western societies and around the globe. HU, and other Western peacebuilding organizations, want to correct the wrongs of their own institutions and change their inherited inequality paradigms. The problem is that constructing peacebuilding approaches from Western idealism and imposing these ideals onto another geographic place and culture who are at another pace of development is asserting a new form of cultural idealism hegemony and imposing an assimilation of values, principles, and ideals.

PEACEBUILDING AND SOFT POWER

A serious ongoing issue within Western peacebuilding organizations, including international organizations like the UN Development Programme and the US Institute of Peace, is their woeful ignorance of their role in tricking the brain into thinking that all institutions have a function for the state's ability to lead in global affairs. Harvard University's Joseph Nye classical book

Soft Power: The Means to Success in World Politics coined the term soft power in the early 1980s, which is now used frequently by political leaders, policymakers, researchers, and academics. During the Cold War, Nye argued that the United States needed to think more creatively than military or economic might—often called hard power. Nye felt that neoconservatives who advise presidents are making a major miscalculation: They focus too heavily on using America's military power to force other nations to do our will, and they pay too little or no attention to our soft power. For Nye, soft power will help prevent terrorists from recruiting supporters from among the moderate majority. And soft power will support the United States in dealing with critical global issues that require multilateral cooperation among states. That is why it is so essential that American policymakers better understand the appropriation of soft power.

State power was the ability to influence the behavior of other states to get a desired outcome. Historically, power has been measured by population size, territory, natural resources, economic strength, military force, and social stability. However, if the United States wanted to maintain a leading role in global affairs by working with both heads of state and local populations, it needed to move from the fear-based thinking and anger of the Cold War period to being an inspiring force on earth. Nye believed the United States needed a vision for global engagement and to do this required being a smart power investing in global goods, CSOs, and institutions. The twenty-first century will need America to cultivate alliances and partnerships with institutions that serve US interests in solving the new century's challenges. This meant a rehaul and reassessing of investments in development and foreign assistance so that it would be more aligned with its interests and people's aspirations worldwide. Nye and other neoliberals of international relations suggested that after the end of the Cold War, the dissolution of the Soviet Union, and the unipolar power of the United States demanded to develop new frameworks and adjust approaches to shifting powers and alliances.

Soft power is the ability to attract people to our side without coercion, specifically, attracting foreign populations (i.e., CSOs) to our side and supporting them to build capable democratic states. To maintain and win global "peace," there needed to be a heavy investment in alliances, partnerships, and institutions at all levels to expand American influence and establish the legitimacy of American action. Effective synchronized soft power ensures that humanitarian operations, foreign assistance, education, cultural diplomacy, legislation, journalists, teachers, and lawyer exchanges directly impact global CSO partnerships. It is through this prism of balancing soft power with hard power that peacebuilding and conflict resolution organizations have a clear and concise role. With soft power dominating foreign assistance, humanitarian aid, and peacebuilding projects from the US Agency for International Development and the US State Department, overseas programs seek alliances with another population during a crisis. So, HU's mission of "working for peace in the Global South, people of color, youth, women, and marginalized groups" or the UN Development Programme's establishing "voices of inclusivity" is an extension of a soft power policy to partner, influence, maintain leverage, and ultimately be the architects of the agenda with global CSOs. Today, in Yemen or Libya's civil war, our so-called peacebuilding efforts use actionable terms like "conflict mitigation," "negotiations," and "conflict transformation" to train women and youth, but this is far from the reality of the thinking of both foreign policymakers and local implementers. This recognizes that the field of peacebuilding and conflict resolution, especially those funded by the US government, are essentially part of serving a function of global soft power politics.

PEACEBUILDING AND CRITICAL THINKING

We owe Socrates a great deal for his contribution to intellectual inquiry. He pointed out that many questions produced confused meanings, self-contradictory beliefs, no evidence, and empty rhetoric. This questioning system by Socrates established the fact that one cannot completely depend upon those in "authority" to have sound knowledge, insight, or even clarity of thinking. He demonstrated that people may have power and be respected for a high position yet be deeply confused and irrational. Socrate's contribution to thinking was establishing the importance of asking deep questions that probe profoundly into thinking before we accept ideas as worthy of belief. He valued the importance of seeking evidence, closely examining assumptions and reasoning, analyzing basic concepts and foundations, and examining implications not only of what is said but of what is done as well. His method of questioning, known as "Socratic questioning," is still the best-known critical thinking teaching strategy. In this teaching mode of questioning, Socrates highlighted the need to think for clarity, logical consistency, and rational discourse.

Socrates set the foundations for the intellectual tradition of critical thinking: to reflectively question common beliefs and explanations and scrutinize those reasonable and logical beliefs from those that serve our interests. For him, real thinking was critical thinking; it involved adequate evidence, rational discourse, and a tested foundation to warrant our belief.

After Socrates's practice of thinking, Plato continued Socrates's thought and approach, then Aristotle, and the Greek skeptics, all of whom emphasized that things are often very different from what they appear to be, and it is only a trained mind that can see beyond the surface or delusive appearances. Beneath the surface of the deeper realities of life, ancient Greek tradition emerged from the need for anyone who aspired to understand the deeper realities to think systematically to trace implications broadly and deeply. For thinking to be comprehensive, it must be well-reasoned, responsive to logical arguments, and survive critical objections.

Today, education specialists emphasize thinking within critical thinking terms. If true education was to be meaningful, students should be able to utilize critical thinking "skills" to effectively evaluate, assess, and understand various complex issues. According to this school, the crisis in national educational reforms is due to the lack of critical thinking skills taught to students. Though students are graduating from colleges with specialized technical knowledge, they lack the ability to analyze and critique methodically. Stephen D. Brookfield, the author of *Teaching for Critical Thinking*, argues that critical thinking is needed across disciplines, and it can be taught by teachers and learned by students.[29] Critical thinking cannot be an abstract philosophical exercise, but it needs to be integrated into all curricula using models such as crisis decision simulation, critical debate, and exemplars and flaws. Brookfield's approach believes critical thinking can be learned by knowing the techniques and tools where students should apply these skills to reading, writing, and debating.

Education reformers claim that students must learn to think as good citizens concerned with the public interest or global citizens. They need to know to be good parents or local community members needs critical thinking. They assert that students graduate from college without the intellectual skills they need to survive the enormous complex realities they face, much less prosper. Critical thinking advocates these skills as a social learning process. By collectively listening to others deconstructing and analyzing complex problem sets, students learn and practice divergent ways to think critically. Critical thinking is divided into three areas: (1) learning to analyze thinking—identifying purposes in thinking, the questions being asked, the information being used, the assumptions being taken for granted, and the concepts guiding the thinking, reasoning, logic, and rhetoric (trivium); (2) learning to assess thinking itself by using intellectual parameters such as clarity, accuracy, depth, breadth, fairness, significance, and relevance; and (3) developing intellectual traits of mind such as intellectual integrity, intellectual humility, intellectual perseverance, empathy, impartiality, comprehension, and an intellectual sense of justice. The trivium and the quadrivium (arithmetic, astronomy, music, and geometry) supported students in the liberal arts to see a unified idea of reality. Commonly called the "Arts of the Word," the curriculum focuses on different ways to navigate words. For instance, grammar is used in logic, which is used in rhetoric. Thinking was how we communicate with the natural order in numbers and quantities. By discerning those natural relationships, we come to better understand the cosmos and our place in the cosmos.

Psychiatrists within critical thinking educationists identify the ability to explicitly self-examine one's thinking as supporting mental health. Richard Paul, Carmen Polka, Brian Barnes, and Linda Elder claim critical thinkers understand egocentricity and socio-centrism and actively combat these biases to improve personal, intimate relationships. There is a deep sense of understanding and balancing of thinking, feelings, and desires. Accordingly, critical thinkers strive to "self-actualize" to have a heightened understanding of themselves. They have emotional healthiness, social intelligence, a deep connection to their communities, easily empathize with others, and view their efforts as aiding humanity's betterment.

Absent in modern trends in thinking or critical thinking is the connection and development of morality, character, and inner guidance within an ethical framework. After Socrates, the ancient Hellenistic schools of philosophy diverged into the schools of Cynicism, Plato's Academy, and Stoicism by Zeno and Epictetus. Stoicism became popular under emperor-philosopher Marcus Aurelius (160–181 BCE). The Stoics adopted Socrates's classification of four aspects of virtue, which they thought were critically interlinked character traits: practical wisdom, courage, temperament, and justice. Practical wisdom allows us to make decisions for a moral meaningful life (eudaimonia). These character traits in Stoicism and Socratic insisted on different virtues that cannot be practiced independently: one cannot be both intemperate and courageous.

Within the Islamic tradition from 700–1350, critical thinkers were less into juristic literalism debates and more concerned with spiritual purification, moral character, and ascetic practices which detached them from worldly distractions. Within the Qur'an and within God's signs in creation, one can find an inner meaning whose implications go further than the exoteric, literal, surface meaning. Critical thinking "spiritualists" like Abu Talib al-Makki's (d.996) *Nourishment of the Hearts* (*Qut al-Qulub*), Ibn 'Abbad's (d.1390) *Letters of Spiritual Direction* (*Rasa'il kubra wa Rasa'il sughra*), Ibn 'Ata Allah al-Iskandari's (d.1309) *The Book of Illumination* (*Kitab al-Tanwir fi Isqat al-Tadbir*), and Abu Hafs 'Umar al-Suhrawardi's (d.1235) *The Benefits of Intimate Knowledge* (*'Awarif al-Ma'arif*) are typical, to name just a few.

Ibn 'Ata Allah's *The Book of Illumination* is an exemplary scholarship within the literature of illumination (*irfan*) but atypical in modern thinking and modern Western theosophical paradigms. Inner and outer knowledge examines the spirituality of "ego economics": how we earn, save, consume, and plan to spend. Ibn 'Ata Allah's works attempt to understand how humans exist with selfish calculations in this world while seeking spiritual illuminations (*tanwir* and *tadbir*). Ibn 'Ata's enlightenment, or "exceptionally high level of thinking," is integrally connected to the inner illumination of the heart. For many scholars, he can be easily regulated to the mystical theology tradition, but this work is an insightful critique of anxious energy situated in an egoistic corrosive soul and the practical wisdom of liberating the self. Central to the spiritual masters within the Islamic tradition is reliance on God, to be his servant, and that all matters are in God's control—whether beneficial or harmful, pleasant or unpleasant, comprehensible or incomprehensible. Thinking is tied to knowing; knowing is connected to obeying; obeying is linked to sufficiency and surrendering the self to divine will. This does not mean critical thinking or questioning does not exist; rather, critical thinking within this context is part of a broader tradition of seeking divine love and contentment. The basis of love is knowledge, and knowledge directs the curious seeker to enter contemplation and deep self-critical assessment (*mushahada*).

In assessing thinking or critical thinking we need to question what approaches, frameworks, and practices are dominating popular trends but, moreover, we also need to examine why moral realism is nonexistent. Why is teaching critical thinking void of moral and ethical foundations? How has the field of studying thinking become dominant in behavioral, psychological, and management sciences but rarely found in religious studies or political philosophy? Is it possible to trace the loss of ethical foundations in thinking from the rivalry of moral realists and moral romantics of the eighteenth century? Moral realists like Jean-Jacques Rousseau were weary of inner weakness, but he emphasized the power of the inner goodness of human beings. As a key thinker of the Enlightenment, he distrusted institutions, tradition, and customs, whereas the Romantic thinkers trusted the self over conventions of the world. It was the power of the individual to logically think about the outcomes of their fate, not the church, government, historical, cultural norms, or popular beliefs. This may or may not be the origin of "thinking" fragmentation. However, modern thinking and critical thinking do not even have the vocabulary of ethics or the literacy of historical moral foundations. Today, experts accept the foundations of thinking to be like a scientist. Adam Grant's works to empower modern thinking to find big ideas, original ideas that are pioneering by designing "new" thinking patterns based on science is not interested in historical contributions to the field of thinking. The advocacy to use the "scientific method" disconnects the broader historical field of thinking and philosophy.

In the pre-modern period, eminent thinkers like Shaykh al-Ishraq Shihab al-Din Suhrawardi (1153–1191) and Ibn 'Arabi (1165–1240) harmonized spirituality and philosophy together. The training of the intellect through philosophy and the disciplined purification of the heart (*tazkiyah*) through *tasawwuf* with illumination which transforms one's being and bestows true knowledge. One of Islam's finest Sufi masters and philosophers, Shihab al-Din Suhrawardi, who wrote *The Theosophy of the Light* (*Hikmat al-Ishraq*) and *On the Reality of Love* (*Fi haqiqat al-'ishq*), created a vast philosophical synthesis of nearly six centuries of Islamic thought. Ishraqi philosophy, commonly understood as theosophy, is essentially the light that orients the metaphysics of human beings. This school advanced the thinking of inner knowledge that none other than the eternal wisdom or sophia perennis illuminates and transforms, deconstructs and resurrects until the individuals understand the essence of the cosmos. During contemplation, the great spiritual masters referred to terms and practices of self-discipline, surrender, poverty, fasting, soul, primordial nature, renunciation, transcendence, reliance, obedience, repentance, etc. This is the way they breathed and the way they lived. If we are going to think, rethink, and find ways to be critical thinkers, then illumination needs to be central to this venture. It appears more than ever that we need to find ways to integrate thinking with the tradition of illumination and ultimately participate in peacebuilding.

NOTES

1. See https://www.facebook.com/uzreport.world/videos/449068877232579/.

2. Mullah Omar was a prominent Afghan militant leader and founder of the Taliban, which ruled Afghanistan from 1996–2001, and then the organization officially returned in August 2021. Born in 1960 in the province of Kandahar, Mullah Omar joined the international *jihad* to oust the Soviets from Afghanistan, and then emerged as the leader of the Taliban organization, a group of seminary students trained as jihadist from the mid-1980s to the 1990s. After intense civil war battles against other Afghan ethnic groups, the Taliban gained control of Kabul in 1996 but not the most western provinces of the country. Mullah Omar's reign of the Taliban hosted several residual jihadist groups from the Soviet war, al-Qaeda's Osama bin Laden being the infamous fighter. Mullah Omar died in 2013, see Bette Dam, *Looking for the Enemy: Mullah Omar and the Unknown Taliban* (New York: HarperCollins, 2021) and Alex Strick van Linshoten (ed.), *The Taliban Reader: War, Islam and Politics in Their Own Words* (New York: Oxford University Press, 2018).

3. Personal interview with Ministry of Technology and Defense Maulvi Attallah Omri, Kabul, April 2022.

4. See Voice of America, https://www.voanews.com/a/almost-30-nations-engage-with-taliban-at-tashkent-conference-/6676107.html.

5. See Lynne O'Donnell, "The Taliban Have Picked Up the Resource Curse," *Foreign Policy*, July 11, 2022, https://foreignpolicy.com/2022/07/11/afghanistan-taliban-mining-resources-rich-minerals/.

6. The Office of Religion and Global Affairs formed by former Secretary of State John Kerry in Shaun Casey's work, *Chasing the Devil at Foggy Bottom: The Future of Religion in American Diplomacy*, 2022.

7. See Shaun Casey, "How the State Department has Sidelined Religion's Role in Diplomacy," September 5, 2017, Georgetown University's Berkely Center for Religion, Peace, & World Affairs, https://berkleycenter.georgetown.edu/essays/how-the-state-department-has-sidelined-religion-s-role-in-diplomacy.

8. For specific offices at the Department of State, see www.state.gov/bureaus-offices.

9. I expand more upon the growing influence of religion and religious communities in international affairs in chapter 4.

10. See UN Children's Fund, 2021 Report, https://www.unicef.org/press-releases/covid-19-pandemic-leads-major-backsliding-childhood-vaccinations-new-who-unicef-data.

11. Craig Zelizer, ed., *Integrative Peacebuilding: Innovative Approaches to Transforming Conflict*, pg. 8.

12. *Report of the United Nation Working Group on Lessons Learned of the Peacebuilding Commission*, 2010, pg. 11.

13. Diana Francis, *From Pacification to Peacebuilding: A Call to Global Transformation* (New York: Palgrave, Macmillan, 2010), pg. 103.

14. M. Moyer, *Development in Afghanistan's Counterinsurgency: A New Guide* (Paris: Organization for Economic Co-operation and Development, 2011), pg. 3.

15. The formative ideas on human security were from UN Development Programme, Human Development Report, 1994, http://hdr.undp.org/en/reports/global/hdr1994.

16. See The United Nations Trust for Human Security Report, 2009.

17. Neil MacFarlane and Yuen Foong Khong, *Human Security and the UN: A Critical History* (Indianapolis: Indiana University Press, 2006).

18. American Anthropological Association Commission on the Engagement of Anthropology with the US Security and Intelligence Communities (2009, October 14).

19. See D. Glenn (2007), "Anthropologists in the War Zone: Scholars Debate Their Role," *The Chronicle of Higher Education*, 54 (14); S. Weinberger (2010, June 22), "Human Terrain Hits Rocky Ground: U.S. Army Social-Science Programme Loses Director," *Nature*, 465 (993); R. Albro and H. Gusterson (2021), "Commentary: 'Do No Harm,'" *C4ISR Journal*.

20. Abdelwahab El-Affendi served as a senior research fellow at the Centre for the Study of Democracy, University of Westminster, and coordinator of the Centre's Democracy and Islam Programme. Dr. El-Affendi was a member of the core team of authors of the *Arab Human Development Report* (2004), a member of the Advisory Board, and a contributor to the *Report on Women's Rights* (2009). He was a member of the Board of Directors of Inter-Africa Group and a trustee of the International Forum for Islamic Dialogue. He was educated at the Universities of Khartoum, Wales, and Reading, and he was the author of *Turabi's Revolution: Islam and Power in Sudan* (1991), *Who Needs an Islamic State?* (1991), *Rethinking Islam and Modernity* (2001), and *For a State of Peace: Conflict and the Future of Democracy in Sudan* (2002).

21. Abdelwahab El-Affendi, *The Conquest of Muslim Hearts and Minds? Perspectives on U.S. Reform and Public Diplomacy Strategies* (Washington, DC: Brookings Institution, 2007), pg. 10.

22. Ibid., pg. 14.

23. Gilles Kepel, *The War for Muslim Minds: Islam and the West* (Cambridge, MA: Belknap Press, 2006).

24. See Humanity United's *Peacebuilding Strategy Report*, August 2023. https://humanityunited.org/wp-content/uploads/2023/09/Peacebuilding-Strategy-Report-2023.pdf.

25. Ibid., pg. 5.

26. Ibid., pg. 7.

27. Ibid., pg. 11.

28. Ibid., pg. 14.

29. Stephen D. Brookfield, *Teaching for Critical Thinking* (Hoboken, NJ: Jossey-Bass Publishers, 2011).

Chapter Two

Peacebuilding in a Globalized World

THE GLOBALIZED WORLD

I traveled to Sulaymaniyah, Iraq, for one week to attend a conference on "The Future of Peacebuilding" with guests from thirty different countries across five continents. Like most conferences, it had a scheduled agenda with panels and break-out sessions for intimate conversations on topics. At the conference, 50 percent of participants were researchers and the other 50 percent were civil society members sharing their ideas and best practices from the field and exploring possible solutions to problems. Participants had cellphones and laptops, had scheduled virtual meetings, communicated with participants with a WhatsApp connection, and utilized a conference-created app to view the agenda and interact with the organizers. Throughout the conference, it occurred to me how I was thinking about how civil society members 'work on the ground' in my own system of thinking and experiences, and the responses I provided were based on these ideas. Civil society members from Sudan, Kenya, Nigeria, Afghanistan, Iraq, Lebanon, Pakistan, and Libya listened keenly to the feedback from the "experts," but behind their courteousness and cultural respect for others, it was clear that the opinions of experts often did not resonate with their local issues. We spoke extensively on interpersonal and intercommunal peacebuilding, gender training, resolving conflicts with reconciliation, improving the role of local community councils to address grievances, and assessing our impact. We used a common peacebuilding language, and all the conference participants knew the work on the ground varied with local geography; however, there was a gap in how we thought about the practices. It was unclear then, but later, I reflected on how we thought of members from thirty countries with similar problems without appreciating the multiple power dynamics within their circles and communities.

Understanding the work and changing environments of peacebuilding is critical to adapting and adjusting to a globalized world. We use the terms "conflict," "war zones," and "fragile states," but these terms have distinct meanings in each geography with its own specific cultural and sociopolitical context. These terms also change meaning with shifts in global power. Ulrich Beck's trilogy's—*The Cosmopolitan Vision* (2006), *Power in the Global Age* (2005), and *Cosmopolitan Europe* (2007)—phase of modernity has already acquired a new shape which he labeled as the "second modernity." The new features include interrelatedness and interdependence of people across the globe, growing inequalities in a global space, and emergence of new supranational organizations in the area of economy (e.g., multinational corporations, politics with the prominence of non-state actors such as the International Monetary Fund, World Bank, World Trade Organization, International Court of Justice, civil society members, and advocacy social movements of global scope such as Amnesty International, Greenpeace, and feminist organizations). Shifting power in a global age created new normative precepts of global risks that include the importance of human rights, new forms of warfare, global organized crime, and terrorism. Their common denominator is "cosmopolitanization" (i.e., the erosion of clear borders separating markets, states, civilizations, cultures, and life-worlds of common people and its consequences: the involuntary confrontation with the "foreign other" all over the globe). Beck does not believe that the world has become borderless, but the boundaries are becoming blurred and indistinct, permeating information, capital, and risk flows.

The globalized world has transformed human society in terms of consciousness, global power, interconnected communities, rapid communications, and engagement—all testing the past ideas of state sovereignty and autonomy. Beck argues that multiculturalism means living side by side with different people within one state; peaceful coexistence and non-interference in internal affairs as principles of international law have implied separate, autonomous, sovereign states; tolerance has meant grudging acceptance, allowance for difference as an unavoidable burden. The cosmopolitan tolerance is more than that: it is not defensive, not passive, but active, open toward others, embracing them, enjoying the difference as enriching and seeing the other as fundamentally the same as us. But the transformation has made old territorial and the new deterritorialized power games overlap and contradict each other. The old categories of state-centered power and politics are becoming defunct categories because they do not capture the new actors, strategies, resources, goals, conflicts, paradoxes, and ambivalent outcomes of economic meta-power, both inside and among nations.[1]

We are not living at the "end of politics" or "end of history" but in a time of global trans-legal metapolitics; the neoliberal world is part of a global experiment of global reform policy, but these reforms are not in the hands of the neoliberals or neoconservative thinkers. The borderless world is foremost pushed forward by capital; let us recall that the 2008 financial crisis in America had an immense impact across major financial sectors across the globe. Monthly reports on unemployment, employment, consumer spending—usually coined as consumer confidence—and the housing market are not just anticipated by experts in a specific territory but rather economists and political analysts study this information to see its impact locally and regionally. Just as the Peace of Westphalia ended the European religious civil wars of the sixteenth and seventeenth centuries by separating state and religion, the national world wars of the twentieth and twenty-first centuries may have created a separation of state and nation. The re-emergence of religion and the flourishing of different religions and cultures possible in the globalized world with the advancement of cosmopolitanism values guarantee the coexistence of transnational identities. In the mid-seventeenth century, a secular state was inconceivable for some European thinkers; this was synonymous with the end of the world. Today a transnational state is almost equally unthinkable because it breaks with the most basic modern political idea of state sovereignty with an international rules–based order.

The globalized world presses us to face fundamental questions: how can we coexist while being equal and different? How can we choose between two destructive alternatives: living together and giving up our differences or living apart in homogenous communities that communicate only through the market or violence? Cosmopolitanism is creating a globalization in politics, society, culture, religion, and identity. Globalized experts, like Beck, believe that where nationalism is about exclusive distinctions and loyalties with unique identities and histories holding the group together, cosmopolitanism is a transgenerational, transregional, not bound by borders and about inclusive distinctions and identities—citizens of the world.

Chapter Two

PEACEBUILDING IN A WORLD OF VIOLENT EXTREMISM

The world of peacebuilding and conflict resolution could not resist the lure of being disengaged from the rising tide of violent extremism (VE) and communities vulnerable to radicalization. While a score of peacebuilding scholars argued against being entangled in the security sector of VE, the vast number of organizations could not resist government funds attached to peacebuilding. Entering this world, peacebuilding scholars naturally wanted to begin with terminology. How should we define "radical"? Or "extreme"? Some wanted to know the definitive meanings of "Muslims," "Islam," or "religion." What consequences may the use of terminology have on research and policy? By 2010, the accepted terms of "radical Islam" and "jihadist" were so prominent that we did not realize that uncritical use of terminology and expressions led to an increasing fear of Muslims, the rise of Islamophobia, and the general othering of Muslims.[2] Mixing terminologies with radical Islam, which was equated with terrorism, were denominations of Islam like Salafis or Deobandis which were to be blamed for nurturing narrow interpretations of religion. Scholars of religion and peacebuilding, as well as practitioners, knew that this reductionism of groups combined with an irresponsible indictment of an entire religion was problematic.

Uncritical use of terminology has concrete social and political consequences. Scholars Jennifer Hoewe and Brian J. Bowe claim: "As the term 'radical Islam' becomes equivalently used and understood with terrorism, it may be a short step to making the term 'Islam' generally equivalent with its radical counterpart."[3] It strengthens the sense of understanding Islam as a monolithic threat to "us"; they stated this is clearly not a neutral terminology. Hoewe and Bowes argue, "The uncritical adoption of this term in news content may make it difficult for counter-frames to emerge, which advances the othering of Muslims in public discourse."[4] Academic associations wrote codes of ethics for their members to abide with. For example, the International Sociological Association stressed that research should be critical and that sociologists should be aware that they may have an impact on society. The International Sociological Association felt the pressures of global affairs and that the research conducted by their members may haven been directly negatively impacting society. "Sociologists should know their assumptions may have an impact on society. Hence their duty is, on the one hand, to keep an unbiased attitude as far as possible, while, on the other hand, to acknowledge the tentative and relative character of the results of their research and not to conceal their own ideological position(s). No sociological assumption should be presented as indisputable truth" was shared at the International Sociological Association annual meeting.[5]

Debates returned to the famous anthropologist Talal Asad's *Genealogies of Religion: Discipline and Reasons in Christianity and Islam*. His work affirmed that there were no universal definitions of religion. Moreover, it is essential to realize that any definition of religion is a construction made from within a specific historical circumstance. Citing Asad, scholars debated that the separation between religion and politics results from the Western separation of domains of power, where religion is understood from a Christian genealogy, and where religion is to be kept separate from political power. Contributing to this position was scholar Mohammed Sulaiman who argued that this view on religion is Eurocentric and that this perspective has dominated the study of Islam and Muslims, and it has, furthermore, constituted the "Western norm" that has affected analyses of some religions as natural and others not. Sulaiman contends that current research on Islam and violence-related questions are divided into two epistemological stances with differing theoretical underpinnings. One is characterized by reductionist (or orientalist) perspectives, where a direct relationship between Islam and violence is sought, for example, through a focus on textual readings and older historical examples. The other is more complex and stresses lived experience and the changing nature of Islam related to the historical situation, and Islam as an explanatory factor is left out of the analysis. As a result, both epistemological stances understand Islamic violence as a "violation of the religious-secular divide," which is the "Western norm."[6]

Sulaiman examined several scholars within the reductionist field, such as Bernard Lewis, Olivier Roy, Emmanuel Sivan, and Samuel Huntington, who manufactured an image of the "good" Muslim as one who reinvents Islam to fit the "Western norm." However, the "real" or "bad" Muslim, or "authentic" Islam, is regressive, ideological, and anti-modern, unlike Christianity, and connected to violence through such a reductionist understanding: "As they interpret Muslim acts of violence to be a consequence of an objective, unmediated and scientific interpretation of classical Islamic texts and as representing a seamless continuity with classic Islamic history, Orientalists provide their readers with what they perceive to be the real, authentic Islam. This unadulterated form of Islam produces the essential (bad) Muslim."[7] Sulaiman argued that "good" Muslims are "only good to the extent that their Islam is reinvented and remodeled to fit within the 'universal' template of Western, liberal modernity."[8] As such, a good Muslim is only one who, by accepting the superiority of Western cultural formations, has managed to depart from the archetype of the bad "real" Muslim. He states that this perspective leads to a generalization of all Muslims, where "every Muslim is deemed to be intrinsically at risk of being 'radicalized,' thus becoming a real threat due to the innate appeal of radical Islam to Muslims."[9]

Focusing on Salafi Sunni Islam as the source of being "bad" radical Muslims with a distorted political ideology as a cause of violence is important to this debate. German scholar of Arab nationalism and global politics Bassam Tibi thought the problem needed to focus on political Islam, commonly called Islamism, which distorted the peaceful nature of Islam. Tibi asserts that Islamism is the real falsification of Islam, and the focus should be on the differentiation between ideology and religion. When political aspirations are inserted into the religion of Islam as an ideology to reconstruct a political system, Tibi understands this as what makes people resort to violence.[10]

The debate turned toward whether Salafism as a whole ought to be considered a security threat. What about Salafi denominations that are comprised of conservative practicing Muslims that explicitly and publicly promote Islam as a nonviolent religion and are simultaneously actively nonviolent, distancing themselves from *jihadi* groups and other violently inclined ideologies? Alex Schmid of the University of St. Andrews asked, "Should we really fear all Salafists in Europe? Are violent and non-VE merely two sides of the same coin?" Salafism varies in different forms but stresses that even "non-*jihadi* Salafis" are "incompatible" with Western European principles of modern liberal-democratic societies. Salafists can be apolitical (quietist), political (reformist), or militant (jihadist); however, even in their non-jihadist variant, their fundamentalist value system is extreme by the prevailing norms of Western European societies.[11] Schmid states that Salafi notions of separation of state and religion, popular sovereignty, gender equality, respect for minority rights, and representative governance contradict the core principles of modern liberal-democratic societies.[12] Presenting the views of security studies and the possible problems of radicalization, Schmid proposed Salafi teachings and practices are anti-democratic and anti-integrative with European society, and, as such, threaten democratic rule. From this perspective, Salafism supports exclusivism tied to a fundamentalist religious value system. These hyper-irrational analyses do not pretend to have biases against religion or the diverse ways religion is practiced. Salafism, a conservative

Sunni sect, now threatens European liberal ideas because the group does not practice liberal representative values within the sect's authoritative bodies. This argument could be applied to the Vatican, Roman Catholicism, Eastern Orthodox Church, Orthodox Judaism, and all the world's great religions.

Concerned with generalized and simplistic "stereotypes" of Islam and Muslims and understanding that fundamentalist religious interpretations are not homogeneous but are just as diverse and complex as any other field of interpretation, Ineke Roex counter-argued positioning Salafis within a security prism. She stated it was important to distinguish between different Salafi types in terms of security policy because it was problematic to present Salafism as a security threat and a threat to democracy. A nuanced analysis illustrates that not all Salafis call for violent *jihad* or agree that the classical interpretations of *jihad* may not even apply in the modern period.[13] In her research, Roex concludes that political detachment or indifference toward politics or participation in liberal democracy among some Salafis may result in societal detachment and group alienation. In her solid empirical research, Roex holds that Salafis are a conservative religious denomination, not a monolithic phenomenon, and not a security problem. She does not consider it "fair to consider the entire Salafi movement as a security threat, and a threat to the democratic system."[14]

Schmid's work on Salafi groups living in Europe focused on their potential leanings toward VE. His assessment of their identities and propensity toward violence or radicalization was based on liberal democratic principles. He suggested that Salafis, who stress purity, piety, and nonviolence as their primary methods, are seen as extremists with maximalist goals, and their peaceful mission (*dawah*) is considered a strategy and a tactical choice to push their Islamic agenda.[15] Tibi and Sulaiman criticized Schmid for his reductionist conclusions, Eurocentric reading, and positioning of religion in security terms, and situating jihadism with non-threatening conservative pious believers.

Despite these debates on security risks posed by Islamism, political ideologies of Salafism, and identifying the sources of violence and VE, the broader peacebuilding community understood that ostracizing a group by disengaging with them would only further their views of alienation. Of course, uncritical use of terminology may have societal consequences, but peacebuilding scholars and civil society members experiencing the tragic horrors of VE did not have the luxury of debating terminology or re-examining Western construction of religion or the "good" Muslim versus the "bad" Muslim. This community was living in real-time with the outcomes of the destruction of radicalism. The Muslim stakeholders living in Muslim-majority communities, who design and execute peacebuilding programs in local communities, needed to understand the mentality, structure, types of personalities altogether, reasons behind the attraction of VE, and what could be done to stop it.

PREVENTING AND COUNTERING VIOLENT EXTREMISM

During the past forty-five years, even before the September 11 attacks on the United States and the Global War on Terror, Muslim-majority communities have been dealing with the virus of terrorism and VE. Within the peace and conflict resolution field, scholars have skittishly delved into terrorism or VE studies believing that they felt experts primarily lead this area in a security-based field for law enforcement, terrorism experts, and political scientist experts focused on military responses to terrorism. Despite these boundaries of expertise, the peacebuilding field found a niche in the areas of prevention, mitigation, de-escalation, rehabilitation, and reintegration. Using prevalent theories on the lifecycle of conflict or the lifecycle of peacebuilding, these frameworks were welcomed by the countering VE (CVE) community to rethink their work with civil society members.

Nevertheless, defining the terms terrorism, VE, and radicalization has been a challenge for governments and scholars alike. For example, the Federal Bureau of Investigation defines it as "encouraging, condoning, justifying, or supporting the commission of a violent act to achieve political, ideological, religious, social, or economic goals."[16] The Department of Homeland Security asserts that CVE is "preventing all forms of ideologically based extremist violence, to include prevention of successful recruitment into terrorist groups. It is distinct from disruptive actions which focus on stopping acts of terrorism by those who have already subscribed to violence."[17] The American humanitarian assistance agency, the US Agency for International Development (USAID), defines CVE as "advocating, engaging in, preparing, or otherwise supporting ideologically motivated or justified violence to further social, economic or political objectives."[18] Even though there is no single consensus on the definition of CVE within the US government or among the United Nations or European Union, for our study, the definition of CVE is "using strategies with non-coercive means to dissuade individuals or groups from violence, and to reduce recruitment for, support of, or engagement in terrorism by non-state actors based on political discontent ideology."[19] Preventing VE (PVE) uses strategies to prevent radicalization from happening or spreading and acknowledges the roles of the rule of law, human rights, and civil liberties. Essentially, PVE aims to prevent radicalization from taking any roots in the first place, whereas CVE examines how radicalized individuals or groups can be interrupted, rehabilitated, reintegrated, and, perhaps, utilized to be change agents against the culture of VE.

Over the past decade, 2012 to 2022, PVE methods have been designed to recognize cultural dynamics, tribal culture, ethnic diversity, and human behavior since these initiatives often work with grassroots civil society organizations. PVE strategies focus on stakeholders on the frontlines of VE to understand the root causes of VE, address its key drivers, adopt crucial community-based approaches to prevent the spread of radicalism, and construct interventions to disengage individuals from violent extremist groups. Whereas some CVE approaches involve security-based measures, PVE program planners incorporate systematic preventive steps to address factors that make individuals vulnerable to recruitment by violent extremist groups.

Given the epidemic rise of violent extremist groups and terrorism in Muslim-majority communities, plus the splintering of violent extremist groups causing immense social, political, economic, development, and psychological damage, this chapter focuses on PVE and CVE strategies and programs to illustrate examples of active approaches in transforming communities. According to the National Counterterrorism Center, the lead US government agency responsible for monitoring terrorism, there are approximately seventy-five active violent extremist groups or designated foreign terrorist organizations actively operating in Muslim-majority communities.[20] The following section explores specific policies in Muslim-majority or -minority communities that involve education, community engagement, the use of narratives and focused messaging programs to prevent recruitment into VE, interruptive disengagement programs designed to intervene in the radicalization process, and how programs operated with the deradicalization, disengagement, and rehabilitation of former fighters.

According to the Global Terrorism Index, which provides a comprehensive summary of global trends and patterns of terrorism, the data indicates records of sixty-six thousand terrorist incidents from 2007 to 2023.[21]

Afghanistan remained the country most impacted by terrorism for the fourth consecutive year, although attacks and deaths fell by 75 percent and 58 percent, respectively. The Global Terrorism Index studies non-state actors' terrorism and does not include acts of state repression and violence by state actors. The deadliest terrorist groups in the world in 2022 were Islamic State (ISIS) and its affiliates, followed by al-Shabaab, Baluchistan Liberation Army, and Jama'at Nusrat Al-Islam wa al-Muslimeen. ISIS remained the deadliest terror group globally for the eighth consecutive year, recording the most attacks and deaths of any group in 2022. Irrespective of this reputation, terrorism deaths attributed to ISIS and its affiliate groups, Islamic State–Khorasan Province, Islamic State–Sinai Province, and Islamic State West Africa, declined by 16 percent. However, there has been a rapid increase in deaths attributed to unknown violent extremist jihadists in the countries where Islamic State West Africa operates, increasing seventeen times since 2017 to 1,766 terrorism deaths. Given the location, many of these are likely unclaimed attacks by Islamic State West Africa. Eighteen Muslim-majority and -minority countries experienced death from terrorism caused by ISIS in 2022, a slight decrease from 20 countries the year prior.

By 2022, the Sahel region in sub-Saharan Africa became the epicenter of terrorist attacks and recruitment for various violent extremist groups. The Sahel accounts for more terrorism deaths in 2022 than all the attacks in South Asia, the Middle East, and North Africa combined. According to the Global Terrorism Index, deaths in the Sahel constituted 43 percent of the global total in 2022, compared to just 1 percent in 2007. The two countries

Table 2.1. 2022 Global Terrorism Index: Overall Terrorism Index Score

Rank	Region	Score	Fatalities
1	Afghanistan	8.822	633
2	Burkina Faso	8.564	1,135
3	Somalia	8.463	755
4	Mali	8.412	944
5	Syria	8.161	447
6	Pakistan	8.16	643
7	Iraq	8.139	174
8	Nigeria	8.065	385
9	Myanmar	7.977	415
10	Niger	7.616	198

The Global Terrorism Index is a composite measure made up of four indicators: incidents, fatalities, injuries, and hostages. The top ten countries impacted by terrorism.

Source: Vision of Humanity, Global Terrorism Index 2023, https://www.visionofhumanity.org/maps/global-terrorism-index.

of concern are Burkina Faso and Mali, which accounted for 73 percent of terrorism deaths in the Sahel in 2022 and 52 percent of all deaths from terrorism in sub-Saharan Africa.[22] Both Burkina Faso and Mali recorded substantial increases in terrorism, with deaths in Burkina Faso increasing by 50 percent to 1,135 and in Mali by 56 percent to 944. Attacks in these countries are more deadly, with the number of people killed per attack increasing by 48 percent from 2021.[23]

One of the major concerns for local CVE experts is that most attacks are attributed to unknown violent extremist groups. Although the extremist groups ISIS and Jama'at Nusrat Al-Islam wa al-Muslimeen operate in these countries, these two groups did not claim many recorded attacks. As with the fear of organized crime, experts of CVE and terrorism are concerned with the problem of the spilling over effect into other countries. As an example, the escalation in violence in Burkina Faso has spread to neighboring countries Togo and Benin. The increase in terrorism in the Sahel has been dramatic, rising by over 2,000 percent in the last fifteen years bringing local governments into strategic discussions with the United Nations, European Union, African Union, and the United States.

ASSESSING FACTORS LEADING TO RADICALIZATION AND RECRUITMENT

Evidence demonstrates that the threat of terrorism from non-state actors is rising and conventional counterterrorism policies do not seem to reduce terrorism worldwide.[24] Governments in Muslim-majority nations have well-staffed departments in counterterrorism, terrorism intelligence, military and police intelligence, and other areas of law enforcement. However, there is a dire need for effective strategies and aligned policies with community programming to disrupt and dismantle the process of radicalization and recruitment into violent terrorism.

During the height of the Arab Spring pro-democracy protests of 2011 and 2012, Libyan leader Colonel Muammar Gaddafi was captured and brutally killed by rival tribes who believed his rule was tyrannical and authoritative. With his death came a vacuum in governance, political authority, and social cohesion, leading to violent extremist groups armed and supported by internal and external organizations. By the end of 2011, several violent extremist groups, including al-Qaeda in the Islamic Maghreb, established their presence in Libya with the support of local partners. In late 2014, the Islamic State of Iraq and the Levant and affiliated groups also officially established their presence, notably in the cities of Derna and Sirte, especially following the return of former militants who fought in Syria and Iraq within the Battar Brigade. Unfortunately, Libya's environment permitted the development of violent extremist groups due to the lack of a central government, weak political institutions, multiple direct military interventions, meddling by regional and global powers, and uncontrolled borders. At times, there was a totally absent judicial system, ineffective law enforcement, the widespread selling of weapons and narcotics, and a growing illicit economy—all of which contributed to the economic hardship for the local population. According to a reputable research institute report dedicated to examining radicalization, the International Centre for the Study of Radicalisation, by the end of December 2013, Libya was among the top five countries sending foreign fighters to Syria's civil war. It was reported that the post-revolution Libya, which was to create an open democratic society, became the site of the "fourth largest mobilization of foreign fighters in modern jihadist history," only behind Tunisia, which had the highest number of foreign fighter recruits coming from Tunisia. Concurrently, the Islamic State increased its recruitment efforts by targeting sub-Saharan African migrants in Libya.

One of the most extensive studies conducted by a team of local Libyan researchers and global CVE experts—supervised by the North African Policy Initiative and UN Development Programme Libya—is the 2022 report entitled, "A Preliminary Assessment of Preventing Violent Extremism in Libya," headed by Jean-Louis Romanet Perroux. This report was shared at the October 2022 conference in Tripoli, Libya, with the Libyan Ministry of Defense, the Ministry of Interior, the Ministry of Foreign, the Department of Justice, the Women Affairs Ministry, and the director of the Libyan Counterterrorism Center. Perroux's team studied civil society members, students, teachers, business leaders, government officials, political parties, tribal leaders, religious leaders, opinion leaders, and other stakeholders to understand the landscape of violent extremist groups better, how radicalization flourishes, and the specific villages, provinces, and localities where VE groups have had an impact.

Different factors influence the proliferation of VE at each level of state and society in Libya. The following are macro, meso, and micro factors and markers of VE.

Macro ("Push")	Country and community wide push factors: governance failures & grievances	Poverty and disengagement
		Overall failure in providing basic services
		Failure to ensure security and justice instability (conflicts and insecurity) corruption
		Close space for non-violent participation in governance
Meso ("Pull")	Community level Factors of attractiveness	Group experience with violence/injustice from authorities
		Group marginalization and/or discrimination
		Disenfranchisement of specific groups Instrumentalization of religion and ethnicity
		Cognitive Factors
		Social ties, group dynamics, material incentives
Micro	Individual level Vulnerabilities and individual experiences	Cognitive vulnerably, identity crisis, uprooting
		Lack of parental guidance (farther absence) Individual experience with violence/injustice)
		Socialization to violence / support for violence
		Failure in being the breadwinner (men)
		Mental health and drug addiction

Source: UN Development Programme Report, "A Preliminary Assessment of Preventing Violent Extremism in Libya."

Meso-level drivers operate at the level of smaller communities and identity groups rather than at the nation level. At this level, research indicates that identity is the critical element, be it religious, ethnic, or else. Among the elements forming an individual identity, the role of religion deserves special attention, particularly in terms of religious ideologies and the weaponization of religion.

The social context in which the subject lives plays an important role, especially if it has high levels of marginalization and discrimination. Living in a post-revolution society like Libya, vital drivers include diminished public services with more militia fighting, increase in the lack of opportunities for civic and political engagement and participation, and fewer opportunities for socio-economic mobility. The report found that adolescents are particularly fragile and easy to influence, and more easily seduced by extremist narratives, particularly if charismatic individuals among family members and friends propose violent extremist thinking. Another individual-level driver focuses on how young men form their identity with masculinity and how their identity may be transformed to meet the "extremist ideal man."[25]

Reprogramming concepts on masculinity and femininity are essential for recruitment by violent extremists. For instance, the "extremist ideal man" idea was drilled and programmed in adolescents as the model identity for Libyan men. Researchers found that teachers impart this distorted male identity to young boys through physical violence so that they learn how to endure pain, inflict it on others, and cope with witnessing acts of violence. These teachings of masculinity promoted the idea that the "ideal man" should be able to fight for a new, equitable society, provide for one's family as a breadwinner, be an excellent candidate for marriage with adequate financial earnings, and adhere to ultra-conservative religious beliefs. Failing to do any of these as a Libyan man was equivalent to being emasculated and useless. Women were equally vulnerable, especially those who struggled financially, were widows, were divorced, and did not have individuals actively involved in the protectors of their homes. Vulnerable women are those most at risk of "spinsterhood," that is, women who remain unmarried, because this is a social taboo in society. VE recruiters capitalized on this taboo by offering vulnerable women the prospect of marriage if they joined their group.

Among violent extremists, there are often "inversions" among the elements that make up an individual identity, whereby religious identity becomes stronger than communal and national identities. Meso-level markers show a social withdrawal and lack of connection with social activities, resulting in greater isolation from others. Micro markers include intolerance toward different opinions, a refusal to engage in dialogue with others, and a refusal to be a part of pluralistic societies writ large. There were definitive markers of intolerance visible through manifest anger, dehumanizing language, hate speech, outright prejudice, and intimidation of perceived enemies. Markers illustrated a mentality of an "absolutist mind" frame where some things must be absolutely rejected and others must be implemented without fail.[26]

The lack of hope of employment is cited as the primary driver of recruitment, reflecting generalized grievances of socio-economic injustice and marginalization. While economic factors, poverty, or the lack of education are the main drivers of recruitment to VE, they are relevant structural reasons. According to an in-depth UN Development Programme 2023 field report on VE in the Sahel region of Africa, "Journey to Extremism in Africa: Pathways to Recruitment and Disengagement," 25 percent of voluntary recruits cited "employment opportunities" as their primary reason for joining, particularly among the sample's male respondents. A total of 73 percent of voluntary recruits expressed frustration with the government in terms of providing employment opportunities, compared to 71 percent of the reference group.[27]

Among those fighters who fought with violent extremist groups, some expressed a widespread attitude of a lack of trust in government and its

Component	Level	Description	Indicator
Markers of Radicalization	Macro	Attitude toward institutions	Political disengagement Lack of trust in institutions Anger toward a group, or "the system" as a whole
	Meso	Attitude toward society	Social withdrawal, de-scholaraization Identity inversions (e.g. religious ID > other IDs)
	Micro	Attitude toward others	Intolerance Religious fundamentalism Lack of trust toward others Lack of support for gender equality

Source: UN Development Programme Report, "A Preliminary Assessment of Preventing Violent Extremism in Libya."

institutions, illustrating a fractured social contract between the state and its citizens. The study found low levels of trust in government institutions, particularly in security actors, and low levels of democratic participation in the outlook of all respondents. On average, voluntary recruits exhibited only marginally lower levels of trust. The dataset revealed a growing fractured social contract between the state and its citizens which opened prospects of an even greater spread of VE on the continent than in recent years, with further associated development backsliding and devastation. Within these attitudes, the UN Development Programme report found deep-seated perceptions of impunity and distrust in the security sector–fueled grievances. These grievances against security actors, notably the police, military, and the justice system, were particularly evident in this study on the Sahel region. A total of 62 percent of voluntary recruits reported having "little or no trust" in the police, with 61 percent expressing a similar negative perception toward the military and police.[28]

The field of VE recognizes radicalization as a highly socialized and dialectical process, influenced by a confluence of factors and conditions, to which a specific trigger event influenced an individual's decision to join, sometimes referred to as a "tipping point." Government action, accompanied by human rights abuses, lack of economic opportunities, state repression, daily occurrences of injustices, and perceptions of absolute corruption accelerated recruitment toward VE. The UN Development Programme report cited 71 percent of the 48 percent who described having experienced a trigger event. It cited government action, including the killing and arresting of family or friends as the specific event that ultimately urged them to join a violent extremist group. Trigger events were also found to be a significant accelerator of recruitment, with higher levels of anger and fear featuring more prominently among those who joined more quickly, compared to those who joined more slowly and reported highlights how recruitment into violent extremist groups presents a unique "pull" opportunity for change and an opportunity to rebel against the status quo. These findings demonstrate that the recruitment of violent extremist groups related to their personal experiences with state repression, state human rights abuses, and experiencing state institutions as failed corrupt entities.

PREVENTION OF VIOLENT EXTREMISM

CVE experts, scholars, and civil society practitioners do not have a single formula or approach to preventing the spread of VE. Among psychiatrists and trained profilers, there is no single explanation as to why one individual is attracted to VE groups while other individuals from the same group do not find it attractive to join a violent extremist group. An agreed definition is that VE is a mobilization that aims to elevate the status of one group while excluding or dominating others based on markers, religion, tribe, gender, culture, and ethnicity. In pursuit of these goals, violent extremist organizations believe they need to destroy existing political and cultural institutions and supplant them with alternative government structures that operate according to the principles of a totalitarian vision of their ideology. Those within the security sector and law enforcement agencies believe that because of the nature of violent tactics used against civilians and the military, resolving this issue requires force to subordinate and dismember VE groups.

According to USAID's 2020 report, "Policy for Countering Violent Extremism through Development Assistance," the organization will work with national and local governments to do the following:

> Build a community of partners with the commitment and capacity to prevent and counter VE in their own countries and regions, engage where US development assistance can have a meaningful impact, and anticipate how VE will evolve and adjust programming accordingly.[29]

USAID's CVE programming aims to foster self-reliance in their partner countries to prevent and counter the violent extremist challenges that threaten to derail their development. The organization designs programs to reduce the risk of recruitment into, and support for, VE while building the capacity and commitment of their partners in government, civil society, youth, and women sectors.[30] It is an updated and revised approach from the 2011 USAID report "The Development Response to Violent Extremism and Insurgency Policy" and the 2016 Department of State and USAID Joint Strategy on Countering Violent Extremism.[31] The policy thinking behind these government assistance–driving CVE programs is to directly target "development tools" to affect an identified or emerging problem with VE. CVE activities should be situated within broader multisectoral development strategies to address political marginalization, weak governance, conflict, fragile social cohesion, threats to religious freedom, reduced economic and educational opportunities, and other structural conditions that lead to the spread of VE.[32] These USAID-sponsored programs attempt to support and enhance local partners' commitment, capacity, and interaction because the organization recognizes that local actors at all levels of society need local ownership. The development agency prioritized supporting stakeholders: government institutions, civil society, customary authorities, religious leaders, women's groups, youth organizations, the private sector, and communities who need to take the lead to protect their communities.

An interesting component of USAID's CVE development approach is assessing the distinguishing contexts of conflict zones by tailoring the programs accordingly. Asserting that "violent extremism most often arises in conflict-affected and fragile states, USAID will consider the relationship between CVE, fragility, and violent conflict and will design, manage, and monitor programming to minimize unintended consequences and maximize positive outcomes."[33] To avoid stove-piping interventions that might inadvertently do harm and exacerbate the problem, USAID will "be vigilant in those places where violent extremism and other forms of violence, state repression, and related governance failures, crime, and mass atrocity mutually influence one another."[34] The development agency's approach is to effectively harness the positive power of youth and other civil society members to inculcate resilience and cohesion, reducing the susceptibility to the attraction of VE recruitment. The agency regularly points to a USAID-funded "Somalia Youth Leadership Initiative" where pre-evaluations and post-evaluations documented that the combination of increased educational and civic engagement opportunities collectively lowered young people's support for, and participation in, political violence.[35]

PVE programs have one overarching theory of change to heavily concentrate on civil society members to have the tools, resources, networks, and international support to be empowered to protect themselves from violent extremist recruitment. But how exactly are these programs supporting empowerment? What do they mean by tools? How do international development agencies understand the process of "bolstering the resilience" of local peacebuilding systems? The key thinking is that local civil society members have raw and underdeveloped capacity to withstand the forces of VE groups. By funding a select group of civil society organizations and community-level partners, they will receive support to increase knowledge and skills, bringing a heightened understanding and strategic thinking on violence prevention and sustaining CVE networks. An often-cited example is the USAID's Office of Transition Initiatives work in the Republic of Niger, which worked with twelve civil society leaders in the Southern Diffa region to create the Nalewa Mada ("We search for peace") network to enhance the resilience skills of local leaders to Boko Haram and the Islamic State West Africa. The network now includes over three hundred religious, traditional, youth, and women leaders in over thirty villages. While conflict is rampant in the region, Office of Transition Initiatives officials claim that communities and local authorities recognize the network as a key contributor to efforts to promote peace and reconciliation. The network created and implemented an early warning system for the Nalewa Mada network to be aware of the presence of VE messaging—either online or visible posters—and of kidnappings of children or attacks on villages. The Nalewa Mada network conducted local-level projects, including supporting communities reintegrating former Boko Haram and Islamic State West Africa fighters with finding temporary employment and rehabilitation processes.[36]

INVOLVING THE COMMUNITY

Despite the support of international development agencies, local civil society members complain about the lack of a sustainable, community-based CVE approach with long-term improvement goals. In a context where the state cannot deliver basic social services or even provide adequate education for its citizens, local civil society members argue that they are fighting an uphill battle with local perceptions of inequality, exclusion, or deliberate discrimination. Civil society organizations argue that unless governments reverse the patterns of poor governance that entrench injustice, corruption, inequality, and exclusion of the marginalized, then the culture of attraction to violent extremist groups will continue to be an option for those who believe this is the pathway for societal change. With little guarantee of citizens' security, human rights, justice, and economic opportunities, local civil society members stress that it is vital to focus on community-based approaches.

Houda Abadi's analysis "Community Approaches to Preventing Violent Extremism: Morocco as a Case Study" explicitly argues that engaging religious actors from the outset and recognizing their role in providing psychological and social support to those vulnerable to recruitment is vital. Trained in the peacebuilding and conflict resolution field and having worked for The Carter Foundation, Abadi researched and interviewed former Islamic State of Iraq and the Levant fighters on how they manipulated local populations with emotional appeal, false hopes, financial incentives, and used propaganda to exploit young men and women from Morocco to join the groups. Abadi directed and designed a three-year locally tailored project that worked with community and religious leaders from North Africa to develop practical applications to prevent VE.[37] These programs centered on amplifying locally credible voices to counter the messaging of VE groups. By focusing on community-led programs on VE, Abadi saw how her local interlocutors, including women and men, mainstream and conservative religious leaders, journalists, academics, activists, and ex-foreign fighters, felt heavily invested in protecting their communities. The training outcome supported participants in developing and launching sixty different projects across multiple sectors, including media initiatives, religious outreach, youth engagement, and gender programming. These community-led projects expanded their local networks across political, gender, tribal, and ideological divisions.[38]

One of the critically important areas in CVE community-based approaches is that field research supports evidence on the benefits of cooperating with religious leaders and faith-based organizations and community leaders because their legitimacy and partnership give credibility. Their authority within local communities reveals a history of relationships within the community, their keen understanding of issues facing them, and their existing knowledge and past experiences in navigating law enforcement, judicial, educational, social, political, and military bureaucracies. Reports suggest that preventative programs and solutions must be anchored with youth as partners from the beginning of the project. Youth are essential in community-based CVE programs because they are invested in PVE from taking root in the community and are thoroughly engaged with opportunities to lead projects from inception. PVE programs led by youth increases ownership tailormade to their local context.

One key concern is how national CVE strategies in Muslim-majority countries are not aligned with law enforcement, the security sector, civil society organizations, and international development agencies. A country may have instituted a national taskforce to address VE and the prevention of the spread of radicalism, but it usually never goes beyond engaging security policymakers and military experts. Since a government's taskforce focuses on assessing, monitoring public security, and the failures of security intelligence, they neglect to incorporate human rights activists, youth, women, family support groups, and the education, social work, healthcare, and religion sectors. This gap contributes toward a trust-building deficit between governments and communities, and it is an important area to develop and implement a comprehensive national CVE strategy. Both UN and USAID reporting indicate that any successful CVE programming at the local level hinges upon stronger relationships with teachers, youth, women, sports, cultural clubs, and integrating religious youths and imams with the broader communities. Often, there is an urban bias in focusing on CVE interventions that neglect rural areas and the community of female leaders, women groups, and faith-based organizations led by female leaders, academics, activists, and female influencers. It is not just a matter of including female civil society organizations or youth groups; instead, it is imperative to empower them with leadership positions in CVE intervention efforts.

NOTES

1. Ulrich Beck, "Reframing Power in the Globalized World," *Organization Studies* 29 (05): 793–96.
2. Jennifer Hoewe and Brian Bowe, "The Impact of Online Network Diversity on Familiarity and Engagement with Social Issues News on Facebook," *The Journal of Social Media in Society* 12, no. 1 (2018): 309–47.
3. Ibid., pg. 15.

4. Ibid., pg. 16.
5. International Studies Association, www.isanet.org.
6. Mohammed Sulaiman, "Orientalism and Anti-Orientalism: Epistemological Approaches to Islam and Violence," in F. Mansouri and Z. Keskin (eds.), *Contesting the Theological Foundations of Islamism and Violent Extremism* (New York: Palgrave Macmillan), pp. 75–95.
7. Mohammed Sulaiman, "Islam, Eurocentrism, and the Question of Jihadism," *Thesis Eleven* (2022), pg. 65.
8. Ibid., pg. 71.
9. Ibid., pp. 76–77.
10. Bassam Tibi, *Islam in Global Politics: Conflict and Cross-Civilizational Bridging* (London: Routledge Press, 2012). For more on Tibi's works on religion, Arab nationalism, and international affairs, see *Arab Nationalism. Between Islam and the Nation-State* (Houndmills: Palgrave Macmillan, 1990) and *The Challenge of Fundamentalism: Political Islam and the New World Disorder* (Berkeley: University of California Press, 1998).
11. Alex Schmid, "Violent and Non-Violent Extremism: Two Sides of the Same Coin," ICCT Research Paper, 2014, pg. 14.
12. Ibid., pg. 16.
13. Ineke Roex, "Should We Be Scared of All Salafists in Europe? A Dutch Case Study," *Perspectives on Terrorism* 8, no. 3 (2014): 51–63.
14. Ibid., pg. 59.
15. Schmid, pg. 18.
16. Federal Bureau of Investigation, "Don't Be a Puppet," (2021), https://www.fbi.gov/cve508/teen-website/what-is-violent-extremism.
17. U.S. Department of Homeland Security, "Factsheet: A Comprehensive U.S. Government Approach to Countering Violent Extremism," (2021), https://www.dhs.gov/sites/default/files/publications/US%20Government%20Approach%20to%20CVE-Fact%20Sheet_0.pdf.
18. Andrew Glazzard and Martine Zeuthen, *Violent Extremism*, GSDRC, February 2016, https://gsdrc.org/professional-dev/violent-extremism/.
19. *European Union Terrorism Situation and Trend Report 2023*, pg. 5, https://www.europol.europa.eu/cms/sites/default/files/documents/Europol_TE-SAT_2023.pdf.
20. See https://www.dni.gov/nctc/ftos.html.
21. See https://www.visionofhumanity.org.
22. Ibid., pgs. 8–9.
23. Ibid., pg. 10.
24. Ronald Crelinsten, *Counter-terrorism* (Cambridge: Polity Press, 2009).
25. UN Development Programme, "A Preliminary Assessment of Preventing Violent Extremism in Libya," 2022, pg. 22.
26. Ibid., pg. 29.
27. UN Development Programme, "Journey to Extremism in Africa: Pathways to Recruitment and Disengagement," 2023, pg. 11.
28. Ibid., pg. 18.
29. USAID, "Policy for Countering Violent Extremism through Development Assistance," 2020, pg. 4.
30. Ibid., pg. 7.
31. For more information on these reports, see USAID, "The Development Response to Violent Extremism and Insurgency Policy (2011) and "The Department of State and USAID Joint Strategy on Countering Violent Extremism" (2016).

32. Ibid., pp. 8–9.

33. USAID, *Policy for Countering Violent Extremism through Development Assistance* (Washington, DC, 2020), pg. 5.

34. Ibid., pg. 12.

35. See USAID, "Promising Practices in Engaging Youth in Peace and Security and P/CVE" (2017).

36. For more information on OTI's Niger work, see https://2012-2017.usaid.gov/political-transition-initiatives/niger.

37. Houda Abadi, "Community Approaches to Preventing Violent Extremism: Morocco as a Case Study," CGP Policy Brief, June 2019, pg. 5.

38. Ibid., pg. 11.

Chapter Three

Rethinking Violence and Countering Violent Extremism

An analysis of violence, nonviolence, peacebuilding, and conflict resolution within the religion of Islam is not a task for the non-specialist or impatient reader. There are over fourteen hundred years of scholarly materials in over four dozen languages written by Muslim religious scholars, theologians, philosophers, mathematicians, academics, and civil society activists. In the modern period, Islamists and other political activists with engineering, medical, or other science training have been confidently compelled to contribute to this topic despite their gap in academic training. In parsing and examining the sources, I purposely tackled the issues of violence and peacebuilding from a scholarly and practitioner perspective where I delved into the primary sources. Moreover, historical writings become alive when we are engaged with prominent Muslim religious scholars specializing in these fields.

IDENTITY AND VIOLENCE

The field of identity studies is rich with interdisciplinary approaches, numerous frameworks, and evolving theories of the meaning of identity in the modern world. One of the major conclusions from this field is the recognition that identities are robustly plural, and the importance of one's identity need not obliterate the importance of others. At the core of this identity question is the issue of choices—implicitly or explicitly—about what relative importance to attach to a particular context, reconciling divergent loyalties and priorities that may compete for your commitment. As individuals examine their identities, it is equally important to identify with others, in various ways, to be connected to living in a society. Amartya Sen argues that there is a role of choice and an inner rational process of decision-making in choosing priorities, values, principles, and ethics in our identity. Reasoning and scrutiny play a major role both in the specification of identities and in thinking through the relative strengths of their respective claims. Sen thinks that when we consider our identities as we see them or as others see us, we choose within constraints. Just as a consumer chooses within a budget constraint—which illustrates constraints and rational decision-making—people choose aspects of their identity within a constraint.[1]

Sen's rational decision-making is tied to choices over alternative identities or a combination of identities, or the limitations tied to those priorities we assigned to it. Also, Sen contests analytical studies that claim that religious identities are the leading or sole principle of people. He thinks this perspective fails to distinguish between various affiliations and loyalties a person has and the religious identity itself. As an individual deciding, manufacturing, and constructing an identity in evolving circumstances, this is connected to their processing of information which may be compatible or incompatible with their inner ethical systems.[2]

An individual's experience with crime may be a formative identity maker: it will vary with the degree of pain and suffering, the severity of pain forced onto the victim, the challenges of recovering from this event, the memory of the violent attack, and to what extent the victim permits the crime take a central role in the identity. Sen believes this process of choosing within constraints also includes important aspects of culture and the dominating force culture plays in interpreting, reflecting, healing, and recovery from any tragic event. In this scenario, violence is perpetrated against a victim who receives the violence; both the perpetrator and victim have been shaped with the instrument of violence but afterward the event subsides, both individuals will need to define the place of violence in their identity decision process. As individuals and groups ask questions about the values, ethics, and sense of belonging that shape our conception of the globalized world, there will be an important dialogue to address individual violence, communal violence, national-sponsored violence, and global violence. These questions are fundamental to our identity and to the way we interact with each other and the global community; the question is not whether we want a world of violence versus nonviolence, but rather can there be a managed coexistence and tolerance with those who advocate violence for change?

The first section of this chapter analyzes the Islamic reasoning for the use of violence and conflict while examining the reconciliation of violence in accordance with the Qur'an and the sayings and deeds of the Prophet Muhammad (*hadith* and *sunna*). The ethics of violence and the interpretation of its use in the Islamic tradition were historically connected to legalists and theologians who colluded, advised, and, in some cases, were employed by the heads of state on these issues. Their reading of the sources to support violence can be explained in three key areas: survival, self-defense, and using force to resist oppression. Historically, the use of violence is defined in terms of the needs of the state: what is good for a secure and prosperous government is good for the religion of Islam. Modern scholars of Islam are revisiting the problem of violence and the weaknesses of classical interpretations in light of pressing contemporary issues like the rights of the unborn, abortion, individual versus communal self-defense, terrorism and foreign fighters of terrorist groups, domestic violence, and related topics like ethnic violence. The scope of this section is to discuss the ideas of harmony and divine unity in Islamic theology and the several important reasons they are crucial to any understanding of violence. Next, I proceed to analyze ideas relating to violence "for" and "against" God in the Islamic tradition and how those ideas fit into the more extensive Islamic theology. Examining essential verses from the Qur'an and sayings of the Prophet that deal with war, conflict, and violence demonstrate that their contextuality is crucial.

THE PROBLEM WITH VIOLENCE: ISLAMIC THEOLOGY, MUSLIMS, AND DIVINE UNITY

The beginning of all Islamic thought begins with God, or more specifically, with the testimony of faith or *shahadah*,[3] the statement that "There is no God but God, and the Prophet Muhammad is the Messenger." This attestation for Muslims is understood to be a unique certainty upon which all other truths depend and exist. With this as the starting point for Islamic beliefs, creeds, and practices, "What is the Islamic perspective on peace and violence as it is related to God and the testimony of faith?" "How have theologians, jurists, philosophers, historians, and other scholars respond to the problems of violence (i.e., destructive behavior to oneself or others by persons who believe that they are thereby serving and surrendering to God)?"

Most readers know that Arabic Islam stems from the root *salam*, or "peace." The literal sense of the word is to be liberated from something or to gain peace in respect to it. It is understood that those who participate in this act of surrendering to the Divine are called Muslims, and through submitting one's will to God's will, one gains safety from error, deviation, and corruption. One is integrally tied into the Divine Unity and is in harmony with the Divine. With this in the background, *al-salaam* or "the peace" is one of the names of God.[4] The Qur'an calls God "the Peace" as in the following passage: "He is God; there is no God but He. He is King, Holy, Peace, Faithful, Preserver, Mighty, Compeller, Sublime. Glory to be God above everything they associate with Him. He is God, the Creator, the Maker, the Form-giver. To Him belong the Names Most Beautiful. All that is in the heavens and the earth glorifies Him. He is Mighty, Wise" (Q: 59:23).

In many ways, this Quranic verse reflects themes that epitomize the essence of Islamic theology. More specifically, it expresses two very important ideas about God which are repeated in the Qur'an. First and foremost, the transcendence of the Divine reality. The name of "Peace" for God signifies that God is free from and infinitely exalted above all defects and imperfections. Perfection is reserved for the divine while errors and imperfections are reserved for His creation, not the Creator. In Himself God knows no violence, hostility, conflict, or antagonism. Second, this verse reflects that Divine immanence is in all created things. He is close enough to His creatures, despite His transcendence, to shape and form all things. All attributes or qualities found in the world derive from Him; so, the Quranic verse "Where soever you turn, there is the Face of God" (Q: 2:115). His creation cannot forget to see and then acknowledge the "face of God" in this world. Again, the words of verse 59:23 quoted earlier—"All that is in the heaven and the earth glorifies Him"—alert us not just to the fact that He is exalted beyond creaturely imperfections, but mainly because every positive and beautiful attribute comes from Him. This idea is constantly repeated in the Qur'an; everything in the universe displays God's "signs" or ayat.[4] For example: "Surely in the creation of the heavens and the earth, and the alternation of the night and day, and the ship that runs in the sea and the clouds compelled between heaven and earth—surely there are signs for people who understand" (Q: 2:164).

To return to my original point, "peace" means that no imperfection, conflict, or violence is found in God. By implication, "there is no God but God" means that "there is no Peace but God" and "there is no perfection but God." Moreover, "everything other than God" (*ma siwa Allah*), which many theologians have defined as the concept of the world (*al-alam*), is different from God. Essentially, everything other than God is imperfect by definition; true peace belongs to God alone, while any peace possessed by His creatures can only be imperfect and perishing.[5] It is a challenge for Muslims seeking complete self-understanding and searching for the "ultimate peace" to access God's self-disclosure.

Within this context, Islam, God's Peace follows upon His Unity: He is one in every respect, so there is nothing in Himself other than Himself that could oppose or contradict Him. His Self is totally unlike the human self, which is understood to be constantly flooded with conflicting thoughts and feelings. In essence, human beings are never wholly at peace with themselves, at least in the way I am using here, because they are composed of opposing faculties, emotions, and energies. According to this line of thinking, peace as such belongs only to God, while its opposite—war, violence, conflict—is to some extent intrinsic to everything other than God, to all created things.

It would be simplistic to assume that if God is absolute Peace, then the world and its creation is "absolute war." The world is only "relative war" or imperfect. But because of God's presence in all things, it is also relatively peaceful too. The world's peace—the harmony and equilibrium that does exist among its opposing forces—is, in Quranic terms, a "sign" or, really, a reflection of God's Absolute Peace. For Muslim theologians, the world is a mixture of opposing forces that may conflict or harmonize depending on the situation. Its relative peace is to be increased or achieved; this can be done only by bringing it closer to the Absolute Peace of God. Islamically speaking, then, does this lead us to rethink whether all types of war, violence, conflict, and all other types of hostility are necessarily wrong? Not according to the fundamentals of Islamic theology because the notion of violence is inherent to the world, and the world is God's good creation. Hence, all conflicts and violence must be working toward God's end, even if they appear evil in our eyes. In other words, conflict, violence, and "opposition" may make up the different dimensions of an equilibrium that escapes our human views. Muslim theologians have historically argued that conflict, violence, and 'opposition' must ultimately derive from God since He created the world and accomplished His aims through all its opposing forces.

GOD'S NAMES

In Islamic piety, that is being in the constant process of surrendering oneself to the one God (Allah), a Muslim has multidimensional varied relationships with God. He is the Life-Giver, the Most Compassionate, the Forgiver, and the Avenger.[6] Creation, specifically human beings, relates to these names and others at any given time. We are connected to the divine because every ontological moment comes from the nature of the divine. Muslim theologians have argued that since we constantly undergo physical, emotional, spiritual, and material changes, God is interested in being involved with His creation and bestows a new relationship with the aforementioned names. For Muslims, each name conveys how God establishes relationships between Himself and us. At times, we may perceive that these ways may conflict at any given moment; it is essential to keep in mind that the complete totality of existence represents the harmony of all the different modes. This is because all existence pours from God's reality, just as a ray of light from the sun. There may be numerous colors of light, yellow, red, or blue, but all of them are essentially the same light from the same source.

The multiplicity of God's names does not infer the pluralistic nature of God but affirms the oneness of Divine unity.[7] To restate an earlier point, the names coexist in God Himself and are harmonious (i.e., essentially "Peaceful"). The names of God are no different from His Being. The "Compassionate" is God, and the "Forgiver" is God, and the "Life-Giver" is also God. While in this world and human perception, the names of the Forgiver and Vengeful appear to be in opposition in conflict with our understanding, the opposition works together in a context of Divine Unity. A common reference in theological texts of the medieval period (e.g., in Ibn "Arabi," is that "All colors in the spectrum are manifestations of the One Light").

For a more straightforward example, God is both Merciful and Wrathful. While on the surface, it may appear that there is a contradiction, the Prophet Muhammad once stated, "God's Mercy precedes His wrath." Muslim theologians have understood that Mercy is before His Wrath because God's Mercy represents the divine nature itself. At the same time, Wrath is an attribute God assumes only in relationship to creatures. It is not only the idea that He is Merciful toward all creatures and Wrathful to some but also that His Wrath must be considered an extension of His Mercy. In addition, in the Qur'an, each chapter (*surah*) begins with the statement: "In the Name of the God, the Merciful (*al-rahman*), the Compassionate (*ar-rahim*)." This reinforces the priority of Mercy in God's nature. One should also note that the words "Merciful" and "Compassionate" stem from the same words, *rahma*, God's Harmony and Conflict with human beings. Also, "Everything in the heavens and the earth glorifies God" (Q: 24:I, 57:I, 61) is a verse found repeatedly in the Qur'an, implying that the glorification of all creatures is a type of work that fosters harmony. On every level of created existence, creatures, particularly humans, need to be harmonious with, not in conflict with, their Creator. For example, in verse 51:56, the Qur'an states, "I have not created jinn and humankind except to worship Me."[8] Our existence in this world means to worship the Creator so that there is harmony, peace, and direct contact between the Creator and His creation. The antagonism and conflicts that come with creation (i.e., with the experience of human beings) is the movement away from worship of the Divine Reality, and toward the worship of this world or, as explicitly stated in the Qur'an, the worship of *al-dunya*. For example, "He has commanded that you worship none but Him. That is the right religion, but most men know not" (Q: 12:40) illustrates a prescriptive command; those who follow it will know and others who disobey will not know. What is unique about human beings as creation, at least as understood Islamically, is their unique sense to grapple with free will, to think, assess, evaluate, and reflect upon God's nature. Human beings, according to the sacred scripture of the Qur'an, choose righteous behavior and steer away from immorality by using reason and Islamic moral principles (*al-Amr bi-al-Maruf wa'l Nahy an al-Munkar*).

While there is no original sin concept in the Islamic tradition, there is an idea that human beings were made with imperfections to overcome them and thereby prove their surrendering to the One God. Connected with this is the idea of forgetfulness or *ghaflah* and its remedy: remembering. One way to be constantly reminded of the Divine is to remember through the signs of creation or through worship.[9]

According to Quranic theology, God made human beings as His vicegerents or representatives (*khalifah*) on earth (Q: 2:30). The Qur'an calls this representation a type of trust that no other creature can carry out (Q: 33:72). The corruption or disobedience of this trust between God and human beings is what brings about evil consequences. This type of conflict and violation leads to further violation of the earth. For Muslim scholars like al-Ghazali (d.1111) and Muhyiddin Ibn 'Arabi (d.1240), the closer human beings are connected to Divine Mercy (*rahma*), the tighter the bond is built on harmony with Divine Peace. However, believers who stray from this bond inevitably fail to be trustworthy custodians. This corruption or *fasad,* mentioned in the Qur'an over fifty times, is produced by human error, human free will, and from being neglectful. The verse in Qur'an 30:41 ("Corruption has spread over land and sea from what men have done themselves that they may taste a little of what they have done: They may haply come back to the right path") demonstrates that God is actively involved with human affairs: whether it is obedience or disobedience, the Creator desires His creatures to witness the result of their capriciousness. Human corruption or the ongoing drama of *fasad* on earth is meant for them to help humans find ways to rectify the corruption they have created.

The Qur'an speaks on this subject of violence on earth that can have a positive return to God through repentance. Human disobedience does not merely bring the misuse of earth's resources and profane violence against the trust, the custodianship of earth, but more importantly, there is another level of human disobedience that fails to affirm God's Unity. At the heart of Islamic theology is the oneness of God (*tawhid*); any association of partners to the One God (*shirk*), or erroneous inclusion of the multiplicity into the single God, the single Source, forces the believer away from the center into dispersion. The association of partners or constructing the "manyness" to the One God is understood to be the ultimate sin in Islam and the very trust God gave to His believers.

THE USE OF VIOLENCE

For pious believers, the doctrine of *tawhid* or the oneness of God is the single prominent feature of professing Divine Unity. Every moment, every level of existence requires the believer to assert *tawhid*. Believers must struggle to conform to God's nature on every conceivable level (i.e., the mind, heart, and soul). Active affirmation of *tawhid* means that believers need to struggle in daily affairs so that, through one's piety and acknowledgment, each moment is connected to the be-ing with the divine.

As a revelation to humankind, the Qur'an commands its believers to work toward establishing a life of *tawhid*, and to establish this realization, it describes it as a human struggle or an effort in a struggle—*jihad*. Usually mistaken as a "holy war against non-Muslims," *jihad* is used repeatedly in the Qur'an 14 in the sense of a striving toward a life of God-consciousness, which often means resisting the attractions of ungodly things. While Muslim caliphs, more accurately called Sultans or kings of the Ottoman, Abbasid, and Mamluk dynasties, applied the word *jihad* to fight and defend their territories either against competing Muslim dynasties or external Christian forces, one cannot compare the "holiness" of striving for an internal harmony with God with that of battling opponents of the state.[10] Quranic verses, such as 22:78 "Struggle (*jihad*) for God as is His due," illustrate a transcendence of the inner soul, which tries to struggle against all distractions away from Divine Unity. The Prophet's saying, "I have come from the lesser struggle to the greater struggle," points out that there are elements of the soul, sometimes called the lower soul, containing caprice, which is the real *jihad* for believers to control.[11] The Qur'an verse speaks of the struggle of the inner soul in surah 29:6, where it states, "Whosoever struggles, struggles only for his soul; surely God is independent of all the worlds." The main point here is to demonstrate that the word *jihad* has been misused and misinterpreted historically and in contemporary times to justify one's political agendas.[12]

To take the word out of its theological context, which is to struggle to preserve *tawhid* awareness[13] in one's faith, is to ignore the way it was intended by the Qur'an and the spiritual model set by the Prophet Muhammad. The inner *jihad* is a struggle to eliminate this internal warfare; by doing this, one attains peace with God. In contrast, the outer *jihad* signifies working toward a fair and non-corrupt society. The trust of being a representative of God or vicegerent is not a symbolic gesture, but often in some classical and modern sources, the primary role of being a believer.

Violence or war against God has inner and outer dimensions (i.e., struggling against corruption, oppression, and non-provoked aggression), which means the individual strives to establish or maintain peace in the world. This war is a war between believers and non-believers, that is, between people who stand to uphold God's unity and justice in this world and those who "prevent" one from being on that path. The inner struggle of a purified heart constantly struggles to maintain a "*tawhid*" awareness. In Quranic verse 4:167, it states, "Surely those who disbelieve and bar from the way of God have gone astray into far error," demonstrating the slippery path of *tawhid*. In Islamic theology, peace in God is the goal of human existence, while war against His enemies, including the inner soul, is one of many ways to achieve this peace. Those who become distant from the Creator are essentially turning their backs upon the vicegerent trust from God.[14] For Islamic theology, to be a complete believer or even to be fully human, one needs to be with Him and constantly struggle against the movement away from the Creator because it is only through proximity with God's Unity that one can attain peace with Him. This explains why most Muslim theologians agree that the ultimate struggle (*jihad*) in the world for believers is to exist in the domain where God wishes you to be, such as in contemplation, prayers, worship, fasting, charity, etc., all these areas bring forth His Peace. In this short theological account of *jihad*, one can see that Muslim scholars have been primarily concerned with how struggling brings (the process) one nearer to God in the context of sharing in a harmonious divine unity.

SCRIPTURE AND VIOLENCE

For some unfamiliar with Islam's sacred text as a revelation, it is difficult to understand why God would include revelations that address the issue of violence. The Qur'an is not a book about the divine but rather a revelation for human beings to redirect their attention to the divine as the sole creator and the source of things known and unknown. As with previous revelations to earlier Prophets, the Qur'an states that there were 124,000 prophets in history, the Quranic revelation was a message for human beings to reconstitute their lives so that they would know what it means to be God-conscious and be aware of those actions that lead one away from the divine.

If a revelation is a communication from God to believers, that is, God revealed Himself through the miracle of the Qur'an, then the holiness of the Qur'an means that it incorporates God's directives and the specific requirements for human beings to establish a sacred relationship with the divine. The Quranic verses that contain detailed instructions on violence are understood as instructions from the divine to preserve order at a particular time and place. For example, two critical references to violence are found in verses 17:33 and 25:68, which state: "*Wa-la taqtulu an-nafs allatt harrama Allah illa bi-li-haqq*," which is translated as "Do not kill the soul that God has made sacred, except for a just cause." The taking away of life means removing the sacredness of life from that soul which God has created. Everyone's life or soul is precious because of God's original creation and, most importantly, He is always present in it. For human beings to interfere in God's work by destroying it is entirely against the desires of the divine. The Quranic verse instructs believers, particularly the new Muslims of the seventh century, not to kill any human life. The condition attached to the end, "except for a just cause," is a direct instruction that conflict or violence is unacceptable unless there is a just cause for it. How is a just cause defined? During the life of the Prophet and the first generation of Muslims a "just cause" was interpreted as a situation in which the lives of Muslims were threatened by hostile aggression. That is, from the earliest Muslim jurists of the ninth century, the use of force was acceptable only if it was used for self-defense and self-preservation.

Quranic references to violence are not only restricted to self-defense or to counterbalance attacks, but also to protect the innocent newborn. For example, verse 6:140: "And do not slay your children for fear of poverty. We provide for you and them." This verse is a good example of how revelations served as instructional practices for new believers so that they know what practices are pleasing to God and which practices are thought to be against God's wishes. Killing infants because of poverty was a normal cultural practice, especially if the family or tribe progressively became poor. Quranic verses revealed to the Prophet were meant to remind humankind of God's presence in all things and alter behavior patterns that met the ethical standard of a loving God. This verse redirects believers to care for their infants regardless of their social standing and to have faith in the one God who is always present to support each soul. "We provide for you and them" reflects an absolute unconditional statement that no one is ever left alone in raising children; in particular, the poor are especially reminded of God's interest in their conditions.

Another example dealing with the death of infants is verse 81:8–9: "And when the female infant buried alive is asked for what sin she was killed" are concerned with changing the practices of female infanticide. Pre-Islamic Arab tribal cultural norms were to prefer a male infant because of a man's primary role in a patriarchal society. Quranic revelations strictly forbade this practice to show that God will provide for each infant born. In addition, these verses wanted to connect a very important theological concept of each believer's accountability, responsibility, and preservation of life. To randomly kill infants without thinking that all actions produce consequences is to not recognize the eventual encounter with the Creator in the hereafter and that everyone will be accountable for each action at that time. Verses 81:8–9 explicitly remind the believer how unjust killings will be assessed; those lives that were unfairly taken away will demand to know why this injustice was done to them.

To demonstrate that the references to violence in the Qur'an are not always a spiritual and temporal guide or a theological reminder of the hereafter, there are numerous stories of the Biblical prophets who were tested for their allegiance to the one God. The story of the Prophet Abraham is viewed in this way: all his trials and tribulations are as a prophet who desired his family and fellow tribespersons to adhere to the single God.[15] The

Qur'an views his achievement, specifically his challenging experiences as an outcast, as a testimony of God's commitment to guiding human beings. Abraham's story in the Qur'an reminds Muslims that even against our own good judgment and desires, there is a level of "violence" needed to prove our love and obedience to God. For example, the Qur'an verses 37:104–13 refer to Abraham's last test to sacrifice his son: "We called out Oh Abraham, you have fulfilled your dream. Thus, do We reward the good. That was indeed a trying test. So we ransomed him for a great sacrifice."

The story of Abraham and his family is a central event for pious Muslims every year in the eleventh month of the Islamic calendar to re-enact Abraham's sacrifice. There are theological reasons for Muslims to reconnect to Abraham's plight to have an annual fresh understanding of what it means to kill for the Lord. This is summed up in the hajj or pilgrimage, which is conducted in the first ten days of the eleventh month of the Islamic calendar.[16] Abraham's paradigm substitutes humans with animals, allowing the believer to view life, life taken away, and the struggle to keep the resistance to death, all as a divine sacrifice. This annual ritual has multilevel lessons for the believer to reflect on the preciousness of life and to whom life ultimately belongs. While the hajj ritual is intended to reconnect to the plight of Abraham and Haggar, it ultimately is concerned with believers returning to the most sacred site for Muslims, which stands under the Heavens, and proving to the divine one's total surrender to Him. On the one hand, pilgrims are astonished at the global community of Islam, and on the other hand, pilgrims are there to satisfy a major religious tenet of faith (i.e., to visit the Ka'ba).

In light of these verses, these examples illustrate the ways in which early Muslims viewed the body, soul, death, life, sacrifice, devotion, worship, faithfulness, and the overall function of the human anatomy in the presence of God. To take life away was to dishonor and disobey the commandments of God. To participate in violence and ultimately in conflict with another human being meant that one was using it as the final alternative to defend oneself against hostility or re-establish a harmonious order.

VIOLENT EXTREMISM AND CONFLICT RESOLUTION FRAMEWORK IN PAKISTAN

Some researchers have argued that the roots of sectarianism in Pakistan are rooted in the partition of Pakistan and India itself, within the Hindu-

Muslim dichotomy and two-nation theory. After establishing an independent Pakistan, a victory for Muslim nationalism in South Asia, sectional identities rapidly resurfaced to challenge the state. Jinnah's Muslim League, traditionally a secular party based on liberal democratic ideals, was challenged by various Islamic parties and ethnic parties, which are all divided on sectarian lines. The more space carved out for Islamic politics, the more the state was a contested territory for religion.[17] Scholars like Hamza Alavi, Ayesha Jalal, and Sugate Bose have argued that Pakistan was never meant to be an expression of Islamic nationalism but rather a safe homeland for a larger Muslim community with South Asian roots, but not at all exclusively for an Islamic religious identity.

Religious extremism and sectarianism in Pakistan are a combination of social forces competing for space and legitimacy in the public sphere, while simultaneously attempting to delegitimize particular religious, liberal, secular, leftist, and ethnic actors. The Pakistani state and society have historically balanced the role of religious political actors within a secular, legal, and institutionalized framework. The state maintains mechanisms for safeguarding human rights, minority rights, and women's rights, through the judiciary at the top and the magistracy at the bottom. However, by the 1970s and well into the 1980s, religious actors who desired an alternative vision of their society were challenging Pakistan's secular tradition and institutions, which some religious actors considered as deeply antagonistic to their identity. Particularly under General Zia-ul Haq's "Islamization" reign (1979–1988) there was a shift in the national debate on Islamic ideology as the central identity for Pakistanis, and how divine rights were the ultimate source for state legitimacy. President Zia's quest to enforce the ideal Islamic state through a vehement program of Islamizing laws, institutions, economics, politics, education, and morals led to an intense "Deobandi Sunnification" of the society.[18]

This was the critical period where domestic powers of the military and intelligence aligned themselves with key religious parties and their institutions to build and assert an Islamic order. The "Mullah-Military Alliance" heightened the power of landlords, military bureaucracy, and key religious leaders in the Jama'at-i-Islami and its affiliated organizations. Zia-ul Haq promoted religious schools (*madrasas*) to garner the religious parties' support for his rule and, more importantly, recruit student soldiers for the anti-Soviet war in Afghanistan. Religious schools' immense networks across the country and region were used for covert training and arms distribution for the war.

State patronage of one Sunni sect, the Deobandis, and ideologically affiliated groups like Ahl-e-Hadith, cultivated greater social, political, economic, and religious mobilization and politicization among the Barewlis, Pirs, Shi'ites, and other Sufi orders. The West needed Zia to fight its Afghan war against the former Soviet Union, and Zia exploited the mullahs' political power to combat secular voices like the Pakistan People's Party, communists, Shi'ites, and other actors who opposed his religious program and regime.

The state's partisanship contributed directly to the increased sectarian conflicts and identity formation based on conflict and enmity. By the 1990s, there were severe clashes between Sunni and Shi'ites, Muslims and Christians, religious and non-religious, and ethnic rivalries. The rise of ethnic groups asserting their identity to protect their community by jockeying for political power and economic resources surged tremendously. The Urdu-speaking Muhajirs, with roots from India, formed the Muhajir Qaumi Mahaz (MQM) in 1984, which by 1997 became the Muttahida Qaumi Mahaz. MQM has student groups called the All-Pakistan Muhajir Students Organization and a subsidiary education and social service group called Khidmat-e-Khalq Foundation working with diaspora communities. MQM and its militant wings regularly clashed with the Pashtun secular party Awami National Party (ANP), which has influence in the provinces of Baluchistan, Khyber Pakhtunkhwa, and Sindh. ANP's strongholds are in the Pashtun areas of Pakistan, particularly in Peshawar valley and in pockets of Pakistan's largest city, Karachi. MQM and ANP's battles are primarily based on socio-economic and political competition, but it is their exclusive identities that celebrate their unique heritage at the expense of the other, which allowed them to dehumanize each other.

SECTARIAN IDENTITIES

Sectarianism reinforces existing social relations or redraws new political and social boundaries. Sectarian identities in Pakistan are crystallized and often consolidated when parties contend for power and legitimacy. Amartya Sen speaks of singular and belligerent identities as primary identity indicators for conflict.[19] But as much as identity serves the purpose of centering oneself in the current world and the past, identities are often remanufactured as cultural constructions to fear the other. Distinguished scholar of religion and international affairs Mark Juergensmeyer asserts that religious violence is a manifestation of feeling one's identity being threatened or attacked by another group or institution. It is a result of religious groups being shaped and programmed to believe that their lives are a struggle between good and evil, and it is tied to a cosmic struggle to preserve a primordial sacred community. According to Juergensmeyer, religious people are not interested in violence or terror as an intrinsic belief; however, when an ultimatum is presented to them, violence is a solution for preserving the sacred order and ridding evil.[20] Identity formation tied to preserving a world order of purity and removing others who oppose this sacredness is a socializing process that continues in Pakistan.[21]

Edward Azar's work on conflict situations characterized by a prolonged and violent struggle by communal groups is less about good and evil; rather, it is tied to deprived social and economic needs. Azar suggests that identities are threatened when basic needs such as security, recognition, acceptance, fair access to political institutions, and economic participation are limited. Azar's protracted conflict analysis explains that groups may experience deep-seated cleavages based upon racial, religious, cultural, or ethnic lines. These divisions are characterized by continuing hostility with unpredictable outbreaks of violence. Violence is caused by the frustration to secure human needs, recognition, self-perseveration, and distributive justice. Ethnic, racial, class, and religious divisions and/or perceived threats may result in the need to dominate the state apparatus and its coalition of elites.[22]

However, as much as deprived economic resources and desire for greater political participation, security, and fair access to justice are critical factors to protracted violence, it is only a partial explanation for the rise of religious sectarianism in Pakistan. Religious sectarianism is seated in a conflict arena gradually contributing to several psychological disorders of religious actors.[23] Renowned psychologist Robert Hare analyzed the behavior of individuals who suffer from psychopathic behavior and display "selfish, callous and remorseless use of others." Those displaying psychopathic behavior consistently demonstrate personality traits such as being chronically unstable, anti-social, socially deviant, and intensely opposed to mainstream values. These characteristics are connected to narcissistic personality disorder, attention deficit disorder, and common expressions of reactive anger and impulsive behavior.[24]

Psychopathic behavior frequently causes harm through direct or indirect actions, since they are not emotionally attached to the people they harm. There is a lack of empathy toward others, and they have difficulty in recognizing and understanding abstract conversations. The inability to connect or understand others creates inner frustrations, leading the individual to think that others are fundamentally wrong on many subjects. Some experts link psychopathic behavior to oppositional defiant disorder, which has traits of persistent anger, emotional outbursts, and disregard for authority. Individuals with oppositional defiant disorder tend to blame others for their mistakes, are temperamental, and do not take responsibility for their anti-social behavior, which they see is normal. Individuals with oppositional defiant disorder are resentful of others, do not appreciate their own lives, and when others irritate them, they move quickly to take revenge.[25]

The combination of these social sciences, religious studies, and psychological approaches to identity-based conflict analysis provides valuable insight into the causes of religious sectarianism and its effects, impact, and manifestations on religious actors. Religious sectarianism contributes to religious extremism and radicalization of the religion; identity-based conflicts are ultimately tied to the social, political, and economic contexts in which these actors operate or live with undiagnosed complex psychopathic disorders.

RELIGIOUS EXTREMISM: MOBILIZING FOR THE STATE AND AUTHENTIC FAITH

During the 1980s with President Zia-ul Haq investing heavily into Deobandi, Ahl-e Hadith, Jama'at-e Islami, and Salafi[26] Islamic groups to fight the Afghan war, Pakistani Barelwi leaders were aggressively trying to reinvigorate a spiritual, theological, social, and religious movement to undermine state patronage of certain Sunni factions. Barelwi politicization and protestation changes projected a more puritan syncretic form of Islam, quite different from Zia-ul Haq's legalist and ultra-orthodox Deobandi version. It is important to recall that there are three main Sunni political parties in Pakistan: the Jama'at-e Islami, the Deobandi Jamiyyat-e 'Ulama-e Islam, and the Barelwi Jamiyyat-e 'Ulama-e Pakistan (JUP). Generally, religious political parties demand that the Pakistan state institutions be governed by the Qur'an, the tradition of the Prophet (*sunnah*), and Islamic law (*shari'a*). Although the three Sunni political parties share these common grounds for establishing an Islamic state, they disagree on doctrinal issues, interpretations of jurisprudence, and the details of establishing an implementing legislative body. While Barelwi JUP was created in 1948 shortly after independence, JUP's reputation reflects both an orthodox tradition with a tolerance toward other schools of thought and religious parties. The Barelwi JUP used to have links with Sufi orders, the network of pirs, shrines, and related institutions, which are all used to gain political legitimacy. An influential JUP leader and thinker, Shah Ahmad Nurani (d.2003) preached the importance for Pakistan to adopt the *Nizam-e Mustafa*, the system of the Prophet, which would protect the state from secularism, materialism, foreign interference, and any corruption.[27]

Several watershed political events in Pakistan and the region intensified the politics of Islamist activities in Pakistan. For example, the 1979 Iranian revolution directly politicized Shi'i identity and Shi'i activism in Pakistan. The Iranian revolution initiated a cold war between Saudi Arabia and Iran, where each state actively attempted to limit each other's influence in the region by funding local groups. The Iran-Iraq war from 1981 to 1988 had detrimental ripple effects on Sunni and Shi'i relations, where both communities aligned their loyalties according to religious sectarian political causes and defended their agendas with militias. When Pakistan became a frontline state in the war against Soviet aggression in Afghanistan, Zia and his senior military leaders directed international funding to train groups to fight in Afghanistan. Deobandi and Ahl-e Hadith religious groups' patronage strengthened ties with the Inter-Services Intelligence (ISI) for the *jihad*.[28] The Saudi monarchy pressured Zia-ul Haq not to allow Barelwis and Shi'ites to participate in the *jihad* enterprise, instead to use this opportunity to marginalize their communities. As the war wound down in Afghanistan in 1989, *jihadi* groups were redirected to a new front in Kashmir, and again ISI and the Pakistan army excluded Barelwi and Shi'ite militia participation. Against ISI's orders, Barelwis covertly initiated their own *jihad* in Kashmir with a group called *Tehreek-e-Jihad*.

Another critical factor that led to the politicization and mobilization of Jama'at-e Islami, Barelwis, and Deobandis was the emergence of the Muhajirs in Karachi. The MQM and its student groups, the All-Pakistan Muhajir Students Organization continue to have intense battles with the Jama'at-e Islami groups, Islami Jama'at-e Tulaba and Hizbul Mujahideen, and with the Pashtun party, ANP.

Barelwi Sunnism

Barelwi Sunnis identify themselves with the broader Sufi tradition with a distinct lineage traced back to the Prophet, the companions, and key saints. All those who belong to this tradition use the general term *Ahl-e Sunnat* wa-l Jama'at (ASJ), and those who do not belong to their school of thought are outside of the Sunni tradition. ASJ refers to those Sunni Muslims who connect with Ahmed Reza Khan Barelwi, the founder of the movement, and stress the tradition of the Prophet as the essential being of a practicing Muslim. ASJ represents the majority of Muslims in Pakistan, if not all South Asia, with over fifteen thousand *madrasas* in Pakistan and global networks regionally and internationally. Over the past two decades, ASJ has had to deal with several internal fractions and dissenting voices. Dr. Tahir-ul Qadri, a trained Islamic jurist, leads the reformed movement Minhaj-ul Qur'an, which has over a thousand schools and a major university. To counteract the Deobandi-influenced Tabligh-e Jama'at, ASJ missionary group is Dawat-e Islami, which is geared to support Barelwi Sunnis to inculcate a love for God while always instilling self-discipline of God-consciousness.[29]

The Barelwi sectarian group, Sunni Tehreek (ST), was established in 1990 by Salim Qadri to defend all Barelwi mosques, shrines, schools, neighborhoods, financial institutions, youth, and leaders. Due to the intense ethnic and religious sectarian riots of the late 1980s, followers of the Dawat-e Islami, Abbas Qadri, Serwat Qadri, and Salim Qadri[30] felt a single Sunni organization needed to protect, promote, and defend the Barelwi tradition. ST organizes major religious events such as the celebration of the Prophet (*milad an-Nabi*), collects and distributes charity (*zakat*), maintains several orphanages, supervises several computer and vocational institutes, operates major hospitals and local clinics, and supplies funds to families who need money for marriages, education, and healthcare. ST's manifesto strives for a "true Islamic welfare state" that promotes national harmony and brotherhood, and protects "real faith and real Islamic rights."[31] In 2001, Salim Qadri was assassinated, which provoked sectarian religious riots for three days in Karachi. Deobandi and Ahl-e Hadith centers were torched to the ground. The brother of Salim Qadri, Abbas Qadri, was appointed as the leader of ST; however, in June 2006 at a *milad an-Nabi* celebration in the Green Park section of Karachi, over sixty top ST and Barelwi scholars were killed, including Abbas Qadri. Deobandi's militant wing, Sipah-e Sahaba,[32] claimed responsibility for the terrorist attacks and warned against future attacks on ST.

Deobandi Sunnism

Deobandi Sunni Muslims claim their historical, theological, and spiritual roots from northern India's famous Darul Uloom Deoband *madrasa*. The major founders of the mid-nineteenth-century reform movement such as Muhammad Yaqub Nanautawi, Muhammad Qasim Nanotvi, and Zulfiqar Ali were trained jurists in the Hanafi school of law and were influenced by Naqshbandi, Qadri, Suhrawardi, and Chishti Sufi Islam. These scholars and successive Deobandi thinkers criticized colonialism, Muslim assimilation into British/Western culture, and compromising the Islamic tradition for political authority, and specifically Hindu and Christian conversion campaigns in South Asia. In post-partition India and Pakistan, Deobandi Sunnis strongly critiqued communism, socialism, the Westernization of Muslim-majority countries, and a post-colonial liberal secularism which they believed was intrinsically antagonistic to religion. With the politicization and mobilization of the Barelwis, Deobandis felt compelled to zealously dismiss and undermine key theological beliefs and practices of Barelwi groups. Reading Hanafi legal texts with a narrow interpretation, Deobandi scholars fiercely argued against Barewli's beliefs and practices within Sufi shrines, the hierarchy of the *pir/murid*, and the public celebration of major holidays connected with the Prophet Muhammad and saints as *shirk* or associating partners with the one divine. They were the natural allies for Zia-ul Haq, and Saudi scholars viewed them as intellectual partners and defenders of the true Islam. The current grand mufti of Pakistan, Taqi Usman, is a prolific scholar of Islamic law and finance and belongs to the Deobandi Sunni tradition and has consistently condemned all expressions of militancy and radicalism, as well as the so-called misguided interpretations of Barewli.

The primary political party for Deobandis is the Jamia'at-e 'Ulama-e Islami founded in 1944, and was led by Samia-ul Haq. Its missionary wing to support Muslims to be more pious is the Tablighi-Jama'at founded in 1927 by the legendary Deobandi scholar and activist Muhammad Ilyas. There are over twelve thousand Deobandi *madrasas* or religious schools in Pakistan; Qari Hanif Jalandari supervises the administrative aspects of Deobandi schools.[33] In collaboration with Pakistan's ISI and army officers, Deobandis formed paramilitary groups to operate in Afghanistan and Kashmir. Originally, these militant activities were to challenge India's control over Jammu and Kashmir by making it costly to the Indian defense establishment to control the province. Others argued that the campaigns in Jammu and Kashmir were payback for India's hand in the establishment of Bangladesh in the 1971 war. For some of the conservative political driven elements of Deobandi Sunni, they believed these activities were tied to establishing a broader Islamic state in South Asia. The Deobandi sectarian groups in charge of militant attacks are the Sipha-e Sahaba-e Pakistan founded in 1985 but banned in 2002; renamed as Millat-e Islamia-e Pakistan and Lashkar-i Jhangwi also banned in 2001; Jaish-e Muhammadi's notorious work attacked Barelwi and Sufi shrines, as well as Shi'ite centers of learning and places of worship.

Ahl-e Hadith Sunnism

Jamai'a Ahl-e Hadith or commonly called Ahl-e Hadith ("The People of the Sayings of the Prophet") is a small reformist movement which started in 1906 in India. In Pakistan, the Ahl-e Hadith's center and political party is called Markazi Ahl-e Hadith based in Lahore, founded in 1956. They theologically align themselves with the first four caliphs of Islam as the only period which contained true practices of the Prophet. They reject the major four Sunni law schools of thought because they believe it treats sayings and customs of the Prophet secondary to legal interpretations. Ahl-e Hadith's subsidiary group, Jama'at ud-Da'wa, primarily conducted missionary work and promoted Ahl-e Hadith Islam. Their student organization is Tulaba Jama'at-ud-Da'wa and mainly operates on college campuses. Probably one of the most famous militant groups to be heard of outside of Pakistan is Lashkar-e Tayyaba (LeT), founded by Hafiz Muhammad Saeed and Zafar Iqbal. Rooted in Ahl-e Hadith ideology, LeT was established in the Kunar province of Afghanistan in 1990 to recruit, train, and protect jihadists for the militant campaigns in Jammu and Kashmir.[34] LeT was accused of training ten jihadists for the 2008 Mumbai terrorist attacks, which killed more than 180 persons. In 2000, LeT claimed responsibility for the Red Fort attacks in New Delhi and another brazen militant attack with Jaish-e Muhammad on the Indian parliament in 2001.[35]

Shi'a Jafriyya

The primary political party for the Shi'a community[36] is the Tahrik-e-Nafaz-e Fiqu-e Jafrriya established in 1979, which transformed itself into the Milat-e Jafariyya in 1993. The primary religious learning center is called Jamia al-Muntazir based in Lahore. The Shi'a community have their own 'Ulama council called the Wafaq-e Shi'a Ulama-e Pakistan and a student group called the Jamia'at-e Tulaba Jafria. The sectarian Shi'a group, Sipah-e Mohammad-e Pakistan, which is officially banned, carries out militant raids against Sunni militant groups like Sipah-e Sahaba, Jaish-e Muhammad, and

LeT. Sipah-e Mohammad-e Pakistan claims they only attack militant Sunni groups because they consistently attack Shi'a institutions. Other related Shi'a radical groups such as Hizbul Momineen and Pasban-e Islam have connections to clergy in Iran and to Hezbollah in Lebanon, and have operated in Kashmir.[37] Pakistani Shi'a militant groups are closely monitored by ISI because of their ties with Iran, and the security establishment is keenly interested in limiting the influence of Iranian soft power in Pakistan.

Tareek-e Taliban Pakistan

The war on terror initiated by the United States and partnered up with the Afghanistan and Pakistan governments was directly aimed at eliminating al-Qaeda, ISIS, and affiliated groups like the Afghanistan and Pakistan Taliban, and the Tareek-e Taliban Pakistan (TTP). TTP was formed in December 2007 when thirteen groups united under the leadership of Baitullah Mehsud and created a base in the Federally Administered Tribal Areas, which border Afghanistan, and the main center was in Waziristan. TTP regularly assassinated key tribal elders, scholars, teachers, preachers, and politicians who were affiliated with the Barelwi and Shi'a communities. TTP is not connected to the Afghan Taliban as Mullah Omar has publicly appealed to TTP to concentrate their efforts in Afghanistan and not against the state or people of Pakistan. TTP has ties to *Tehreek-e-Nafaz-e-Shariat-e-Mohammadi* founded by Sufi Muhammad and *Harkat-ul-Jihad-al-Islami* formerly led by Ilyas Kashmiri, an anti-Soviet jihadist. TTP militant activities are against the Pakistan state, and all of these institutions, including police academies, military institutions, judiciaries, naval bases, and intelligence agencies. In addition, TTP continues to attack Barelwi shrines, mosques, leaders, schools, shops, and social service groups. Also, TTP is striking Shi'a mosques, shops, and specifically detonating bombs during Shi'a religious rituals during the month of Muharram in Lahore, Karachi, Jhang, Swat Valley, and Hangu district. ASJ and the larger Sufi community have suffered immensely from TTP's attacks, as there were over thirty-five attacks on shrines and mosques in 2010.[38]

A FRAMEWORK FOR PEACEBUILDING DURING VIOLENT EXTREMISM

Pakistan's religious extremism and sectarianism are complicated by external and internal factors: the external risk factors include the global economic crises, border disputes, cross-border trafficking, and international interference in domestic matters; the internal risk factors include rising inequality, religious intolerance, marginalized youth, gender-based discrimination, legacies of violence, presence of militant groups, availability of weapons, and unattended trauma. Additional risk factors are institutional weaknesses, and the trend has demonstrated that countries are more likely to revert to conflict if they suffer from institutional weaknesses. These weaknesses include a lack of functioning state structures, corruption, unreformed security sectors, a lack of judicial and electoral reform, the penetration of the state by criminal and mafia actors, and a lack of progress in economic reform and job creation.

Pakistan and the international community can only achieve limited success with these challenges with the coordination of stabilization, peacebuilding, and development interventions. To address these complex challenges, scholars and researchers in conflict resolution strongly recommend peace processes as an increasingly common tool to address armed conflicts, while resolving domestic economic, social, and political issues. According to *The Yearbook on Peace Processes*, about 80 percent of armed conflict in 2007 and 2008 consisted of some form of dialogue, formal negotiations, and mediation, including back-channel contacts. The remarkable work of the Uppsala Conflict Data Project highlights that peace agreements—along with military victories and ceasefire—are one of the main types of conflict ending between 1990 and 2005. Other Uppsala data shows that the 132 armed conflicts that occurred between 1989 and 2009 involved 183 peace agreements.[39]

During religious extremism and sectarianism in Pakistan, there needs to begin an official peace process addressing conflict and ending conflict. It must be a high-level initiative from the president, the Pakistan National and Provincial Assembly, and the judiciary. This effort needs to be comprehensive with the support of the international community. Prior to the peace process, a team of experts of conflict analysts must serve as advisors to steer the initiative. If we examine the Human Security Report Project, between 1990 and 1999, 43.9 percent of negotiated settlements saw a recurrence of the conflict within five years. In the period 2000 to 2005, this percentage declined to 11.8 percent.[40] This pattern of conflict recurrence has been explained by various factors including the increasingly protracted nature of armed conflicts, the rising number of actors in conflict zones, a lack of ripeness of a conflict for its resolution, a lack of commitment by the parties to end the conflict, and insufficient implementation of peace accords.[41] Studying the Human

Security Report Project and Uppsala Conflict Data Project will provide best practices and lessons learned for the Pakistani peace process.

Some researchers have argued that the fragility of peace processes is due to the "give war a chance" thesis which holds that "too many wars nowadays become endemic conflicts that never end because the transformative effects of both decisive victory and exhaustion are blocked by outside intervention."[42] Clearly, Pakistan is a case study where the war thesis has thrived, yet Pakistan is anything but stable. Recent research has also highlighted that peace agreements have tended to be stronger in providing incentives for former combatants than threats to potential peace spoilers. As a result, peace agreements have been less effective in containing those actors who want to undermine a peace process.[43] The Uppsala Conflict Data Project's Conflict Termination Data holds that "intrastate conflicts are less likely to recur after government victories and after the deployment of peacekeepers."[44] Monica Toft argues that between 1940 and 2000, "military victories had a strong tendency to stay ended" but acknowledges that military victories often do not establish peace because the winning side is not viewed as a legitimate actor by a great part of the population.[45] Overall, there is a need for strategies that balance incentives and threats to forge transitional pacts and deter spoilers.

A PEACEBUILDING FRAMEWORK

The practice of peacemaking has changed drastically over the last decades. While domestic actors and their national institutions should drive peace processes, the increasingly global transnational connections in conflict zones opened them to broader external influences and interests. Peace processes have become so complex that they involve dozens of actors and multiple agendas that must be balanced. A precursory glance at mediation efforts over the last decade suggests that there are five emerging trends regarding divisions of labor between official and nongovernmental organization (NGO) mediation actors in different contexts. First, official actors tend to dominate peacemaking in state conflicts. Second, NGO actors tend to focus on internal conflicts. Third, NGO actors tend to engage at earlier stages of peace processes and are not very much included in the latter part of the process. Fourth, NGO actors have more access to conflicts of lower strategic priority. And fifth, the comparative advantages depend on personal characteristics of lead mediators and associated personal contacts in specific regions.[46]

If Pakistan initiated a peace process to address sectarianism and religious extremism, it should utilize all international resources including the UN initiative: the UN Development Programme's Bureau of Conflict Prevention and Recovery's work on conflict prevention. This is an Inter-Agency Framework Team for Preventive Action that involves twenty-two UN agencies and departments and assists UN Resident Coordinators and Country teams in developing integrated conflict prevention strategies. The UN Department of Political Affairs on Building National Capacities for Conflict Prevention supports the implementation of the Framework Team's initiatives in politically unstable settings through confidence building with key national stakeholders. For example, in 2009 the UN Department of Political Affairs and UN Development Programme jointly deployed thirty peace and development advisors in twenty-four countries.[47] The Bureau of Conflict Prevention and Recovery's experience underscores the importance of long-term approaches and partnerships for addressing conflicts and building new capacities for local and national conflict management frameworks.[48] Also, the Commonwealth Secretariat maintains mediation support activities in nine countries.

There are several examples where mediators, state, and civil society utilized mediation support resources. In the Philippine-Mindanao conflict, the Malaysian mediation team created an International Contact Group, which included states and two international NGOs with various support resources. The two-decade civil war in Sri Lanka pressed international and domestic actors to create a Group of Friends for Sri Lanka led by former State Department official Richard Armitage. The Group of Friends ensures a more long-term vision of resolving the conflict.[49]

Another important trend has been utilizing the so-called insider mediators to contact conflict parties in formal or informal dialogue forums. Insider mediators are trusted and respected insiders at all levels of a conflict zone who have a deep knowledge of the dynamics and context of the conflict, and a serious sensitivity in their contribution to finding solutions that all parties recognize.[50] These individuals are viewed as legitimate players at a high level because of their position in society, personality, and skills. They are accepted in mediation roles because of who they are and their community contributions. Inside mediators can play various peacebuilding roles, such as human rights advocates, conflict analysts, professional interveners, conveners, trainers, and coordinators. A successful example of the use of an insider mediator is in the National Architecture for Peace in Ghana, where the coordination of national local political leaders, civil society members, and UN Development Programme and UN Department of Political Affairs[51] established a nationwide system of local peace councils to provide space for eminent personalities to mediate local disputes.[52]

A LONG-TERM APPROACH TO RESOLVING CONFLICT

In framing a peace process for Pakistan, one needs to calculate a long-term approach to peace processes that meticulously focuses on the continuous peacemaking efforts needed to foster locally owned conflict settlements and peacebuilding through nonviolent methods of conflict. This approach is built on the notion that the ending of a conflict and the securing of peace are part of a continuous transformation process.[53] For the past three and half decades, Pakistan has continued to experience religious extremism, ethnic divisions, separatist movements, and sectarianism; it is vital to shift from a short- to long-term view on peace processes. The administrations of Zia-ul Haq, Benazir Bhutto, Nawaz Sharif, Pervez Musharraf, and Asif Ali Zardari have demonstrated that short-term deal-making efforts have backfired and only have resulted in shortsighted policies of appeasing or utilizing violent actors and extremists. Whether it be the policies in Kashmir, Afghanistan, Federally Administered Tribal Areas, or Baluchistan, the short-term deals are intended to silence the noise for the moment. Short-term approaches have limited the efforts of civil-state actors to broker effective pacts, support practitioners to strengthen post-conflict recovery, fortify the rule of law and judiciary sectors, and invest in institutions that can contain protracted conflict.

Pakistani security and civilian leadership must recognize that peacemaking is a continuous political process that does not unfold along a neat sequence of calculated phases. Peace processes are hard to control, are intensely political, and involve dozens of competing self-interests.[54] Despite these challenges to sustain peace processes, there must be an understanding of a continuous peacemaking process with clear outcomes in different phases of the process. There are many recent examples when a conflict is placed within the international spotlight but the attention disappears after a peace agreement has been signed.[55] However, the hard work of implementing, evaluating, monitoring, and re-examining its effectiveness comes with continued attention to the people involved in the process.[56]

The long-term approach to implementing peace processes asserts that effective conflict resolution should be based on local parties while the international community serves as facilitator and convener of the process. Continued international engagement with the country's political elites, stakeholders, and civil society members must encourage governance reforms and expand political participation beyond the feudal landlords. Any success of international assistance to peace processes is measured by its ability to build capacities within Pakistani society and its ability to resolve conflicts in a self-sustainable manner. Resolving conflict with religious actors, ethnic groups, and/or separatist groups in Pakistan will consist of peace agreements, but this is one part of a long political and transition process. It is an instrument, not an end in itself. The cessation of violence must be followed up with a detailed roadmap of mediation, development, and security for stakeholders across the various stages of peace processes.[57]

In the peace process, it is important to calculate the challenging political economies that block the development of peaceful transitions. Within Pakistan, policymakers and international mediators need to factor in patrimonial governance, the influence of feudal landlords, the competition for power and resources by all actors, the influence of criminal and terrorist interests, a culture of overpromising, and incessant corruption. While stakeholders face the difficult choice of accepting these factors for the sake of peace and stability, addressing these issues early is critically important for transitional change.[58] This pragmatic approach recognizes the inherent complexities, risks, and limitations connected to resolving armed conflict; however, it simultaneously strengthens post-conflict recovery and development.[59]

In dealing with the current religious extremism, a "countering violent extremism" strategy is a short-term policy for Pakistani security establishment and Western allies. It is at the expense of civil stability, a downward-spiraling economy, loss of human capital and international investments, and more importantly, the loss of innocent lives. Religious extremists, whether it is TTP, LeT, or Sipah-e-Sahaba, are like any civil society actors whose self-interests, agendas, and behavior can be modified with an active engagement strategy. First, there needs to be a well-structured dialogue between the development, diplomatic, peacebuilding, and security communities to develop a common understanding of peace processes. This chapter has already underscored the importance of intersectorial partnerships for identifying the main points of a peace accord that will reinforce that a non-military option is the only solution to extremism. Such a strategy will need to develop a mutual understanding of approaches, mandates, and detailed guidance about the roles of different communities in the various phases of the peace processes.

The strategy will need to focus on the short-term goals and long-term approaches, practical approaches to cultivating local peace councils, and how to design and implement an "architecture of peace processes" that will factor in disruptions by spoilers, conflict economies, competitive interests, corruption, weak institutions, and vacillating political will.

Second, religious communities and religious leaders must be involved at every phase of the peace process. To delegitimize extremist religious ideology, national religious leaders must be united to stand together in unison against extremism. The religious leaders not only bring an alternative narrative to counteract the extremist messaging, but they reinforce a mainstream national identity. Key religious leaders from the Barelwi, Deobandi, Shi'a, and Ahl-e Hadith communities may serve as insider mediator roles on a national level or as a facilitator to resolve local conflicts. It is critical that religious leaders, as other civil society actors working toward a peaceful resolution, have protection from extremist threats and that their institutions are equally protected from extremist infiltration.

Third, engaging civil society through a broader conflict resolution framework, and not solely a counterterrorism or counter-violent extremism agenda, will reduce the ideology of radicalism. Terrorism is neither an ideology nor a discrete form of conflict; rather, it is a strategy or tactic of political violence used by actors in a wider context of conflict to achieve political goals. Pakistani policymakers should treat terrorism as a symptom, and not the sole cause, of any conflict. Focusing exclusively on acts of terrorism limits the analysis and understanding of the broader range of issues at work in any given situation. Using a conflict resolution framework, one can comprehend the broader set of issues, actors, and behaviors involved, as well as the history of a conflict and the grievances that terrorism is tied to—grievances that need long-term political, social, cultural, and economic solutions. To counter ideological support for terrorism, fellow religious actors within the ideological community must be supported to speak out against radicalism and have continual messages to counteract extremist propaganda. This means including religious leaders and the larger religious communities. Secular approaches tend to neglect religious leaders or only use certain religious leaders in an exploitative strategic manner, and this has proven to damage any peacebuilding process.

Fourth, mediation training and developing the capacity of local NGOs, religious and non-religious, is crucial in mitigating violence. Regular peace mediation training for the diplomatic, development, and religious communities will strengthen their capacities in peacebuilding work. These trainings will enhance technical skills, provide a deeper analysis to scenario reconstructions, and foster a serious understanding of the latest research on thematic issues and best practices.[60]

Fifth, peacebuilding is a multidimensional, highly complex process that involves the coordination of numerous actors—not only religious actors—simultaneously working at different levels and in different areas of society. No single organization in Pakistan can own all peacebuilding tasks. Peacebuilding efforts promote human security in conflict societies and strengthen the capacity of societies generally to manage conflict without violence. To Pakistan, peacebuilders need to concentrate on both negative and positive peace; that is, the absence of physical, verbal, and psychological violence as well as the presence of structural, cultural, political, economic, and legal conditions that allow individuals to realize their potential. Concurrently, there is a need to promote cooperative conflict resolution, whereby conflict parties or individuals are encouraged to collaborate in developing a solution that supports all involved, rather than creating competition or threats. Fostering a new cadre of peacebuilders will need to critically assess, understand, and respond to the root causes of violent conflict, including structural inequities.

Sixth, peacebuilding efforts to eliminate religious extremism need to re-center attention on providing real problem-solving skills to religious leaders and constituents who can analyze their problems, identify reasons for violent conflicts, formulate solutions to complex problems, and use practical mediation skills to facilitate change in their communities. Practitioners need to devise a comprehensive understanding of the context in which they implement programs; only partial analysis—or an only intuitive understanding of the situation—could lead to negative consequences or costly mistakes. Pakistan religious leaders need to ask crucial and fundamental questions to examine what a conflict is about; what needs to be done to prevent further harm; what local, regional, and international forces are involved; and what were their respective roles in contributing to religious extremism and terrorism.[61] The difficult answers to these questions will assist practitioners in using peacemaking tools, frameworks, and models in their specific contexts. Since analytical tools for conflict prevention, mediation, transformation, and peacemaking are lacking in Pakistan, trainers must distinguish between program effectiveness and the effectiveness of peacebuilding. Meeting specific program goals is important but should be linked to the bigger picture and its ultimate effect on society. Goals must be outlined with criteria to ensure that specific ends are linked to the large and long-term goal of peacebuilding. Trained peacemakers must measure their effect on their communities for them to quantify, or at least map, the progress or relapse of their work. Specific analytical tools are desperately needed to strategically characterize the situation, create taxonomies, and define new ways to assess and evaluate the problem to understand and eventually implement peacemaking activities.

Finally, security and stability in Pakistan and any nation heavily rests on human capital; ignoring the problems associated with human development and human security neglects the core drivers of instability. Developing and improving water, sanitation networks, and agricultural irrigation systems can alleviate water shortages. All peacebuilding efforts must be tied to serious national and international community efforts in investing in infrastructure development, especially after the floods of 2010 and the persistent energy and water crisis in Pakistan. Human development includes diagnosing and treating psychopathic disorders. In Pakistan, psychological counseling is in its infancy and rarely are people treated with disorders; there needs to be an investment in counseling centers and cultivation of the field of psychoanalysis. In addition to expanding the network of peacebuilding work on the ground, it is important to underscore the critical value of research by analysts and practitioners and the need to support their efforts to disseminate their work to policymakers, local peacebuilding organizations, and students of conflict resolution in Pakistan.

NOTES

1. Amartya Sen, *Identity and Violence: The Illusion of Destiny* (London, Penguin Books, 2006).

2. Ibid., pg. 41.

3. The *shahadah* was established during early period of the Prophet's missionary work. The belief that "There is no God but God. and the Prophet Muhammad is the final Messenger" was perceived to be hostile to the religious practices of the Arab Bedouin polytheistic culture. What distinguished the new Muslim converts was that they publicly affirmed this new testimony of faith by rejecting contemporary cultural and religious norms of idolatry.

4. In the Qur'an, each verse is referred to as or a sign to illustrate that God's signs are in the word itself as well as all around His creation. The spiritual insight to see and understand the communication of these signs shows that one understands Him through an unfolding process of God-consciousness awareness. One may see a sign but not connect the significance of it until it is seen in conjunction with other signs. Ayats for pious Muslims speak about ongoing communication with the Divine while trying to structure a life around Divine unity.

5. Quranic verse "All things perish except His Face" (Q: 28:88) illustrates the idea that imperfection rests in creation not in the Creator. For more on this theme see Fazlur Rahman, *Major Themes of the Qur'an*.

6. The Qur'an attributes ninety-nine names to God, for example, The Merciful, The Truth, The Guider, and so forth. A custom of the Prophet Muhammad was to recite, contemplate, and reflect upon these names, which would bring the individual closer to God, and this proximity gives a stronger sense of God-consciousness. See Kenneth Cragg's *Taddabur al-Quran: Readings and Meaning*.

7. This controversy concerning God's names and attributes was taken up by a ninth-century intellectual movement called the Muta'zilites, literally "those who cut-off." For more see, Farhad Daftary, ed., *Intellectual Traditions of Islam*.

8. Jinn are beings made of fire, while the angels are made of light and humans are made of clay, an essential element of earth. Jinn are semi-spiritual and semi-corporeal. Just as fire is neither pure light nor pure clay or the like, human beings are given free will and they can also use it to obey or disobey God, whereas angels cannot disobey God. According to this narrative in the tradition, Iblis was the first fallen angel not to have obeyed God. See C. E. Constance Padwick, *Muslim Devotions*.

9. For a good analysis on *ghaflah*, particularly chapters 2 and 3 of Seyyid Hossein Nasr's *Ideals and Realities of Islam*.

10. This reasoning to use *jihad* to defend borders and aggression or "state-driven *jihad*," as I refer to it, was common in revolutionary Iran and its war against Iraq. See Ayatullah Ahmad Jannatf, "Defense and Jihad in the Qur'an."

11. For more specific *hadiths*, see Muhammad ibn Isma'il Bukhari, Sahih al-Bukhari, or the biography of the Prophet by the famous eighth-century biographer, Ibn Ishaq, Al-Stra al-nabawiwa.

12. Within the Sunni legal tradition, the consensus is that the most senior jurists can issue the call for a "*jihad*" but only after only another consensus is conducted with other scholars, policymakers, senior advisors, and military strategists. Historically, independent nationalist movements used this as a battle cry against colonialism. In recent times, despotic rulers such as Saddam Hussein, Colonel Ghaddafi, Bashir Asad, and known terrorist organization leaders like Osama bin Laden and al-Baghdadi attempted to be the authorities in using the term for their agenda. However, Muslim scholars and non-scholars alike recognize their weak appeal and baseless rational grounding.

13. "*Tawhid* awareness" is a term coined after becoming familiar with the Buddhist tradition, particularly the Mahayana text called the *Dhammapada*. In the *Dhammapada*, it is written, "All we are is the result of what we have thought," which is to strive toward the ideal bodhi wisdom or boddhisattva. For more see Philip Kapleau, ed., *The Three Pillars of Zen*, and Shunryu Suzuki, *Zen Mind, Beginner's Mind*.

14. The Qur'an refers to those who have rejected God's message numerous times by using anatomical metaphors such as deaf ears, sealed hearts and blinded eyes, and blinded sight. For more see Qamar-ul Huda, "Anatomy in the Qur'an" in *The Encyclopaedia of the Qur'an*.

15. For more on this subject, see Toshihiko Izutsu, *Ethico-Religious Concepts in the Quran*, and Bruce Lincoln, *Death, War, and Sacrifice*.

16. For a more in-depth study on the Islamic pilgrimage, see F. E. Peters, *The Haj: The Muslim Pilgrimage to Mecca and Holy Places*.

17. See Hamza Alavi, "Pakistan and Islam: Ethnicity and Ideology," in *State and Ideology in the Middle East and Pakistan*, edited by Fred Halliday and Hamza Alavi (Monthly Review Press, 1991).

18. Vali Nasr, "Military Rule, Islamism and Democracy in Pakistan," *The Middle East Journal*, 2004, 58 (2): 195–209; Shahid Javed Burki and Craig Baxter, *Pakistan Under the Military: Eleven Years of Zia-ul Haq* (Boulder, CO: Westview, 1991); and Arshi Saleem Hashimi, "Use of Religion in Violent Conflicts by Authoritarian Regimes: Pakistan and Malaysia in Comparative Perspective," *Journal of South Asia and Middle Eastern Studies*, 2007, 30 (4): 22–49.

19. Amartya Sen, *The Argumentative Indian* (London: Allen Lane, 2005).

20. Mark Juergensmeyer, *Terror in the Mind of God: The Global Rise of Religious Violence* (Berkeley: University of California Press, 2001).

21. See Mohammed Waseem, "Sectarian Conflict in Pakistan," in K.M. de Silva (ed.), *Conflict and Violence in South Asia: Bangladesh, India, Pakistan and Sri Lanka* (Kandy: International Ethnic Studies Centre, 2000) and Muhammad Qasim Zaman, "Sectarianism in Pakistan," in Ian Talbot (ed.) *The Deadly Embrace: Religion, Violence, and Politics in India and Pakistan, 1947-2002* (Karachi: Oxford University Press, 2007).

22. See Oliver Ramsbotham, "The Analysis of Protracted Social Conflict: A Tribute to Edward Azar," *Review of International Studies*, 2005, 31 (01): 109–11.

23. I am not making a blanket claim that all religious leaders have psychopathic behavior problems; rather, based on my experience with religious peacebuilding activities I have encountered many religious leaders who appeared undiagnosed with psychopathic and personality disorders.

24. Robert Hare, *Manual for the Revised Psychopathy Checklist*, second edition (Toronto, Canada: Multi-Health Systems, 2003) and David Cooke and Christine Michie, "Refining the Construct of Psychopath: Towards a Hierarchical Model," *Psychological Assessment*, 2001, 13 (2): 171–88.

25. See Lee Anna Clark, "Assessment and Diagnosis of Personality Disorder: Perennial Issues and an Emerging Reconceptualization," *Annual Review of Psychology*, 2007, 58: 227–57, and John C. Nemiah, "The Psychodynamic Basis of Psychopathology," in Armand M. Nicholi, Jr. (ed.), *The Harvard Guide to Psychiatry* (Cambridge, MA: Harvard University Press, 1999), 203–19.

26. There is a distinct school of thought called the Salafi, a response to modernity and postcolonial secularism. It is common for the non-specialist to use "Wahabbi" interchangeably with Salafi, but this is an inaccurate depiction of the group. Barelwis in particular use the term "Wahabbi" in pejorative terms and to accuse the other Sunni sect to be practicing aspects of faith unfamiliar to the Islamic tradition.

27. For more, see Jamal Malik, "The Luminous Nurani: Charisma and Political Mobilization among the Barelwis in Pakistan," in Pnina Werbner (ed.), special issue on "Person, Myth and Society in South Asian Islam" *Social Analysis*, 1990, 28: 22–43; Usha Sanyal, Ahmed Riza Khan Barelwi: In the Path of the Prophet (Oxford: Oneworld Publications, 2005) and the official website, http://www.ahlesunnat.net/.

28. There are numerous definitions attributed to *jihad*; in this case I am using the term as used by the Pakistani security strategists who applied *jihad* as a war to fight Soviet aggression and to use all resources to support the people of Afghanistan. For more on the variations of the term of *jihad*, see Asma Afsaruddin "Recovering the Early Semantic Purview of Jihad and Martyrdom: Challenging Statist-Military Perspectives," in Qamar-ul Huda (ed.), *Crescent and Dove: Peace and Conflict Resolution in Islam* (Washington, DC: USIP Press, 2010), 39–51.

29. For more, see Alix Philipon, "Sunnis Against Sunnis. The Politicization of Doctrinal Fractures in Pakistan," *The Muslim World*, 2011, 101 (1): 347–68.

30. All individuals mentioned are followers of the Qadriyya Sufi order, which Abdul Qadir Jilani founded in the mid-twelfth century.

31. Interview with Dr. Tahir-ul Qadri, Alvi Haider, and central executive committee member of ST Mohammed Shaheed Ghori. Interviews were conducted between 2009 and 2011 in Islamabad, Lahore, Karachi, and Hyderbad.

32. The Sipah-e Sahaba violent extremist wing eventually merged with the modern Lashkar-e- Jangvi group.

33. For more on Deobandi Sunni Muslims, see Barbara Metcalf, *Islamic Revival in British India: Deoband 1860–1900* (Princeton: Princeton University Press, 1982) and Muahmmad Qasim Zaman, *The Ulama in Contemporary Islam: Custodians of Change* (Princeton: Princeton University Press, 2002).

34. Mohammed Waseem, *Dilemmas of Pride and Pain: Sectarian Conflict and Conflict transformation in Pakistan*, Working Paper 48, 2010, University of Birmingham.

35. See Ashley J. Tellis, "Bad Company—Lashkar-e-Tayyiba and the Growing Ambition of Islamist Militancy in Pakistan," Carnegie Endowment for International Peace, Washington, DC, 2010.

36. In Pakistan, and in the larger South Asia region, there are several Shi'a communities such as Ismailis, Zaidis, Bohras, Daudis, and Ahmadiyyas; however, for the purpose of this chapter I am only concentrating on the largest Shi'a community called Jafriyya or elsewhere referred to as Itna Asharis.

37. For more on Pakistani Shi'a community, see Vernon James Schubel, *Religious Performance in Contemporary Islam: Shi'i Devotional Rituals in South Asia* (Columbia: University of South Carolina, 1993) and Dietrich Reetz, "Migrants, Mujahidin, Madrassa Students: The Diversity of Transnational Islam in Pakistan," The National Bureau of Asian Research, Seattle, April 2009.

38. See Zahid Hussein, *Frontline Pakistan: The Struggle with Militant Islam* (New York: Columbia University Press, 2007) and Abbas Hussain, *Pakistan's Drift Into Extremism: Allah, then Army, and America's War on Terror* (Armonk, NY: M.E. Sharpe, 2004).

39. Lotta Harbom and Peter Wallensteen, "Armed Conflicts, 1946-2009," *Journal of Peace Research*, 2010, 472 (4): 501–09.

40. Human Security Report Project, *Human Security Brief 2007* (Vancouver: Simon Fraser University, 2007), pg. 35.

41. See Stephen Stedman, "Spoiler Problems in Peace Processes," *International Security*, 1997, 22 (2): 5–53; Scott Sigmund Gartner and Jacob Bercovitch, "Overcoming Obstacles to Peace: The Contribution of Mediation to Short-lived Conflict Settlements," *International Studies Quarterly*, 2006, 40 (4): 819–40; and B.F. Walter, "The Critical Barrier to Civil War Settlement," *International Organization*, 1997, 51 (3): 335–64.

42. Edward Luttwak, "Give War a Chance," *Foreign Affairs*, 1999, 78 (4): 36–44.

43. Monica Duffy Toft, *Securing the Peace: The Durable Settlement of Civil War* (Princeton: Princeton University Press, 2010), pg. 151.

44. Joakim Kreuz, "How and When Armed Conflicts End: Introducing the UCDP Conflict Termination Dataset," *Journal of Peace Research*, 2010, 47 (2): 243–50.

45. Monica Duffy Toft, *Securing the Peace: The Durable Settlement of Civil War* (Princeton: Princeton University Press, 2010), pg. 151.

46. A. Griffiths and C. Barnes (eds.), *Powers of Persuasion: Incentives, Sanctions and Conditionality in Peacemaking* (London: Conciliation Resources, 2008), pp. 9–14.

47. UN Development Program, *Preventing and Reducing Armed Violence: What Works?* (New York and Oslo: UNDP and the Ministry of Foreign Affairs of Norway, 2010).

48. UN Development Programme Bureau of Conflict Prevention and Recovery 2009.

49. T. Whitfield, *External Actors in Mediation: Dilemmas and Options for Mediators* (Geneva: Centre for Humanitarian Dialogue, 2010), pg. 15.

50. R. Smith and S. Deely, *Insider Mediators in Africa: Understanding the Contribution of Insider Mediators to the Peaceful Resolution of Conflicts in Africa*. Summary Report of Phase 1 (Prangins: PeaceNexus Foundation, 2010).

51. UN Development Programme, *Annual Report 2008 of the Bureau for Crisis Prevention and Recovery* (New York: UNDP, 2009).

52. UN Development Programme, *Preventing and Reducing Armed Violence: What Works?* (New York and Oslo: UNDP and the Ministry of Foreign Affairs of Norway, 2010), pg. 16.

53. B.W. Dayton and Louis Kreisberg (eds.), *Conflict Transformation and Peacebuilding: Moving from Violence to Sustainable Peace* (London: Routledge, 2009); Mats Berdal and Achim Wennmann, *Ending Wars, Consolidating Peace: Economic Perspectives* (London: International Institute for Strategic Studies, 2010).

54. In particular to conflict zones is the need to balance the "top-down" approach versus "bottom-up" approach in order to mange existing power structures, customs, and procedures. See W. Reno, "Bottom-Up Statebuilding?" in Charles Call with Vanessa Wyeth (eds.), *Building States to Build Peace* (Boulder: Lynne Reiner, 2008), pp. 143–62.

55. Some examples are the Good Friday Agreement in Northern Ireland; Dayton Accords with Bosnia-Herzegovina, Croatia, and Serbia; and the Oslo Accords between the Israeli and Palestinians.

56. Pakistani policymakers and mediators would benefit from a comparative analysis of conflict reduction and implementing peace processes. See Dorina Bekoe, *Implementing Peace Agreements: Lessons from Mozambique, Angola, and Liberia* (New York: Palgrave Macmillan, 2008).

57. For an excellent analysis of mediation, development, and security, see Nicole Ball and Tammy Halevy, "Making Peace Work: The Role of the International Developmental Community," Policy Essay 18 (Washington, DC: Overseas Development Council, 1996).

58. Christopher Cramer, "Trajectories of Accumulation through War and Peace," in R. Paris and T.G. Sisk (eds.), *The Dilemmas of Statebuilding: Confronting the Contradictions of Post-War Peace Operations* (London: Routledge, 2009), pp. 129–48.

59. Katia Papagianni, "Mediation, Political Engagement, and Peacebuilding," *Global Governance*, 2010, 16 (2): 243–63.

60. See Dean Pruitt and Jeffrey Rubin, *Social Conflict: Escalation, Stalemate, and Settlement* (New York: McGraw-Hill, 1986); Herbert Kelman, "Interactive Problem-Solving: A Social-Psychological Approach to Conflict Resolution," in John Burton and Frank Dukes, eds., *Conflict: Readings in Management and Resolution* (New York: St. Martin's Press, 1990).

61. See Martha Minow, *Between Vengeance and Forgiveness: Facing History after Genocide and Mass Violence* (Boston: Beacon Press, 1998); Ruti G. Teitel, *Transitional Justice* (Oxford: Oxford University Press, 2002); Dinah Shelton, ed., *The Encyclopedia of Genocide and Crimes against Humanity* (Detroit: Macmillan Reference, 2004).

Section II

RELIGION AS AN INFLUENTIAL FORCE

Chapter Four

Religion and Civil Society

RELIGION AND PEACEBUILDING

In my twenty-five years working in the field of religion, peacebuilding, and conflict resolution, it never ceases to surprise me when policymakers, thought leaders, researchers, global civil society organizations (CSOs), and practitioners ask if it is possible to integrate religion and peacebuilding. Scott Appleby's *The Ambivalence of the Sacred: Religion, Violence, and Reconciliation* ushered in new thinking on how religious actors can be peacemakers and participate in human suffering. Despite these contradictory responses, religion brings both benevolent and destructive outcomes. While religious beliefs may inculcate acts of compassion, ethics, moral goodness, and a propensity toward social justice, they can concurrently justify intolerance, violence, and conflict. Appleby's work then created the Catholic Peacebuilding network, an ambitious way of connecting Catholic peacemakers—scholars and practitioners—to increase peacebuilding collaboration. Catholic organizations, such as Pax Christi International, the Sant' Egidio Community, and Caritas Internationalis, were highlighted for their peace and nonviolent activities, advocacy work on human rights, disarmament, peaceful alternatives to war, humanitarian work, mediation, and promotion of interfaith dialogue.[1]

In the past forty years, researchers have produced a vast literature on religion and peacebuilding and positioned the visibility of faith-based organizations in global forums; however, policymakers and scholars still question whether faith-based actors can advocate for peace or if they will exacerbate conflict. They wonder if religious stakeholders in conflict zones can effectively work with secular institutions and are trustworthy enough to integrate into broader peacebuilding activities. Apprehensive, if not paranoid, questions come to the fore about whether religious organizations are inherently biased against gender rights, inclusiveness, and equity. Just as in the broader secular approach to peacebuilding and conflict resolution, there are pernicious assumptions that religious communities and faith-based organizations are the causes of harmful and destructive conflicts. Besides these biases against religion, funders and peacebuilding organizations argue that religious leaders do not have the necessary capacity, organization skills, and monitoring abilities, and because of their fixed belief system, it is an obstacle for them to engage outside of their communities.[2]

In retrospect, in examples like Northern Ireland and South Africa, religious leaders were integral in framing and designing what appeared to be fragmented peace efforts by the international community. While the religious leaders' roles were diverse, the inspirational individuals were integral in the conversations, leading to a peace agreement and initial reconciliation phases. A distinctive feature ascribed to religious peacebuilders is their understanding of reconciliation and forgiveness and how they could transcend it from the pews of the churches to the public arena. South Africa's Truth and Reconciliation Commission was initially tied to secular thinking but was later infused with inspiration and symbolism from the church. It is also recorded that the healing process after World War II in Europe and worldwide was partly due to the Pax Christi and Moral Rearmament. The approach to reconciliation involved spiritual guidance, listening, apology, and visions of a better future. Again, in Mozambique, traditional reconciliation practices based on indigenous beliefs were utilized to establish a post-conflict transition.[3]

Religion is now recognized as a central fabric of the broader landscape of civil society members. In terms of terminology, I use the term religion broadly; the terms "religion," "faith," "spiritual," "secular," "transcendence," "faith-based," and "faith-inspired" are contested terms. This chapter will not address the variety of ways these terms are distinguished or understood in academia. Instead, for preciseness and simplicity, I use religion, religious, and faith-based leaders with the understanding that such terms can be easily associated with a Western understanding of religion and the way religion is understood and practiced in Muslim-majority communities.[4] However, religion or faith-based actors are defined here broadly, including formal and informal religious actors, individuals, and institutions. Some examples of religious actors include *'ulama*, imams, preachers, religious schoolteachers, Muslim women and youth groups, humanitarian relief groups, mediators, as well as international religious organizations such as the World Muslim League, the Muslim World Congress, the Organization of Islamic Cooperation, The Red Crescent, or Islamic Relief.[5] In addition, millions of Muslims practice Islamic mysticism; an estimated more than 30 percent of Sunni Muslims participate in these orders as either followers of a Sufi guide of an order (*murid*) or affiliated with a Sufi order (*mutabarrikin*). Most notable of these historical Sufi orders are the Naqshbandi, Chishtiyya, Qadiriyya, Tijaniyya, Shadiliyyah, Rifa'iyyah, Mawlawiyya, Suhrawardiyya, and Kubrawiyya. Therefore, religion and religious communities refer to the multitiered dimensions of all these religious institutions and their respective histories and communities.

This chapter focuses on how Muslim religious institutions and religious leaders play a critically important civil society role in contributing to peacebuilding and conflict resolution. As civil society members, they actively foster peace through interventions in active conflict zones and identify ways to prevent sectarianism. Muslim religious organizations, leaders, and broader religious institutions operate within inherited historical, moral principles of their faith tradition, whereby the involvement of religious actors contributes to integrated peacebuilding, conflict mitigation, social services, education, humanitarian relief, peace negotiations, mediation, trauma healing, development, reconciliation, disaster relief operations, countering violent extremism, and reconstruction. Even though Muslim religious leaders and communities were recognized as players in peacebuilding more than a decade ago, among the civil society industry and international aid community, they are still neglected or sidelined at many levels. This is demonstrated in the world's most complex conflict situations, such as Libya, Syria, Yemen, or Sudan, where Muslim religious leaders are integrated into the planning, coordination, execution, monitoring, and other central decision roles.

CIVIL SOCIETY

As societies have modernized and moved toward postmodernity, the relationship between religion and society has evolved in many ways. For instance, notions of who are civil society members and what their roles and contributions to society have changed with modernity. Currently, religiously plural societies are becoming the complex norm around the world. Religion is a factor in intercommunal violence in Nigeria, Afghanistan, Iraq, Egypt, Sri Lanka, Nigeria, India, Northern Ireland, Sudan, Pakistan, Lebanon, Libya, and Uganda. Negative perceptions of religion, such as religion being used to motivate the violent conflicts that drive communities apart, have predominated. Still, if caused by the influence of religious leaders, their traditions play constructive roles in counteracting extremism, aiding in reconciliation, and cooperating with the broader secular civil society network. Scott Appleby calls this dual role of religion's power to create a spiritual commitment to peace and violence.

The civil society network comprises organizations unrelated to the government—including schools and universities, advocacy groups, professional associations, churches, mosques, foundations, advocacy groups, philanthropies, and cultural institutions. CSOs play multiple roles and are an important source of information for both citizens and government. They monitor government policies and actions and hold government accountable. They advocate and offer alternative policies for the government, the private sector, and other institutions. They deliver services, especially to the poor and underserved communities. They defend citizen rights and work to change and uphold social norms and behaviors. Civil society is an essential building block of development, national cohesion, and supplier of social services programs and contributes toward the development of the society. After government and commerce, when civil society is effectively mobilized, it is referred to as the "third sector," and has the power to influence the actions of elected policymakers and businesses.

In times of crisis and peace, religious leaders and faith-based groups offer more than religious guidance: they are vanguards of traditions of spiritual enrichment, being interconnected, serving their communities and others, and resolving conflict daily. Like other civil society members, religious communities are a vital form of social capital for their communities. Mosques and churches serve as places of worship, places of refuge, and community centers. Religious leaders run complex institutions such as schools, hospitals, clinics, youth centers, vocational centers, and businesses with elaborate and complex social networks and resources on local and international levels. In the absence of strong governance, the delivery of social services to communities, weak public education, and bleak opportunities for the youth, the roles of religious leaders and faith-based organizations are especially critical to the community. Scholar and peacebuilding practitioner Andrea Bartoli highlighted the strengths of religious mediators, stressing four key factors:

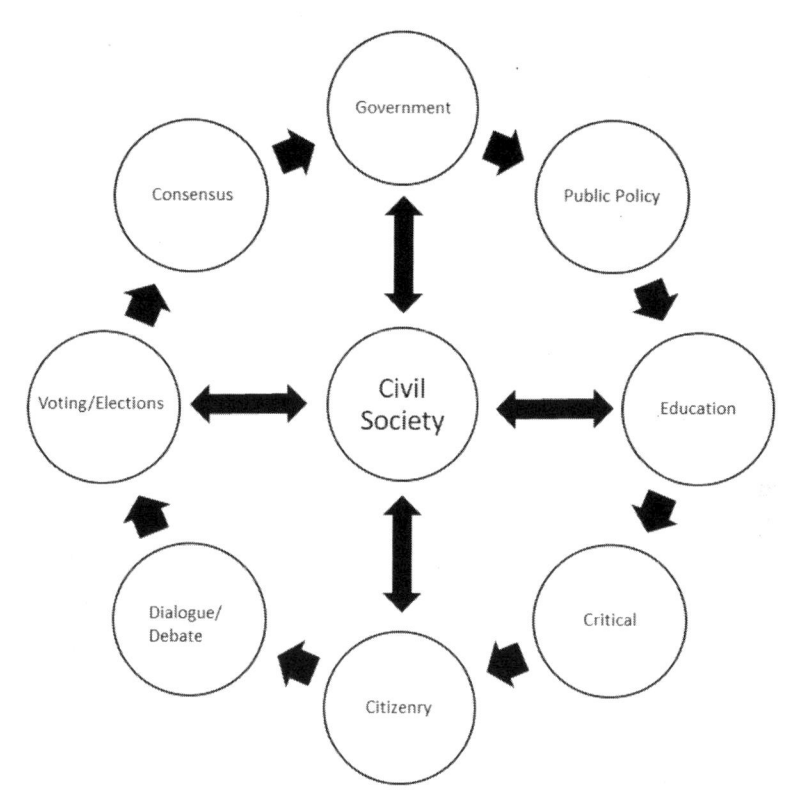

[Diagram: Civil Society at center, connected by double arrows to Government, Public Policy, Education, Critical, Citizenry, Dialogue/Debate, Voting/Elections, and Consensus arranged in a circle, with arrows flowing clockwise between outer nodes]

(1) religious leaders possess intimate knowledge of the culture and language of peoples in conflict; (2) these leaders have deep roots in the community, providing negotiators with firsthand information as conflict changes on the ground; (3) religious leaders and faith-based groups have access to a vast network of political expertise, locally and internationally; and (4) many of these religious leaders have developed short-term and long-term visions of peace which were adapted to their society.[6]

Muslim religious leaders and faith-based organizations are often the first to hear and observe erratic behavior and opinions on the ground before a conflict erupts. Due to their wide networks, these leaders are acutely sensitive to intolerance, hate speech, and organized activities planning to disrupt their communities. As leading civil society members, these leaders will need to confront bigotry, hatred, and dehumanization of any group before the presence of law enforcement. As such, religious leaders are involved in advocacy, protection, mediation, interventions, and peacebuilding education awareness programs during various stages of conflict. Muslim religious leaders engaged in peacebuilding activities already agree upon tackling the roots of conflict at the community level, which activates conflict management programs. They understand that interdisciplinary approaches are required to confront the causes of the social breakdown, establish a multiparty participation process, and apply a multiprong engagement program with affected communities. They are not only operating on their faith-based ethos of justice and ethical principles but also seek to learn from other CSOs explicitly involved in these complex peacebuilding efforts.

In Muslim-majority and -minority communities, peacebuilding work without the cooperation of religious actors may well lose legitimacy with the very people they are trying to help. They draw on a network of meso-religious communities and leaders who cooperate and build upon years of common experiences and shared values. It is not so much understanding the daily problems and conflicts of the community; these events need regular participation by leadership, who must host timely dialogues to resolve them. Religious peacemaking scholarship highlights the many cases where religious leaders have transformed conflict peacefully and cultivated a "culture of peace" in war-torn regions. In Jordan, the Royal Hashemite Kingdom assembled over three hundred leading Muslim scholars and jurists from across the Islamic world to discuss indiscriminate violence in the Middle East and the broader Islamic world. They agreed to work together against the rise of extremism and the irresponsible, illegal act of calling other Muslims who disagree on certain positions apostates (*takfir*). The resulting "The Amman Message" stated, "Islam honors every human being, without distinction of color, race or religion."[7]

CIVIL SOCIETY MEMBERS IN WAR— JAMMU AND KASHMIR, INDIA

The Indian province of Jammu and Kashmir has been disputed since independence in 1947. India has gone to war with Pakistan three times over control and supervision of the province. Human rights groups, activists, journalists, academics, religious leaders, lawyers, teachers, students, and broader civil society groups have documented, prosecuted, brought attention to, and reproduced material that has repeatedly highlighted the violence and politics of the Indian State and the everyday militarized reality of Jammu and Kashmir. As of 2016, according to an extensive report, "Structures of Violence," the Indian government has caused systematic violence against Kashmiri civil society, amounting to the disappearance of eight thousand persons, over seventy-five thousand deaths, another six thousand unresolved cases, the uncovering of mass graves, and cases of torture and sexual violence.[8] This includes the fact that Indian State actors have gone with impunity where there have been no trials of the armed forces for human rights violations in Jammu and Kashmir. In the quest for complete domination of Jammu and Kashmir, human rights and civil rights reports provide evidence, through extensive case studies, that there is no process or political will to give justice to the families, the deceased, and the victims of Indian military brutality.

Kashmiri civil society members are regularly identified as threats to national order, incarcerated, and viewed as prisoners of the state. Since 1988, there has been an intensive militarization of the Jammu and Kashmir province in India, authorized through the legal system, producing patterns of impunity that exceed and operate beyond the law. Regular national debates on protecting democracy and national interests through the military have placed Kashmiri civilians as a national security concern.[9] The 2012 report "Alleged Perpetrators" identified five hundred named officials as perpetrators responsible for 214 human rights violations in Jammu and Kashmir. Other reports written by the International Peoples' Tribunal on Human Rights and Justice in Indian-Administered Kashmir and The Association of Parents of Disappeared Persons have argued that Indian State, Indian army, and Indian paramilitary units such as the Border Security Force, Central Reserve Police Force, Jammu and Kashmir Police, and government underground militias were responsible for illegal detentions, torture, rape, killings, and forced beatings. The same group issued a 2009 report, "Buried Evidence," documenting North Kashmir's unmarked and mass graves. All these reports find that the Indian political state and its forces have conspired and executed these human rights violations in the name of national security.[10]

Researchers on the ground in Jammu and Kashmir documented how civil society members were regularly harassed, monitored, and beaten on the streets and on university campuses, and prevented from gathering in public. In interviews, high school and university students expressed how the police regularly disrupt their youth groups, and students as young as thirteen years old are arrested for gathering. Youth gatherings and professional meetings, such as lawyers' or humanities professors' meetings, are viewed as acts of resistance to the state, allowing for forced disruptions and arrests.[11] Not only are the assembly of civil society youth groups not permitted, but there is regular vetting and banning of books, magazines, and films, limited access to the internet, and university libraries have become scaled down to vocational materials or the promotion of Indian nationalism. Sheikh Shawkat Hussain, a law professor at Kashmir University in Srinagar, reported that the state shut down research institutes like the Kashmir Institute, which promoted research, conferences, workshops, and sponsored student-led research. It's common for classes to be interrupted by police action.[12] In the disguise of national security and counterterrorism operations by the Indian military, civil society in Jammu and Kashmir has all but been eviscerated and systematically demolished. In their military operations to crack down on Kashmiri Islamist groups, like Muslim Mujahideen, Hizbul Mujahideen, Ikhwan ul-Muslimeen, or non-Islamist Jammu Kashmir Liberation Front, Indian forces allegedly carried out abductions of youth like Nahida Imtiaz, daughter of the ex-parliamentarian Saifuddin Soz.[13]

Kashmiri youth are not allowed to create or sustain a culture of dialogue and collaboration or congregate to think about ways to resolve their conflict. International development agencies like the UN Development Programme (UNDP), the US Agency for International Development, or the Red Cross are prohibited from supporting any activities in Jammu and Kashmir nor attempting to establish relationships with civil society groups. While the UNDP, the Red Cross, and Amnesty International have tried to initiate national and transnational youth networking to link youth with each other, across cities and across countries, to promote civic and policy engagement, develop critical thinking, and foster national dialogue and cooperation, they are prohibited from these programs in this province.[14] Attempting to duplicate cross-national participatory workshops or roundtable discussions in critical cities in Libya, Tunisia, Algeria, and Morocco, the UNDP has been refused access to Jammu and Kashmir to strengthen existing local capacity to train and support youth. North African civil society activists and policy leaders operate in dangerous and repressive environments, and youth struggle to find economic resources to work, meet, train, and engage with their communities; the UNDP, US Agency for International Development, and the Red Cross have access to civil society members for peacebuilding activities.

Within these conditions, researchers and practitioners argue that it is nearly impossible for local CSOs to affect policies and to move the Indian government. Indian-administered Jammu and Kashmir has nearly choked any viable activities of civil society members, plus the lack of visibility, communication, and linkages with the global peacebuilding community has, in effect, isolated them. It is no wonder that, for these and other reasons, frustrated youths withdraw, becoming invisible; worse, they join extremist or criminal groups that offer better prospects for addressing their needs and expectations. Indian repressive policies against civil society demolished safe places and opportunities for learning, dialogue, and cooperation among themselves and other parts of India. This weakened the social fabric, undermining participatory governance and trust in social, political, and economic institutions. Kashmiri civil society members face astonishing challenges: repressive policies, illegal detentions, human rights violations, closure of schools, random arrests, monitoring of all human activities, deliberate isolation from other Indian states, and the prevention of the global community to maintain contact.[15]

In this repressive context arose a leader, Syed Ali Shah Geelani (1929–2021), who formed the All Parties Hurriyat Conference in 1993. Accused of being a pro-Islamist leader who wished an independent Jammu and Kashmir to be an Islamic theocracy, Geelani founded the Tehreek-e Hurriyat party in 2004, where he served as chairman of the party. Elected as a Jammu and Kashmir Legislative Assembly member, other Kashmiri politicians accused Geelani as the source of increased militancy and promoting youth to adopt separatist ideologies.[16] However, Geelani was an avid believer in nonviolent action, public protests as resistance, and boycotting elections when there were apparent discrepancies in transparency and fairness.[17] Interested in engaging youth to his party and ensuring they had access to uninterrupted education without interrogation, Geelani believed that Jammu and Kashmir's repression would stop once India and Pakistan could resolve their differences over the territory.[18]

Geelani worked not only to have Kashmiri voices represented in the legislature of Jammu and Kashmir, but he had an international reach with the Organization of Islamic Conference, European Union, UN Human Rights Commission, and other international bodies. He staunchly criticized the EU delegation for not meeting with him during their travel to India and for not engaging with Kashmiri activists to express their concerns about human rights violations. Geelani said his frustrations with the Organization of Islamic Conference's Kashmir Contact Group work was ineffective and too slow to make change for his people. As a local Indian activist, politician, civil society organizer, and an inspiring leader for a population to not lose hope amid repression, Geelani's legacy is to ensure civil society members did not become obscure and fall into oblivion in India's history. Geelani sought training workshops for Kashmiri youth to gain knowledge from local and national experts to share their knowledge with their younger peers. He wanted civil society activists to receive the same opportunities offered to Indians in major urban centers like New Delhi, Mumbai, Hyderabad, and Kolkata. He knew youth training workshops provided by international organizations were politically driven, and only certain cities keen on developing and connecting with global organizations benefited from these connections. He witnessed India move from an underdeveloped agricultural society to a competitive, technologically driven, and globally connected society; however, those advancements were relegated to certain Indian states, and Jammu and Kashmir was, according to Geelani, purposely being left behind as an underdeveloped state.

Geelani did not do enough for many critics, and his political activities did not produce the vision he spoke about. However, Geelani vividly advocated for an active, enriched civil society with resilient social, political, and economic institutions. In one speech, he wanted Jammu and Kashmir to develop hubs for youth to learn vocational skills and build their capacity-building training in entrepreneurship programs or rapid incubation programs to increase the technology knowledge of the youth. The emergence of the technology boom in southern India and the competitive technology educational centers, like the Indian Institute of Technology, was one of his long-term objectives to build a sustainable ecosystem. Geelani believed in helping youth identify markets of their local and surrounding cities and tailor education programs toward skills required in the sectors of focus. He wanted Kashmiri youth to be rooted in Jammu and Kashmir but to imagine themselves in various sectors, such as construction, education, agriculture, transportation services, oil logistics, technology, information systems, medicine, etc.

When Syed Ali Shah Geelani died in September 2021, most of the obituaries wrote about his political life, his feuds with other Kashmiri politicians, how Indian politicians portrayed him as an agent working for Pakistan, or his dissent within the political party he founded. The obituaries did not attempt to cover the man's contributions to his community or how the Kashmiri youth admired his activism. The media coverage neglected his behind-the-scenes peacebuilding efforts of ensuring those arrested received legal representation, the victims' families compensated for their loss, or teaching students to be tenacious, imaginative, and relentlessly committed to their studies. He witnessed two generations ready to leave India for more lucrative opportunities overseas, leaving their families and communities behind. Geelani was disturbed about the present condition of Jammu and Kashmir and the future of India and Indian society. He recognized that the gap between the wealthy and the have-nots was even more apparent during the early 1990s' liberalizing the economy. Most did not listen to Geelani's nuanced vision of economic, social, and political independence because they only saw him as an Indian politician. He struggled, like many colleagues; he was imprisoned, and the authorities tried to isolate his voice from the community. But, when one sat alone with Syed Ali Shah Geelani and listened to his dreams and vision for his community, Geelani spoke of another world based on peaceful coexistence and security for his community.

QUAGMIRE OF INTERNATIONAL FUNDING

Islamic peacebuilding efforts have increased at many levels and in many regions of Muslim-majority countries. These peacebuilding activists operate with their faith as the central pole of all ethical activities. They believe humanity has a common origin and human dignity must be recognized and respected, regardless of religion, ethnicity, or tribe. They cherish diversity within and outside of their tradition: diversity among people encapsulates the richness of traditions. An important element in Islamic peacebuilding is the desire to improve their community and the world, they want to cooperate, collaborate, and engage in dialogue with others and among themselves to foster and sustain peace. In each of the cases studied, peacebuilders using their faith tradition as the primary framework does not mean to be exclusivist; instead, it requires to be engaged with others respectfully. Muslim peacebuilders not only desire to practice good deeds and strive toward justice for only the Muslim community, but these values must be evident in everyday dealings with all human beings. These essential principles do not contradict Western approaches or Christian approaches to peacebuilding. Instead, similarities allow for more common ground in working together.[19]

Interestingly, broad concepts of civil society serving as the third sector or a watchdog for government are not the reality of most CSOs in developing and Muslim-majority countries. Countries range in different stages of development: Western versus Eastern, peaceful versus conflict, secular versus faith-based, authoritarian or liberal democracy, monarchy or pseudo-democracy. First, it is essential to point out that using the term civil society in Muslim-majority countries—a mix of post-colonial developing states, neoliberal democracies, monarchies, and military authoritarian—is not the same as civil society in Western liberal democracies. First, an area of concern is that legitimate governance in democratic societies requires public participation in policy decision-making and representation in the rule of law institutions. In addressing justice, undoubtedly, the formal security sector has little oversight or accountability, so any discussion of security sector reform processes will depend on civil society members participating without impunity.

Second, the combination of international aid agencies and the influence of international financial institutions directing, if not micromanaging, how civil society members operate in these societies is a concern. In Muslim-majority countries, civil society members and CSOs are heavily monitored with their activities: active surveillance of communications on mobile and laptop devices, regular monitoring of their funding received from the international community, and the intelligence community is represented in CSO workshops and trainings to monitor conversations and activities.

Considering the volume and international financial support from the United States, United Kingdom, Canada, the European Union, Scandinavian countries, and other Western countries to CSOs in Muslim-majority or -minority communities, it imparts a responsibility on their respective governments to ensure its programs serve the right and intended purposes without doing harm to local civil society members. This engagement with local CSOs should consider the following nine forms of engagement: (1) consulting with local CSO and local and national governments on the partnership; (2) bringing in local civil society members into the early process of needs assessment, planning, coordination, and execution stages of the projects; (3) the international donor agency ensures an adequate degree of protection and emergency plan for the CSO; (4) serving as a partner and bridge between local and national government to ensure that local civil society members are operating within national laws and transparency; (5) considering scenarios that will do harm to local civil society members and have an immediate rescue plan; (6) engaging local civil society faith-based members can create tensions for them and their religious networks, so conduct a thorough review of scenarios to protect this engagement; (7) designing a process for engaging independent civil society on matters other than security cooperation or countering violent extremism to minimize challenges and the risk of exposing civil society representatives to government reprisals; (8) instead of creating competition and resentment among local civil society members on funding of projects, it would benefit all parties if donors empowered local CSOs with transparent processes, planned projects, and a strategic plan for the next five years; and (9) while funding local CSOs is part of the donor agency's soft power politics, local CSOs should not feel that their livelihoods can be endangered with impulsive change of policy or funding.

While respective donor agencies have their internal guidelines for a policy framework for operating with local, independent civil society members, there should be essential common principles directing appropriate engagement, rules for protection, and abide by the do-no-harm policy.

CHALLENGES

Yet religion cannot be neglected with Samuel Huntington's assertion that the world faces a clash of civilizations with strong religious dimensions, forthcoming realities of religiously framed wars or genocides, religiously inspired terrorists, and overt tensions and bitter conflicts among religious groups. While there is enough media and academic coverage of negative dimensions of religious impact in conflict zones, the case of more positive impact, both local work by religious leaders and transnational efforts that cross regional boundaries, must be better understood. I've studied that the work of religious peacebuilders usually gets unrecognized, especially within Islamic communities. Sometimes, the combination of memory and unchecked bias of secular approaches toward peacebuilding can persuade the conscious that religious tensions are the source of all conflict and cannot be a source of peacebuilding.

The main challenge facing the peacebuilding industry is deepening the understanding of religious peacebuilding authentically and finally recognizing and supporting the nuanced differences in how religious leaders and faith-based organizations contribute to resolving conflict. There was a time when we thought the global order after the September 11 attacks and subsequent wars in Iraq, Afghanistan, Yemen, and Syria solidified the debate over religion's role in politics, international affairs, and the conflict resolution field—for some thinkers the first ten years after 2001 reinforced notions that religion can mobilize individuals toward extremist actions or intolerant ideology. For those hanging onto modernization theory, where religion was to have a minimalist and vanishing role in politics and the public sphere, scholars now contend that the many-faceted forms of "secularism" may have contributed to the rise of religious resurgence and mass appeal. The study of religion in international relations seems to have swayed from one end of the pendulum of being completely neglected or an afterthought in global affairs to being immensely central to understanding security, terrorism, and threats facing fragile states. For example, in the early analysis of the Arab uprisings of 2011, there were countless questions on the role of the Muslim Brotherhood in Egypt, Tunisia, Libya, and Yemen would permit religious radicals to hijack the nonviolent civil unrest to create an Iranian-style theocracy. With the election of Muslim Brotherhood's Mohamad Morsi in Egypt, which was then overturned after one year with an army intervention, and the current Tunisian crisis of ousting and imprisoning pro-Islamist politicians, the verdict of entrusting religious political actors governing the state is unquestionably negative.

What is positive is how Western social scientists are so deeply committed to classical liberalism that any reference to religion and religious actors conjures up potentially destabilizing negative scenarios. Understanding the role of religion and religious actors in peacebuilding illustrates vividly that religion is part of a multilayered matrix of complex institutions where some religious leaders contribute to exacerbating conflict, while others work aggressively to mitigate violence and build institutions for peaceful purposes. Religious leaders and faith-based organizations are much of the fabric of civil society and are critical contributors to social, economic, educational, humanitarian relief, political functions, and peacebuilding efforts. The roles played by religious actors and faith-based organizations are diverse, ranging from high-level mediators to peacebuilding through development at the grassroots level. Religion is not restricted to the confines of a church or mosque; religious organizations in Muslim-majority communities are very much part of the development, humanitarian, conflict resolution, and social welfare sectors. Their immense networks and strategic capacity as transnational actors have enabled them to mobilize effectively and rapidly support their war-affected communities, mediate between conflicting parties, and serve as primary civil society actors contributing to reconciliation, dialogue, and reintegration.[20]

One of the critical challenges within social sciences is analyzing the connection of the resurgence of religion with terrorism, political activism, and contributors to an ultimate clash with liberal democracies. Let us recall that terrorism is neither an ideology nor a discrete form of conflict; instead, it is a strategy or tactic of political violence used by actors in the broader context of conflict to achieve political goals. Analysts should treat terrorism as a symptom and not the sole cause of any conflict. Focusing exclusively on acts of terrorism limits the analysis and understanding of the broader range of issues at work in any given situation. Using a conflict resolution framework and not a counterterrorism prism can present a more comprehensive set of suitable issues, actors, and behaviors and deal with the history of a conflict and the grievances that terrorism feeds upon.

It is recognized that religious leaders have firsthand knowledge of local issues, and most often, they and their organizations can gain local cooperation easily and have direct access to disputants. When designing a focused peacebuilding strategy, it is necessary to identify the right-size responsibility for religious leaders and faith-based organizations on their role in the conflict zone. It is not just simply to include them in the peacebuilding operations, but there needs to be a clear vision and methodology to be included in the relationships, in implementing conflict prevention practices, and supporting post-conflict development and social well-being. As members of the civil society, there will be a need to smooth and lessen the competitive nature among CSOs when religious leaders are integrated. Like other civil society actors, religious leaders need to be trained and incorporated into the wider field of peacebuilding with a long-term commitment to a comprehensive approach that focuses on the local community while engaging the middle and top levels of leadership.

At the end of the day, religious leaders are just that—leaders in their communities whose voices and words hold meaning and value for those who follow them. In times of a powerful focus on extremist violence and resort to costly, counterproductive military solutions, the international community of peacebuilding needs to recognize the full scope of religious leaders' standing, access, and credibility, which can be channeled for peaceful and tolerant purposes. The challenge is for existing secular peacebuilding organizations—with a devout dedication to secular culture—to self-transform themselves to recognize the importance of religious communities and faith-based organizations while appreciating their peacebuilding activities and integrating them as resourceful civil society members.

NOTES

1. The Community of Sant'Egidio is a global network that began as a student initiative inspired by the 1968 ethos of rebellion against authority and what a small group saw as the spiritual call to meet the needs of immigrant populations in Rome. During the time of Pope John Paul II, the community developed a relationship with the Catholic Church as an independent lay community that focused on the poor and excluded in Italy and later in other regions, including Africa. Sant'Egidio worked with prisoners, immigrants, children, and marginalized communities. Sant'Egidio worked on mediation in Mozambique, negotiations in Sudan, and public health issues like HIV and AIDS. See Sahiri Constant Lohourougnon, *The Community of Sant'Egidio and the Mozambican Conflict* (Our Knowledge Publishing, 2004) and Roberto Morozzo della Rocca, *Sant'Egidio's Dream* (Georgetown University Press, Washington, DC, 2023).

2. For a discussion on the prominence of secular approaches and the domination of Christian and Catholic peacebuilding approaches contributing toward biases within the peacebuilding field, see chapter 1.

3. See D. Philpott (ed.), *The Politics of Evil: Religion, Reconciliation, and the Dilemmas of Transitional Justice* (Notre Dame, Indiana: University of Notre Press, 2006) and H. Corbin, *Amnesty after Atrocity* (2007).

4. These terms include the activities of women, men, and youth in Muslim-majority communities.

5. Outside of academic circles, mainly within Muslim-majority academic and non-academic communities, the terms "religious actors" or "religious stakeholders" are perceived as pejorative. I have had extensive conversations with colleagues, practitioners, nongovernmental organization and CSO leaders, and religious leaders on this topic I am conscious of this poor construction and will try to limit the use of these terms.

6. See Andrea Bartoli, *Negotiating Peace: The Role of Non-Governmental Organizations* (Republic of Letters, 2013) and idem., "Mediating Peace in Mozambique: The Role of the Community of Sant'Egidio," in C. Crocker, F.O. Hampson, and P. Aall (eds.), *Herding Cats: Multiparty Mediation in a Complex World* (Washington, DC: USIP Press, 1999), pp. 245–74.

7. See Amman Message, www.ammanmessage.org, and The Royal Institute for Inter-Faith Studies, 2004.

8. International People's Tribunal on Human Rights and Justice in Indian-administered-Kashmir, and Association of Parents of Disappeared Persons, *Structures of Violence: The Indian State in Jammu and Kashmir*, 2015.

9. Haley Duschinski, "Destiny Effects: Militarization, State Power, and Punitive Containment in Kashmir Valley," *Anthropological Quarterly*, 2009, 82, no. 3: 691–717.

10. International People's Tribunal on Human Rights and Justice in Indian-administered-Kashmir and Association of Parents of Disappeared Persons, *Buried Evidence*, 2009.

11. Mohamad Junaid, "Death and Life Under Occupation: Space, Violence, and Memory in Kashmir," in *Everyday Occupations: Experiencing Militarism in South Asia and the Middle East*, edited by Kamala Visweswaran (Philadelphia: University of Pennsylvania Press, 2013), pp. 158–90.

12. Haroon Mirani, "Academic Dissent Stifled in Kashmir," *University World News*, May 1, 2011.

13. *Structures of Violence: The Indian State in Jammu and Kashmir*, pp. 28–32.

14. F.A. Dar, *Living in a Pressure Cooker Situation: A Needs Assessment of Youth in India Administered-Kashmir* (London, UK: Conciliation Resources, 2011); Amnesty International, *India: "Denied": Failures in Accountability for Human Rights Violations by Security Personnel in Jammu and Kashmir* (London, United Kingdom: Amnesty International, 2015).

15. See Mridu Rai, "Making a Part Inalienable: Folding Kashmir into India's Imagination," in *Until the Freedom Has Come: The New Intifada in Kashmir*, edited by Sanjay Kak (Haymarket Book, 2015), pp. 250–78; Rekha Chowdhary, *Jammu and Kashmir: Politics of Identity and Separatism* (New Delhi: Routledge, 2016).

16. "Omar Farooq Lash out at Geelani," *The Hindu*, Chennai, India, April 29, 2007.

17. Abdul Hakeem, *Paradise on Fire: Syed Ali Geelani and the Struggle for Freedom in Kashmir* (London: Kube Publishing, 2014), pp. 130 44.

18. "India Should Accept Five Conditions on Kashmir: Geelani," *Business Standard India*, March 23, 2015.

19. See Qamar-ul Huda, *Cresent and Dove: Peace and Conflict Resolution in Islam* (Washington, DC: USIP Press, 2011).

20. T. Bouta, Ayse Kadayifci-Orellana, and Mohammed Abu-Nimer, *Faith-Based Peace-Building: Mapping and Analysis of Christian, Muslim and Multi-Faith Actors* (The Hague, Netherlands: Institute of International Relations, 2005).

Chapter Five

The Discourse of Islam and Peacebuilding

WHAT DO WE MEAN BY ISLAM?

When my good friend Shahab Ahmed asked me to provide feedback for his manuscript *What Is Islam? The Importance of Being Islamic*, I wanted to discuss this with him at a coffee shop in Cambridge, outside of the Harvard University campus, to listen to his reasons for writing the book. Ten years earlier, Shahab Ahmed's academic contribution addressed the historicity of Salman Rushdie's *Satanic Verses* in scripture and complex historical commentaries surrounding this event. But now, in 2014, Shahab was more interested in unpacking modern notions of the self; he said, "Religious identity, let alone identity, is a complex topic that is understudied in Islamic studies, unfortunately, the field of identity studies is in an epistemological abyss of based only about thinking power, post-structuralism frameworks and has little or no connection to any of the Islamic canonical sources." This is how Shahab spoke to friends: direct, blunt, and with genuine intellectual integrity. As an undergraduate student studying Arabic, global politics, and Islamic studies, I met Shahab at the American University in Cairo in the 1980s. We spent lots of time admiring Mamluk architecture, walking together in old Cairo, making countless trips to the Egyptian Museum, and spending many long nights attending remembrance (*dhikr*) rituals in different parts of the city. In many respects, his journey in exploring religious identity and the meaning of orthodoxy may have started with interfacing and critically thinking about the legacy of Islamic civilization in a context of relentless bombardment of unfiltered news headlines on Muslims, Islam, and unintelligible responses by pundits, Orientalists, and Salafi-Islamist political talking heads.

Ahmed's meticulous research into the historical works in defining Sunni orthodoxy involved studying various sources and discovering and making sense of arguments, explanations, narratives, and persuasive descriptions of debates in the classical period of Islam. Conveying knowledge is one exercise, but trying to persuade the fundamental principles of orthodoxy to be adopted by a community is another challenging exercise. Academic scholars did not miss the opportunity to criticize Ahmed's theoretical framework, missing historical sources, not emphasizing Shi'ism, or, as one scholar stated, "the failure to make sense of all kinds of phenomena; the inculcation of virtues, the development of embodied sensibilities, the achievement of spiritual states and so on."[1] Academic scholars and researchers were lining up to pounce on Ahmed for not examining specific fields, misreading or not including certain texts, not identifying other—or their own—scholarly works on power and institutions, and so forth. In *What is Islam?* Ahmed argued three key points: the text of the Qur'an, the context of lived ideas and culture produced by actual Muslims, and the nature of the universe itself against which the Qur'an is revealed, which Ahmed called the pre-Text. For him, Islam retains its coherence because rather than a law, religion, culture, or discursive tradition, Islam is a hermeneutical engagement with the pre-text, text, and con-text of revelation (i.e., the Qur'an). He notes that contradictions are inherent in Muslim intellectual traditions and the lived religion. Ahmed claims that the religion of Islam is not a single monolithic entity, as contended by Salafi orthodox scholars; instead, the religion is a constellation of multitudes. These multitudes incorporate a philosophical inquiry into reality, the mystical experience of seeking the divine, aesthetics and arts expressing this journey toward the divine, the scientific study of nature, and a passion for exploring true love. Indeed, Ahmed described a bold sixth school (*madhab*) of Islamic law beyond the orthodox five: the *madhab* of love.[2]

For this book when referring to Islam or an Islamic community, I am speaking about Muslims operating in any of these six categories: (1) Muslims affiliated with the major accepted schools of law outwardly practicing their faith built on irrepressible transcendent ideals based on a firm belief that a single divine entity is responsible for the transformation of all life; (2) Muslims emphasizing the importance of spirituality, the inner, experiential dimensions of the religion, and the spiritual journey and the quest for a deeper connection with the divine; (3) Muslim communities with common inherited institutions, culture, architecture, infrastructure of identities, and historic linguistic and ethnic interconnections; (4) Muslims actively seeking common ground and understanding among different religious traditions, cultures, societies, ethnic and tribal affiliations, class, gender, and in the areas of interfaith and intrafaith dialogues; (5) Muslims studying, preserving, transmitting, and sharing of classical intellectual-spiritual-ethical Islamic heritage while accepting and being conscious of the wide range of challenges and contradictions of the modern secularism; and (6) Muslims firmly believing and acting as stewards of the earth, environment, ecology, and protectors of other human beings, creation, and the climate.

GLOBAL ISLAM

In contemporary comparative politics and international affairs, the term "global Islam" is used to illustrate that the religion of Islam is not the only perspective to consider in discussing Islam; rather, in a globalized world, transnational interconnectivity global considerations are needed. Oliver Roy's *Globalized Islam: The Search for a New Ummah* and John Esposito's *Islam and Globalization: Exploring the Views of Muslim Publics* speak to the issue of the global Muslim community undergoing transformations with globalization, technology, and access to swift communications. The global Islamic community, often referred to as *ummah*, is not restricted to a geographical space and is facing globalization's challenges. Muslims are rapidly changing with the contours of globalization's technology, with interconnected international economies, and Muslims are utilizing technology and not fighting against it.

Akbar Ahmed's *Journey into Islam: The Crisis of Globalization* and Tariq Ramadan's *Western Muslims and the Future of Islam* are examples of two Muslim intellectuals who find the age of globalization a significant challenge for Muslims because religious traditions are becoming less attractive for the youth. They claim that the age of globalization comes after two important imposing experiences of modernization and Westernization, which challenged identity, the maintenance of Islamic values, traditional gender roles, traditional roles of authority, adherence and respect to Islamic law, and intellectual heritage. Ramadan concisely tackles the tension between religious Muslim practices of fasting, daily prayers, charity, and community while living and engaging in secular, multicultural, pluralistic environments. Ramadan underscores the point that Western Muslims living in an age of globalization may not feel the same belonging to Muslim-majority countries, which will decrease their affinity to these cultures and original points of heritage.

Juan Cole's *Engaging the Muslim World: A Road Map for U.S. Policy in the Middle East* was written after the September 11 attacks and when the United States was actively at war in Afghanistan and Iraq. Beginning with a historical context from the twentieth century, Cole begins with the United States's various policy decisions in the Middle East and the political, social, and cultural dynamics of responses to these decisions. Affirming the age of globalization, Cole believes the United States needs to use a less militaristic approach to resolving conflicts in and around the Middle East and use less forceful democracy promotion. Instead, countries should design democracy, or any other desired form of government, by indigenous processes and not external pressure. Engaging the Muslim World recognizes civil society movements for democracy and against authoritarian regimes, and it is time for the United States to support these grassroots movements. Similarly, Asef Bayat's *Making Islam Democratic: Social Movements and the Post-Islamist Turn* highlights the way the globalized world with instantaneous information and networks of interconnectivity is influencing the younger generation in Muslim-majority countries to think about freedom of expression and assembly, democracy, and social movements centered on social justice. Not viewing Islamist parties and Salafism as a solution to their society's problems, Bayat believes that "Islamic democratic" movements will influence the direction of the future of these societies.

One exceptional book on global Islam is by Peter Mandaville, *Global Political Islam*. This book is a meticulous study of contemporary Islam practices across borders. Affirming the new age of communications interconnectivity, issues facing Islam (i.e., Muslims) transcend national boundaries and impact regional and international politics. After evaluating the changing nature of political Islam in Egypt, Jordan, Tunisia, and Turkey, Mandaville studies the evolving dynamics of political Islam and its impact on governance and social movements. Interestingly, he covers how Muslim-majority countries portray Islam as a global image while using public diplomacy for soft power purposes. According to Mandaville, globalization and modernity are not on the edges of Muslim lives; instead, they intersect at the heart of their identities, causing new ways of adapting or resisting global realities.

Nile Green's *Global Islam: A Very Short Introduction* believes the term global Islam comprises contemporary Muslim communities that reflect a general continuity with time-honored traditions among Muslims, such as the traditional law schools and institutional Sufism. Green thinks global Islam refers to the doctrines and practices promoted by transnational religious activists, organizations, and states during the era of modern globalization. For him, modern technologies, organizational forms, and infrastructure have significantly shaped the proliferation of reformist Islam and global Islam; therefore, it is a modern configuration of Muslim thought and practice at the intersection of globalization and Islamic reform.

Building upon these works on global Islam, I also recognize that contemporary Islamic tradition is a complex multifaceted tradition with diverse cultures, divergent interpretations, and layers of diversity in the fields of ethics, aesthetics, art, music, ethnic groups, and tribes. Muslim-majority communities consist of complex histories of interfaith relations with the Eastern Orthodox Churches, Roman Catholicism, Coptic Church, and Protestant Churches, as well as the Sephardic Jews and Dharmic Buddhist and Hindu communities. Each religious tradition contains spiritual, sacred sites believed to be a direct connection to the divine or the work of the messengers of God. Not only are these sacred sites spaces for pilgrimage, veneration, worship, and social interaction, but these sacred sites provide historical cultural significance, memories, and rituals that re-enact, embody, and reinforce identities.

STUDYING ISLAM AND PEACEBUILDING

There are seminal works in the field of Islamic peacebuilding that seeded theory and practice, as well as deepened the scholarship on religious peacebuilding and conflict resolution. In 2001, Abdul Aziz Said, Nathan Funk, and Ayse Kadayifci's edited book *Peace and Conflict Resolution in Islam: Precept and Practice* analyzed several important aspects of conflict resolution, ethics, history, and politics in the Islamic tradition while highlighting Sufism as a key area Islamic practice containing paradigms of peacemaking. Scholar and practitioner Mohammed Abu-Nimer wrote *Nonviolence and Peace Building in Islam: Theory and Practice*, positioning the Islamic peacemaking field within the conflict resolution field of study. Abu-Nimer demonstrated that fundamental principles of Islam support peacebuilding and nonviolence and that these basic assumptions, values, and beliefs are derived from text, scripture, historical narratives, culture, and daily human experiences. After establishing fundamental principles, he used case studies to demonstrate how traditional dispute resolution methods in Arab-Muslim communities are applied to daily nonviolence and peacebuilding practices. This work is built upon his earlier work, *Dialogue, Conflict Resolution and Change: Arab-Jewish Encounters in Israel*, leading to another impressive publication with co-authors Amal Khoury and Emily Welty, *Unity in Diversity: Interfaith Dialogue in the Middle East*, which discusses the intricate relationships between interfaith activities and religious identity. In 2005, Abdul Karim Bangura published *Islamic Peace Paradigms*, where he identified key themes, such as dialogue, love, law, and nonviolence, to illustrate essential modalities in promoting peace in Islamic cultures.

Interfaith dialogues evolved as an essential practice because these transformative dialogues recognized the interdependence of a globalized world. Works on interfaith dialogue claimed that individuals with faith created powerful links to the larger community across the globe, to which religion acts as a governing principle. Studies showed that participants in interfaith dialogue were interested in honoring the differences of the other while, at the same time, they recognized similarities. Interfaith dialogues were classified as cognitive or affective: cognitive dialogues primarily seek to learn more information about the other faith tradition, whereas affective dialogues are interested in developing, healing, and empowering relationships. Islamic peacebuilding consisted of various works examining how interfaith dialogues are utilized as an important platform for peacemaking. David Singh and Robert Schick's *Approaches, Foundations, Issues and Models of Interfaith Relations*, Raimon Pannikar's *The Intra-religious Dialogue*, and Bruce Feiler's *Abraham: A Journey to the Heart of Three Faiths* were common texts used.

The field of Islamic peacebuilding continues to advance important idealism of nonviolence to affirm unambiguously that killing any innocent being is not acceptable or legitimate. Acknowledging the enormous body of scholarly literature on the rules and limitations of killings within Islamic law, Chaiwat Satha-Anand, an influential scholar and practitioner of nonviolent Islamic peacebuilding, asserts that violence is completely unacceptable in Islam and that Muslims must use nonviolent action to fight for justice and reconciliation. Satha-Anand states, "Islam itself is fertile soil for nonviolence because of its potential for disobedience, strong discipline, sharing and social responsibility, perseverance, self-sacrifice, and the belief in the unity of the Muslim community and the oneness of mankind."[3] Satha-Anand disputes status quo perspectives on Islamic just war theories, particularly the use of defensive violence, by once again reviving the nonviolent aspects of the Islamic tradition. He challenges scholars and peacebuilding practitioners to be critical of historical positions justifying violence and apply an alternative thinking framework.

These scholars use scripture, historical texts, commentaries, and other narratives to demonstrate that at the heart of Islam is a message of nonviolence, tolerance, and respect for all creatures. However, one key problem is that the academic study of Islamic peacemaking is not only rooted in Western conflict resolution studies but is essential to note that it is influenced by scholars trained in sociology, anthropology, and political science fields of study. One key underlying issue is the foundational perspectives on approaching Muslims, Islam, religious communities, and Islamic culture. Affirming that Islamic peacebuilding and conflict resolution practices are embedded in Muslim culture, these values and principles of conflict resolution are reinforced regularly in cultural practices. Since peacebuilding activities are seen and visible to outsiders, it is obviously a living component of their human experiences.

Similarly, the current political reality of existing violent extremists within Muslim-majority communities has been an opportunity for scholars to point out that these interpretations are misconstrued, grossly out of context, and selectively used to justify their violence and political agenda. Some scholars of Islam have argued that if extremists and their ideologues could be convinced of the more accurate interpretation of texts and historical narratives, then there would be a euphoric realization of their errors and actions. Imparting "proper and accurate" information will enlighten them to a historical context with a nuance of a wide range of divergent views within this discourse. On the other hand, ideologues of the violent extremist school vociferously claim that the approach is flawed because the opinions of past thinkers are viewed as illegitimate and authoritative. This brings us to the point that one of the qualities of scholars of the idealogues is their belief in the absolute nature of their understanding of Islam, and this absolutism constructs a worldview that ties the self to the sacred.

Muslim scholars trained in theology and religious studies commonly begin training with the Qur'an and examples from the Prophet's life as the starting point and illustrate it as authentically Islamic. While other scholars in Islamic peacebuilding will not be restricted to an established religious precedence, vast religious literature, or scholarly debates, their foundational ideas on peacebuilding are inherent to moments in human experience, in cultural contexts, where there is a "human connection" in the activity. Stating that there are multiple cultures within Islam, and Islamic culture is not homogenous, either across the world or in any community, these moments of human connection illustrate a higher consciousness of peacebuilding. This is prominent among cultural anthropologists who argue that cultural habits consist of inherited experiences from previous generations but are, in turn, organized and interpreted by individuals in the present generation.[4] Culture is a discourse that allows individuals or communities to express religious, psychological, social, political, and economic experiences—including through violence. Eminent scholar of conflict resolution John Burton argues that the root causes of violence in any culture or civilization lie in unmet human needs of security, identity, shelter, primary resources, and acceptance of others.[5] Black, Scimecca, and Avruch stress that cultural considerations matter a great deal in conflict resolution; individuals in conflict zones need to alter their own perceptions as well as the attitudes of the parties involved to ensure that they cognitively understand their power in mediation and the process of transforming the conflict.[6] These approaches are exemplified in the Islamic peacebuilding works of Abdul Aziz Said, Nathan Funk, Abu-Nimer, Ayse Kadayifci, Amal Khoury, and Emily Welty.

THE RELIGIOUS SCHOLARS: *ULAMA* AND PEACEBUILDING

When University of Erfurt scholar of Islam Jamal Malik initiated a two-year project entitled "Religious Pluralism and Religious Plurality: Towards an Ethics of Peace" from 2016 to 2018, his university hosted *madrasa* teachers and students from Pakistan's major religious sects: Sunni Barelvi, Deobandi, Ahl-i Hadith, Jama'at-i Islami, and Jafari Shi'ites. The workshop examined critical religious studies, pluralism in Islam, and historiography. The collaboration was designed to contest stereotypes and prejudices about the religious other and reflect upon traditional concepts within scholarly frameworks of modernity. Similarly, Ebrahim Moosa of Notre Dame secured funding for the "Contending Modernity: Madrasa Discourses" project, which consisted of engaging with Pakistan *madrasa* teachers, students, and younger leadership on scriptural hermeneutics, theories, and methods on Western approaches to religious studies, and ways in which the modern experience impacts thinking on juridical interpretation. Malik and Moosa's academic engagement with the *madrasa* institution was an attempt to broaden the thinking of Islamic seminaries by engaging them with topics, methods, and theories that are not usually taught in these institutions, and their educational experiences are limited to traditional methods of learning. Each scholar's project, situated on two different continents, believed the vanguards of Islam are the seminary students being trained to be the future's religious scholarly class (*'ulama*) and that their respective projects will produce favorable outcomes of change in their thinking.

These scholars operate within a set of perennial questions in Islamic studies: with whom do we engage, and does the party have an authentic voice genuine legitimacy within the Muslim community? For Western government policymakers, turning to religious authorities is not the first place for engagement; instead, they turn to government counterparts or vetted nongovernmental organizations with a track record of impact in the community. Among journalists covering stories in Muslim-majority communities, interviewing seminary teachers or religious leaders is not on their radar for information gathering or situational analysis.

However, both scholars are based in the Western world with academic training in religious studies or the history of religions, and they astutely understand that in the postmodern globalized world, religious institutions and religious scholars in Muslim-majority communities still undoubtedly maintain recognizable authority and power with the community of believers. Unlike in Christianity, the *'ulama* are not a clergy class that acts as an intermediary between the divine and human beings. Instead, the *'ulama* is a historic institution with expertise in Islamic sciences of jurisprudence, scripture, theology, Quranic studies, the life of the prophet, and related subjects, and has held powerful positions to advise the state, military, and political economies. While the *'ulama* views themselves as authentic custodians of a living religious tradition, there are postmodern questions about whether they are the sole group of Muslims to engage with for peacebuilding and conflict resolution. The unambiguous answer is no. Muslim-majority religious scholars explore academic and applicable contemporary questions of jurisprudence and the practice of religion, but they are not on the frontlines of conflict mitigation, nor are they situated in the global industry of peacebuilding work. With the rise of conflicts in Muslim-majority conflicts, there are more *'ulama* writings about peace and conflict, but overall, as a group, the *'ulama* are not structured or intellectually trained as their counterparts in peacebuilding civil society organizations (CSOs).

One issue of concern is not only the emphasis on the *'ulama* class but, as Muhammad Qasim Zaman articulates in *The Ulama in Contemporary Islam*, that there is an exclusive focus on modernists *'ulama* and with those *'ulama* affiliated with Islamist political parties. Zaman demonstrates that the *'ulama* was never a monolithic scholarly group seeking consensus or passively wielding authority without internal debates. In fact, the legitimacy of the *'ulama* authority and its authenticity is related to the institution's ability to demonstrate engagement with the tradition and respond to the changes of the times with impactful, meaningful discourse. This discursive engagement with tradition, argues Zaman, is not the same with the modernist and Islamist *'ulama*—who are more concerned with sovereignty, the nation-state, the community adhering to Islamic codes of conduct according to law, and ensuring Muslim spiritual lives are not eviscerated with modernity.

Connected to the question of authority and legitimacy in the Muslim-majority community, SherAli Tareen's *Defending Muhammad in Modernity* tackles this subject at two levels: the problem of religious identity and religious difference. Tareen argued that what is essential for the *'ulama* is how they defend themselves and construct an identity of legitimacy. Whether the *'ulama* navigates conversations on science and religion or sectarian intrareligious or interreligious violence, Tareen states there is a "constellation of theological contestations" over divine sovereignty (*tawhid* and *shirk*), and, more importantly, protecting the normative legacy of the Prophet Muhammad's life (*sunnah* and *bid'a*). This internal need to defend Islamic identity in changing landscapes of colonialization, independence, modernity, and postmodernity results from competing political theologies within the *'ulama* class and simultaneously remaining relevant in a growing secular world.

Contrasting to the works of Zaman and Tareen is a creative research work by Simon Wolfgang Fuchs's study of Pakistani Shi'i *'ulama* religious communities, institutions, and the importance of transnational networks. Fuchs argues that the Shi'a in South Asia *'ulama* resolves issues at the local level by drawing on their connections with authorities in Iran and Iraq. Having been trained in leading seminaries (*hawzas*) in Shi'a centers of learning in Qom (Iran) or Najaf (Iraq), these South Asian Shi'a *'ulama* understand the need to consult a central body of authorities who have more expertise on contemporary issues. By doing this, they are purposely maximizing their transnational connections to ensure their statements are accurate and validated, and at the same time, they empower themselves to stay connected to a broader globalized community while serving their respective communities. Central to this point is how Sunni and Shi'a *'ulama* differ in structure, hierarchy, and historical differences in viewing religious authorities with knowledge and expertise.

It is important to note that the state is extremely involved in Muslim-majority communities and controls religious affairs. The lack of fundamental freedoms of speech, assembly, association, being able to criticize authorities, or having the freedom to think and publish without retribution is common. These markers are daily reminders of how power is asserted at the micro level—family, workplace, school, marketplace, community centers—and the macro level—institutions, bureaucracies, military, media, and business sectors. These reminders reinforce the *'ulama* that the powers associated with hierarchies and, more importantly, all citizens understand their place in society and the limitations upon them. So, when there are severe criticisms of the *'ulama* and religious institutions, outsiders neglect to recognize that religious leaders need to seek approval from their superiors, ministries of religion and foreign affairs, office managers, family members, mosque leadership, and intelligence agencies. In many cases, intelligence officers demand a pre- and post-workshop interview to determine the qualifications of the religious scholar. I have witnessed intelligence officers overseeing the work of peacebuilding workshops in Afghanistan, Pakistan, Iraq, Egypt, Jordan, Turkey, Morrocco, Tunisia, Malaysia, Indonesia, and Bangladesh.

Cooperating, teaching, and designing peacebuilding projects with *'ulama* has reminded me of their limitations imposed on them, and more importantly, their curiosity in the peacebuilding field has informed me of their unique ways of thinking. First, religious scholars, like most civil society stakeholders, want to define, design, measure, and evaluate according to their own thinking frameworks. There are notions that peace is viewed as a top-down process, created and implemented by ruling elites—the officials with the political power to make peace. There is an agreement that all members of society must adhere to the authority of the political power and agree that each citizen is responsible for maintaining peace. However, during the workshop meetings, the *'ulama* unequivocally stated that they are not the ultimate decision-makers and do not possess the power to make a change. This is not always the case; these views vary with geography and scholars' power levels.

Their understanding of conflict is connected to their ability to change society. Muslim religious leaders view conflict as an inevitable component of life, beginning with using the creation story as an example of conflict between the divine and the angels. Using the Islamic version of creation, they cite that God created Adam out of clay (earthly material) and asked the angels to bow down to the new creation. One angel, Iblis, refused to bow down, believing that man was a lesser form of creation. Religious leaders refer to this narrative to argue that conflict has always existed and that it is impossible to create societies without conflict. With scriptural reasoning and theological argumentation, they believe the best we can do is minimize the conflict that arises in life.

One area of concern for *'ulama* in peacebuilding activities is: does this work bring justice to the victims? Will the conflict situation be morally and ethically resolved by the principles of law? According to religious leaders, justice is the primary issue in resolving conflict. Unless conflicting parties take part in resolving the problem and simultaneously receive justice from the appropriate authoritative institutions, conflict can be expected to continue eternally. In Islamic thought, the concept and practice of justice are synonymous with peace.

PEACEBUILDING WITH AFGHANISTAN'S *'ULAMA*

During the period of Ashraf Ghani, I served as an expert consultant for a three-year project to engage with Afghanistan's *'ulama* in peacebuilding, a national reconciliation program, and national dialogues to advance their role in peacebuilding efforts in the country. This project included the Afghanistan Ministry of Religious Affairs and the Afghanistan's Reconciliation Committee, and the external co-sponsors were The Netherlands, United Arab Emirates Islamic Affairs and Endowments, Qatar Ministry of Islamic Affairs, and the US Agency of International Development. The project contracted with six local organizations to organize the logistics. From the beginning of the project, I sensed that there were hesitations on the part of both Afghanistan and Western partners to engage with religious leaders, religious institutions, imams, and the more extensive religious networks because there was a fear of aggravating tensions or just not knowing how to work with religious leaders with this level of diversity.

During this time, the national government of Afghanistan remained weak, poor governance was transparent, corruption was uncontrollable, and the insurgency of the Taliban was gaining ground in half of the country. In addition, there were still fears of terrorist groups, such as al-Qaida, IS-Khorasan, and other fringe groups present in the area. The underlying hesitation in this peacebuilding project is that the religious leaders, imams, and *'ulama* would still be living in violent extremism and conflicts, which means they risk being subjugated to extremist ideologies. As unprotected civilians, they need to maintain their network of colleagues and identify networks and institutions to reinforce a pluralistic interpretation of the religion. The peacebuilding project aimed to create a network of religious leaders to be effective agents of change in their communities, be resilient to the growing culture of radicalization, prevent youth from being attracted to violent extremism, and empower the trained religious leaders to uplift their communities against violence and conflict while serving to be models of peacemakers.

Clearly, Afghanistan's civil society alone did not have the will or capacity to promote peace and stability in their local communities. Not only was there a great deal of mistrust of CSOs connected to Kabul politics and national politics, but religious leaders affiliated with Kabul's flourishing CSO industry were viewed as profiteers. In this context, the project intentionally focused on western, southwestern, and southeastern provinces to ensure attention and focus was on the neglected areas. Then, the trust deficit with national and provincial governments meant a greater trust in community-based councils, tribal assemblies of elders, and traditional networks, such as mosques, religious schools, religious institutions, and shrines.

The peacebuilding program included classes and training in Islamic principles of tolerance, pluralism, and acceptance of others. Resources for the program were based on Islamic ethical principles, such as forgiveness, love, generosity, compassion, openness to learn from others, openness to discussion, allowing debate to bring out diverse views, and recognizing diversity of ideas, ethnicity, religions, languages, and groups. The workshops comprised over two dozen experts leading the meetings for five or seven days. In addition to integrating local Afghanistan religious scholars and university professors, Muslim scholars who co-authored the training material flew in from Turkey, Egypt, the United Arab Emirates, the United States, Qatar, Morocco, and Malaysia. Afghan religious leaders and scholars were graduates of Al-Azhar University in Egypt and the International Islamic University in Malaysia. Teachers from the famous Morocco Academy for Imam Training Program on Pluralism spoke about their five-year curriculum on teaching and training imams on non-religious subjects like economics, social history, accounting, computer programming, and Arabic literature.

We established an international committee of practitioners and scholars to support the trained religious leaders and scholars in Afghanistan to increase regular communications and greater collaboration with the Afghanistan 'Ulama Council and the Afghan Islamic Affairs Department. The international committee sought to encourage the participants in their daily challenges in their villages and provide appropriate action to resolve conflicts. Within eight months, the Afghanistan Ministries of Religious Affairs and Reconciliation, the body supervising National Dialogues, were competing for funds or became entangled with Kabul's politics, which ultimately minimized the work of the international committee. The committee could not coordinate essential communications with the trained religious leaders, and they felt the committee lost interest in their lives. To further the education of the imams and religious leaders, the program established local programs with local academic centers, colleges, and universities.

The program was built on a single change theory that the religious leaders, scholars, and imams could learn peacemaking skills that would create a process of self-examination, healthy self-criticism, and self-empowerment to transform themselves and their communities. Regardless of their circumstances, they can serve as peacemakers in their communities. The change theory assumed that peacemaking efforts focused upon cognitive perceptions of the individual and the multiple ways an individual can contribute to society as a peacemaker. The critical problem in this program was that it was heavily focused on expanding skills and capacity building in specialized topics of peacebuilding, and if the participants mastered these areas, then they could, or would want to, advance these ideas forward. One such topic was increasing the participants' ability to display more empathy (*ma'arifat alghayri*) toward others who need emotional support. It was assumed that using a skills enhancement approach would enrich their knowledge of peacebuilding and position them in the broader field of peacebuilding efforts. All intercultural, interfaith, diplomatic, or corporate dialogues require a long-term commitment by the parties involved. To have dialogues to be impactful and influential in society, all stakeholders must be synchronized; religious institutions, civil society, media, youth organizations, educational institutions, the business sector, and the government must have the same vision for dialogue. For constructive, effective, and impactful peacebuilding dialogues to materialize, we must prepare our *'ulama*, imams, and religious institutions to develop a formal and informal dialogue curriculum on interfaith. As education specialists have pointed out, all educational experiences involve engaging teachers, peers, curricula, clubs, activities, and sports—essentially a total education culture or formal education. However, religious leaders, like other members of society, are simultaneously learning informally from social media, role models from home and the public sphere, media, sports, opinion makers, and thought leaders. The project neglected this essential component: the combination of formal and informal education needs to have foundational values and principles of dialogue. That is, dialogue needs to be appreciated as an intrinsic value to learn, grow, prosper, and become a generous, compassionate citizen.

We thought that the training materials were the core resources for learning; however, we failed to understand that dialogue is an intrinsic value needed to foster, cultivate, nurture, and constantly reinforce this value in culture, religion, business, and public spheres. Instead of being overly curriculum-centric, the program needs to sustain effective dialogues and monitor their effectiveness; there needs to be safe and neutral spaces for dialogue, where the space is appreciated for the genuine sharing of opinions. Most importantly, there was a dire need to have in place models, methodologies, and manuals to implement in dialogues struggling with conflict and everyday situations. These resources must contain content that addresses dialogue as a platform for resolving conflicts and teaching skills that enhance trust building.

In retrospect, an *'ulama*-centered peacebuilding dialogue program needed to focus on shifting cultural norms toward self-evaluation, self-criticism, and heightened self-awareness in dealing with other human beings. This would involve an intense commitment to evaluating curriculum, religious instruction, religious formation, and an interreligious education that teaches coexistence, nonviolence, reconciliation, dialogue, conflict prevention, and mutual respect. Designing programs to enhance knowledge and skills for *'ulama* in the field of peacebuilding is valuable only if this venture corresponds to ensuring that the value of dialogue and intrafaith dialogue are intrinsic principles.

ISLAMIC WOMEN PEACEBUILDING

Muslim women's participation in Islamic peacebuilding does not receive enough attention in research and in supporting grassroots CSOs. In Muslim-majority communities and Muslim-minority communities, Muslim women's contributions go beyond peacebuilding and conflict resolution, including finance, politics, technology, medicine, education, law, architecture, engineering, and all other fields. Since the 1980s, Muslim women writers have been articulating and developing theories on Islamic feminism, often subject to international debates. Some point out that the debate is partly due to how it is embedded in the broader discourses concerning women's rights and Islam and the position of women in Muslim-majority societies and of Muslim women in societies where Muslim populations constitute a minority. Also, the debate is often entangled with controversies between the labeling practices and controversial personalities seeking to contribute to the topic. For instance, who is entitled to speak and name someone else as an "Islamic feminist"? How are these labels accommodated, contested, or resisted? Other controversies on not the subject being explored or the personalities involved but instead if Islamic feminism is mirroring or mimicking theories used by Western feminists of the 1970s and 1980s and if this juxtaposition is at all an authentic inquiry within the tradition of Islam. Nevertheless, the term "Islamic feminism" has multiple definitions concerning different ways of conceptualizing feminism or different feminisms and the debates concerning "Islamic" or "Islamist" in connection with feminisms. One single agreement is challenging patriarchal readings of the Qur'an and the *hadith* literature and how these interpretations have allowed and enabled patriarchal traditions to persist.

It is crucial to capture the essential debates and issues involved in Islamic feminism to understand how their perspectives structure new concepts in Islamic peacebuilding. Two leading scholars, Asma Barlas and Margot Badran, are indebted for further feminist readings of Islamic texts. Asma Barlas, who does not want to be labeled as a feminist because it has ethnocentric implications and a history of racist undertones, conducted an important "unreading" of the patriarchal interpretations of the Qur'an where her critical hermeneutics illustrated egalitarian idealism in the revelations. Historian Margot Badran elaborated upon these readings of Islamic feminism and argued for feminist discourses grounded in an Islamic paradigm. Badran asked: "How (can we) support the struggles of others when one cannot claim ownership in these struggles?" Rejecting the idea of societies composed of closed and separate identities and communities, another scholar, Pepicelli, argued that participation of both Muslims and non-Muslims in the debate is necessary given that these questions touch upon the societies constituted in pluralist terms: the societies in which we live.

Raja Rhouni argued the possibilities of post-foundationalist feminist hermeneutics by analyzing the famous Moroccan feminist writer Fatima Mernissi's work on women's rights in Islam.[7] Rhouni believes that Islamic feminism should move beyond the search for truth and authenticity—what she calls foundationalism—toward "post-foundationalist Islamic gender critique." This means engaging in dialogue with the tradition and applying the contextual approach to expand the exegesis methodologies rather than undermining foundations and traditions. Rhouni contests the ideas of renowned Islamic studies scholar and reformer Nasr Hamid Abu Zeid, who argued on the issues of women in Islam; Islamic thinkers are unable or unwilling to transcend "the crisis of interpretation and counter-interpretation." Abu Zeid was precisely saying that proponents and opponents of gender equality employ the same strategy (i.e., finding Quranic passages that fit their arguments and identifying them as foundational [asl] points of truth).[8] Along with rethinking gender in Islamic thought, Rhouni argues that the contextual approach would aid in disrupting the discourse of political and ideological instrumentalizations of religious texts.[9]

Moving from the academic debates of Islamic feminism and their potential areas of impact within traditional interpretations of scripture, we turn to scholarship on Muslim women peacebuilders in Muslim-majority countries. In this area, Ayse Kadayifci-Orellana has been a trailblazer both as a peace scholar and practitioner on peacebuilding in conflict zones. Her scholarship has highlighted insights into the profound importance of religion and culture in conflict resolution and the role of women in peacebuilding and reconciliation processes. When attention was absent to the vital role of women in Islamic peacebuilding, she explored how Muslim women participate in conflicts and transform conflicts given the restraints in their culture, tribe, and geography. Her work has provided erudite evidence on the Islamic tradition's broad scope for women's full participation in social and political life, their contribution to peacemaking, and the vast opportunities to contribute to peacebuilding. Her case studies from Palestine, Uganda, Kenya, Nigeria, Pakistan, Philippines, Afghanistan, Indonesia, Iran, and Muslim-majority communities have bridged the gap in the research.

Kadayifci-Orellana's fieldwork research demonstrates the multiple ways Muslim women peacebuilders have and continue to contribute to resolving conflicts and building sustainable peace in their communities. She has illustrated the diverse and creative ways in which Muslim women peacebuilders engage their religious and cultural traditions to prevent violent conflict and establish the foundations of a peaceful society. She states, "Since the inception of Islam as a religious tradition, women have participated in social, political, economic, and intellectual life as poets, Islamic scholars, spiritual teachers, warriors, heads of state, and businesswomen. Though Muslim society, like virtually all traditional agrarian societies, developed a clear patriarchal structure, women's experiences were by no means monochromatic."[10] She has written about witnessing conservative Muslim women and men engage in peacebuilding activities together, quoting scripture (Qur'an 3:195), "I shall not lose sight of the labor of any of you who labors in My way, be it man or woman; each of you is equal to the other," emphasizing equality. According to Kadayifci-Orellana, these conversations underscored no contradiction in affirming the spiritual equality of men and women while upholding separate gender roles. The Quranic norm demonstrates righteousness as the single most important standard for defining the dignity and worth of a person, yet essential differences between the sexes require different distributions of rights and responsibilities. In essence, Kadayifci-Orellana argues that women are spiritually and morally equal, but they have separate societal roles, usually defined by their status within the family unit as mothers, wives, sisters, and daughters. Their understanding of the "equal before God, unequal before man" interpretation leads to strong preferences for a gendered division of labor and opens opportunities for cooperation, not competition.[11] Her work studied Sakena Yacoobi, founder and director of the Afghan Institute of Learning, working toward conflict resolution and educational programs to rebuild Afghanistan; Soraya Jamjuree, an eminent activist who was reconciling strained communal relationships between Muslim and Buddhist communities in southern Thailand; the late Dekha Ibrahim Abdi, who was a Kenyan Muslim peacemaker and recipient of the Right Livelihood Award, also known as the alternative Nobel Prize, for her peace and conflict resolution work in Kenya, Somalia, Ethiopia, Sudan, Uganda, and other parts of the world, and who was a founding member of the Wajir Peace and Development Committee, which was formed to address the violence that erupted after the 1992 drought; and the outstanding work by Mossarat Qadim of Pakistan, who sought creative and imaginative ways to engage with mothers of violent extremists to prevent the spread of radicalism and initiate a process of healing in their respective families.[12]

Houda Abadi is the executive director of Transformative Peace based in Morocco, which works on inclusive peace processes, women, peace, security, and human-rights-based approaches to preventing violent extremism.

Her contributions to Muslim women's peacebuilding and conflict resolution have immensely broadened the thinking and practice of gendered inclusive approaches and feminist security frameworks aimed at ceasing all forms of violence, including ecological physical violence. Building upon Fatima Seedat and Yaliwe Clarke's works[13] on reconfiguring structures to integrate women in the conflict resolution field, Abadi's work focuses on creating more inclusive spaces and agendas to ensure Muslim women's meaningful participation in peace processes. She studied ways to develop inclusive strategies to overcome barriers and skillfully utilize constitutional mechanisms that empower and protect women. In working toward equal inclusion of women as a prerequisite for building sustainable and transformative peace in conflict zones, Abadi's work illustrates that local communities accept the use of indigenous and Islamic peacebuilding approaches.

By emphasizing the inclusion of local customs, cultural norms, and indigenous practices with Islamic peacebuilding frameworks, Abadi stresses the importance of including women not as a way of symbolism, savior mentality, or tokenism but instead based on evidence that when women participate in peace processes the agenda is designed with critical concerns to equality and equitable outcomes for all parties. Women's voices and perspectives on conflict, peacebuilding, post-conflict development, reconciliation, reconstruction of society, and the laborious process of writing a new constitution produce wider in-depth perspectives on protecting children, young women, marginalized communities, and communities not represented in the process.[14]

STRIVING FOR JUSTICE AND WOMEN'S RIGHTS IN AFGHANISTAN

During the twenty years of the American and International Security Assistance Force intervention in Afghanistan, from 2001 to 2021, the global Western aid industry believed it was a momentous opportunity to empower civil society, particularly women's groups, to advance Afghanistan into a democratic society. From the 1950s to 1979, Afghan women were active on university campuses, and there were established women-led groups within the Afghan Communist Party, the Jama'at-e Islami Party, the Afghan Socialist Party, the Afghan National Party, and other Afghan national and ethnic political parties. The presence of women was visibly vibrant in the education, engineering, mathematics, medicine, law, and hospitality sectors.

After two and half decades of war, by 2001, women were rarely visible in the significant public and private sectors, and the global community actively sought partnerships to begin a new era. In addition to identifying women to establish civil society groups, Western organizations like the US Institute of Peace, Asia Foundation, Mercy Corps, Caritas, and National Endowment for Democracy understood that they needed to work with tribal leaders, religious leaders, and community council leaders—Afghan men dominated all. Their practical challenge was identifying credible local religious leaders and tribal leaders who believed in the work of gender justice and gender equality. The work of the US Institute of Peace and Asia Foundation mapped out religious leaders, their community network, and their ability to influence specific geographical areas and social networks. The project aimed to work with men, especially men with religious authority, to build trust and convince them to protect women's rights and for girls to attend school.

These projects were led by Afghan women who needed to engage men as equals in a dialogue they neither had nor expected. Palwasha Kakar of the US Institute of Peace Religion and Inclusive Societies Program encountered a complex challenge: First, convincing a Western organization that working with religious leaders does not mean cooperating with radical extremists or letting them take control of a program. Second, collaborating with Afghan religious leaders did not mean she needed to convince them to agree with all principles of democracy or equality but asking them to understand the fundamental rights of women in the Islamic tradition would educate them to be advocates of women's rights. Third, most interesting, US Institute of Peace's Washington, DC, and Kabul offices were not keen on trusting Afghan religious leaders or faith-based organizations with their broader activities with civil society, such as training, facilitation, monitoring of progress, maintenance of financial records, and supervising a transparent operation. Not only were there the foundations of secular bias within the conflict resolution, but there was the cultural and professional disposition of not trusting or allying with religion. The institution in the early years of the US invasion of Afghanistan was not interested in reaching out or developing relationships with new religious leadership on the protection of women's rights or peacebuilding activities.[15] Rather, it tilted toward working with "moderate religious voices" to strengthen indigenous movements of change on women's rights. "Moderate voices" in the context of a post-Taliban Afghanistan meant that the institution would vet those religious men who received approval from the intelligence and security sectors. In essence, this directed Muslim women to carefully and selectively engage religious leaders as the agents of change on women's rights and human rights because it reduced the potential popular backlash to what might otherwise be perceived as advancing Western ideas and morality.[16] Kakar researched Afghanistan's Asia Foundation activities which illustrated that traditional male leaders tend to rule in favor of women as a party to a dispute on such matters as inheritance, choice of spouse, child custody, and divorce.

This team of Muslim women peacebuilders found it compelling to first approach local leaders who are known to share a broad goal of women's empowerment; once this relationship is established, then it is only feasible to develop trust-building steps forward. Even before engaging with traditional or religious leaders, Muslim women peacebuilders astutely connected with local stakeholders by discussing a needs assessment and an assessment of which religious and tribal leaders were suitable and had common goals. By first doing a human mapping and establishing relationships with key stakeholders, they understood which leaders were open to collaboration, who was interested in discussing women's rights, and what types of collaboration were possible.[17] One of the most important lessons for Muslim women peacebuilders was that genuine dialogues and engagement with religious leaders are time-consuming and involve significant short-term and long-term investment to build trust, ownership, and the implementation of a vision. Equally important, the lessons from Muslim women's peacebuilding projects are that Afghan religious leaders need to be included and consulted in developing these projects from the very beginning stages of the project. They need to be part of a meaningful and inclusive process, especially to have ownership of the process, products, and outcomes. Another lesson learned is that women's rights and access to justice are not exclusively a matter for any one sector. There needed to be combined and coordinated efforts among civil society groups, the police, security forces, judiciary, academic research centers, and traditional justice mechanisms.

In 2020, the Afghanistan Research and Evaluation Unit issued an insightful report entitled "Women's Participation in the Afghan Peace Process," funded by the UN Women organization in Afghanistan. During the Hamid Karzai and Ashraf Ghani periods (2001–2021), women became more involved with government ministries and civil society peace efforts at the local, provincial, and national levels. The report acknowledged the wide range of activities, including peace messaging campaigns, women's participation in nongovernmental peace councils and local community councils, and their involvement in dialogues with insurgents. The Afghanistan Research and Evaluation Unit report documented a series of women-led peacebuilding initiatives that cultivated a network of peace activists and trained conflict resolution experts. It gave credit to the work of civil society women groups and Muslim women peacebuilders who also served on Afghanistan's High Peace Council, local committees resolving disputes, and women leaders who designed, developed, and conducted workshops, conferences, and advocacy programs on protecting women's rights.

This report studied four provinces that had women participation in the Afghanistan peace process of 2017 to 2021. The case study's findings indicate that a lasting peace was only possible where women's voices and views were included through the peace process. Examining the peace process, the participation of Afghan women in and support of the national peace efforts enabled a more robust engagement with peacebuilding and reconciliation issues. From 1990 to 2014, as many as 130 peace agreements were signed, but only thirteen peace agreements included women with signatory authority. All agreements with women as participants at a signatory level were more durable than those only signed by men. Additionally, the involvement of women in peace processes resulted in a stronger integration of human rights, transitional justice, national reconciliation, and subsequent women's involvement in the decision-making processes at the local and national levels.[18]

The Afghanistan Research and Evaluation Unit report delved into improving the space for civil society members to operate without harassment or intimidation. They argued that Afghan CSOs need to sustain their efforts to hold the main political parties accountable for regular transparency, anti-corruption, and illegal activities, including compromising on protecting women's rights or violating the constitution. The report provided data on the growing trends of CSOs in the urban centers but was lacking in the rural areas. More was needed to advocate for meaningful participation and inclusion of women in national peace efforts without siloing women groups to women's rights alone. It criticized domestic Afghan CSOs for not coordinating their work, identifying more opportunities to collaborate on common projects while considering formal networking alliances. Suggesting that an alliance of peacebuilding CSOs would have concentrated their efforts in the different stages of the peace process, especially on critical issues related to disarmament, reintegration of fighters into communities, transitional justice, political integration, and ceasefires—all ensuring that women were involved in each area of the process.

The report recommended that the Afghanistan government: (1) create a national priority program on women's political participation with ample funding to address the challenges that women are facing across provinces, strengthening women's political participation at the national and subnational levels, and seeking women's meaningful participation in the program design and delivery; (2) actively support women's meaningful participation in national peace efforts by guaranteeing 33 percent women's involvement in the negotiation team, and select women committed to the advancement of Afghans' rights; (3) promote a national dialogue addressing the constraints on women's rights; and (4) treat women's rights as a national concern for peace, prosperity, and security.[19]

Effective and lasting peacebuilding strategies and conflict resolution practices by Muslim peacebuilders continue to develop new theories and praxis within an Islamic framework. While most researchers have agreed that strategies begin with interpreting Quranic and prophetic evidence, recent studies are using additional resources and narratives, such as considering how Islamic jurisprudence contributes to peace or violence, as well as examining essential foundational doctrines, creeds, beliefs, and practices of the religion. More recently, questions deliberately questioning the meaning of "Islamic" opens the door to identity, inherited definitions, and balancing past constructions of Muslim identity with current evolving individualized conceptions of identity; modern ideas of equity, diversity, and inclusiveness in identity; and shifting boundaries of identities no longer bound to a specific culture, geography, ethnicity, tribe, or denomination of a faith tradition. The combination of the quest for an identity, or more accurately, seeking individual ownership for identity formation, is a defining marker of a globalized age with cosmopolitanism driving an interconnected world.

Acknowledging a rapidly changing world within Muslim-majority communities, Islamic peacebuilding still has fundamental approaches to resolving conflict to return to a culture of peace. Across the board, Muslim peacebuilders acknowledge that all humanity has a common origin; human dignity must be recognized and respected, regardless of religion, ethnicity, or tribe. With an interconnected world, the planet's diversity is more evident than before. This diversity among people encapsulates a richness of traditions that need to be engaged with dialogues. For these peacebuilders, striving to improve the world requires core values of cooperation, collaboration, and an authentic engagement in dialogue with others and among themselves to foster peace. Peacebuilders in Muslim-majority communities agree that their faith tradition, indigenous cultures, and customs are not items to discard to emulate Western societies. While there are strong affections and admiration of Western values of openness, equality, and for the individual to self-actualize dreams, however, Muslim peacebuilders—like other peacebuilders—are expressing the desire to retain and build upon their cultures and faith traditions. There are more forums, virtually and in person, for local and international dialogues and debates to exchange ideas. Finally, practicing good deeds, modeling peacebuilding attitudes and behavior, and striving toward justice must be present in everyday dealings with all human beings. These essential principles are a synopsis of critical ingredients of Islamic peacebuilding.

NOTES

1. Alireza Doostdar, "Review of Shahab Ahmed, *What Is Islam? The Importance of Being Islamic*," *Shi'i Studies Review*, 1 (2017): 277–82; also see, Khalil Andani, "Review of *What Is Islam? The Importance of Being Islamic*," *Islam and Christian-Muslim Relations*, 2017, 28 (1): 114–17; Anna Bigelow, "*What Is Islam?* A Celebration and Defense of Contradiction, Perplexity, and Paradox," *Marginalia* 24, August 2016; Ali Altaf Mian, "Shahab Ahmed's Contradictions: A Critical Engagement with *What is Islam*," *Der Islam*, 2020, 97 (1): 233–96.

2. See Noah Feldman, "An Extraordinary Scholar Redefined Islam," *Bloomberg Opinion*, September 20, 2015, https://www.bloomberg.com/opinion/articles/2015-09-20/an-extraordinary-scholar-redefined-islam.

3. Satha-Anand, "The Nonviolent Crescent: Eight Theses on Muslim Nonviolent Actions," in Paige, Satha-Anand, and Gilliatt, *Islam and Nonviolence*, pg. 23.

4. Kevin Avruch, *Culture and Conflict Resolution* (Washington, DC: US Institute of Peace Press, 1998); Peter Black, Joseph Scimecca, and Kevin Avruch, *Conflict Resolution: Cross-Cultural Perspectives* (New York: Greenwood Press, 1991).

5. John Burton, *Conflict: Resolution and Prevention* (New York: St. Martin's Press, 1990).

6. Dean Pruitt and Jeffrey Rubin, *Social Conflict: Escalation, Stalemate, and Settlement* (New York: McGraw-Hill, 1986); Herbert Kelman, "Interactive Problem-Solving: A Social-Psychological Approach to Conflict Resolution," in John Burton and Frank Dukes, ed., *Conflict: Readings in Management and Resolution* (New York: St. Martin's Press, 1990).

7. Mernissi's book is considered as one of the first works that displayed a new way of doing feminism, one which does not stigmatize Islam or tradition. Fatima Mernissi, *Beyond the Veil: Male-Female Dynamics in Modern Muslim Society* (Bloomington: Indiana University Press, 1975).

8. See Abu Zeid and Nasr Hamid, .*Qadiyyat al-mar'a bayna Sindani al-hadatha wa mitrakati a-taqalid* (Cairo: Alif Publications, 1999); and *Reformation of Islamic Thought* (Amsterdam: Amsterdam University Press, 2006).

9. Raja Rhouni, "Rethinking 'Islamic Feminist Hermeneutics': The Case of Fatima Mernissi," in Anitta Kynsilehto, ed., *Islamic Feminism: Current Perspectives* (Tampere Peace Research Institute Paper No. 96, University of Tampere, Finland, 2008), pp. 103–16.

10. Ayse Kadayifci-Orellana, "Muslim Women Peacemakers as Agents of Change," in Qamar-ul Huda, *Crescent and Dove: Peace and Conflict Resolution in Islam* (Washington, DC: US Institute of Peace Press, 2011), pg. 179.

11. Ibid., pg. 184.

12. Ibid., pg. 199.

13. Y. Clarke, "Gender and Peacebuilding in Africa: Seeking Conceptual Clarity," *Africa Peace and Conflict Journal*, 2013, 6 (1): 87–91; F. Seedat, "Women, Religion and Security," *Agenda*, 2016, 30 (3): 3–10.

14. Houda Abadi, "Seeking an Islamic Framework towards Peacebuilding and Women's Inclusion," Firoz Lalji Institute for Africa, London School of Economics, UK, 2022, pg. 22.

15. Based on professional experiences with US Institute of Peace's Afghanistan team, 2005–2010.

16. Palwasha Kakar, *Engaging Afghan Religious Leaders for Women's Rights*, PeaceBrief #175. (Washington, DC: US Institute of Peace Press, June 2014).

17. Ibid., pg. 3.

18. Shukria Azadmanesh and Ihsanullah Ghafoori, "Women's Participation in the Afghan Peace Process," Afghanistan Research and Evaluation Unit, Kabul, September 2020, pg. 9.

19. Ibid., pg. 15.

Chapter Six

Living in Peace

Spiritual treatises, manuals, and scholarly texts were primarily written for a diverse audience of educated spiritual aspirants and religious scholars who would understand contemporary and historical theological issues of Sufism. There was always a topic quoting the Prophet, examples from his life, and other significant figures, and quotes from the Qur'an. The most important aspect of the organization of some free tax is not its external arrangements but the unifying mental structures that provide interconnecting themes to the reader so that each topic is related to the larger whole. Sufi treatises and textbooks contained more than legal opinions or esoteric principles; these textbooks were a source for disciples to interpret and engage with the tradition so that it would structure their lives to bring them closer to the divine.

According to the major canon of Sufi treatises, love for oneself is a self-destructive path that leads the Sufi away from proper observance of the spiritual path. The highest type of love is the one that is not for the individual but for the divine. When a spiritual aspirant completely surrenders their love to the divine, only then can the individual access all things associated with that path. Spiritual masters have opined that when people direct their special love in the proper ways, they become interested in the things associated with the divine things. This is because love is charitable, and the lover and beloved become attached to each other.

Contrary to popular associations or stereotypes of the Sufi spiritual path that it is soaked in emotionalism, irrationality, and influenced using intoxications, the literature and contemporary teachings by Sufi scholars stress the need to develop an internal and external structure for disciples and urge them to use their intellectual faculties to comprehend the path. Historian of Islam Ira Lapidus stated that the pursuit of knowledge, *'ilm*, in the Islamic world was not merely the scholarly practice of researching and writing on knowledge or being active in the general discipline of intellectual inquiry. It is the search for insight: to find the essential meaning in the revelations so that it bears the truth from God. It encompasses the spirit behind searching for knowledge that will lead the individual's sacred quest to better understand the self in relation to the divine.[1]

In this field of the Islamic religious sciences and epistemology, from as early as the eighth century onward, Sufis treated their spiritual and intellectual quest with great importance as integral to their encounter with God. In the matrix of *adab*, many of the monumental Sufi masters, such as as-Sulami (d.1021 CE), stated irrefutably that "the whole of Sufism is entirely based on the ways of behavior (*at-tasawwuf kulluhu adab*)."[2]

Aside from commentaries on the Qur'an, Sufi scholars wrote upon their esoteric experiences, biographies, and manuals containing specific and complex guidelines of law, customs, and detailed ways to conduct oneself in the Sufi tradition (*tasawwuf*). Influential works by Abu Nasr as-Sarraj (d.988 CE), author of *Kitab al-Luma'*, and 'Ali al-Makki's (d.996 CE) *Qut al-Qulub* categorized the practices of Sufism and connected such practices with a proper *adab*. The sections of Sufi *adab* were written in the context of disciplinary rules for spiritual seekers so that they might connect the tenets of Sufism with *adab*. In these early Sufi texts, the themes of *adab* were prominently connected with the different states (*ahwal*) or stages (*maqamat*) in which Sufis achieved their mystical virtues and encounters. These texts outlined precise ways for disciples to practice the proper ways of behavior for novices (*adab as-suffiyya wa adab al-muridin*). The Sufi journey toward God and meeting the creator meant that Sufi disciples had to master and embody the perfect practices of *adab*. Sufi *adab*, unlike other "secular" types of *adab*, worked within an esoteric and exoteric epistemological context, and the search for truth was more than a contemplative or an intellectual exercise; rather, it forced Sufi disciples to structure their inner and outer lives around a mystical *adab* theology.

Prominent scholar Shaykh Abu Hafs Umar al-Suhrawardi (d.1234) viewed the inner esoteric tradition (*tasawwuf*) as the way to perfect devotion in which one can fully embrace divine beauty; at the heart of the Suhrawardi *tasawwuf* was the reconnection with the divine the human soul had previously experienced in a preexistent time. This did not mean that Suhrawardi Sufis could not lead a practical life; rather, they were encouraged to enjoy the benefits of this world and not reject the world. Within his own Sufi order, al-Suhrawardi preached a balanced code for Sufi living, for which the Prophet Muhammad set an example. For him, there were only a few advanced devotees who were able to pray all night and work all day. According to al-Suhrawardi, most believers had to maintain prayers and specific Sufi practices, such as meditational spiritual exercises (*dhikr*), as part of their daily routine. On the controversial issue of whether Sufis should maintain celibacy, he felt that only Sufi masters were qualified to judge whether their disciples were spiritually equipped to take on that challenge. He obstinately opposed anyone defending or advocating the life of the antinomian, nomadic, begging Qalandars, who were intensely ascetics. The Qalandars were extremely controversial at this time because of their anti-social characteristics, for not practicing the basic articles of the faith, and for their outward disrespecting adherence to the law (*shari'a*).

For this study on reaching peace within the individual, al-Suhrawardi stressed proper moral conduct (*adab*) was mainly connected with his concern that Sufis develop an internal and external discipline that mirrored the Prophet's life. To him, the physical world was very much related to the spiritual world, and for spiritual seekers to perfect their spirituality, their physical customs had to reflect their internal condition. Shaykh al-Suhrawardi's ideas on *adab* stemmed from the belief that it is necessary to obey the law entirely because it is a manifestation of divine order.[3] Some have suggested that his efforts in creating a perfect, harmonious society required an intensely structured model.[4] *Adab* was a critical element in his ideal world because all the minute details of an individual's behavior could be controlled. For al-Suhrawardi, Sufis were practicing more than spiritual purity, for in the larger scheme, Suhrawardi Sufis were attempting to reunite with the divine, and this required them to uphold the *shari'a*. According to al-Suhrawardi, one needed to be prepared to carry out this extraordinary responsibility by planning one's thoughts and actions for every moment and place.

Sunni and Shi'a literature, including Sufi texts, contain a great deal of elaboration on theories and practices of proper moral Sufi conduct. His main concern was to ensure that Suhrawardis, and any other Sufi group, would not be neglectful of obeying *shari'a* and the guidance of the mediating shaykh. Current theories on *adab* practice suggest that the knowledge learned from a senior Sufi shaykh (*al-'ilm as-sahih as-sama'i*) needed to have established boundaries to ensure that the master–disciple relationship would not be threatened and that disciples would not transgress their limitations with the authority of the shaykh. It is not completely convincing that this *adab* theory applies to Sufi hierarchies or other structures in Islam; it is known that Sufi masters felt that it was important that disciples understand that their training entailed both the inner and outer realms. If any aspect of *'ilm* was disrespected by improper *adab*, then the resulting disequilibrium of law and spiritual training would cause an imbalance in the goal of reuniting with God.[5]

For al-Suhrawardi and other legal-minded Sufi scholars, the spiritual training required disciples to adhere to the *adab* prescribed by the guiding shaykh and to the regulations of the Sufi order. Hierarchies and rankings of Sufi disciples and shaykhs mattered in many ways; aside from the realities of set roles in the Sufi order, these distinctions marked the level of mystical knowledge attained, the in-depth understanding of *irfan* (gnosis), and, more importantly, the comprehension (*dhawq*) of the Qur'an and God's presence (*hulul*). Al-Suhrawardi stated:

> The Prophet stated that God had taught him good etiquette. *Zahir* (outer) and *batin* (inner) etiquette are needed for a civilized world. If people embrace *zahir*, they will learn to be a Sufi with etiquette *adab*. But, several things are difficult for a person to achieve completely. Until the untrained persons fully immerse themselves in proper manners, i.e., the manners rooted within the Prophet's tradition, they will remain ill-mannered. If people's appearances are like those who indulge in the world, their manners will reflect that. For example, when people do not change their manners, they also do not change, then their manners are copied from elsewhere. Let us remember what the Qur'an tells us: In God's creation, there can be no changes.[6]

The Sufi shaykh expands upon several concepts on the continuity of proper moral conduct derived directly from God and was transmitted to the prophets. He asserts that the *adab* tradition is rooted in when God taught the prophets adequate guidance so they might redirect their complete attention toward God. Within the Sufi and broader Islamic tradition, Prophet Muhammad is the figure par excellence who embodies the perfect way of directing oneself toward God and concentrating on becoming closer to the divine.[7] The Qur'an calls the Prophet the "seal of prophets" (*khatam al-anbiya*), and just as God taught proper *adab* to Prophet Muhammad, the Prophet used the same methods to teach his companions the same *adab*. Al-Suhrawardi's applied and moral theology situated *adab* at the center of Sufi thought and practice in order to ensure that his Sufi disciples fully comprehended *adab* as a transformative medium between the inner and outer worlds. For the broader Islamic tradition, it was these Sufi scholars who elaborated upon an "*adab* theology," which was less about the physical, psychological, and temporal dimensions of moral conduct; instead, *adab* was—and still remains—more concerned with accentuating the constant opening of the heart that inspires a real journey toward encountering God.[8]

Al-Suhrawardi quotes a well-known saying of the Prophet that speaks clearly to followers about how important *adab* is to God:

> And an even better point is that people are against changes to manners and proper etiquette, and this is why the Prophet said to make friends with one's *adab*. This is why God created human beings and allowed them to correct themselves when needed. And in this, it is virtuous. God has shown His majesty to humankind through these virtues (*adab*). These virtues are from personal training to light the flints to set fire to a pure and virtuous life. In this way, human beings will become strong in their values, and strength is a character instilled into human beings by the will of God.[9]

The focus on *adab* represents many aspects of the law and order for disciples to follow in society; it was the real reenactment of the Prophet's life in this world. The Prophet in every way represented the "perfect human being" (*insan al-kamil*): he mastered social relationships, political challenges, tribal conflicts, financial stresses, and religious tolerance; he was divinely chosen as the last Prophet; he was the only Prophet to ascend to heaven to dialogue with God; and he brought God's final book of guidance to humanity. In every moment of the Prophet's existence he was being taught by Allah the proper conduct of behavior and being spiritually trained by God. Each aspect of the Prophet, from speech (*kalam*) to his worship (*'ibada*) to his daily actions (*'amal*), is derived from him witnessing the divine face (*mushahadat al-wajh*) and of God's essence being manifested (*tajalli ad-dhat*) to him.

Scholars and disciples viewed *adab* as the cornerstone of spiritual training, which consisted of thinking, acting, and experiencing the closeness of the Prophet. The strong emphasis on *adab* was also a celebration of the Prophet's life; his life was the model to emulate, embody, and sustain a spiritual life not consumed with fear, anxiety, suffering, or worldly retributions.

VIRTUE ETHICS

The broader field of contemplation studies is a foundational area of study within Islamic theology and, of course, in Christian theology. Exploring self-examination, meditation, self-transcendence, and moral philosophy has been a cornerstone for spiritual exercises, as Ignatius of Loyola termed it: exercitia spiritualia. Just as in Roman Catholic spiritual orders, Muslim Sufis and non-Sufis undergo a regimen of spiritual exercises to neutralize or master the power of the passions. Islamic virtue ethics based on spiritual exercises such as self-examination, mediation, silence, fasting, prayer, and supplications aim to reorient the self toward a clearer understanding of the true nature. In this process we recognize our human imperfections and passions such as inattention, greed, anger, pride, envy, prejudice, impatience, and intolerance. For many eminent Sufi scholars, these passions needed to be tamed and managed to strive toward a goal of self-perfection.[10]

In the Muslim world and among Muslim diaspora, there is a surge in rediscovering the mystical spiritual legacies of classical scholars such as al-Kharraz (d.847), al-Muhasibi (d.857), Sahl at-Tustari (d.896), al-Junayad al-Baghdadi (d.910), Abu Talib al-Makki (d.998), as well as some of the later luminaries, such as al-Ghazali (d.1111), Ibn 'Arabi (d.1240), and Jalal ud-din Rumi (d.1273). More academic and popular translations have opened the door for access and deeper analysis of their works and nurtured a renaissance in these spiritual practices. Examining their ethical imperatives in their spiritual quest, Sufism has moved beyond the association of miracles, paranormal experiences, visions, and higher states of the mind in their path.

Atif Khalil notes that eminent Sufi scholar al-Makki believed that the traveler progresses on the spiritual path by practicing virtuous acts and obeying God. Al-Makki asserted that finding joy may be difficult in the beginning of practicing spiritual practices but through the habituation of friendliness and magnanimity, one uncovers this joy of virtuous acts. Khalil thinks al-Makki asserted that it is not "enough to simply know a virtue or practice it with a heart that delights in its exact opposite." Instead, the critical idea is that when a person strives to attain ethical perfection, then the person must actualize the latent goodness of the self because morally good is sweet, and all that is evil is repugnant.[11] Actualizing goodness and reminding ourselves of the place of living a virtuous life is the Sufi response to the time-honored question, "What does it mean to be human?"

One of the major differences between modern-day Islamic ethics of the Sunni Salafism or Sunni Deobandi schools is they focus on "rules-based" ethics tied to the commentaries by modern jurists. However, Sufi scholars like Rumi, al-Makki, and Zarruq emphasized an ethical narrative that points directly toward the ethical subject's intention, circumstances, intersubjectivity, experiences, or telos, which influence our moral decision processing and decision-making. For instance, Catholic theologian MacIntyre articulates poignantly that the rules-based ethics in John Rawls's "distributive justice" and the libertarian ethics of Robert Nozick's "personal entitlement" both neglect the character of the self and the circumstances that influence the individual experiences, and both downplay telos. By avoiding the intention of the person (agent), MacIntyre reminds us that society is composed of individuals seeking to advance self-interest and identify the best possible ways to live ethically.

HUMILITY

In Islamic scholarly literature theological concepts on piety (*tawadu* or *khushu*) are a central place to contrast against Quranic figures who displayed pride (e.g., Pharoah or Iblis). Scholars have elaborated on the defining characteristics of this virtue, its signs, and even the dangers of misusing piety for personal gain. For spiritual aspirants on the path, it was important to recognize how humility can be a slippery slope between conceit, pride, self-loathing, self-hatred, or excessive self-admiration. The ability to cultivate a consciousness of the process of humility, sustaining the proper type of humility, and embodying the precise nature were major areas of concentration for Sufis.

Modern scholars of moral philosophy, such as Hare and Richards,[12] note the obvious displacement of humility in the works of the Enlightenment; from Montaigne and Spinoza to Nietzsche, the emphasis on one's self-worth, self-esteem, and ability to untap into the individual's profound creativity. Noting that humility was perceived as a "religious" virtue that extolled inferiority and ignoble qualities, which prevented reaching unlimited self-esteem. Hare states that "the [academy] has been largely indifferent or even hostile to the character of humility"[13] because humility was seen as meekness, lowliness, and not even aligned with the Enlightenment. Contemporary ethicists and moral philosophers attempt to rehabilitate the place of humility and virtues to recognize our human mistakes and imperfections and instill an openness to accepting criticism and new ideas for higher self-actualization. There is a recognition that to self-correct oneself, to mediate on the mistakes and poor decisions effectively, then the cultivation of humility helps to reprioritize our thinking. Within this context and the broader context of the individual seeking to foster inner and outer peace, we turn to the values of humility in the Islamic contemplative tradition.

Famous Sufi master al-Darqawi's letters warned disciples on the spiritual path to be aware that humility does not draw you to self-loathing or toward self-admiration, stating, "I am nothing, do not say I am nothing or say I am something, rather say you turn towards God to seek wonders." Another spiritual master, Dhu al-Nun, said, "he who desires humility should face towards the majesty of the divine."[14] Humility is a virtue within the contemplative tradition to not forget or abandon relationships with others or relinquish one's obligations to the community or family, but it was seen as a process of self-actualization. Humility was not a preoccupation of being insignificant compared to something else. Scholars argued against the dangers of practicing humility so that the person is consumed with lowering the self, and perhaps, becoming obsessed with it and obsessing it as a form of narcissism.

Saeko Yazaki's "Morality in Early Sufi Literature" and Cyrus Zargar's *The Polished Mirror: Storytelling and the Pursuit of Virtue in Islamic Philosophy and Sufism*[15] are two excellent works identifying the diversity of thought and practices on the virtues of humility. The obsessive incorrect practices of humility can turn humility upside down yet remain humble. This is the prime reason in Islamic contemplative ethics why this virtue, the inner struggle, is to constantly strive to cultivate humility in every state, both with God and all human relations. The virtues of humility find a connection with the divine names such as gratitude, compassion, forgiveness, benevolence, gentleness, patience, and mercy—these are all qualities that signify an important state of poverty and the need to be in front of God. Reciting these divine names inculcates these virtues of humility in your heart. Another aspect of humility is how it creates a shield of protection for the individual. It is understood that as these virtues of humility create an inner space within the individual it is protecting them from the distractions away from the path of God.

The eminent Moroccan Sufi master Muhammad al-Jazuli (d.1465) and his infamous work *Dala'il al-Khayrat* ("Guide to Goodness") is a celebrated book of prayers and blessings upon the Prophet, which has become one of the essential books for devotion. Humility is not just a virtue to possess for the self; instead, these virtues demand to be perfected by serving others (*khidma*), particularly by identifying ways to support the cultivation of humility in their lives. Al-Jazuli's book consists of supplications to recite blessings or *salawat* to the Prophet. These supplications are offered at specific times and dates of the year, and al-Jazuli speaks of the rewards of reciting these blessings while seeking spiritual benefits and closeness to God through these spiritual practices.

Mohammed Rustom's translation of al-Ghazali's (d.1111) *Kitab Dhamm al Kibr wa-l-'Ujb* ("On Condemnation of Pride and Self-Admiration") is a valuable contribution to understanding the debates, arguments, reasoning, and counterarguments on the virtues of humility. Al-Ghazali cautions disciples about virtues existing in isolation and creating an imbalance within the soul. There were concerns about the harmony of the virtues, where no virtue can exist on its own because it could negatively impact other existing virtues. Humility is not only a required virtue of increasing closeness to God, but the prime reason to cultivate and nurture this virtue is to combat pride, egoism, greed, and self-admiration. According to al-Ghazali, fostering piety should not come at the price of integrity and self-respect or the contempt of others, nor should it be self-denigration or humiliation. The process of inculcating humility had obstacles to overcome, and the disciples of the contemplative tradition needed to understand the vices and potential grandiose self-posturing in front of others or the demonstration of a hero complex.

SUPPLICATIONS

The role of supplications in Islam is a powerful concept for pious Muslims because it underscores dependency on and deliverance by the creator.[16] The Qur'an consists of two verses in which dependency and deliverance are explicitly made. In Q 2:186, the Qur'an states, "I answer the call (*da'wa*) of the suppliant (*da'i*) when he calls upon Me (*da'ani*)," and in the Qur'an 40:60, God states, "Call upon Me (*ud'uni*), and I will answer you." Muslim theologians commented on these supplicatory prayers (*du'as*) on how the believer knows if God is answering and if He is even obliged to respond to these prayers. Medieval theologian Fakhr al-Din al Razi (d.1209) stated, "We know there are many pious believers exerting energy in reciting *du'as* and requesting humble petitions (*tadarru'*) without receiving a response." The theological conundrum examines whether unanswered prayers relate to a strong or weak faith of the believer and whether they reflect a more profound concern for the inner spiritual healthiness of the believer. This section examines the role of the *du'a* in the believer's journey to establishing inner peace and how supplicatory prayers are interpreted and incorporated into daily life.

Scholars understood the purpose of *du'a* in the Quranic context of verses 2:186 and 40:60, where God is saying He answers the call of the suppliant and states emphatically that "I will answer you." Al-Razi thought this meant the believer calls the divine to repent from sins.[17] He explains that one tends to reach the divine during a time of repentance. Before Razi's time was theologian Zamakhshari (d.1144), who asserted that God's presence in listening and responding to supplicatory prayer is definitive, especially for those aware of their daily sins.[18] However, other theologians noted that *du'as* are not just for repentance for sins; instead, it is a direct dialogue between the believer and the divine to express adoration, love, and a deep yearning for connection. The repetitive words in *du'as*, "O God! There is no deity but You," or "O God, you are Peace, you are Light, You are all-Forgiving, You are the Merciful God I seek your forgiveness," illustrate a desire to be praised. It was understood that any act of praising God through words of adoration would elicit an undeniable response in the form of a reward.

Second, theologians expounded upon the meaning and types of function of *du'a* as a form of worship (*'ibada*). This was usually qualified to state explicitly that reciting *du'a* does not substitute or minimize the importance of maintaining regular liturgical prayers.[19] However, the idea that supplicatory prayer is worship (*al-du'a huwa al 'ibada*) was built upon the interpretation that any act of worship involving human beings calling out to and reaching God through it must be viewed as an act of worship. There are, however, two different ways of conceptualizing *du'a as-'ibada* in these verses. However, for some scholars, equating *du'a* with a form of worship posed problems with liturgical prayers and the general expression of devotional piety. To this extent, the act of reciting *du'as* needs to be an authentic petition proving to be an act of surrender rather than an exercise of seeking things from the divine. The *du'a* required to include specific formulas requesting forgiveness, repentance, surrender, and obedience to the creator.[20]

Qur'an 7:55 states, "Call upon your Lord, humbly beseeching Him and silently (*khufyatan*), verily God does not love transgressors (*mu'tadin*)." This is a reinforcement of an all-forgiving God who forgives transgressors. Pious Muslims know that the fundamental concept of a *du'a* is a petition with an act of self-surrender. Humility is a necessary characteristic for the suppliant to express the *du'a*. Many classical and contemporary scholars speak about the importance of the inner state (i.e., the spiritual state), which should be in absolute humility during the supplicatory prayer. The contemplative tradition stressed the disciple's complete presence of the heart (*hudur al-qalb*).[21] Al-Ghazali cited a *hadith* explicitly pointing out that one's *du'a* petition should not be conditional or qualified statements: "My Lord grant me this, If You provide this" or "My Lord forgive me if You will." Al-Ghazali and

Razi believed that the prayer is bracketed with a certain degree of "self-sufficiency" (*istighna'*) by the individual, and supplicatory prayers need to display absolute reliance, poverty, and "destitution" as if a slave is standing in front of a master. Another point to be aware of is the use of firm, resolute (*'azm*) words in the petitioning; for example, "My Lord, grant this to me," illustrates impatience and arrogance on the part of the spiritual aspirant. Reciting a *du'a* with *hudur al-qalb* is essential to seeking God's generosity, guidance, and mercy.[22]

Rumi's grand masterpiece Mathnawi-i ma'nawi ("Couplets of Inner Meanings") reminds disciples of the rites of pilgrimage to Mecca when pilgrims approach the holy Ka'aba reciting "*Labbaik, Allahumma labbaik, labbaika la shareeka laka labbaik, innal hamda wanne'matah laka wal mulk, la shareeka laka*" (Here I am, O Allah! Here I am; Here I am, there is no partner unto You, Here I am; all praise and sovereignty belongs to you, there is no partner unto you). The mandatory ritual pilgrimage for Muslims does not have origins in a single *du'a* or series of petitions, but in the fact that all prayer is a response to the call of God.

TRAUMA FROM EXTREMISM

When we examine the discourse on trauma, it needs to be understood from within the framework of its historical events. Trauma as a concept, with its own language and cultural experiences, often refers to any stress-inducing situation. Trauma can be caused by natural disasters, human-made disasters such as conflict or war, forced displacement of people, domestic violence, and circumstances caused by social, political, and economic instability. Within this definition is prolonged tyranny, and oppressive practices against the population, such as torture, imprisonment, systematic rape, mass executions, and bombardment of civilians, can be considered traumatic experiences. Whether it be an invasion of a country or the ethnic cleansing and sectarian cleansing that happened in Syria, Iraq, Myanmar, Yemen, Afghanistan, and Libya, there is sociological, emotional, and cultural scarring of victims. The emergence of terrorist groups such as the Taliban, al Qaeda, Boko Haram, al-Shabab, and the Islamic State of Iraq and Syria are psycho-pathological groups that utilized sustained trauma against various populations. Unfortunately, in Muslim-majority countries psychological support services to address trauma or attempt to reverse traumatic experiences are limited; it remains unpopular to address mental disorders. These populations incurred catastrophic destructiveness and experienced devastation from violent extremist groups.

One of the primary goals of using trauma on a population is to inflict more terror by weaponizing trauma to act as an ongoing weapon in the mind and the victim's body. One can be in the classroom listening to a lecture or working in a professional environment, believing this is a calming event separate from past traumatizing events. Psychologists have identified moments from a sound, scent, odor, visual reminders, music, and even particular uses of phrases in a conversation that could trigger memories of trauma. Viktor Frankl,[23] a survivor of the Holocaust who became a psychologist in the field of meaning, said that human beings are always in search of meaning and of ultimate meaning, and when people's meanings are torn apart, they suffer immense emotional pain. Frankl says that when meaning structures are damaged, causing a loss of meaning, people need to struggle to find new meaning in life and unknown reasons to live. According to Frankl, to overcome trauma, the individual needs to reform the internalization of trauma and convert it into reasons to survive and overcome past destructive events. This recovery involves developing a new discourse, giving meaning to life while articulating a new inner discourse that makes sense for a new chapter of life. The international communities' efforts to prevent and counter violent extremism and enter former militants into rehabilitation and reintegration programs have failed to support traumatized populations from the wrath of terrorist groups. Programs aiming at civil society to prevent violent extremism are primarily interested in inoculating the population from radical recruitment and spreading of radical ideologies. These preventative programs to combat violent extremism are also based on assumptions and ensure communities are resilient and safe from militant penetration and the spread and acceptance of radical ideas, and to inform authorities about any presence of radicalization. However, programs designed and funded by the United Nations, the US Agency for International Development, several Scandinavian development programs, and development programs based in the United Kingdom, France, Italy, Germany, Japan, and several others focused on psychological therapy for the perpetrators of terrorism and not the victims who suffered at the hands of terrorism.

HEALING

Libyan theologian Aref Ali Nayed believes that healing from the civil war and terrorism can be learned from one of the greatest spiritual masters of

North Africa, the Sufi Shaykh and eminent scholar Abu al-'Abbas Ahmad ibn Ahmad Zarruq al-Baurnusi al-Fasi (1442–1492), also known as Sidi Shaykh Ahmad Zarruq. Shaykh Zarruq was a trained scholar in jurisprudence, Sufism (*tasawwuf*), Qur'an, and *hadiths*, and during his time, he was considered to be an intellectual force and called a "renewer of the Muslim community" or a mujaddid. His legacy as a Sufi master remains powerful in several modern Sufi orders, including the Shadhili and Naqshbandi orders. Originally from Fes, Morocco, he was recognized as an accomplished jurist of the Maliki school of law and a contemporary of prominent scholar Muhammad al-Jazuli.[24] One of his important works includes the *Qawa'id al-Tasawwuf* (*The Principles of Sufism*), his exceptional commentaries on the intricate complexities of Maliki jurisprudence, and the famous commentary upon the *Kitab al-Hikam* written by the well-known Egyptian scholar Ibn 'Ata Allah al-Iskandari (1259–1310).[25]

Shaykh Zarruq heavily incorporated and built upon Ibn 'Ata Allah's works of *Kitab al-Tanwir fi isqat al-Tadbir* (*The Illumination on Abandoning Self-Direction*), *Al-Qasd al-mujarrad fi ma'rifat al-Ism al-Mufrad* (*The Pure Goal Concerning Knowledge on the Unique Name*), and astonishing *Unwan at-tawfiq fi adab at-tariq* (*The Sign of Success Concerning the Discipline of the Path*).[26] In the thirteenth century, Shaykh Zarruq was buried in Misrata, Libya, and in 2012, his tomb was raided and the mosque was burnt down by Salafi terrorists who felt visiting shrines and practicing Sufism were antithetical to Islam. Shaykh Zarruq and Ibn 'Ata Allah's works were directed toward disciples to lead a spiritual life, a purposeful, meaningful life to construct meaningful interaction with others. Shaykh Zarruq's book *The Principles of Sufism* (*Qawa'id al-Tasawwuf*) is an analytical guidebook for Sufi practitioners to maintain their commitment and to have a sincere orientation (*sidq al- tawajuh*) or intention because this controls the inward being and is the source to guides the disciple. Without an authentic degree of sincerity and authenticity of commitment, nothing can be achieved, and as a result, the Sufi disciple will be a useless imitator without a genuine reality in his beliefs on the path. Equally important is the spiritual aspirant, who must be fully equipped with the correct inner knowledge of the *shari'a* rules governing his outward being. Shaykh Zarruq warns disciples of being ignorant or lackadaisical about religious commitment because ungenuine and dishonest understanding will lead to mistakes in practice.

Shaykh Zarruq states that knowing the principles of the Sufi path in which he follows because these principles are based on the Qur'an and the *sunnah* of the Prophet. He quotes a renowned Sufi scholar, Abu al-Qasim al-Junaid, who said, "This is our science is founded on the Book and the *Sunnah*. He who does not listen to the sayings (*hadith*) and sit with the disciples (*fuqaha*), and receive his instruction from the learned, will harm whoever follows him, and following him is unlawful."[27]

Nayed believes healing begins when the individual has an elevated vision of living (*uluw al-himma*), where the person is searching for a transcendental life and is not stuck in the mundane world of materialism. Nayed notes that the Sufi master Zarruq wrote profoundly on compassion (*al-rahma*) because the faith of Islam and the Prophet of Islam are all manifestations of compassion. Transcendental compassion can be accessed internally to operate in the best interests of the self, community, and broader world. Seeking transcendental compassion empowers the individual to heal the wounds they inherited by culture or family or wounds inflicted on the person by a group or state. The second principle Nayed thinks is essential for Libyans and others to heal is to understand and uphold the responsibility of preserving the sacred in our lives and this world. *Hifdh al-hurma*, upholding sacredness, means the individual understands what God holds as sacred and is committed to finding what is holy to preserve. As Immanuel Kant[28] elaborated on moral philosophy, people should not use another person for a means for the benefit of oneself. According to Kant, to treat another merely as a means is to do something morally impermissible; it is to act wrongly because the other is being used immorally. In the same line of philosophical thinking, Nayed believes people are not mere things; people cannot and should not be exploited, regardless of their philosophical, social, political, or tribal orientation; each person is worthy of respect and dignity without any hesitation.

According to Nayed, the third principle of healing from Zarruq is the call for service, or the perfecting of service to others, *husn al-khidma*. Not only is Nayed excavating classical Sufi wisdom from the classical period of Islam about the principle of service to others, but Zarruq focused on how *shari'a* was not intended to focus on obeying the rules or fearing the repercussions of violating law-based rules; rather, the law was meant to support individuals to serve others. It is through service to others that the self begins to see, hear, and feel the connection to humanity, and it is this connection that opens the heart to be more empathetic with others. Service to others for no monetary compensation or seeking to exploit or manipulate another for personal gain raises awareness of the soul. Being in service to others brings a mirror to oneself to ask if one could do more to alleviate the pain of others, thereby relieving some of the pain of oneself.

Nayed's fourth principle toward healing is pulling from Zarruq's spiritual prescriptions on resilience and persistence (*nufudh al-azma*). In the inner struggle against egoism, selfishness, and shortcomings with the self and others, this type of persistence is to realize the long path toward managing the ego's ability to direct and dominate the soul. In trying to live a life of compassion and love, treating others with unconditional dignity and respect, this is the meaning of Zarruq's spiritual persistence. The fine art of practicing and managing the ego is not to underestimate the pain from trauma or minimize the degree of deep, excruciating suffering. Instead, *nufudh al-azma* recognizes that there are methods and practices to use to ensure the ego does not intensify, worsen, and seed the pain longer than it is.

The fifth principle from Zurruq's spiritual works is gratitude and appreciation of gifts in (*shukr al-ni'ma*) life. The appreciation of gifts is meant for two levels: the first level is to appreciate the ability to be alive at the moment, live with your loved ones, and identify the preciousness of time spent with others. The second level is living in an environment filled with diverse creatures, diverse beings, and the multitude of things the world we live in has to offer. Finding ways to appreciate suffering is probably a tall order to ask of someone who has experienced detrimental trauma. Even in trauma, suffering, pain, and in the recovery of healing, Zurruq's principles of *shukr al-ni'ma* point toward the *rahma* (mercy) of the divine as the source of recovery.

NOTES

1. Ira M. Lapidus, *A History of Islamic Societies* (Cambridge: Cambridge University Press, 1988).

2. Sayyid Imran (ed.), *Sulami, Tafsir al-Sulami wa huwa haqa'iq al-tafsir* (Beirut: Dar al-Kutub al-'Ilmiyya, 2001), 2: 212.

3. 'Abu Hafs 'Umar al-Suhrawardi, *'Awarif al-Ma'rif* (Cairo: Maktabat al-Qahira, 1973), pp. 202–25, hereafter cited as AM.

4. Claude Cahen, "Notes sur l'historiographie dans la Communauté Musulmane Idéale," in *Revue des études Islamiques* 13 (1977), pp. 81–88; Herbert Mason, trans., *The Passion of Husain Ibn Mansur Hallaj* (Princeton: Princeton University Press, 1982).

5. For further discussion on the variety of uses of the term *adab*, see Ian Richard Netton, "The Breath of Felicity: Adab, Ahwal, Maqamat and Abu Najib al-Suhrawardi," in Leonard Lewisohn (ed.), *The Heritage of Sufism* (London: Khaniqahi Nimatullahi Publications, 1993), pgs. 457–82.

6. AM, pg. 247.

7. Stephen Hirtenstein, *Patterns of Contemplation* (Oxford: Anqa Publishing, 2021).

8. Seyyid Mahjub Hasan Wasti, "Hazrat Shaykh-ul Shayukh wa 'Awarif al-Ma'arif," in *Suhrawardi Silsila Risala*, edited by Shah Owais Sohrawardi (Lahore: Sohrawardi Foundation, 1989), pp. 5–22.

9. AM, pg. 250.

10. See Qamar-ul Huda, *Striving toward Divine Union: Spiritual Exercises for the Suhrawardi Sufis* (London: Routledge Press, 2003).

11. Atif Khalil, *Repentance and the Return to God: Tawba in Early Sufism* (Albany: SUNY Press, 2018), pg. 158.

12. Stephen Hare, "The Paradox of Moral Humility," *American Philosophical Quarterly*, 1996, 33 (2): 235–41; Norvin Richards, "Is Humility a Virtue?" *American Philosophical Quarterly*, 1998, 25 (3): 253–59; Hellmut Ritter, *The Ocean of the Soul: Men, the World and God in the Stories of Farid al-Din 'Attar*, translated by John O'Kane (Leiden: Brill, 2003).

13. Douglas Seanor (ed.), *Hare and Critics: Essays on Moral Thinking* (Clarendon Press, 1988).

14. Bilal Orfali and Atif Khalil (eds.), *Mysticism and Ethics in Islam* (Beirut: American University of Beirut Press, 2022).

15. S. Yazaki, "Morality in Early Sufi Literature," in *The Cambridge Companion to Sufism*, edited by Lloyd Ridgeon (Cambridge: Cambridge University Press, 2015), pp. 74–97; Cyrus Zargar, *The Polished Mirror: Storytelling and the Pursuit of Virtue in Islamic Philosophy and Sufism* (London: Oneworld Academic, 2017).

16. For more on supplicatory prayer and prayers, see Annemarie Schimmel, "Some Aspects of Mystical Prayer in Islam," *Die Welt des Islams*, 1952, 2, no. 2: 112–25; cf. Schimmel, *Mystical Dimensions of Islam*, pp. 155–67; Constance Padwick, *Muslim Devotions: A Study of Prayer Manuals in Common Use* (London: SPCK, 1961).

17. Fakhr al-Din al-Razi, *al-Tafsir al-Kabir* (Beirut: Dar al-Kutub al-'Ilmiyya, 1990), 5:86.

18. Zamakhshari, *Kashshaf* (Riyadh: Maktabat al-'Abikan, 1998), 5:307.

19. See 'Abd al-Qadir al-Jilani, *Ghunya* (Damascus: Maktabat al-'Ilm al-Hadith, 2001), pp. 407–12; Qurtubi, *Tafsir al-Qurtubi* (Beirut: Dar al-Kutub al-'Ilmiyya, 2004); Muhammad b. Jarir al-Tabari, *Jami' al-bayan 'an tafsir al-Qur'an* (Beirut: Dar al-Ma'rifa, 1992), 25:30–31; Qushayri, *Risala*, ed. 'Abd al-Halim Mahmud and Mahmud b. Sharif (Damascus: Dar al-Farfur, 2002); and Muhammad b. 'Ali al-Shawkani, *Fath al-Qadir* (Damascus: Dar Ibn Kathir, 1998).

20. Sulami, *Tafsir al-Sulami wa huwa haqa'iq al-tafsir*, edited by Sayyid Imran (Beirut: Dar al-Kutub al-'Ilmiyya, 2001), 2:212.

21. Fakhr al-Din al-Razi, *al-Tafsir al-Kabir* (Beirut: Dar al-Kutub al-'Ilmiyya, 1990), 5:86.

22. Al-Ghazali, *Ihya' 'ulum al-Din* (Aleppo: Dar al-Wa'i, 1998), 1:522.

23. Viktor Frankl, *Man's Search of Meaning* (Boston: Beacon Press, 2006).

24. For more on Morocco Sufism, see Vincent Cornell, *The Way of Abu Madyan* (Cambridge: The Islamic Texts Society, 1996) and *Realm of the Saint: Power and Authority in Moroccan Sufism* (Austin: University of Texas Press, 1998).

25. For more on Shaykh Ahmed Zarruq, see Ali Fahmi Khashim, *Zarruq, The Sufi: A Guide in the Way and a Leader to the Truth: A Biographical and Critical Study of a Mystic from North Africa* and Scott Kugle, *Rebel Between Spirit and Law: Ahmad Zarruq, Sainthood, And Authority in Islam* (Bloomington: Indiana University Press, 2006).

26. For more on Ibn 'Ata Allah, see O. Siddique, *The Illumination on Abandoning Self-Direction* (Sydney, 2022); K. Williams, *The Pure Intention: On Knowledge of the Unique Name* (Cambridge: The Islamic Texts Society, 2018); Victor Danner, *The Book of Wisdom* (Mahwah, NJ: Paulist Press, 1978); A. Durkee, *The School of the Shadhdhuliyyah: Vol 1 Orisons* (Malaysia: The Other Press, 2005); and E. Geoffroy (ed.), *Une voie soufie dans le monde: la Shadhiliyya* (Paris: Maisonneuve & Larose, 2005).

27. Ali Fahmi Khashim, *Zarruq, The Sufi*, pp. 40–41.

28. Paul Guyer and Allen Wood (eds.), *The Cambridge Edition of the Works of Immanuel Kant in English Translation*, sixteen volumes (Cambridge: Cambridge University Press, 1992).

Chapter Seven

Intrafaith and Interfaith Dialogue and the Challenges of Pluralism

There are many lenses through which Muslims see themselves as believers and as a faithful community under God's order. Historical, philosophical, theological, mystical, and juridical literature has illustrated that the Qur'an as a revealed scripture is the most important authority for Muslim identity, self-understanding, soteriological and ontological, and all matters related to religious practices. Scriptural authority and authenticity are critical for Islam as it brings the believers closer to the essence of the divine. The remembrance of God is the struggle of constantly bringing greater attention to God in all moments of our lives. While remembrance of God is not restricted to the textual life of the Qur'an, I have shown that the customs and life of Prophet Muhammad are also crucial for Muslims to obey and surrender themselves to the one God. For Muslims, the Prophet Muhammad is the last of all messengers, "the seal of the Prophets," because he completed the revelations in their purest form. He transmitted the Qur'an to a community and ensured it was compiled, memorized, and written down in his lifetime. In addition to being the throne carrier for the last revelation, the Prophet's life is a real model for Muslims to embody, emulate, and strive to capture in daily spiritual life.

Shaikh Zakariyya Baha ud-din's meditational exercise instructions on connecting with God require the seeker to purify the heart of any other desires and to concentrate on our essence ilah-lah "There is no God but God." The purified heart creates the space for the divine to rest and to be reunited with the ultimate reality. The seeker is often called an *ashiq* or lover by poets because only lovers of God can truly prepare themselves for the encounter and *ashiq* seekers are only invited by God. Many Muslim writers have referred to this as an unveiling process whereby each level of deeper knowledge of God brings about another level or station of encounter. These practices of attempting to reunite with God, either through the intercession of the Prophet or the direct mediation of one's own spiritual teacher, affirm a particular identity that is unique to the Islamic tradition. This is not to say that other traditions do not have their methods of encountering God, but within each religious tradition the ideas and religious practices used to reach enlightenment are integrally tied to the specific realities of that tradition. Cultivating a compassionate heart, loving the Prophet in multiple expressions, using poetry for deeper reflection, and incorporating supplications in addition to daily ritual prayers are at the core of the Islamic path of increasing the knowledge of the divine.

The specific references to other traditions in the Qur'an highlight and acknowledge other religious traditions and their uniqueness. The nature of revelations, at least Islamically, is not to refute or dismiss the wisdom of other religious traditions. Instead, it is to align itself with previous traditions in new innovative ways to forge a community of unity. While there are verses to the People of the Book to appeal to correct their ways in understanding God and to adhere to the message of the Prophet, the core relationships with Jews and Christians is instructional for Muslims. It is instructional for Muslims to work with the challenges of theological exclusivity and claims of private covenants with the divine. The Quranic revelations are not exclusive for Muslims but for believers of the one God, and this is another mechanism used by the scripture to create a tolerant and accepting community. The verses directed specifically at Jewish and Christian communities do pose interesting questions of "us" and "them" and the problems of identifying the fine lines of those weak definitions. One of the main areas where I think the Qur'an attempts to question the religious authorities of *ahl al-Kitab*, specifically how they were designated to be "authorities" and whether their knowledge of their own tradition is more important than scripture itself.

For Muslim exegetes, the Qur'an and the life of the Prophet determine the tone and fundamental understanding of Jewish, Christian, and Muslim relationships, and some commentators have primarily used or misused those definitions in viewing the other tradition. Whereas traditionally the religious dialogue among the Abrahamic traditions has been restricted to polemical debates and theological counter-debates, I have demonstrated that there is an enormous range to work within areas of interreligious dialogue. My understanding of the Qur'an and of the customs of the Prophet was not to create further obstacles for a common community to worship the same God, but rather to build upon and continue the rich tradition of surrendering the selves together in this mission. I read the verses on Jesus's birth, life, and removal from the earth as an earnest invitation by revelations for individuals and communities to refocus on the divine and our place with Him. As much as the return to Allah in the Islamic tradition has intrinsic cultural affirmations from within, there is overwhelming evidence from Quranic scripture not to privatize the covenant of God and to be exclusive throne carriers of God. Certainly, this is done all the time in the Islamic religion, but historical and textual evidence points to a religious pluralism that I think obliges Muslims to tolerate others and to learn new innovative ways to create a community of unity. For Muslims, the spiritual struggle is to keep the Prophet's model at the center of their lives; it is unfortunate if proponents of religious exclusivity did not see that the Prophet's commitment of loving all and bringing forth a community of mutual respect was at the heart of his message. While the voices of exclusivity and cultural chauvinistic identities are the most vocal for the moment, this does not mean that true interreligious dialogue between the Abrahamic or Dharmic traditions cannot flourish to counteract the ignorance of intolerance. The Islamic tradition that I refer to (i.e., surrendering the self to journey toward God's self-disclosure) is integrally tied to an internal reconciliation and, more importantly, a reconciliation with other traditions to create a community of faithful committed to each other.

THEOLOGICAL DIALOGUE

Among the theological areas of contention between Muslims and Christians have been over the divine nature of Jesus and his death. First, the Qur'an does not state categorically that Jesus died naturally; rather, it focuses on dismissing the notion that Jesus was crucified on the cross. In sura 4:157–158, it states "though they did not kill him and did not crucify him (*ma salabu-hu*), though it so appeared to them. Those who disagree in the matter are only lost in doubt. They have no knowledge about it other than conjecture, for surely they did not kill him. But God raised him (Jesus) up in position and closer to Himself; and God is all-mighty and all-wise." According to Islamic revelations, both Jews and Christians agreed that Jesus was killed by capital punishment because he "threatened" the religious authority of the Jewish rabbis. At least these were the commonly held views by Jews and Christians living in seventh-century Arabia. According to Islam, however, Jesus was an extraordinary prophet who was sent a message from God to return to worshipping him without the superstitions and religious innovations created by human beings. The Qur'an contests the position that Jesus was crucified on the cross by asserting that he was saved from the hands of his tormentors and God raised him to himself (*bil rafa'a Allah 'alayhı*). What does the Qur'an mean by "God raised him to himself"? And more importantly, what are the theological problems of Jesus's death on the cross?

The classical Muslim interpreter of the Qur'an 'Abd Allah ibn 'Umar ibn al-Baydawi (d.1286) stated that at the moment when Jesus was going to be captured to be killed, God thereupon informed him that he would take him up to heaven. Jesus then asked his disciples which of them would be willing to have his likeness cast upon him and be killed and enter paradise.[1] One of them accepted and God put the likeness of Jesus upon him and instead an impersonator was crucified. Al-Baydawi believed it was Judas who betrayed Jesus that was crucified.[2] The Quranic verse 3:54 states: "But the unbelievers contrived a plot, and God did the like; and God's plan is the best. When God said: 'O Jesus, I will take you to Myself and exalt you, and rid you of the unbelievers, and hold those who disbelieve till the Day of Resurrection. You have then to come back to Me when I will judge between you in what you were in variance.'" Al-Baydawi's thought is consistent with the teachings of the Qur'an and the Prophet in that he does not contest Jesus's death on the cross; rather, he was interested in elaborating on the time and place of Jesus's return to God.

Another eminent commentator, 'Abu Jafar Muhammad ibn Jarir al-Tabari (838–923), stated that Jesus was taken up to heaven after Herod gave the order to kill Jesus. At that very moment, Jesus was removed from earth and a Jewish leader who brought Jesus to Herod named Joshua took on the resemblance of Jesus and was crucified instead of Jesus. Joshua stayed on the cross for seven days, and each night Mary and the disciples mourned incessantly at the foot of the cross thinking it was originally Jesus who was crucified.[3] On the eighth day, with God's mercy and compassion for the community of mourners, Jesus descended from heaven to console Mary and the apostles with a feast and later returned to heaven. Just like al-Baydawi, al-Tabari's interpretation of the moment of the crucifixion event is focused on the ways in which Jesus was removed from the earth in the living flesh and how his removal simultaneously deceived the apostles, the community of observers, the Jewish leadership, and Herod's officials.

These commentators reflect general Islamic views that Jesus was alive when God brought him to heaven and that he still exists with God until his ultimate return back to earth. But why could Islam not accept Jesus's death on the cross? Islam's understanding of the history of prophets and the reason for having messengers is God's answer to redirecting his creation to worship him. When human beings error to follow another Supreme Being(s), God chose a prophet among them to communicate their wrong beliefs and to guide them back to the one single God. In his eternal love and commitment to his creation, prophets serve as modus operandi for God's speech on earth or as stated in the Qur'an vicegerent of God (*khalıfa*).[4] This being said, messengers and prophets have a unique position as human beings and chosen as the vehicle for the divine's message.

The divine will allows prophets to experience the pains and ordeals of being chosen to spread the word of God, but God will not allow any prophet to be destroyed by the community of creation. Death on any one person or anything is purely decided by the divine, and Jesus's death sentence by Herod or his entrapment by the religious authorities was not conducive to divine mandate. For Herod and rabbinic authorities (i.e., creation) to conspire and kill a prophet is to transgress against the divine order of creator and creation. Only the divine has the power to select and send prophets and decide on their fates; to contest this system is to challenge God's authority. Given these parameters, commentators have limited their work on expanding on the "substitute Jesus" at the time when God pulled him up to heaven. Traditionally, exegetes focused on specific figures surrounding Jesus to identify the moment he was removed from the earth. Since the Qur'an is firm on Jesus not being crucified, the literature works on what the Qur'an does not specify and that is what could have happened in his absence.

CONTEMPORARY ISLAMIC–CATHOLIC DIALOGUE

One of the primary challenges for Muslim–Catholic interreligious dialogue in the modern era is to deal with the past and forge a vision of the future. In confronting the past record of hostility, the two religions must address apologetic denunciations, harmful polemics, and indifference toward the other tradition as an invisible entity. The key challenge for the future is to understand the truths of real dialogue that will transform how our traditions officially view one another, and how these new understandings inform the communities to rethink, recreate, and reforge a vision of a common future. In retrospect, one such step toward this goal was the monumental work of the

Second Vatican Council, which opened the way for real constructive Catholic dialogue with non-Christians, particularly Jews and Muslims.[5] However, the immediate task has been locating authentic mechanisms and sincere religious authorities to promote mutual understanding in the two communities. Despite the gains of dialogue since the Second Vatican Council (Vatican II), with delegated authority from the Pope the Congregation for the Doctrine of the Faith issued in September 2000 a declaration entitled *Dominus Iesus* that set out the official faith position of the Church and condemned other views contrary to the Catholic faith. With complete support from the Vatican, *Dominus Iesus* created a lively controversy among Christian theologians (Orthodox, Catholic, and Protestant) because of its truth claims by the Catholic authorities and references to other Christian churches as not authentic in the "proper" sense. This section examines Muslim–Catholic relations since Vatican II and analyzes some critical steps taken by members of the religious traditions in dialogue and studies some new questions for Muslim–Catholic interreligious dialogue.

The dialogues between the Roman Catholic Church and Islamic religious leaders in the past fifty-five years have had their highs and lows, but if there was any one moment in recent times that spurred on the movement of serious dialogue between the religious authorities in both traditions, it is undeniably the groundbreaking work of Vatican II. In the Declaration on the Relation of the Church to non-Christian religions, *Nostra Aetate*, it is stated unambiguously that:

> One is the community of all peoples, one their origin, for God made the whole human race to live over the face of the earth. One also is their final goal, God. His providence, His manifestations of goodness, his saving design extend to all men. . . . The Church, therefore exhorts her sons, that through dialogue and collaboration with the followers of other religions, carried out with prudence and love in witness to the Christian faith and life.[6]

As in other parts of the Vatican II documents, the constitutions, the declarations, and the decrees, there is obvious evidence of a conciliatory intention to connect with other religious traditions to improve the conditions of humanity and, in particular, work together for healing and social justice. This is evident in the Second Vatican Council's Declaration on Religious Freedom or Dignitatis Humanae, where it is stated that: "The Council declares that the right to religious freedom has its foundation in the very dignity of the human person as this dignity is known through the revealed word of God and by reason itself. This right of the human person to religious freedom is to be recognized in the constitutional law whereby society is governed and thus it is to become a civil right."[7] In Vatican II, there was an obvious commitment to a new vision for the modern period—a vision of unity, peaceful cooperation, and a progressive, thinking Church that embraced pluralism, gender inclusivism, religious tolerance, reconciliation with Jews and Muslims, and a spirit to focus on social justice for all humanity.[8] It was in this spirit that the Council emphasized the following:

> The Church regards with esteem also the Muslims. They adore the one God, living and subsisting in Himself, merciful and all-powerful, the Creator of heaven and earth, who has spoken to men; they take pains to submit wholeheartedly to even His inscrutable decrees, just as Abraham, with whom the faith of Islam takes pleasure in linking itself, submitted to God. . . . The sacred Council now pleads with all to forget the past and urges that a sincere effort be made to achieve mutual understanding; for the benefit of all, let them together preserve and promote peace, liberty, social justice and moral values.[9]

Nostra Aetate stressed the importance of the Catholic Church's relations with non-Christians and its shared spiritual, ethical, and religious beliefs and specifically identifies "unity and love among men" as one of the primary reasons for cooperation. But it takes another daring step forward by emphasizing the importance of forgetting the past and thinking and acting in conciliatory terms.[10] While Pope Paul VI did not lay down concrete methods for reconciliation or dialogue, which is common in papacy writings, he did endorse a culture of openness to recognizing the holy in other religious traditions and the desire to understand and respect the different ways in which each tradition connects with the divine. For instance, "We cannot truly call on God, the Father of all, if we refuse to treat in a brotherly way any man. . . . Man's relation to God the Father and his relation to men and his brothers are so linked together that scripture says: 'He who does not love does not know God.'"[11]

If we fast forward to the interreligious dialogue era of Pope John Paul II, there was more advanced interreligious dialogue with Muslims and other religious traditions by establishing the Pontifical Council for Inter-Religious Dialogue. Michael Fitzgerald's "Twenty-five Years of Dialogue: the Pontifical Council for Inter-Religious Dialogue" documents that Catholics were encouraged to seek and explore the wisdom and spiritual knowledge of other religious traditions, but also argued that John Paul II made this message a visible obligation for the faithful during his travels.[12] For instance, in a 1981 trip to the Philippines, he addressed a congregation of Muslims: "I wish you to be convinced that your Christian brothers and sisters need you and they need your love. And the whole world, with its longing for greater peace, brotherhood, and harmony, needs to see fraternal coexistence between Christians and Muslims in a modern, believing, and peaceful Philippine nation."[13] John Paul II was aggressively pressing the need for improved relations between Christians and Muslims at every human level. For him, forging interreligious dialogue was not a doctrinal issue that needed to be understood intellectually, but rather it was tied to faith being practiced or applied faith.

It is common for Muslim theologians to present their interpretations of faith publicly in answer to modern questions on such subjects as artificial intelligence or organ transplants; these statements are legal commentaries and these reasoned opinions must not contradict the statement in sacred texts. Similarly, in trying to understand the theological claims of *Dominus Iesus*, one must not forget that it is mainly intended for Christian believers. Nevertheless, some statements refer to the "others"—presumably non-Catholic Christians and non-Christians—who still benefit from the "mysterious relationship between the Church and the Holy Spirit."[14] For example, *Dominus Iesus* states:

> For those who are not formally and visibly members of the Catholic Church, salvation in Christ is accessible by virtue of a grace which, while having a mysterious relationship to the Church, does not make them formally part of the Church, but enlightens them in a way which is accommodated to their spiritual and material situation. This grace comes from Christ; it is the result of his sacrifice and is communicated by the Holy Spirit. It has a relationship with the Church, which, according to the plan of the Father, has her origin in the mission of the Son and the Holy Spirit.[15]

When I read this statement from *Dominus Iesus*, it does not appear to recognize the fact that other religious traditions do not adhere to the belief in a Holy Spirit communicating with believers. According to Islamic theology, all work and communication are performed by the one and only God. This is even consistent in Sufi Islam, where saints (*awliya*) can intercede on behalf of the believer, but the divine is at the center of all work performed.

Dominus Iesus does not answer the question: if Muslims do not believe in the Holy Spirit or the salvific work of the Catholic Church, how can they benefit from grace working in the mysterious relationship of Church and Holy Spirit? With the obvious disagreement between Muslims and Catholics on the function of the Church and the salvific nature of the Holy Spirit, genuine interreligious dialogue will need to focus on how the divine works in each other's tradition and not at the expense of each other.

If the *Dominus Iesus* document is meant to affirm the Church's function in salvation, it would be an area of dialogic exploration Muslim–Catholic relations. For some Muslim scholars, an institution to be the sole source for salvation could be interpreted as an invalidation of other religious traditions and their respective ways of understanding salvation. Again, the interpretation from a non-Catholic scholar could read this *Dominus Iesus* section as an attempt to dismiss other religious traditions by speaking about their prayers, rituals, sacred scriptures, and general beliefs as not genuinely salvific. That is, other traditions may have "some spiritual element" but in fact, this is merely preparing for the truth of the Gospels. For example, *Dominus Iesus* section 21 states: "It is clear that it would be contrary to the faith to consider the Church as one way of salvation alongside those constituted by the other religions, seen as complementary to the Church or substantially equivalent to her, even if these are said to be converging with the Church toward the eschatological kingdom of God."[16] While one accepts that the primary intention of *Dominus Iesus* is to reaffirm the true distinctions of Catholic doctrine for the faithful, it is an area for dialogic exploration to examine exclusive claims on salvation and its unique possession of truth in a post–Vatican II world.

The *Dominus Iesus* paragraph does not stop at sole custody of salvation but even goes on to undervalue other religious traditions by claiming that they have inherent obstacles to obtaining salvation. For instance, some prayers and rituals of the other religions may assume a role of preparation for the Gospel, in that they are occasions or pedagogical helps in which the human heart is prompted to be open to the action of God. One cannot attribute to these, however, a divine origin or an ex opere operato salvific efficacy, which is proper to the Christian sacraments. Furthermore, it cannot be overlooked that other rituals, insofar as they depend on superstitions or other errors, constitute an obstacle to salvation.[17] One possible response to *Dominus Iesus*'s assertions from the perspective of Quranic theology is that

God made human beings as His vicegerents or representatives (*khulafa*) on earth (2:30). The Qur'an calls this representation a type of trust that no other creature can carry out (33:72). As human representatives overseeing this world, obedient human beings need to beware of losing the trust given to them by the divine. The corruption of, or disobedience to, this trust between God and human beings is what brings about evil consequences. It factors in free will and the choice humans make every day and every moment between upholding the trust mandated by the divine or choosing to neglect the trust and suffer the unforeseeable consequences. This inner conflict and violation lead to further violation of the earth and the community. For medieval Muslim theologians such as al-Ghazalı (d.1111) and Ibn Arabi (d.1240), the closer human beings are connected to Divine mercy (*rahma*), the tighter the bond to harmony with divine peace. However, Muslims understand that if believers stray from this bond, they inevitably fail to be trustworthy custodians. This corruption, or *fasad,* mentioned in the Qur'an over fifty times, is produced by human error and the abuse of human free will. Islamically, then, God is actively involved with human affairs and desires his creatures to accept their submission to Him—for example: "Corruption has spread over land and sea from what men have done themselves that they may taste a little of what they have done: They may haply come back to the right path" (Q. 30:41). The Creator desires his creatures to witness and experience the result of their capriciousness. Human corruption or the ongoing drama of human *fasad* on earth is meant to help human beings find ways to understand and rectify the corruption they have created. The Qur'an speaks of violence on earth (*fasad*) as having the potential to bring about a positive return to God through repentance. Human disobedience is not only a violation of the trust of custodianship of the earth but, more importantly, a failure to affirm God's unity and completely surrender to divine will.[18]

CONTEMPORARY ABRAHAMIC DIALOGUE

Most Muslim scholars, religious leaders, nongovernmental organizations, and governments denounce religiously motivated violence, and they condemn and detest the abuse of their religion. Evidence of this can be seen in Muslim leaders' widespread condemnation of terrorism and religiously motivated violence worldwide. With the rise of radicalism and unprecedented conflicts in Muslim-majority countries, paradoxically, the world has witnessed astonishing efforts of many Muslim organizations and leaders to promote more frequent and effective dialogues to enhance mutual understanding and create practical steps to improve relations. Efforts are underway in many places to vigorously educate Muslim youth about the core Islamic teachings of tolerance, peace, and pluralism. Even governments and institutions in Muslim-majority countries are working to reeducate, rehabilitate, and reintegrate Muslim extremists about the falsity of the doctrines they advocated and to find alternative nonviolent methods to express their discontent. For too long, Muslim religious leaders and scholars lectured on the higher goals of peace in Islam by defining the goals with scripture and *hadith*, prophetic sayings and actions, and attempting to demonstrate that peace is a pillar of the faith. Ironically, with the rise of violence in Muslim global communities, we have witnessed a surge of publications, podcasts, social media, and organizations dedicated to peacemaking. Muslim religious leaders (imams) and scholars recognize their essential roles in reinforcing pluralism within Islam worldwide. *'Ulama*, researchers, and Muslim leaders are promoting nonviolence, pluralism, and tolerance with immense intensity, and they should be recognized and their vital efforts publicized.

WHY DIALOGUE?

Several Muslim faith-based organizations worldwide are engaged in interfaith, intrafaith, intercultural, peacebuilding, and educational dialogues. Dialogue efforts by *'ulama* will tend to start with the discipline of peacemaking as it exists within the tradition of Islam. Historically, according to Muslim jurists, Islamic law seeks to preserve and protect life, religion, property, rights, and intellectual expression. These fundamental objectives of the Islamic faith, *'ulama* engaged in the dialogic process with others to learn the importance of younger Muslims to know these fundamental values and how to live accordingly. The development of interfaith dialogue institutions, like the King Abdulaziz Center for National Dialogue in Riyadh, The Royal Institute for Inter-faith Studies and The Aal al-Bayt Institute for Islamic Thought in Amman, The World Muslim Congress for Global Communities in Abu Dhabi, Kalam Research Institute in Dubai, and Abdurrahman Wahid Center for Interfaith Dialogue and Peace in Indonesia, has set in motion a cultural, religious, social, and historical shift toward prioritizing interfaith dialogues and the acceptance of others. These dialogic interactions and engagements illustrate subtle and immense changes for *'ulama* authorities who have experienced new understandings of the other. All types of dialogue, whether interfaith or intrafaith, are increasingly recognized as proven tools for learning and self-teaching because they connect people from different groups in a safe space for mutual sharing and listening. Dialogue is a structured process with a trained facilitator who can manage and supervise discussions with clear goals and learning objectives, and evaluate the impact of the dialogue. Interfaith dialogues need to be a facilitated dialogic process to address intergroup tensions, correct stereotypes, encourage mutual acceptance, and develop relational bonds that help to bridge intercommunal divides.

These dialogues are not designed to debate or determine which group has the authentic perspective, and it is not asserting one's faith as superior to another. It is not about proving one's tradition is more authentic than another tradition. Instead, effective dialogue transforms participants beneath the surface to deeper, more honest reflection to better understand the faiths and experiences of others and their own faith and assumptions on a much more intimate level. Uncomfortable topics must be addressed to bypass regular obstacles; unfortunately, religion is used to fuel tensions, legitimize violence, and justify divisions and exclusions. The religious peacebuilding field strongly advocates that a practical approach to transforming these destructive religious dynamics is to operate within the framework of meaning for those during conflict—the language in which they interpret their reality. That is, when *'ulama* dialogue with their religious counterparts they should use a religious framework to counteract religiously inspired conflict and to assert peacebuilding approaches based on religious principles of peace.

An important example in our time of Muslim interfaith dialogue is the Common Word document written by Muslim theologians asking for greater serious dialogues and improved relationships between Christians and Muslim religious leaders and their congregations.[19] The Common Word was sponsored by the Ahl al-Bayt Institute for Islamic Thought in Jordan. Typically, when the future of the Christian–Muslim dialogue is discussed, it is in abstract terms, with no clear agenda or specific vision for an actionable plan. However, Common Word authors sought to build upon a common heritage with the basis of the love of God and the love of neighbor as two essential cornerstones of our traditions. One scholar has described the euphoric moment as "the Vatican II for Christian–Muslim relations." If this is accurate, then it is critical to profit from the "Vatican II" dialogic spirit by thinking strategically, carefully, and with attention to global Christian–Muslim communities.

In the early years of the Common Word process, there were critics who cautioned on moving forward because the document contained many complex and unresolved theological issues; in particular, many Christian denominations in the West disputed among themselves some of the Christian responses.[20] There were some Christian scholars and clergy who argued that the Common Word defined the parameters of interfaith dialogue too narrowly without the consultation of Christian clergy. However, most Christian religious leaders believed it was a beautiful invitation to engage with Muslim *'ulama* scholars and imams. The Muslim theologians and scholars of the Common Word aimed to foster a global culture of dialogue with Christians, which was undeniably an invitation to move the two communities toward a common good, toward common interests, and to recall our common heritage of loving God and our neighbor. The common good agenda, as it has been called, is not limited to theological debates and historical views of the other, but it insists on moving toward specific peacemaking goals. There are immense lessons from the Common Word interfaith dialogue experiences in the past decade, and in any dialogue, learning lessons and gaining sight from these experiences will only enhance the goal of peaceful relationships. While *'ulama* and Christian clergy focused on scripture, textual sources, and historical interpretations of those sources, it was only a step in the dialogue. One lesson is clear: for too long, Christians and Muslims have extended immense effort in identifying sources to love each other, to dialogue with one another, and to argue a case for dialogue instead of the actual work of dialogue.

The Common Word experience forced the Muslim and Christian participants to work through resources and scriptures—which is just one specific type of dialogue—but beyond this, the issue was how to delve into the actual practice of dialogic engagement. In retrospection, the Common Word dialogue experience raised critical questions about how little participants would share their own real-life experiences connected to interfaith encounters and how our experiences are filled with or absent of fundamental divine directives like loving others. Muslim and Christian participants of the Common Word interfaith dialogues realized the heavy burden of scripture and their original intent on loving God and loving their neighbor. This awareness of loving others is not to be minimized. However, the dialogues needed to continue to pursue the personal human experiences of Muslims and Christians. This dialogue experience is a powerful reminder of a divine mandate to faithful believers in each tradition; in essence, it reinforces the importance of loving God as a fundamental aspect of the traditions of Islam and Christianity. When this conference asked participants to share the higher goals of peace in Islam, it undoubtedly must include the lessons of the Common Word because, in many ways, the experience helped us become more sensitive, empathetic, caring, and nurturing of the other person in our lives. The dialogic experience pushed us to take what is in scripture and apply it to our daily lives. It is summed in the Qur'an 2:152: "So remember Me, and I will remember you. And show thanks to Me, and do not deny Me."

INTERFAITH DIALOGUE CHALLENGES

Suppose the primary objective of dialogue is to learn from another while transforming oneself. In that case, we need to acknowledge that this requires empowering individuals to challenge themselves in ways that will make them active peacemakers. Peacemaking training programs rely on the content of the skills to change the participants' perceptions of the situation and their understanding of the self in relation to the larger society. Dialogues in peacemaking consist of understanding the nature of peacemaking, how to think about peacemaking strategically, mediation, real dialogue, reconciliation, and nonviolence. In *Crescent and Dove: Peace and Conflict Resolution in Islam*, I argued that if we can enhance *'ulama* skills in peacemaking, we can advance in real dialogue. Fundamental peacemaking dialogue skills include topics of religious ethics, theology, principles and practices of forgiveness, compassion, justice, love, dignity, reflection, patience, solidarity, service, tolerance, and reconciliation. If *'ulama* and imams alike can learn peacemaking skills, then this will create a process of self-examination and healthy self-criticism, and self-empowerment to transform themselves, and in their communities, regardless of their circumstances, they can serve as peacemakers. It is built upon the basic idea that peacemaking efforts focus on cognitive perceptions of the individual and the multiple ways an individual can contribute to society as a peacemaker. In the Qur'an 2:34, "Remember, when We asked the angels to bow in homage to Adam, they all bowed but Iblis, who disdained and turned insolent, and so became a believer." Iblis responds in Qur'an Kareem 7:12, "I am better than him (Adam), You created me from fire, and him You created from clay." In the Islamic verses of creation, God created Adam out of clay (earthy material) and asked the angels to bow down to the new creation, but one angel, Iblis, refused to bow down, believing that it was a lesser form of creation. *'Ulama* consistently refers to these verses to argue that conflict has always existed since the creation and that it is impossible to create "conflict-less societies"—the best we can do is to minimize the amount of conflict that arises in life. These interpretations must be taken seriously because dialogues are critical in identifying counter-narratives for finding solutions to violence and intolerance.

One of the many aims of religious peacebuilding is to recognize and co-exist with religious pluralism, dialoguing with other faiths in an age when interreligious dialogue is an established practice. On the one hand, religious leaders want to establish authority in a world where believers are leaving behind their faiths, and religious institutions need to be the source for the believers to gain deeper insights. However, on the other hand, contemporary interfaith dialogue tied to religious peacebuilding efforts attempts to reassert a new definition of expressing faith while acknowledging the presence of others in their own lives, challenging the sovereignty of their faith independent of the Catholic tradition. *Dominus Iesus* states: "This truth of faith does not lessen the sincere respect which the Church has for the religions of the world, but at the same time, it rules out, in a radical way, that mentality of indifferentism characterized by a religious relativism which leads to the belief that one religion is as good as another."[21] It is not so much the zealous language used to affirm the Christian faith that is objectionable but the way the document claims the supremacy of the Catholic faith over other religious traditions existing in the world. For Islamic theology, this is not a new claim and the Qur'an addressed the exclusive claim to be within God's domain, referring to the claims made by Jewish and Christian religious leaders who felt that they were not like any other people God created, that their special covenant had elevated their status before Him and that they were "friends of God to the exclusion of other people" (Q. 62:6). Alongside this unique status before God came inherent purity and the belief that the afterlife was exclusively reserved for them. For example, the Qur'an says: "They claim to be children of God and His beloved" (5:18) and "considered themselves pure" (4:48). The Qur'an consistently repeats that only God can make an exclusive claim, which is to say that no religious group has the authority or the power to judge any other people because it is God who decides the fate of all created things. It says: "And they say: None shall enter paradise unless he is a Jew or a Christian. Those are their vain desires. Say to them: Produce your proof if you are truthful. Remember, whoever submits his whole self to God and is a doer of good will be rewarded with his Lord" (Q. 2:111).[22]

This is not only a reminder for Muslims of how other religious groups previously made exclusive truth claims, but more importantly, it shows that Muslims themselves need to beware of proclaiming a divine exclusivity and eschatological absolutism because everything is dependent on God's will and it is He who has power over all things (Q. 5:19). Of course, this does not mean that Muslims have never made exclusive claims to faith with authentic direct relations with the divine, but the question to examine is whether it might be possible to raise the issue of divine exclusivity in interreligious dialogue to study the language we apply to our traditions. The crucial point for the Muslim–Catholic interfaith dialogue process is to discover the "other" in our own experiences and on our own spiritual paths. The virtue of loving your neighbor as yourself becomes the personal realization that human traditions do not and cannot live in isolation, separated from each other by walls of mistrust.[23] For many critics of dialogue and the search for real answers to questions of religious pluralism, this argument threatens the uniqueness of the truth claims in their tradition. However, the heart of the matter is not to measure each other's truths against our litmus test but to see how the others live as spiritual persons and are spiritually touched by their concept of love, justice, and truth.

After sixty years of Vatican II and *Dominus Iesus*, it is time to redefine a new dynamic purpose of interfaith dialogue and religious peacebuilding, which involves moving beyond accumulating information, data, and facts about the other and dismissing myths about each other. Our attention should be on thinking about innovative approaches to dialogue between Muslims and Christians that will reach new levels of sensitivity through which we come to a conceptual and real understanding of the holy transcendental nature of each religious tradition.[24] A new sensitivity forces us to think, act, believe, and relate to ourselves in a fresh-spirited way that presses us to respond to whether what we really know of our faith tradition is possible without knowing the other religious tradition. Is it possible to assert complacently: "God wants everyone to be saved and reach full knowledge of the truth" (1 Tim. 2:4) when we do not even appreciate how others also love God? While Catholicism and Islam are unique traditions, each religion must explore how it shares patterns of theological reasoning in interreligious, comparative, dialogical, and confessional areas. No doubt, dichotomizing the specific codes of faith sets up barriers to dialogue, but an honest theological inquiry and reasoning will carry us over to a more profound knowledge of God. In this journey of mutual dialogue, where we come to know religious traditions other than our own, we grow intensely sensitive to the religious wisdom of our neighbors who seek the compassionate mercy of the divine.

Vatican II initiated Muslim–Christian dialogues that stressed understanding the essential meanings of each other's religious tenets and beliefs. Since then, participants in the dialogue have recognized the importance of cooperating in several religious and non-religious areas. As a result, the two communities have moved closer to each other by seeing what is involved in collaboration. One of the lessons learned from these past sixty years of dialogical collaboration is that the so-called other is not so independent from the broader us and that we are touched by another set of beliefs in many ways. We experience a realization that our neighbor's religious tradition not only challenges us to articulate our own faith in new terms and new contexts, but in this very process, it enriches our own religious understandings. For too long, we have lived alone as spiritual hermits only immersed in our religious traditions uniquely expressed in their own transcendental truths. This has given us a distinct cultural, ethnic, and religious identity on one level. Still, on another level, it has created barriers to recognizing each other's traditions as a valuable source of self-knowledge. Ultimately, some of our new understandings that point to the differences that separate us are potentially within the world of our religious convictions. Differentiations in how divine truths are expressed are often set out in terms of the failure of other religious traditions to answer specific theological questions. This activity of engagement, this notion of a real interfaith Muslim–Catholic dialogue, has revealed that the human face and human experience of the other are no longer left to the imagination. The other religious tradition has and can provide a greater understanding of my own tradition and its interconnectedness to other traditions. It is appropriate to take up the traditional Jesuit Catholic notion of theology as faith-seeking understanding because the endeavor of dialogue is truly about understanding the life of faith. Perhaps, if Muslim–Catholic realities are moving toward mutual enhancement and complementarity, redefining dialogue as praxis seeking understanding may be more accurate and not faith-seeking understanding.

An example of interfaith peacebuilding is renowned Catholic monk Thomas Merton, whose extensive dialogue work argued that the two greatest sins of interreligious dialogue were apologetics and syncretism. Within the interfaith dialogue, the first area is a matter of the participant's desire to identify common ground; the second is a matter of purpose and essential telos of interreligious dialogue.[25] Through honest interfaith dialogue, we are working on mutual interpenetration of each other's religious traditions, an ever-deepening spiral movement of mutual enrichment. The dialogical process does not imply a loss of the uniqueness of one's tradition. Instead, it proves that religious traditions consist of individuals interested in stretching their imaginations and striving for a world where faith traditions act to unite common communities. This honest dialogue calls for a movement to and from each other's traditions that requires serious reflection and a critical understanding of our holiness. It cuts through the talk of eschatological exclusivism and the private ownership of divine truths by forcing us to create a dialectical vocabulary for dialogue. The combination of dialectical dialogue and the dialogical movement of self-reflection compels us to be courageous in new ways of knowing and makes us think of dialogue as both spiritual and epistemological.[26] Religious peacebuilding participants need to comprehend that interreligious dialogue aims to reach a fundamental understanding between the different religious traditions, not to win over the other or that they are trying to agree on shared issues.

Dialogue seeking illumination may be another level of interfaith dialogue that has yet to be explored in interfaith relations or religious peacebuilding. While remaining faithful to our religious traditions and relating to one another as partners in the same global community, interfaith dialogue could bring illumination. Some of these questions point to one of Islam's distinguished philosophers and Sufi saints, Ali ibn Uthman al-Jullabi al-Hujwırı (d.1070), who wrote an influential treatise still used in some parts of the Islamic world entitled *Kashf al-Mahjub* ("Unveiling the Veiled"). In his instructional manual for disciples training in the spiritual path, al-Hujwiri wrote about specific techniques for achieving union with God; with the success of each inner practice, the Sufi removes one more of the veils that divide the believer from the Creator. He wrote: "Bowing oneself in prostration forces humility and the prostration of the head brings about self-knowledge, and the profession of faith is an intimate statement. The true and real salutation takes the place of detachment from the world and escapes from the problems of stations."[27] From this perspective, the dilemmas posed by interreligious dialogues on the exclusivity of the religion appear to establish worldly positions to make truth claims for one's tradition while disregarding the other as just another misguided religious entity in the world. However, since we have established a desire to achieve an honest, sincere interreligious dialogue, we must move beyond the stagnant stations of faith pronouncements toward the mutual humble process of removing the veils that divide us from each other and God.

'ULAMA IN DIALOGUE

"A faith-seeking understanding" framework for interreligious dialogue could position 'ulama and religious leaders to engage them robustly and meaningfully. However, attempting to engage 'ulama in dialogue or peacebuilding activities should begin with assessing their understanding and purpose of dialogue and exploring their assumptions, principles, and values. Religious participants may believe peacebuilding is a foreign venture by not taking a basic inventory of their knowledge of this field. The sooner the audience is engaged in theories of achieving peace and why religious leaders need to be active in this field, the more willingly they will be engaged and take ownership of the process. Interestingly, I've observed numerous Western programs where the trainers underestimated or miscalculated the religious participants' ability to converse on specific cognitive, social, political, or religious obstacles to peacebuilding.

Peacebuilding interfaith dialogues and conferences are built on the idea that knowledge and skills are a tool to nurture an awareness of conflict and peace indicators. Workshops for religious leaders usually discuss open communication, interfaith dialogue, religious pluralism, tolerating other opinions, and the basics of conflict resolution. However, these workshops rarely enhance their skills in interfaith dialogue. Instead, peace trainers use basic themes and never move forward with more sophisticated skills. For example, understanding when a conflict arises involves a knowledge-based approach but applying specific skills to de-escalate conflict to ensure stability is as, if not more, important. To develop practical peacebuilding skills for Muslim religious leaders, expanding more practical models to implement peacebuilding work is necessary. Religious leaders in conflict zones require skills that allow them to evaluate, negotiate, and mediate conflict effectively and know how to change their situation structurally. In many peacebuilding workshops where I was asked to support as a trainer, to my surprise it was common for the organizers to ask 'ulama to make structural and institutional changes during the time of conflict. This illustrates an ignorance of what religious leaders can do in their communities and reflects an insensitivity to what the 'ulama and religious leaders can do within their own communities. In essence, if there were ways to reframe peacebuilding programs for Muslim religious leaders, 'ulama would benefit immensely from capacity building of practical skills to transform their conflict in sustainable ways. Critical skills in negotiating through a conflict are essential tools in peacebuilding, but equally important is whether religious leaders can apply the skills in challenging conflict scenarios.

Across twenty-five Muslim-majority countries and with over fifteen years of working with *'ulama* and Muslim religious leaders in peacebuilding, I've realized they must have a combination of knowledge of the field and the essential tools for organizational structure. On the one hand, peacebuilding programs emphasize that the *'ulama* understand the principles of conflict prevention, mediation, negotiations, conflict management, conflict resolution, and post-conflict stability, and their effectiveness depends on their ability to function in that conflict. Second, they must understand the fundamentals of organizational management.

Those *'ulama* without basic organizational management skills cannot even operate successfully in interfaith, intrafaith, and intercultural dialogues. They are part of institutions that have not educated these skills, and more often, *'ulama* are dependent on staff to perform the most straightforward duties. For example, they have no exposure to strategic planning or developing long-term goals and plans that exemplify the organization's mission and vision. There is a need to support *'ulama* in basic problem-solving skills that identify issues, analyze them, and develop practical solutions to problems. Belonging to a historical institution with internal hierarchies and a central body overseeing their activities, *'ulama* have no or little exposure to fostering teamwork, collaboration, team cohesion, or team building processes. These organizational management skills are essential to making informed decisions by analyzing various factors and predicting potential outcomes. *'Ulama*—imams and religious scholars alike—are trained in understanding legal boundaries and the repercussions of violating these laws; however, the issue is not textual or scriptural mastery; it is if they have strong verbal and written communication skills to convey rational, logical ideas as leaders of the community. And, as leaders of the community with religious authority, there is the fundamental issue of inspiring others and motivating their colleagues and community toward a common goal. I've witnessed astonishing imams and *'ulama* capable of fostering teamwork, being open to change, and adjusting their strategies and tactics to evolving circumstances. This involves examining creative ways to attract parties to a reinvigorated process of negotiation and designing exercises to balance power between and within parties. Strategic planning for conflict intervention and conflict transformation involves advanced training in conflict intervention, management, and transformation; examining sources of leverage, the role of third-party mediators, use of neutral space, and international resources for support; and establishing guarantees, assurances, and specific conditions with a timetable. They can adapt and adjust to rapidly changing problems while managing their emotions and the emotions of others as effective leaders. But these skillful religious leaders are few.

Religious leaders and *'ulama* are aware of the various dynamics at play in their societies and illustrate their insights on these issues. Peacebuilding programs need to reinforce the point of individual accountability in peacebuilding as often as possible since religious participants belong to hierarchical and non-individualistic structures. Some dialogue forums promote establishing community-based peace councils as a creative and brilliant response to political stagnation. New community-level mechanisms can handle a range of disputes, improve communication between conflicting parties, and increase access for the disenfranchised. Community peace councils create a new generation of leaders to prevent and transform conflicts, and these leaders feel empowered to act, as they are no longer waiting for a response from a distant dysfunctional government institution.

'Ulama with fixed values tied to belief systems are accused of being unable to accept, recognize, and welcome perspectives or other differences. This narrow perspective within the peacebuilding field is that the more individuals are involved or cherish their own traditions, the more difficult it is for them to participate in dialogues. Muslim religious leaders do not have an issue with dialogues. The critical problem for them is how dialogues are structured without consultation, creating imagined insults, threats, and the thinking that the other is trying to control them. Religious leaders and scholars of the Islamic faith have participated in local, regional, and international dialogue conferences to improve mutual recognition and acceptance. Despite opposition or challenges from within, *'ulama* understand and appreciate the process of inquiry and learning from the other. They know that gatherings with other religious leaders are a moment of public recognition, an important symbol of peace and cooperation. Several international Islamic religious dialogue organizations operate on a global scale and are committed to dialogue. Within these meetings, Muslim scholars and leaders meet with other religious leaders from different traditions and those without faith traditions. Andrea Bartoli and Charles Gardner wrote about these global dialogue conferences consisting of cultural dialogues, relational dialogues, public dialogues, spiritual dialogues, and encounters with people from very different settings and life experiences. Individual religious leaders feel they are representing their tradition, feel they need to represent the most authentic views of that tradition, and feel the need to defend criticism, but there is a moment when these individuals find

their personal engagement with others to be an opening of self-discovery.[28] If the forum for dialogue permits creativity and flexibility, then the dialogues reflect the space created. Suppose the forum for dialogue is structured with endless lectures and pronouncements that diminish the space and process to learn from others. In that case, it's common to see Muslim religious leaders disengaged within the mutual dialogues.

Intrafaith and interfaith dialogues for the *'ulama* and Muslim religious leaders encourage them to see others in themselves and to create a deeper connection with others. The dialogues foster an appreciation of human life as inherently diverse with limitless potential and dignity of all people. Bringing religious scholars to express their respect for human dignity, understand, and communicate with others on this basis is to transform division into collaboration. Courageous dialogue does not contest or limit one's faith or authority in the religious tradition; instead, it provides a nurturing of a culture of dialogue that will increase the values of peace and peacebuilding.

NOTES

1. Abd Allah ibn 'Umar ibn al-Baydawi, *Anwar al-tanzil wa-asrar al-ta'wil alma'ruf bi-Tafsir al-Baydawi* (Beirut: Dar Ihya al-Turath al-Arabi, 1998).

2. Ibid., pg. 339.

3. Abu Jafar Muhammad ibn Jarir al-Tabari, *Jami al-bayan 'an ta'wil ay al-Qur'an*, edited by Muhmud Muhammad Shakir and Ahmad Muhammad Shakir, sixteen volumes (Cairo: Dar al-Ma'arif, 1969).

4. *khalifa* (pl. *khala'if*) literally means vicegerent or viceroy as in 2:28–30: "I am setting in the earth a viceroy" and in *sura* 38:26: "David, behold, We have appointed you a viceroy." *khalifa* is used a total of nine times (2:28–30, 6:165, 7:67–69, 7:72–74, 10:14–15, 10:73–74, 27:62, 35:39, and 38:25–26). However, the verbal noun *khalafa* "to succeed or to be a successor" occurs six times and the passive participle *istakhalfa* "to make one a successor" as in *sura* ̂ 24:54 "even as He made those who were before them successors" occurs six times.

5. For documents related to Roman Catholic interreligious dialogue, see An Encyclical by John Paul II, *Redemptoris Missio* (1990) and *Dialogue and Proclamation* (1991), produced jointly by the Pontifical Council for Inter-Religious Dialogue and the Congregation for the Evangelization of Peoples; and the Pontifical International Commission for Theologians' *Christianity and the Religions* (1996).

6. *Nostra Aetate*, pp. 1–2.

7. *Dignitatis Humanae*, pg. 2.

8. See F. Provost, "From Tolerance to Spiritual Emulation: An Analysis of Official Texts in Muslim–Christian Dialogue," in R. Rousseau (ed.), *Christianity and Islam* (Scranton, PA Ridge Row Press, 1985); F. Gioia (ed.), *Interreligious Dialogue: the Official Teachings of the Catholic Church, 1963–1965* (Boston, MA: Pauline Books and Media, 1997).

9. *Nostra Aetate*, pg. 3.

10. The reference "to forget the past" implies that Christians and Muslims are not being asked to neglect historical animosities and conflicts but rather to proceed to a fresh moment of forgiveness and reconciliation so that actual healing would occur in both communities. See F. Schuon, *Christianity/Islam: Essays on Esoteric Ecumenism*, translated by G. Polit (Bloomington, IN: World Wisdom Books, 1985).

11. See, 1 John 4:8, and *Nostra Aetate*, pg. 5.

12. M. Fitzgerald, "Twenty-five Years of Dialogue: The Pontifical Council for Interreligious Dialogue," *Islamochristiana*, 1989, 15.

13. Pontifical Council for Inter-Religious Dialogue, *Recognize the Spiritual Bonds which Unite Us: 16 Years of Christian–Muslim Dialogue* (Vatican City: Pontifical Council for Interreligious Dialogue, 1994), pg. 23.

14. *Dominus Iesus*, § 18.

15. Ibid., § 20.

16. Ibid., § 21.

17. Ibid.

18. For more, see Muhammad Ahmad al-Sarakhsı, *Sharh kitab al-siyar al-kabır* (Beirut: Dar al-Kutub al-Ilmiyya, 1997), 4:186; Abu al-Walıd Ibn Rushd, *Bidayat al-mujtahid wa-nihayat al-muqtasid* (Cairo: Dar al-Fikr, n.d.), 1:279; and Abu al-Hasan al-Marghinanı, *Al-hidayat sharh al-bidaya* (Cairo, n.d.).

19. For a Common Word document, see https://www.acommonword.com/.

20. For a complete list of Christian responses to the Common Word, see https://www.acommonword.com/christian-responses/.

21. *Dominus Iesus*, § 22.

22. For similar verses, see also Qur'an 2:111–13, 7:169, 3:24, and 4:53–55.

23. See E. Schumacher, *A Guide for the Perplexed* (New York: Harper & Row, 1976); A. Olson and L. Rouner, *Transcendence and the Sacred* (South Bend, IN: University of Notre Dame Press, 1981).

24. Useful texts to consider to innovative interfaith dialogue: Marianne Moyaert (ed.), *Ritual Participation and Interreligious Dialogue* (New York: Bloomsbury, 2015); Paul Hedges (ed.), *Contemporary Muslim-Christian Encounters: Developments, Diversity and Dialogues* (New York: Bloomsbury, 2017); Vladimir Latinovic and Gerard Mannion (eds.), *Religious Dialogue in the Twenty-First Century* (New York: Palgrave Macmillan, 2015); S. H. Nasr, "Islamic–Christian Dialogue: Problems and Obstacles to be Pondered and Overcome," *Muslim World*, 88 (1998): 218–37.

25. See Merton's letter to Kilian McDonnell in Patrick Hart, sel and ed., *The School of Charity: The Letters of Thomas Merton on Religious Renewal and Spiritual Direction* (New York: Farrer, Straus, Giroux, 1990), pg. 189; Thomas Merton, *Dancing in the Water of Life: Seeking Peace in the Hermitage*, Journals of Thomas Merton 5, edited by Robert E. Daggy (San Francisco, CA: HarperSanFrancisco, 1997), pg. 22.

26. See Francis Clooney, "The Interreligious Dimension of Reasoning about God's Existence," *International Journal for Philosophy of Religion*, 1999, 46: 1–16; and *idem*, "The Study of Non-Christian Religions in the Post-Vatican II Roman Catholic Church," *Journal of Ecumenical Studies*, 1991, 28: 482–94.

27. Ali ibn Uthman al-Jullabi al-Hujwiri, *Kashf al-Mahjub*, Urdu translation by Ulama Fazal ud-Din Gohar (Lahore: Zia al-Qur'an Publishers, 1989), pg. 410.

28. Andrea Bartoli and Charles Gardner, "Dialogue and Mutual Recognition: The Practice of Interreligious Encounters," in Peter Stearns, *Peacebuilding Through Dialogue* (Fairfax, VA: George Mason University Press, 2018), pp. 187–202.

Section III

PEACEBUILDING WITH PEACE EDUCATION

Chapter Eight

Peace Education

Within the peace and conflict studies field, a peace education curriculum comprises vital concepts of nonviolent debate, critical thinking skills, and fostering the appreciation of diverse perspectives; these concepts are interconnected to peace education. A relatively young field of fifty-five years, peace education was primarily established by Johan Galtung, one of the founders of the International Peace Research Association. Galtung was adamant that peace needs to be learned, practiced, and reinforced in the educational system. For peace to be practiced, it must be taught at the earliest school levels for society members to comprehend and practice peace.

Distinguishing between negative peace and positive peace, Galtung asserted that positive peace is a condition where nonviolence, ecological sustainability, and social justice remove the causes of violence. A positive peace curriculum requires both the adoption of a set of beliefs by individuals and the presence of social institutions that provide for an equitable distribution of resources and peaceful resolution of conflicts. Soon afterward, Quaker mathematician Lewis Richardson established precedents for tracking and statistically assessing data for comparative research. By the mid-1970s, the establishment of organizations such as the Stockholm Institute of Peace Research and the Peace Research Institute of Oslo, the outstanding work of Galtung, Ruth Sivard's publications on military expenditures, and Peter Wallensteen and Karin Axell's works on the costs of the Cold War illustrated how little resources were allocated toward peace education.

By the Cold War in the 1980s, conflict researchers were acutely concerned about the threat of nuclear war, interstate conflict, and human rights atrocities. In this milieu, three essential books were produced to set the stage for peace education: *Education for Peace by a Norwegian*,

Comprehensive Peace Education, and *Peace Education*.[1] Specifically, Brocke-Utne pointed out the devastation of militarism, war, and how male violence affects females and argued that feminism is the starting point for effective disarmament. Reardon argued that the core values of schooling should be care, concern, and commitment, and ultimately, the fundamental concepts of peace education are about planetary stewardship, inculcating humane relationships and global citizenship. As an educator, Harris proposed the importance of peace education to understand violent behavior, develop intercultural understanding, provide for future orientation, teach peace as a process, promote a concept of peace accompanied by social justice, stimulate respect for life, and end violence. During this time, Harris was a proponent of a cutting-edge pedagogy based on cooperative learning, democratic community, moral sensitivity, and critical thinking skills. This peace education pedagogy focused on student-teacher learning relationships as the cornerstone for reimagining peace.

Concurrently, the field of peace education was influenced by environmental educators who advocated that students and faculty become aware of the ecological crisis, the necessity to provide tools to create environmental sustainability, and the ability to use resources in a renewable way.[2] These educators argued that the deepest foundations for peaceful existence are rooted in environmental health and that ignoring global trends in violence against the environment is detrimental to the planet.[3]

A pivotal meeting in November 1995 where 186 members of the Twenty-Eighth General Conference of the UN Educational, Scientific and Cultural Organization stated that the major challenge at the end of the twentieth century was transitioning from a culture of war and violence to a culture of peace. In November 1998, the UN General Assembly adopted a resolution for the culture of peace and another declaring the year 2000 the International Year for the Culture of Peace and the years 2001 to 2010 to be the "International Decade for a Culture of Peace and Nonviolence for the Children of the World." From this mandate, the UN Educational, Scientific and Cultural Organization developed eight action areas necessary to transition from a culture of war to peace.[4] The first is "Culture of Peace through Education," which states that nonviolent peace education is the only way to fight violence. However, as global organizations and educators focused on the nonviolent curriculum as the primary foundation to rid violence, peace education took different shapes as educators attempted to address other forms of violence in various social, cultural, political, and developmental contexts. In countries of the Global South, where the problems of poverty and underdevelopment cause violence, this form of education has often been referred to as "development education," where students are taught about different strategies to address problems of structural violence. But, in Ireland, peace education was referred to as "Education for Mutual Understanding," as Catholic and Protestant peace educators try to use educational strategies to undo centuries of enmity.[5]

Peace educators adhering to the human rights tradition are guided by the Universal Declaration of Human Rights, which provides a statement of values to be pursued to achieve economic, social, and political justice. Some human rights peace scholars believe these rights are derived from concepts of natural law, a higher set of universally applicable laws superseding governmental laws. Narrowly construed, the study of human rights is the study of treaties, UN institutions, and domestic and international courts, and addressing rights against discrimination based upon gender, disability, sexual orientation, minority status, and tribal or religious affiliation.

The theoretical, pedagogical, conceptual, and practical parameters of developing a nonviolent dialogue, debate strategies, and critical thinking peace studies curriculum in Muslim-majority communities vary on region, ethnicity, economics, social and political stability, the complex bureaucracy of the education ministries, and related other internal and external factors. This chapter uses evidence from a case examining Libya, addresses essential concepts of a peace studies curriculum, and analyzes the challenges in implementing a peace education curriculum in the classroom.

PURPOSE AND ESSENTIAL CONCEPTS

Researchers and educators of peace studies agree that children need formal training in dealing with the multidimensions and multimanifestations of violence. One of the critical assumptions in instituting a peace studies curriculum is to ensure teachers have extensive training in peace and conflict studies. Hence, they create innovative curricula and extracurricular activities for students to value nonviolent dialogues. The assumption starts with the knowledge base of teachers, who should be able to design, implement, and develop the students' ability to debate with reason. Therefore, using logic will open the mind to embrace pluralism inside and outside the classroom. However, theoretical assumptions usually neglect the reality of the professional and personal lives of the teachers, as well as the institutional support needed for professional development.

Also, within this assumption is that K–12 and secondary school teachers have the ability, access to funding, unconditional support of their administration, and approval of the education ministries from the local province and capital. There needs to be a manager directing the many pieces of the puzzle to be aligned before any peace studies curriculum can be implemented. These peacebuilding activities address the issues of anger management, social perspective taking, decision-making, social problem solving, peer negotiation, conflict management, valuing diversity, social resistance skills, active listening, and effective communication to express oneself clearly and succinctly. This education provides students with peacemaking skills that they can use to manage their interpersonal and intrapersonal conflicts. The following are the essential concepts extrapolated from peace education research studies that aim to cultivate broader diversity perspectives, foster nonviolent dialogue, debates, and critical thinking skills, appreciate pluralism, and foster peaceful communities.

Alternative to Violence

Peace educators are interested in violence prevention to get students to understand that anger is a normal emotion that can be handled and managed positively. Peace educators must deal with violence with alternative narratives or reframing techniques to counter hostile behaviors learned in the broader culture. Students are taught anger management techniques that help students avoid fights in school and resolve angry disputes in their immediate lives. Acknowledging that images of violence in the mass media are disturbing and intriguing to young people and that many of their students live in violent homes, it is essential first to recognize various forms of violence. Once identified, students are taught to develop practical skills in mitigating and transforming anger as a necessary component of peace education.

Violence Prevention

While it may appear self-evident for a peace education curriculum to stress violence prevention, this theme was meant to provide young people with alternatives to physical fighting. The first curriculum provided students with information about violence and homicide. Teaching students to be peacemakers involves creating a cooperative context that encourages disputants to reach mutually acceptable compromises and not dominate each other—preventing conflict skills involves recognizing incompatible goals and rising tensions within discussions and role-playing specific methods in de-escalating discord with dialogue. Students role-play anti-bullying or victim activities to practice ways to assert themselves to avoid becoming subjugated.

Community Development

This theme aimed to build peaceful communities by promoting an active democratic citizenry interested in equitably sharing the world's resources. This form of peace education teaches peacebuilding strategies that use nonviolence to improve human communities and an appreciation of the diversity in the schools and broader community.[6] This section of a peace curriculum stressed how to determine the needs of the community leaders and more general community members and understand the factors that tilt toward a positive or negative reception of ideas by the community.

Virtues of Peace

Peace and conflict studies educators promote a pedagogy that models open, peaceful, democratic classroom practices. They desire that through education, people can develop specific thoughts and dispositions leading to soft, nonviolent behavior. Essential virtues and dispositions include kindness, tolerance, cooperation, and caring for oneself and others. While developing such virtues is integral to peace education, it is not the complete picture. As much as the problems of violence lie in the individuals and communities suffering from violent conflict, peace educators advocate for people to understand how to live these virtues, considering broader social forces and institutions that must be addressed. For example, violence in schools mirrors the violence in society. It is exacerbated by the availability of guns, urban and rural poverty, drug and alcohol abuse, and domestic abuse—the teaching here is that a person can live with the virtues of peace despite institutional violence.

Dialogue

Peace educators use the teaching and learning processes as an act of peacebuilding where students are engaged in modeling and practicing dialogue as an active process allowing for the development and recognition of individuals' voices.[7] Dialogue refers to both a quality of relationship arising, however

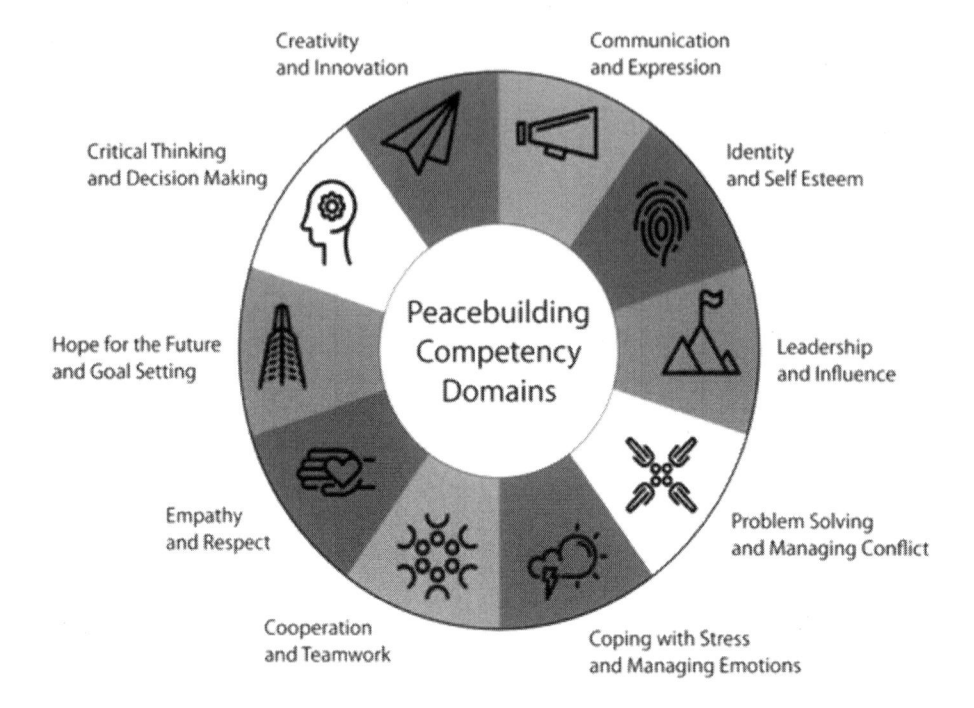

Peacebuilding Competency Domains:
- Creativity and Innovation
- Communication and Expression
- Identity and Self Esteem
- Leadership and Influence
- Problem Solving and Managing Conflict
- Coping with Stress and Managing Emotions
- Cooperation and Teamwork
- Empathy and Respect
- Hope for the Future and Goal Setting
- Critical Thinking and Decision Making

briefly, between two or more people and a way of thinking about human affairs highlighting their dialogic qualities.[8] Based on this definition, dialogue refers to any processes (e.g., speaking, writing, and body language) allowing for creating and sharing meaning. As an active process, students understand the complexities of dialogue, how it can be misappropriated, and how to use dialogue strategically as an asset in appreciating and valuing others.

Culture of Peace

Educators in peace education believe they are not only changing the framework of thinking of violence and nonviolence. Instead, they are engaged in a broader mission of changing cultures to transform them to be peaceful. This means working toward securing a future against further violations of human rights, whether based on ethnicity, religion, gender, sexual orientation, or disability. Through a wide variety of perspectives, including the sociological, historical, philosophical, psychological, cultural, religious, political, anthropological, gender, and linguistic perspectives, this approach examines how people are empowered to forge a new vision of the future.

Critical Thinking

Peace educators assert that critical thinking skills are one of the goals of their curriculum. While definitions vary, fostering necessary thinking skills is the process of applying reasoned and disciplined thinking to a subject and is different from the formal transmission of facts and ideas. It involves examining assumptions, identifying hidden values, and assessing evidence to reach conclusions. It is an essential element of the peacebuilding curriculum as it helps people understand and resist propaganda or political manipulation.[9]

Integrating Critical Thinking

Peace and conflict researchers agree that critical thinking is needed across disciplines, which teachers in various fields can teach. It is understood that critical thinking cannot be an abstract philosophical exercise. Instead, it needs to be integrated into all curricula.[10] This approach holds that critical thinking can be attained by learning its techniques and tools, and students should apply it to reading, writing, and debating. Education specialists insist that data reveals that students will thrive as thoughtful citizens concerned with the public interest or as global citizens interested in peacebuilding in local communities.

Examining History

Peace educators assert that students must critically examine, evaluate, and assess their national and global histories. They pose questions: Who are the authors of history? How was the history recorded? Is the information based on reliable sources? Was history recorded with a broad or narrow framework? These sets of questions are meant to help students understand how we are shaped by history based on writers who were commissioned by monarchs or imperial powers to analyze and record war, battles, victories, land acquisitions, imperial power, and the struggle between global forces.

Identity

Peace studies scholars are sensitive to the issue of identity and how identity was developed. Since identity formation is directly interconnected with the nation's process of forming citizens with proud national identities, scholars know this could be challenging political power. Nevertheless, a peace studies curriculum examines the construction of gender, federal, tribal, intellectual, class, and even religious and non-religious identity. In the classroom, students are pressed to recognize how values and beliefs are formed. The postmodern era positions individuals in a globalized community where lines of exclusion and inclusion are blurred, and individuals have more access to information to make decisions than before. What do we do with this information? How do we use data to reinforce our identity? Are identities becoming more informed with access to technology and global information? Can students recognize when individuals and communities self-examine their identities to choose some areas over another?

The Art of Debate

Within the peace curriculum, discussions, debate, and critical thinking are taught as a social learning process, a process that only improves knowledge and skills if only practiced often. Disagreements are encouraged under a thoroughly designed curriculum, accepting that bias and hatred will not be permitted as arguments. Identifying assumptions of peers, the teachers, and texts are examined; then assumptions are reviewed for accuracy and context; nonviolent debates and discussions uncover evidence, test generalizations, and identify if examples of evidence are supportive. Students learn various debate methods and critical thinking through teachers modeling them and repeated practice.

The curriculum supports students in thinking about their commitments, their place in the community, and, ultimately, their place in the world. Raising more complex concepts and problems for students leads to a sophisticated level of self-examination and reflection. The challenges arise when students refuse these academic exercises because of the psychological trauma of others' fears. Other critics have suggested that being critical brings out "negative" attitudes toward authority and the world order. The field has a "hyper-criticism" element built into the theory and practice of peace education. Critics claim that this "hyper-critical" focus creates anxiety in students to mistrust information, miscalculate messages in personal relationships, and stay on a trajectory of misreading the world.

These themes illustrate fundamental themes, approaches, and questions to implement a curriculum for debate, dialogue, and critical thinking skills to be used inside and outside the school. The curriculum stresses the importance of teachers modeling debate, discussion, and critical thinking to demonstrate how it is done effectively and ensure the sequencing is understood correctly. Identifying alternative perspectives, self-examination, checking assumptions, and taking informed actions fosters a shared understanding of critical thinking and helps students in various disciplines.

A peace education curriculum is designed to bring forth more analytical thinking and to rely less on rote learning or memorization of the materials. Analytical thinking seeks to identify objectives and reflect upon the questions, the information being used, and the underlying assumptions being taken for granted. Students are guided to rethink the concepts driving the thinking, reasoning, logic, and supporting evidence. The curriculum is purposely designed to pedagogically bring the teacher and student together to collaboratively assess intellectual parameters such as clarity, accuracy, depth, breadth, fairness, significance, and relevance. In each category, students are asked to examine the pieces of the puzzle and whether these pieces have a logical and reasonable place in the context.

Furthermore, teachers perform another noble act of the student's educational development in teaching peace studies. In addition to the content, students learn academic honesty by developing intellectual traits such as integrity, humility, perseverance, empathy, impartiality, comprehension, and an intelligent sense of justice. These are not just traits or learned qualities from a meaningful curriculum. Instead, the teacher is purposefully instilling an intellectual code of ethics accompanied by learning and seeking meaning.

THE PEACE EDUCATION TEXTBOOK BENEFITS

The peace education textbook consists of modules that empower students and teachers to critically rethink, reframe, and reapproach the nature of learning special topics, such as dialogue, debate, and critical thinking, which can be applied to their lives outside the classroom.

Peace education learning modules are designed to make the student an active learner in their education journey and to check assumptions, theories, and frameworks generally accepted on the surface.

The nature of learning changes as the student engages in role-playing, simulations, and practical exercises to build empathy, broaden one's appreciation of diversity, and appreciate pluralistic perspectives.

Peace education supports and promotes civics, human rights, equality, respect for divergent ideas, appreciation of the environment, and inculcates peacebuilding and conflict resolution skills.

APPROACHES TO BASELINE ASSESSMENTS

How exactly do peace educators and researchers evaluate the effectiveness of the curriculum? This is an area contested within the field of scholars because there is a question as to what it means to be effective. To be effective means measuring the impact on a student's life or their quality of life within the community. Is effectiveness measuring learning and retention of the peace materials, or is it the teacher's ability to find new innovative ways for students to understand critical thinking skills? Are the data collected compared to previous data points? The field of peace education and conflict resolution studies has numerous baseline assessment frameworks available for teachers to use. However, given the multidisciplinary nature of the peace education discipline, there is no single consensus on using one framework. Some researchers agree that a questionnaire for a focus group of participants (i.e., knowledge, attitudes, and practices surveys) provides insights into a focused group's core thinking and competencies. Many believe that a diagnostic assessment is the preferred system because it is a barometer for how much preloaded information a group has about a topic. In this baseline approach, the word diagnosis is defined as an analysis of the nature or condition of a situation. Diagnostic assessment tests help researchers understand how much the group knows specific quantitative and qualitative information. This information helps in lesson planning, learning objectives, and identifying areas needing more or less time.[11]

In teaching peace education programs, researchers used another baseline assessment approach called the formative assessment, which helped researchers understand the participants' learning. At the same time, they teach and provide them with information to adjust their teaching strategies accordingly. It is the understanding that meaningful learning involves processing new facts and concepts, adjusting assumptions, and drawing nuanced conclusions. As researchers Thomas Romberg and Thomas Carpenter noted: "Current research indicates that acquired knowledge is not simply a collection of concepts and procedural skills filed in long-term memory. Rather, the knowledge is structured by individuals in meaningful ways, which grow and change over time."[12]

The formative assessments support the researchers in tracking the student's knowledge, which is growing, evolving, and changing in real time. Some examples of criteria used in the formative assessment process include:

Portfolios
Regular journal entries
Group projects
Progress reports
Class discussions
Short and regular quizzes
Presentations by students
Mini-group presentations
Group debates
Group simulations and scenario exercises[13]

LIBYA AS A CASE STUDY

The case study of Libya was conducted with the coordination of the UN Development Programme based in Libya, the European Union, the International Rescue Committee, and the North African Policy Initiative based in Tunisia. After the fall of Colonel Muammar Ghaddafi's regime in 2011, Libya has been experiencing ongoing social, economic, and political chaos. There are various factions of Libyan armed groups based on tribal affiliations vying for power and control of the country. The fractured politics has led to civil conflict as various armed militias struggle for control. With minimal political resolution on the horizon, Libya's governance and state institutions are extremely weak and poorly managed due to the lack of stable authority. The absence of a working government, pervasive corruption, and weakened institutions have contributed to law and order problems for the government to provide essential services.

Libyans suffered from poor or absent essential services, a weak education system, and difficult socio-economic conditions. All these factors lead to deteriorating living conditions. The political divisions that have been plaguing Libya since 2011 and the weakness of the state institutions have led to an administrative atomization: local state and non-state authorities are left alone to govern the country at the local level without sufficient resources from the national government, and often with minimal human and infrastructural capacity.[14]

The international community saw an increased presence of violent extremist groups by the end of 2011, including al-Qaeda in the Islamic Maghreb, which also established its presence in Libya with the support of local partners. By 2014, the Islamic State of Iraq and the Levant and affiliated groups also officially established their presence, notably in Derna and Sirte. There was an influx of returning Libyan veterans who had fought in Syria and Iraq with the Battar Brigade.[15] By this time, counterterrorism scholars identified Libya as an environment for developing violent extremist groups due to the lack of a central government, weak political institutions, porous borders, multiple direct military interventions, and indirect meddling by regional and global powers.[16] There was a failed judicial system, widespread availability of weapons, a flourishing illicit economy, and increasing hardship for the local population.[17] According to a report by the International Centre for the Study of Radicalisation, Libya was among the top five countries sending foreign fighters to Syria by December 2013.[18] Post-revolution Libya became the site of the "fourth largest mobilization of foreign fighters in modern jihadist history," with the highest number of recruits from Tunisia.[19] In addition, the Islamic State increased its recruitment efforts by targeting sub-Saharan African migrants in Libya.[20]

Since Libyan youth were recruited by violent extremist organizations, militias, and criminal gangs, there was a concerted international effort to create an alternative environment with peace and conflict studies. With armed militias and violent extremists operating with impunity, contributing to rapid lawlessness and civil conflict, the Libyan peace and conflict education program was designed to bring stability and prevent the influence of violent extremist propaganda from spreading among the disillusioned youth. As most Libyan youths were not already engaged in gainful, purposive livelihoods, there was the concern that their lack of purpose—combined with financial incentives from violent extremist organizations—would culminate in a wave of Libyan youth joining violent extremist groups.

The research conducted by peace educators in the past thirty-five years suggests that students who enrolled in a vigorous curriculum on peace studies, conflict resolution, strategic peacebuilding, and mediation successfully navigated various interpersonal, communal, national, and international conflicts. These students used analytical skills and frameworks in their professional and personal lives and became leaders in their fields to design and execute solutions for their respective organizations and communities. A peace education curriculum for Libya used current methodological and interdisciplinary assessment practices to evaluate its effectiveness. An initial assessment methodology needs primary objectives to learn from the participants: to take stock of their knowledge of the peace studies field and compare this knowledge dataset with known information afterward.

Peace Education 199

The objectives of a baseline assessment survey were:

- To become more informed about focus group participants' understanding, recognition, and comprehension of basic terms and concepts of violence, peace, nonviolent debates, and debating strategies. We wanted to know which areas or words, cognitive constructs, or imagery were used to define stability and critical thinking skills.
- To be better informed on how participants understand the significance of nonviolent debates and peace education with clarity, accuracy, depth, and reasoning, and can we measure the relevance of peace education to their lives.
- To understand to what extent participants are interested in developing their interests in peace, violence, tolerance, peace education, and fostering pluralistic communities.

The researchers used a multiple choice questionnaire with essential concepts from the peace education field to inventory participants' knowledge of diverse perspectives, nonviolent dialogue, debates, pluralism, and critical thinking skills. The team was conscious of tainting the data results, so an independent monitoring team was utilized to ensure that data was timely, harmonized across implementers, and fed directly into learning and adaptive management opportunities. Through regular meetings, tasks were organized and a schedule was created for regular, systemic monitoring and monitoring support services.

Table 8.1. **Data Collection and Monitoring Process**

Data Collection Method	When Useful
Key Interviews and Focus Group Discussions	Gauge perceptions, understand dynamics, identify critical actors or unanticipated outcomes, and delve into nuanced descriptions of how something happened
Secondary Data	Cost-effectively track established measures, triangulation
Surveys	Aggregate and compare data across a broad range of actors
Score Cards	Rapid, participatory feedback for accountability regarding peace studies
Participatory Appraisal	A participatory approach to incorporate community input and feedback into new activity design as well as for feedback during implementation
Electronic Data Capture	Boost response rates under challenging environments, track fluctuating indicators, and include crowdsourcing of information when appropriate
Direct Observation, Photos, and Videos	Verify implementation processes/procedures and triangulate other data
Online Collection	Cost-effectively capture data from more isolated populations

In addition, the team of research evaluators used the framework "outcome mapping," which has several different benefits as a monitoring, evaluation, and learning approach, including unpacking other uses of information at different levels of program implementation, helping to develop a common language around progress markers, and going beyond monitoring to inform adaptation throughout the performance. It helped the baseline assessment to be rapid and flexible monitoring.

THE INDICATORS

The first indicator of this baseline assessment was focused on seven geographical areas defined by the UN Development Programme: Murzuq, Kufra, Ghat, Sebha, Bani Walid, Zuwara, and Misrata. The UN Development Programme team project lead predetermined these seven municipalities as sensitive focus areas where the organization determined that these vulnerable cities needed immediate support. The second indicator consists of participants of the project (i.e., students, teachers, and administrators from schools from the seven municipalities). We organized three focus groups with students, teachers, and administrators, consisting of twelve individuals in each focus group from each of the seven municipalities.

The third indicator was the schools themselves. We focused on the baseline assessment on three levels of schools: ten to fourteen years of age (middle school), fifteen to nineteen years of age (high school), and twenty to twenty-four years of age (university level). The baseline assessment focused on three school levels in seven municipalities or twenty-one schools. The fourth indicator focused on the Ministry of Education and members from local governing councils to assess the variety of their services and their assessment of the importance of implementing a peace education curriculum and curriculum reform. The team interviewed five members from the Federal Ministry of Education based in Tripoli to receive their input on the survey. In addition, the team interviewed three senior ministers from the local governance of the seven municipalities or a total of twenty-eight members.

Managing the information generated by peace education monitoring, evaluation, and learning approach involves several types of knowledge. The team needed to properly work with teacher and student assessments, evaluations, analytics of monitoring data, interviews, and surveys from teachers, administrators, and the offices of the provincial and central ministries. By instituting a data hub for information management and sharing, the team had easy access to understand the data, which aided in creating action plans for the different peace education teams. The Libyan Peace Education team developed and maintained a roster of sectoral stakeholders to consider for thematic consultations while implementing the learning agenda—whether through learning event deep dives, research key participants, or other consultative efforts.

RESULTS

After reviewing all the surveys, evaluations, videos, and information gathered from the data hub, the team learned about attitudes toward introducing peace education and conflict resolution courses to schools. The results demonstrated that when a peace curriculum was introduced to public or private schools, these courses did not always have the full support of the administrators; the teachers felt they did not have the appropriate support needed to develop the curriculum; the teachers felt their participation in the peace curriculum program would benefit their teaching career; at the same time, teachers expressed that they received insulting sarcasm and intimidating conversations from colleagues and administrators because they participated in a UN peace studies program.

However, the survey results demonstrated that the student participants favorably desired more peace education courses but without the heavy hand of local and national education ministries overseeing the curriculum. In Libya, with the support of the education ministries, the international community could proceed with the peace curriculum. Student evaluation forms expressed favorable peace topics on gender justice, conflict mitigation, values, ethics assessment, and different approaches to dialogue. There was a desire to have more exercises on understanding interfaith and Islamic approaches to peacebuilding and identifying strategies for interpersonal peacebuilding. Evaluators and Libyan nongovernmental organizations (NGOs) expressed frustrations regarding the lack of follow-up courses or extracurricular activities and that the program should have considered expanding the peace studies program to include the broader student community. Unfortunately, the curriculum did not have the funding or organization capacity to be outside the classroom to include the involvement of parents, community leaders, civil society organizations, or cultivating partnerships with the private sector.

However, with extensive interviews and surveys of participants, students, teachers, and administrators involved in the Libyan peace and conflict studies pilot program, there was reason for concern about the program's efficacy, which had short-term funding cycles. In private discussions, some teachers expressed that they knew there were no funds allocated for the following academic years, so school administrators needed to have a plan to move forward with peace studies with international financial support or technical guidance. Others who discontinued teaching the peace studies curriculum expressed the weak, tenuous partnerships between the education ministries, administrators, teachers, students, and implementing Libyan NGOs.

Surveys revealed that student participants were dissatisfied with the peace education curriculum's structure and planning and wished for more consultation with local Libyan educators. They expressed that there needed to be a better match between what the students expected in courses versus what teachers were trained to teach. There were explicit comments stating that the teachers were not appropriately trained in the specific topics, could not delve deeper into the desired subjects, or the teachers did not express the desire to follow-up on the students' requests. Student participants expressed profound views on the nature of peace education; if peace was to be taught in the classroom, the actual instructors should model the curriculum inside and outside. This repeated criticism of teachers and instructors for not embodying the "peaceful teacher" is a critical cultural marker that was not considered in the design stages of the program. After reviewing the evaluations, researchers realized that the content and delivery of the peace curriculum were more stressed than the actual reputation of and quality of teachers in the schools.

Survey results expressed that several teachers resented the criticisms by administrators and local Libyan NGO partners because they felt they "outperformed and -excelled" in the conflict conditions they were teaching and within the timeline of the peace studies curriculum. In other evaluations, local Libyan NGO partners criticized the international donor community for their expectations of regular reporting, financial disclosures, and being held responsible for the capacity of teachers and education administrators.

REFLECTIONS ON THE PEACE STUDIES INITIATIVE

Attempting to bring educational reforms to a conflict zone like Libya is challenging because of the numerous political, social, economic, tribal, and educational bureaucratic systems. The UN program to bring sustainable peace and security through peace education programs had several stakeholders to collaborate with and receive approval from, and financial and capacity limitations. The need to have a dozen or more stakeholders for consensus on a peace studies program posed a wide range of challenges because each stakeholder used their influence to benefit from other agendas. If the United Nations needed the Ministry of Education's approval and support, the ministry's staff would determine how to direct this initiative to support their specific tribe or province. This parochial bias was again applied within the schools; administrators selected favored or teachers connected with the Ministry of Education. It became even more complicated when the teachers picked specific students they favored or felt could excel in the peace studies program because of their family relationships. We learned that administrators and teachers collaborated on selecting students for the peace studies program based on their ability, family connections, tribal affiliation, and whether their respective families held a high status in the community. Against these biases ingrained in this structure of the education system and within the community, the peace studies program was used as an instrument to benefit an inner group.

In reflecting upon the peace studies curriculum initiative, there are noticeable institutional, bureaucratic, societal, and donor agency fault lines. On the one hand, the United Nations can only operate in a country when they are invited by the host country, which means that the UN personnel and broader team are working within constraints beyond the conflict itself. The United Nations has internal bureaucratic challenges that are beyond the scope of this study, but it is worth mentioning that an international organization that believes it is working "on the ground" with local participants brings its own bureaucratic structure to the field, which at times is detrimental to the progress of any the host of the country. The international organization brings a cultural organization management system that lacks cohesiveness, clear lines of decision-making, communication gaps, internal office politics by staff members trying to undermine the other's programs, and essential ability to manage communications with all the stakeholders. The problems within the organization are not kept a secret, and the host country bureaucrats and ministries exploit these fractures to advance their interests.

Since the United Nations needs to operate with several ministries at the same time, that have their institutional ruptures too, the education initiative would have benefited if it started in the beginning with a working relationship with local civil society organizations, school administrators, and teachers to create a workstream in establishing ties, managing professional expectations, and ultimately, listening to their concerns about education and the problems of implementing reforms. A preliminary assessment with these stakeholders would have informed the organizers of the critical issues involved while understanding which stakeholders are aligned with parochial biases.

Wilfred Dolfsma's work on a strategy of change, *Institutions, Communication, and Values*, illustrates the need for institutions to understand their impact on economic behavior, incentives, and predicting outcomes.[21] The communications and relationships of these organizations, in turn, influence the development and maintenance of local relationships by the values they promote. Therefore, a thorough internal analysis of the interplay between institutions, communication, and values is necessary to understand if any education initiative will succeed. Dolfsma's research on bringing innovative change with social networks requires mastering how relationships and interactions among individuals and organizations—including knowledge of various constraints with tribal, cultural, religious, class, and bureaucratic values—can open an exchange of new innovative ideas.

Upon reflecting on the peace education initiative, it is clear that despite the negative evaluations, there was a positive change in the teachers and students as the team saw an astonishing capacity for growth learning and having a growth mindset. It is a positive reminder that there is a hunger to learn new ideas in conflict zones, opening a journey of self-improvement, a profound sense of fulfillment, and this transformation of well-being. The training of their teachers revealed their enthusiasm to receive professional development in new areas outside of their specialty because teachers received very little professional attention from the Ministry of Education. The teachers expressed immense gratitude for their newfound optimism and determination to use their learned pedagogical skills in the classroom. Not found in this program's evaluation forms was visible motivation to pursue growth and change in the schools and the communities. Both teachers and students expressed a spirit of resilience to overcome obstacles, learn from their experiences, and create a new shared vision for a harmonious culture and society. This optimism to transcend adversity gave them new energy to confront uncomfortable truths within their communities and embrace new thinking to deal with the uncertainty of the future. It is a reminder, even to the pessimists working within organizations with exceptional bureaucracies, to consider the capacity for change and growth while fostering positive change in people and how the relationships we forge can transform lives and communities.

It is not clear if the specific content topics of the peace education curriculum were the source for positive change, if it was an external international organization reaching out to a neglected group stuck in conflict, or if it was the meaningful experiences that supported new ideas and perspectives. It may be a combination of all these interactions; however, the education program contributed to one specific area that is often neglected or ignored in conflict studies: it contributed to the human need for repetitive positive dialogue and positive reinforcement of ideas to replace self-doubt, negativity, and the culture of pessimism. The team of peace education experts and trainers, in cooperation with the support of the UN team, injected a self-awareness in the program to recognize strengths, weaknesses, moments of lapse in judgment, evaluating setbacks, and reminder that despite these daily problems we bring dignity, integrity, patience, gratitude, and an openness to learn more for personal growth. In the broader scheme of this education project to bring sustainable peace, among the participants and organizers, there were genuine conversations about embracing change instead of resisting it because new obstacles challenge our opportunities to learn and evolve. In a culture immersed with conflict, sectarianism, tribal rivalries, civil war, and uncertainties with social services like water, electricity, and supplies, one cannot expect instant gratification or change, but there were powerful times of human connection among the stakeholders.

NOTES

1. Ian Harris, "Types of Peace Education," in A. Raviv, L. Oppenheimer, and D. Bar-Tal (eds.), *How Children Understand War and Peace* (San Francisco: Jossey-Bass, 1999), pp. 299–318.

2. Frank Verhagen, "The Earth Community School (ECS) Model of Secondary Education: Contributing to Sustainable Societies and Thriving Civilizations," *Social Alternatives: Peace Education for a New Century*, 2002, 21, no. 1: 17.

3. C. A. Bowers, *Education, Cultural Myths, and the Ecological Crisis* (Albany, NY: SUNY Press, 1993); Stephen Sterling and John Huckle, *Education for Sustainability* (London: Routledge Press, 2014).

4. David Adams, "Toward a Global Movement for a Culture of Peace," *Peace and Conflict: Journal of Peace Psychology*, 2000, 6, no. 3: 259–66.

5. John Whyte, *Interpreting Northern Ireland* (Oxford: Clarendon Press, 1991); Smith and Robinson, *Education for Mutual Understanding: Perceptions and Policy* (University of Ulster: Centre for the Study of Conflict, 1992).

6. M. Pilisuk, "The Hidden Structure of Contemporary Violence," *Peace and Conflict: Journal of Peace Psychology*, 4 (1008): 197–216.

7. Herbert Khol, *Growing Minds: On Becoming a Teacher* (New York: HarperCollins Publishers, 1984).

8. Kenneth Cissna and Rob Anderson, "Theorizing about Dialogic Moments: The Buber-Rogers Position and Postmodern Themes" in *Communication Theory*, 8 (1998): 63–104.

9. Susan Fountain, *Peace Education in UNICEF*, United Nations Working Paper, June 1999.

10. S. Brookfield, *Teaching for Critical Thinking: Tools and Techniques to Help Students Question Their Assumptions* (San Francisco, CA: Jossey-Bass, 2012).

11. A. Smith and A. Robinson, *Education for Mutual Understanding: Perceptions and Policy* (Coleraine, University of Ulster Centre for the Study of Conflict, 1992).

12. Thomas Romberg and Thomas Carpenter (eds.), *An Integration of Research* (New York: Routledge Press, 1993).

13. Elizabeth Cohen, *Designing Groupwork Strategies for the Heterogeneous Classroom*, second edition (New York: Teachers College Press, 1994), pg. 44.

14. J.R. Allen, H. Amr, D.L. Byman, V. Felbab-Brown, et al., "Empowered Decentralization: A City-based strategy for rebuilding Libya," The Brookings Institution, Washington, DC, 2019.

15. Frederic Wehrey and A. Alrababa'h, "Rising Out of Chaos: The Islamic State in Libya," *Syria in Crisis. Carnegie Endowment for International Peace*, 2015, 5.

16. Monty G. Marshall and Benjamin R. Cole, "State Fragility Index and Matrix," Center for Systemic Peace, Vienna, VA, 2014.

17. M. Cherif Bassiouni (ed.), *Libya: From Repression to Revolution: A Record of Armed Conflict and International Law Violations, 2011–2013* (Leiden, Martinus Nijhoff Publishers, 2013).

18. Aaron Y. Zelin, "ICSR Insight: Up to 11,000 Foreign Fighters in Syria; Steep Rise among Western Europeans," International Centre for the Study of Radicalisation, King's College London, December 17, 2013.

19. Aaron Zelin, "The Others: Foreign Fighters in Libya," The Washington Institute for Near East Policy, 2018.

20. Multiple author interviews with migrants in Libya, 2018–2020; Inga Kristina Trauthig, "The Current Situation in Libya and Its Implications for the Terrorism Threat in Europe," paper presented at the third conference of the European Counter Terrorism Centre Advisory Network on Terrorism and Propaganda. Europol's headquarters in The Hague, April 9–10, 2019; Jean-Louis Romanet Perroux, "Human Trafficking, Smuggling and Governance in Libya: Implications for Stability and Programming," USAID and NORC at the University of Chicago, May 2020.

21. Wilfred Dolfsma, *Institutions, Communication and Values* (London: Palgrave Macmillan, 2009).

Chapter Nine

Islamic Peace Education

PEACE EDUCATION IN MUSLIM-MAJORITY COMMUNITIES

The debate on Islamic religious schools and public schools in Muslim societies since September 11, 2001, focused mainly on ideological indoctrination for terrorist organizations or religious institutions incapable of dealing with modernity.[1] American policymakers, in particular, repetitively linked *jihad* movements or the support of *jihad* with *madrasa* networks in Pakistan, Afghanistan, Yemen, Somalia, and Indonesia.[2] Similarly, policymakers and policy decision-makers in Europe were confronting the combination of a rising tide of right-wing Islamophobic public discourse on immigrant assimilation, the building of mosques, the Danish cartoons, the wearing of the veil or *niqab* (fully covered dress for women), the two wars in Iraq and Afghanistan, and the clash between secularism and Islamic traditions. This intense debate in Europe undoubtedly contributed to anti-Western sentiments by European Muslims in France, Denmark, Germany, the United Kingdom, Switzerland, Italy, and other places, which complicated the objective examination of peacebuilding and conflict resolution practices within Muslim communities.

There has been abundant attention given to the role of Islamic boarding schools or seminaries (*madrasas* or *pesantrens*) in contributing to militancy and the growth of radical movements. Analysts claim that the governments of Pakistan, Indonesia, Egypt, Yemen, and other states have failed to provide adequate education in which students should be nurtured to be responsible civil society members; instead, analysts assert that seminary graduates have been insulated from diverse views and are educated in to be intolerant of others. Unfortunately, these critiques immaturely linked traditional Islamic seminary curriculum to fostering narrow worldview views, and neither provides space for creativity and intellectual curiosity nor to develop citizenship skills. These scholars contest that the seminary curriculum uses pre-modern texts to teach traditional Islam, and these outdated, non-inclusive texts have little or no relevance to contemporary issues or values. Furthermore, the religious studies curriculum offered in Islamic seminaries does not prepare graduates for practical employment opportunities.[3] According to the critiques, these factors contributed to intolerant views of others, extremist interpretations of their religious tradition, a greater propensity toward violent behavior and attitudes, a self-centered view of the world, and, ultimately, a ripe milieu for anti-social behavior and radicalism.

Other critics, such as Diego Gambetta, Steffan Hertog, Klaus Seitz, and Tariq Rahman, pointed out that public education in conflict zones in predominantly Muslim societies in the Middle East, South Asia, and Southeast Asia centers around technical and vocational training of medicine or engineering programs which intellectually promote the world as either black and white terms or good versus evil. That is to say that mechanical or vocational education does not provide critical thinking or cultivate self-inquiry appreciation. Corrine Graff questions the hypothesis of connecting essential thinking skills to vocational studies because the attention needs to be on the institutions that function within weak fragile states, on the socio-economic conditions of poverty, the perennial problem of poor development, and abysmal investment within the educational sector in these countries.[4]

Studies on Islamic religious institutions by Peter Bergen, Swati Pandey, Mumtaz Ahmed, Saleem Ali, Christine Fair, Tariq Rahman, and Rebecca Winthrop examined several dimensions of curriculum content, socio-economic background of students, teacher training and pedagogy, the social environment of religious schools, statistics of the number of enrolled students and registered institutions, and ineffective feeble efforts by different governments to reform these institutions.[5] The tenuous link between *madrasa* or *pesantren* education to radical thinking or extremist behavior has been documented to demonstrate that Islamic seminary education in itself does not teach intolerance, radical interpretations, or promote hatred against any tradition or civilization; rather, a tiny percentage of seminaries are exploited by jihadist groups to spread radical ideas.[6] However, despite the preponderance of the evidence, there is enormous scholarly and policy attention to linking Islamic religious education and public education in Muslim societies to greater intolerance, and the "closing of the Muslim mind" is more connected to reforming education that would model the Western experience.[7]

PEACE EDUCATION IN MUSLIM COMMUNITIES

One of the many arguments proposes that education systems can either intensify or conversely mitigate constituents' grievances against their government, which can make citizens turn toward supporting dissent or rebellion movements. On the other hand, educational specialists assert that education systems can positively shape the students' worldviews and formidably instill a constructive identity where individual and collective responsibilities are shared. Considering weak autocratic states where the education sector is hardly supported and is the most easily manipulated with unaccredited private schools, education specialists argue that teaching peace citizenship knowledge and skills and civic education for students to resolve conflicts and understand nonviolent alternatives to mitigate conflict peacefully is vital.[8]

However, there is a missing dimension in the literature studying Islamic seminaries and educational systems in Muslim-majority societies, which is how educational nongovernmental organizations (NGOs) and Muslim educational specialists and practitioners have been making immense achievements in developing pluralistic values and global citizenship textbooks through the discipline of peace education. Despite the criticism of security studies policymakers and the inability of weak states to invest critically in the education sectors, there has been an increased number of peacebuilding education academic programs and NGOs dedicated to this field. Muslim NGOs in Pakistan, Afghanistan, Bangladesh, Indonesia, Egypt, Turkey, Malaysia, Kenya, and many other countries have developed educational modules, manuals, and teacher training guides to support primary, secondary, and tertiary peace education. NGO education specialists have immense classroom experience, yet they recognize that ministry of education bureaucracy prohibits them from introducing a peace education curriculum easily. Instead, NGOs have successfully offered teacher training and supplemental courses on peace education and conflict resolution.

One exemplary model is an Afghan NGO, the Sanyaee Development Organization (SDO), which has been dedicated to peacebuilding education for over thirty-three years in Afghanistan, especially during the turbulent period of the war against the Soviet Union and the Afghan civil war years in the 1990s. In SDO's peace education manual, it states:

> Peace education is an essential component of quality basic education. Peace education is the process of promoting the knowledge, skills, attitudes, and values needed to bring about behavior changes that will enable children, youth, and adults to prevent conflict and violence, both overt and structural; to resolve conflict peacefully, and to create the conditions conducive to peace, whether at an intrapersonal, interpersonal, intergroup, national or international level.[9]

Muslim educational NGOs, like SDO, frame peace education curricula as not limited to the thinking that the absence of violence, referred to as "negative peace," but within the framework of positive peace to explain social, economic, and political injustice.[10] Amid war and severe violence against civil society members, Muslim NGOs have creatively devised manuals to train students and teachers in peacebuilding, and concepts and practices are developed from a local context. For example, in describing the issues of poverty, discrimination, unequal access to economic opportunities, and gender violence, SDO's peace manual situating this section entitled "Structural Violence in Society" reinforces the values of Islamic/Afghan ethics against these injustices.[11] In training teachers and students in peacebuilding, organizations like SDO are conscious of the fact that each member of their society is a victim of war, and no one in the past thirty years has been left untouched or unharmed by the effects of war. They believe in their peace education workshops to train teachers and students in preventing and resolving all forms of conflict and violence, whether structural or from the interpersonal level to the societal and global level.

In the neighboring country of Pakistan, the leading NGO on peace education is the Peace Education and Development (PEAD) Foundation directed by education expert Sameena Imtiaz.[12] PEAD's mission statement is "to educate and empower people by promoting values of peace, nonviolent conflict management, and inculcating democratic values for responsible citizenry."[13] PEAD's activities are in underdeveloped areas in Pakistan, such as the rural areas of Punjab, Khyber Pakhtunkhwa, and the Federal Administered Tribal Areas, where peacebuilding peace projects focus on youth mobilization, health education, active citizenship, and using arts and the theatre to raise awareness of the danger of ethnic bias and stereotypes. PEAD's three-volume training manual for primary to secondary levels is entitled *Living Together: Value Education Manual*, written in collaboration with the National Commission for Inter-Religious Dialogue and Ecumenism and Caritas Germany. These three volumes include exceptional peacebuilding educational materials because the framing of evaluating and confronting bigotry, prejudice, racism, sexism, violence, provincial thinking, and abuse is not used in other schoolbooks. The first volume explicitly helps the school define its core values and how the teachers reinforce them to students. The manual provides examples of values such as justice, respect for others, cooperation, forgiveness, and trust.[14] These values are not passing themes during the day; the PEAD manual stresses the importance of integrating these core values in each subject, extracurricular activities, role-playing exercises, breakout sessions, and artistic and poetic competitions. PEAD's emphasis on values-based peace education is effective because for behavior, attitudes, and thought to be grounded on respect and tolerance of others, there must be shared values of loving oneself. Stressing the development of ethics as the foundation of peace education is not universally shared by public education experts; however, in Muslim societies where the public space values humility and the demonstration of ethics, this approach is making an impact.

Another captivating Pakistani education NGO is the Insan Foundation Trust. Insan means humanity in Urdu. Based in Lahore and Rawalpindi, Insan uses peace education training workshops to achieve the following goals: (1) support political and economic viability of gender equality and women's empowerment with the involvement of women, communities, and government and nongovernment institutions; (2) mobilize, educate, and train youth groups and communities to ensure healthy development of deprived youth and children; and (3) enable stakeholders to protect, support, and promote democratic values, negotiated peace, and sustainable development.[15] Insan's peacebuilding curricula incorporate specific curricula for classroom instruction and sports to cultivate intracultural and intraethnic harmony. The organization builds upon local cultural customs of poetry competitions, artistic campaigns, and street theatre performances to enhance the message of peacebuilding.[16]

In Bangladesh, two highly regarded peacebuilding NGOs using peace education are Ain O Salish Kendra[17] and the Bangladesh Inter-Religious Council for Peace and Justice.[18] The peacebuilding curriculum of these NGOs emphasizes the topics of human rights, interreligious harmony, and identifying ways to deal with cultural and social biases. Specific programs educate Bangladeshi religious leaders about illegal forced marriages, human trafficking, gender bias, and ecological stewardship. The organization developed tailored peace education curricula using scripture and religious texts for the imams and seminary students. Their manuals and educational pamphlets are designed to be instructional and practical, and their work is often recognized because of their ability to be very much involved with grassroots issues. The advocacy work by Ain O Salish Kendra has earned them recognition from community leaders and politicians who turn to them as regular resources for peacebuilding interventions.

PROBLEMS IN PEACE EDUCATION

The strong emphasis on transforming the behavior and attitudes of students and teachers is widely mentioned as a central objective of the peacebuilding process. Scholars like Boyden and Ryder consider it the primary underlying assumption of peace education: "That conflicts are the result of learned attitudes and learned behavior and that it is possible to change both attitudes and behavior through educational interventions."[19] One strong criticism against peace education is the generally poor evaluation record and weak mechanisms to evaluate progress or regression. Due to limited funding and staff resources, Muslim NGO educators, like SDO, PEAD, and Insan, have had to rely on their trained teachers to use surveys, student interviews, and progress reports to track their projects.

Other significant areas of concern facing peace education NGOs in Muslim societies may not be unique to their local cultural geographies. Across the spectrum, NGOs using peace education manuals face the problem of program design, program implementation, balancing the use of Western models versus indigenous models of peacebuilding, and the sustainability of their respective programs. Many struggling NGOs, Muslim or non-Muslim, are supported by international donors whose timetable and concept of a project may not be entirely in line with the local NGO. Very often, donors are project-driven, that is, engaged only on a short-term basis, and not invested in a long-term strategic program plan; this restricts the long-term impact of the NGO to communities, institutions, students, and ultimately the aim of cultivating a culture of peace. As funding for short-term projects is exhausted, there are typical problems with few technical resources to evaluate the impact of the peace activities.[20]

Another critical area facing Muslim NGOs in implementing peace education programs is the actual content of curriculum development and the specific resource material for teacher training. Being acutely aware of the biases in the textbooks and teachers, Muslim educational NGOs incorporate pluralistic stories, non-Islamic holidays, and religious rituals of non-Islamic traditions, emphasizing women's roles in each section. However, regardless of the specific content of the peace education materials, the courses are still offered as supplemental courses and need to be integrated into the more extensive curriculum. Leading Muslim educational NGO administrators have expressed that teacher training is ineffective unless the entire curriculum is overhauled and a new curriculum is redesigned so that peace education is the central experience for students. NGO evaluations demonstrated that trained teachers in peace education attempt to incorporate what they learn but face resistance from their superiors or patronizing criticism from other non-trained teachers. Despite these experiences, trained teachers felt they made an impact in improving teacher-student relationships and in areas of developing an interest in topics that were uncommon in the curriculum. Trained teachers also stated in interviews that with fundamental changes in the curriculum to integrate peace education, students would fully internalize their newly acquired information about peace education. In addition to these issues, both Muslim educational NGOs and trained teachers complained about how few refresher courses or professional development seminars were available. Public and private schools do not have merit-based advancement structures whereby teachers would enroll in professional development courses to receive a credit or certificate, which would count toward their seniority. Educational NGOs are the primary source for public and private school teachers to learn, adopt, and integrate new subjects such as human rights, peace education, and civic citizenship courses.

Another structural problem for Muslim educational NGOs was the inability to monitor and evaluate their work accurately and statistically measure their impact in the classroom and on the broader culture of the institutions. With support from external donors, NGO administrators surveyed student and teacher experiences and practices and used the recommendations by trained teachers; however, this monitoring and evaluation component needed a more accurate, quantifiable analysis. Whether one can attribute inconsistent monitoring and evaluation reporting to the skills of NGO staff members, the accuracy of reporting by teachers and students, or the lack of funds allocated to the NGO to conduct these procedures correctly, regrettably, evaluating projects is usually rare. It is unusual for donors and NGOs to design a project in consultation with teachers or educational administrators. This would be helpful because the process would already have integrated monitoring and evaluation, finance management, and organization coordination into the project's lifecycle. The monitoring and evaluation process should be systematized, and a pre-test and post-test should be made mandatory for reviewing the impact of peace education.[21]

ISLAMIC PEACE EDUCATION

Islamic peace education is a relatively new field within peace education. There are three reasons for the development of Islamic peace education: first, in the past twelve years, Muslim educational NGOs have primarily worked with public and private English-medium schools and neglected Islamic seminaries. Some have argued that this neglect is an example of the NGOs' secular bias and the NGOs' secular nature or the design of the peace education textbooks. The second reason for Islamic peace education is that political elites in Muslim societies and the West viewed Islamic seminary graduates as incapable of integrating their knowledge and skills into society. Their religious education did not prepare them for other vocational skills nor provide critical thinking skills needed for significant employment sectors. According to this perspective, seminary graduates were vulnerable to unchecked radical ideologies and easily exploited by jihadist movements. The third reason is the internal demand for peace education by leading seminaries who felt international and domestic pressure to diversify their curriculum. This internal demand by Islamic seminaries is not solely due to political pressure but a realization by seminary education boards that the current static curriculum would not allow their students to be competitive in a world of globalization.

There is no single approach to Islamic peace education; at this time, approximately fifteen manuals, modules, or textbooks are being used in nineteen different Muslim countries or predominant Muslim communities. Each is constructed for local cultural, religious, and sociological needs. In a 2011 and 2017 international meeting of Islam Peace Educators in Mindanao, Philippines, forty-five participants shared their experiences developing, designing, and implementing an Islamic peace education textbook or teacher manual.[22] The teachers, activists, NGO members, education specialists, scholars, and education policymakers discussed various models and approaches to Islamic peace education employed by Muslim seminary teachers in the classroom. Acutely aware of the widespread perception of Islam as a religion of violence and intolerance, this workshop brought together Muslim educators to focus strategically on effectively using peace education curricula to promote peacebuilding activities from an Islamic perspective.[23]

Examining several Islamic peace education modules, textbooks, and manuals, there are several trends of approaches and methodologies in these texts. First, these texts establish the philosophical, scriptural, theological, and ethical principles of peacebuilding by the Prophet Muhammad, his companions, and his family as the primary source of Islamic peacebuilding. Second, the spiritual and temporal dimensions of these actors serve as an educational model to retrieve, re-embody, and re-enact these customs of peacebuilding; it is not merely an academic exercise. Third, peace is not viewed as an absence of conflict, nor restricted to Western notions of structural violence, nor is the understanding limited to the legal definitions by Muslim jurists; instead, the texts make an explicit connection between Islamic peace and metaphysics, cosmology, politics, and culture. Fourth, texts situated the theology of peace with the culture of inner and outer peace. Fifth, citations from scripture; *hadiths* (sayings of the Prophet Muhammad); eminent theologians; philosophers; and Sufi saints like al-Ghazali, Ibn-Arabi, Jafar as-Sadiq, Abu Hafs 'Umar al-Suhrawardi, or Maulana Rumi were all integrated into the text as a way to illuminate their contributions to peacebuilding. Sixth, the stress on Islamic values of nonviolence, compassion, collaboration, justice, forgiveness, self-sacrifice, and ethics of service were placed within a religious peacebuilding framework. Seventh, specific historical events during the time of the Prophet Muhammad, such as the Constitution of Medina or the Hudaybiyyah Agreement or the peaceful return to Mecca in 630, are highlighted and analyzed extensively as practical peacebuilding events. And, eighth, the texts analyze factors leading to conflict, solutions to violence, understanding violence, and its connection to being a devout Muslim.[24]

The Islamic peace education texts stressed the practice of dialogue, discussions, and role-playing—often found in private English-medium elite schools. All of the Islamic peace textbooks had included or involved local Muslim religious scholars (*'ulama*) as either contributors to the peace textbook or as consultants to the project. In all cases, the Muslim NGOs approached local Muslim religious scholars and leaders in the community to involve them in the project, as well as receive their endorsements in teaching peace education from an Islamic perspective. In countries with Sunni and Shi'ite communities, the Muslim NGO sought a representative from each sect to be represented in the development and implementation of the program. Muslim NGO representatives spoke positively about their experiences of including *'ulama* as partners in the peace education project. They were even praised for their ability to translate complex theological, philosophical, and metaphysical concepts of human-divine vertical relationships to personal issues such as anger management, effective communication, and paying attention to equality for all living creatures.

One of the areas Muslim peace educators found challenging in *madrasas* or *pesantrens* was issues of pedagogy in the classroom. Most Islamic seminaries are hierarchical, where the teacher is viewed as the final authority over the material and other parts of the student's life. Islamic peace education training focused on retraining teachers as mentors and not as tyrannical authorities with a rod in hand. Simulations, role-playing, and sharing of personal experience were used to support seminary teachers in the basics of peace education. There were teacher training courses in bias awareness and understanding how human beings inherit prejudices from family, tradition, community, language, culture, literature, and other sources. There was particular emphasis on increasing teacher-student relationships and shifting the culture to be more favorable toward the needs of students. Seminary teachers could not have accepted these trainings if the manuals and workshops were not based on Islamic texts and tradition. Trainers needed legitimate Islamic seminary certificates or education to be accepted by the seminary teachers. There were many cases where the trainers were Western trained in peacebuilding or had little knowledge of the *madrasa* or *pesantren* culture, which caused greater suspicion among seminary staff and students.

Qari Haneef Muhammad Jalandhari, president of Khairul Madaris in Multan and the executive director of the Deobandi Sunni *madrasa* system in Pakistan, which consists of approximately fifteen thousand *madrasas* or one million seminary students, expressed the implementation of an Islamic peacebuilding program within his institutions where all administrators, teachers, staff, and students would take these courses. My interviews with Muhammad Jalandhari, his senior staff members, and teachers from the four provinces of Pakistan revealed that they were concerned that the trainers might understand the field of peacebuilding but needed an understanding of integrating the topic with the institution. In the Islamic peace education manuals examined, there was the standard approach of explaining how peace education tries to arouse the students' creativity in resolving conflict without violence so that conflict can have positive impacts on life.

Islamic peace education programs were developed from an Islamic-centric perspective and emphasized local values and local problems, as reflected in the socio-cultural reality of that society. For example, South Asian peace education materials for *madrasas* needed to consider the rich intellectual history of the madras institution and how the curriculum prepares young seminarians to be religious leaders. South Asian *madrasas*' core curriculum, Dars-e Nizami, was first standardized by Mulla Nizamuddin (c.1747) at Farangi Mahal, India. The Dars-e Nizami consists of approximately eighty books in twenty subject areas broadly divided into two areas of study: revealed knowledge and rational sciences. Revealed knowledge studies are the fundamental courses for all students, and they consist of reading, memorizing, and recognizing sentence structure of the Qur'an, Quranic exegesis, *hadith*, and jurisprudence. Advanced students will enter the 'Alim level and, afterward, university-level courses called takasuss. The courses offered within the rational sciences studies consist of Arabic, literature, grammar, Urdu language and grammar, prosody, rhetoric logic, philosophy, dialectical theology, the art of argumentation, spirituality, astronomy, mathematics, and homeopathic medicine.[25] Understanding that South Asia *madrasa* institutions are identified with a specific Islamic sect or school of thought (*madhab*) within the larger Sunni Hanafi or Shi'a school of thought is vital. For example, the primary Sunni sects are Deobandi, Barelwi, Ahl-e-Hadith, and Jama'at Islami, and for Shi'a Islam, there are Jafari and Ismaili schools. A federation for the school (*wafaq*) supervises the affiliated *madrasas* by ensuring that the curriculum is followed, academic standards are observed, examinations are administered, and appropriate diplomas are issued to students. The *wafaq* school board is tied to ensuring teachers are certified in their specialized field; for instance, if a particular school hires a teacher to teach the memorization of the Qur'an, then the teacher should possess the supporting documents that demonstrate evidence of mastery of the subject.

The major *madrasa* federations in Pakistan are Wafaqul-Madaris for Deobandi Sunnis, Tanzim-ul-Madaris for Barelwi Sunnis/Sufis, Wafaq-ul-Madaris-al-Salafi for Ahl-e-Hadith Sunnis, Wafaq-ul-Madaris for Jafria Shi'ism, and Rabitatul-Madaris-al-Islamia for the Jama'at Islami Sunnis. The Rabitatul-Madaris-al-Islamia is directly connected to the Jama'at Islami political party and its founder, Maulana Abul Ala Maududi (1903–1979), who felt a reformed *madrasa* institution was needed to train religious leaders in modern studies with a teaching methodology that uses self-criticism and reflection.[26] These sectarian divisions and their affiliation with educational federations contribute significantly to the success of any peace education program because the federations have the power to alter the curriculum and create incentives for their respective *madrasa* sect.[27]

In addition to Islamic sources for Islamic peace education, the textbooks contained the basics of conflict resolution, negotiation, mediation, facilitation, arbitration, and conflict management. There were specific chapters with student-based exercises on the following practical topics: counseling, psychology, family and psychological analysis, anger management, positive and negative approaches to peacebuilding, stages of violence, root causes of conflict, the complex practices of pluralism and dialogue, the rule of law, and understanding the impact of violence on children. The Urdu Pakistani Islamic Peace education textbook dedicated three chapters to "Inter-Personal Communication," whereby the following topics were examined: avoiding condescending body and oral language, avoiding pointing out the weaknesses of others, being an active listener, using self-critical thinking for personal development, examining one's positive and negative qualities, and using self-criticism for self-awareness. These chapters strongly advocated the need to have empathy and ways to understand the suffering of others, the appreciation of diversity, appreciation of aesthetics, ways to forgive oneself, and ways to express appreciation effectively.[28]

ISLAMIC PRINCIPLES IN PEACE EDUCATION

The Dars-e Nizami and advanced takassus curriculum heavily focus on linguistics, syntax, grammar, morphology, semantics, pragmatic semantics, and syntactic structure. The curricula examined for this study reviewed grammar courses studying classical Arabic, Quranic Arabic, Persian, and Urdu languages. Building upon this course work, the peace education manuals consisted of sections entitled Islamic approaches to dialectic argumentation or disputation (*al-jadal*), the art of disagreement (*al-ikhtilaf*), and the diversity of expressing discord, dissension (*al-shiqaq*). Lessons started with verses from the Qur'an 19:37, "But the sects differ among themselves" and Q: 11:118, "If your Lord has so willed, He could have made mankind one people: but they will not cease to dispute." There were sections examining why human beings are stubborn and why there is an innate need to be persistently correct in one's opinions. This section addresses why individuals or parties defend positions because they do not want to appear less knowledgeable or acknowledge their weak points. According to these lessons, disputation (*jadal*) in Islamic jurisprudence and philosophy has guidance on not being contentious to harm the other person or party. During disputes, the lesson firmly states that one cannot force others to take your position in disputes.

The lesson on *al-shiqaq* cites Q: 4:35, "If you fear that a breach (*shiqaq*) might occur between a [married] couple, appoint an arbiter from among his family and an arbiter from among her family; if they wish for peace, Allah will cause their reconciliation." The lesson continues to cite Q: 2:137, "And if others come to believe in the way you believe, they are indeed on the right path; and if they turn away, it is only they who are in the wrong or schism (*shiqaq*)." Interwoven in this topic is subject heading "*al- ikhtilaf fi'Islam*" or (The art of disagreement in Islam) where it expands first elaborates upon the etymology of the term *ikhtilaf*, its Arabic roots, and talks about taking a different position from another person either in opinion, utterance, or action and expanding on the idea that differences between people may begin with a difference of opinion over an issue which may lead to argument or be elevated to controversy, discord, and intense schisms. When this happens, the moment is no longer concerned with finding out the truth or clarifying the finer points of the opinion. In this moment, one needs to recognize that one is not involved in a dispute for a higher understanding but is involved in making the other person appear insignificant. In this case, practicing *ikhtilaf* requires being mindful of the direction of the dispute, recognizing the words being used and how they are being used to attack and not being used for wisdom.

THE PROPHET AS A MODEL

Examining the sources in Dars-e Nizami Islamic peace textbooks heavily relied upon the two primary sources: the Qur'an and *Sunnah* of the Prophet; quotes from the significant legal thinkers, commentators of the Qur'an; renowned commentators on the life of the Prophet; and quotations of the significant thinkers, philosophers, mystics, theologians, and scholars of jurisprudence.

Since Muslims attempt to emulate and embody the Prophet's model, his statements on deeds and actions inform ways to shape spiritual life. The following are sample statements used in the textbooks:

> The Companions of the Prophet (peace be upon him) used to be steadfast to the Islamic norms of behavior during argumentation. They discussed matters politely and amicably, avoiding using vile and insulting language. Each was prepared to listen attentively to the other.
>
> The Prophet (peace be upon him) used to point out to his Companions what was right and wrong regarding controversial questions. The Companions had mutual trust in the genuineness of each other's judgment. This approach guaranteed the preservation of mutual respect among fellow Muslims who had different opinions, but this method restrained bigotry and fanatic ideas.
>
> The Companions were entirely trained by the Prophet (peace be upon him), who taught them to be God-conscious and avoid personal agendas in pursuit of truth. When true statements were said, it did not matter who voiced it.

The lesson positions the Companions as the first generation of Muslims who memorized the Qur'an from the person who received the revelations, the Prophet. This personal intimate "training," "encounter," or "guidance"—words used in the textbook—positions the Companions at a higher level than any other generation of Muslims. The textbook suggests that it is critically important to follow in their footsteps since they are primary sources of the Prophet's legacy. For instance, on the issue of tolerance in accepting other faith traditions, Q: 22:17 states, "Those who believe (in the Qur'an), those who follow the Jewish scripture, the Sabians, the Christians, Magians, and Polytheists, God will judge between them on the day of Judgement: for God is the witness of all things." The lesson cites Q:5:69: "Those who believe in the Qur'an, and those who follow the Jewish (scripture), the Sabians, and the Christians, any who believe in God and the Last Day, and work righteousness, on them, shall be no fear, nor shall they grieve." The lesson is a continuity of several juridical sources that state the Qur'an recognizes the existing faith and non-faith traditions of the time of the Prophet, and it is this recognition of plural beliefs that affirm the necessity to live with others in light of different beliefs, traditions, and historical communities.

The lesson cites a famous Companion and second Caliph, Umar ibn Al-Khattab (c.586–644): "He heard from the Prophet (peace be upon him): The value of deeds is just in their underlying purposes. So, when you go towards something or do anything with worldly purposes, you are going towards what you have in heart, or when you go towards a woman with whatever purpose, you go towards your intentions." I asked the teacher of the Dars-e Nizami peace textbook if he could explain this section to me because the lesson did not elaborate on it. The teacher explained the saying of the Prophet: if we commit wrong deeds with good intentions, our acts are considered correct. Instead, the meaning is that even when we know what is good (from the Qur'an and *shari'a*), we must conduct those good things accompanied by true intention and purpose. The teacher explained that the lesson teaches students to be reminded that despite a lapse in our intentions and actions, we are never confident that God accepts our good deeds. It is in this light, according to the instructor, that students need to dedicate their entire spiritual, intellectual, and physical capacities and capabilities to be informed and make the most informed decision.

The fundamental Islamic principles of peacebuilding in the Islamic textbook include the pursuit of preserving the sacredness of human life; equality; the quest for peace (individual, interpersonal, communal, regional, and international); peacemaking via reason, knowledge, and understanding; creativity; forgiveness; proper deeds and actions; responsibility; patience; collaborative actions and solidarity; inclusivity; doing good; and living and seeking justice. Dars-e Nizami peacebuilding textbook's beginning chapter on understanding disputes and the art of disagreement realizes that the starting point is dialogue, which must always remain nonviolent in peace. The focus on recalling the scripture, the Prophet's life, commentators on the Qur'an, mystics, and a wide range of scholars is to bring attention to discipline, obedience, self-sacrifice, personal and social responsibility, and the belief in the oneness of humankind.

The chapter on "Responsibilities of Tolerance, Patience and Forgiveness" begins with Q:49:9, which states, "And if two factions among the believers should fight, then make a settlement between the two. But if one oppresses the other, fight against the one that oppresses until it returns to the ordinance of Allah. And if it returns, then make a settlement between them in justice and act justly. Indeed, Allah loves those who act justly. The believers are but brothers, so make a settlement between your brothers. And fear Allah that you may receive mercy." The chapter uses this Quranic citation to initiate the lesson on the nature of responsibility and proceeds to dissect the various etymological meanings in the three languages: *maswuwlia* in Arabic, *zamandari* in Urdu, and *masooliyat* in Persian. The instructor leads a lesson on individual and collective responsibilities in the three languages. To achieve these responsibilities, the individual must understand their duties of obedience and love for God. One is misdirected without this basic understanding of the self's direction toward the divine. The second part of the lesson continues with the individual's responsibility to live by the *shari'a* so one is in harmony with the broader community.

The Islamic peace education field is emerging rapidly because of the demands of Muslim institutions and the pressures by domestic and international forces to reform these institutions. While each Islamic peace education project in nineteen countries has its contextual narrative, in general, Muslim educators and Muslim educational NGOs are striving to teach students that the knowledge of peace can enhance their dignity and individuality, and this does not contradict Islamic tradition or values. The projects underscore the value of diversity and the common origins of the human family, adopt mutual understanding as a fundamental religious ethical value, and cultivate open-mindedness in all aspects of life. As much as the content of the textbooks and manuals is extremely important to understand, equally important is how Islamic peace education workshops are creating space to support teachers and students alike in the classroom, especially in deprived, underdeveloped, and neglected institutions. These workshops have brought added recognition and dignity to *madrasa* and *pesantren* teachers, who often need to gain the respect of the more significant profession. Islamic peace education textbooks and trained teachers promote intellectual curiosity within traditional and non-traditional boundaries while fostering personal responsibility, constructive critical thinking, positive attitudes toward all, appreciation of pluralism, and striving to be visionaries in creating peace in their societies.

NOTES

1. Religious schools in Muslim-majority communities are either called *deeni madrasa* in South Asia; *maktab* in Arabic countries; and *pesantren* in Indonesia.

2. Jessica Stern, "Pakistan's Jihad Culture" in *Foreign Affairs* 79, no. 6 (2000): 115–26; Christopher Candland, "Religious Education and Violence in Pakistan," in Charles H. Kennedy and Cynthis Botteron (eds.) *Pakistan 2005* (Oxford: Oxford University Press, 2006), pp. 230–55; Mathew Nelson, "Muslims, Markets, and the Meaning of a 'Good' Education in Pakistan," in *Asian Survey* 46, no. 5 (2006): 690–720; Marc Sageman, *Understanding Terror Networks* (Philadelphia: University of Pennsylvania Press, 2004).

3. Ali Saleem, *Islam and Education: Conflict and Conformity in Pakistan's Madrassahs* (Karachi: Oxford University Press, 2009); Jayshree Bajoria, "Pakistan's New Generation of

Terrorists. New York City," Council of Foreign Relations, May 2010; National Commision on Terrorist Attacks Upon the United States, *The 9/11 Commission Report* (Washington: 9/11 Commission, 2004), pp. 365–67; Tariq Rahman, *Denizens of Alien Worlds: A Study of Education, Inequality, and Polarization in Pakistan* (Karachi: Oxford University Press, 2005); and Zia Mian and Iftikhar Ahman, *Making Enemies, Creating Conflict: Pakistan's Crises of State and Society* (Lahore: Mashal Books, 1997).

4. Diego Gambetta and Steffen Hertog, *Engineers of Jihad: The Curious Connection between Violent Extremism and Education* (Princeton: Princeton University Press, 2007); Klaus Seitz, *Education and Conflict: The Role of Education in the Creation, Prevention, and Resolution of Societal Crises-Consequences for Development Cooperation* (Eschoborn: Deutsche Gesellschaft fur Technische Zusammenarbeit, 2004); Tariq Rahman, *Denizens of Alien Worlds* (Karachi: Oxford University Press, 2005); Corrine Graff, "Poverty, Development, and Violent Extremism in Weak States," in Susan Rice, Corinne Graff, and Carlos Pascual (eds.), *Confronting Poverty: Weak States and U.S. National Security* (Washington, DC: Brookings Institution Press, 2010).

5. Peter Bergen and Swati Pandey, "The Madrassa Scapegoat," in *The Washington Quarterly* 29, no. 2 (2006): 117–25; Tariq Rahman, *Denizens of Alien Worlds*, 2005; Ali Saleem, *Islam and Education: Conflict and Conformity in Pakistan's Madrassahs* (Karachi: Oxford University Press, 2009); and Rebecca Winthrop and Corrine Graff, "Beyond Madrasa: Assessing the Links Between Education and Militancy in Pakistan" (Washington, DC: Brookings Institution, 2010).

6. Tahir Andrabi, Jishnu Das, Asim Ijaz Khwaja, and Tristan Zajonc, "Madrassa Metrics: The Statistics and Rhetoric of Religious Enrollment in Pakistan," Unpublished paper, 2008.

7. Robert Reilly, *The Closing of the Muslim Mind: How Intellectual Suicide Created the Modern Islamist* (Intercollegiate Studies Institute, 2010).

8. Alan Smith and Tony Vaux, *Education, Conflict, and International Development* (London: DFID, 2003); Peter Buckland, *Reshaping the Future: Education and Post-Conflict Reconstruction* (Washington, DC: World Bank, 2005).

9. Sanyaee Development Organization (SDO), *Peace Education Training Manual for Teachers*, Vol. 1 (Kabul: SDO Press, 2000), pp. 3–6.

10. Peadar Cremin (ed.), *Education for Peace* (Dublin: Educational Studies Association of Ireland, 1993); John Paul Lederach, *Preparing for Peace: Conflict Transformation across Cultures* (Syracuse: Syracuse University Press, 1993); Betty Reardon (ed.), *Educating for Global Responsibility: Teacher-Designed Curricula for Peace Education, K–12* (New York: Teachers College Press, 1988).

11. SDO, Ibid., pp. 16–24.

12. Sameena Imtiaz served as the executive director of the PEAD Foundation, as well as the author of *Aman ki Janin Pehla Qadam* ("First Step Towards Peace") in Urdu, 2010. As an educator and civil society trainer, Imtiaz regularly conducts workshops on human rights, gender peacebuilding, and minority rights.

13. Peace Education and Development (PEAD) Foundation, see www.pead.org.pk.

14. Sameena Imtiaz and J. William, *Living Together: Value Education Manual, Module 1* (Islamabad: PEAD, 2007).

15. Insan Foundation Trust website, http://www.insan.org.pk.

16. Insan Publications, *We Must, We Can* (Lahore, 2009) and *Rapid Situation Analysis of Gender Reform Action* (Lahore, 2008) and other publications, see www.insan.org.pk.

17. See www.askbd.org.

18. See www.bicpaj.org.

19. Jo Boyden and Paul Ryder, "The Provision of Education to Children Affected by Armed Conflict" (unpublished paper obtained by authors) (Oxford: Refugee Studies Centre, 1996), pg. 51.

20. David Hicks, "Understanding the Field" in David Hicks (ed.) *Education for Peace: Issues, Principles, and Practice in the Classroom* (London: Routledge, 1988), pp. 3–19; Frank Hutchinson, "Young People's Hopes and Fears for the Future," in David Hicks and Richard Slaughter (eds.), *World Yearbook of Education: Futures Education* (London: Kogan Page, 1988), pp. 133–47; James Turner Johnson, *The Quest for Peace: Three Moral Traditions in Western Cultural History* (Princeton: Princeton University Press, 1987).

21. I am grateful to Sameena Imtiaz, Rashad Bukhari, Kishwar Sultana, Uzma Tahir, Murad Akbar, Amina Rasul, Asna Husin, Raz Muhammad Dalili, Lili Munir, Mohsen Youssef, and Aziz Naderi for sharing their experiences on funding, monitoring, evaluating, and the gaps in project implementation.

22. This conference was sponsored by the US Institute of Peace and organized by the Philippines Council for Islam and Democracy; for more, see http://www.usip.org/in-the-field/international-islamic-peace-education-workshop-held-in-davaocity-philippines.

23. To read an assessment of Islamic Peace Education in Ache, Indonesia, see Asna Husin, "Islamic Peace Education: Changing Hearts and Minds," in Qamar-ul Huda (ed.), *Crescent and Dove: Peace and Conflict Resolution in Islam* (Washington, DC: USIP Press, 2010), pp. 151–78.

24. See the Peace Education Program project 2005; Philippines Council of Islam and Democracy, *The Islamic Model for Peace Education* (Manila, Philippines: Council of Islam and Democracy, 2009); Iqra Asia's work in peace education, http://www.iqra-asia.com/.

25. See Muhammad Qasim Zaman, *The Ulama in Contemporary Islam: Custodians of Change* (Princeton: Princeton University Press, 2007); for a historical account of *'ulama* of northern India and their contributions, see Francis Robinson, *Ulama of Farangi Mahall and Islamic Culture in South Asia* (London: Orient Longman, 2001). To access a well-known Karachi-based Deobandi curriculum online, see www.binoria.org.

26. Abul Ala Maududi was a prominent Islamist figure of the twentieth century who publicly stated that the *madrasa* system "fails to stimulate any imaginative and creative intellectual thought and Islam was confined to the observance of a few prescribed rituals without any understanding and appreciation of Islam's revolutionary message." Mathew J. Nelson, "Muslims, Markets, and the Meaning of a 'Good' Education in Pakistan," *Asian Survey* (2006), 46, no. 5: 690–720.

27. It is important to understand the fierce independence and multiple sectarian divisions of Islamic religious and educational institutions in South Asian history and how it differs greatly from West Africa, the Arab Middle East, Turkey, Southern Europe, Central Asia, China, and Southeast Asian religious educational systems.

28. Qamar-ul Huda, et al., *Islam mein qiyam aman aur hal-e tanaza't -Peacebuilding and Conflict Resolution in Islam: A Textbook for Teachers and Students*, second edition (Islamabad, 2014), pp. 137–49.

Section IV

ETHICS, MUSIC, AND THE SACRED

Chapter Ten

Modern Islamic Ethics in a Global World

ETHICS AND LEARNING IN PEACEBUILDING

I begin with examining ethics to explore critical questions facing Muslim-majority communities and the broader community of humanity. One can find ethics classes taught in business, law, and medical schools, and in accounting, computer science, biology, philosophy and religion, sports medicine and coaching, political science, and sociology classes. To major in the field of ethics as an undergraduate, the courses will probably be based in the religious or philosophy studies department and emphasize an interdisciplinary framework. A history of ethics course will consist of Western moral approaches starting with Plato, Aristotle, David Hume, Immanuel Kant, John Stuart Mill, Rene Descartes, and Thomas Hobbes. If one wants to learn more about religious traditions, then "religious ethics" courses examine major ethical and scriptural themes from the Abrahamic and dharmic traditions. In essence, these courses introduce a history of intellectual attempts to answer questions like "why be moral?" "what is good versus evil?" and "what is a meaningful life?" Ethics teachers are interested in instilling students to critically engage with the Ancient Greek philosophers and modern philosophers on ethical topics. However, ethical courses in themselves do not pretend to be a substitute for moral education, or moral formation, instead, instructors state clearly in syllabi that the reading materials are meant for reflection and criticism; that is, the course is interested in finding problems in the sources and examining their worthiness. Since ethics are not mandatory for students, nor are ethical seminars part of employee orientation, is the teaching ethics enterprise by universities and corporations reaching their similar goals of cultivating holistic citizens capable of confronting personal conflicts efficiently? Is teaching ethics not a pedantic exercise in understanding past ethical and moral formulations only to become familiar with them but not to be applied in personal introspections?

During the research of this book, there were frontpage stories of misusing personal information sold by Facebook, the laundering of funds by powerful politicians as revealed in the Panama Papers, and Harvard University's admissions process of historical favoritism of wealthier candidates; these are usually portrayed as a story of a few bad apples giving the industry an ugly name. In some sense, this narrative of a few bad apples provides comfort for those invested in the institution's success—whether it be the largest technology company, democracy, or one of the oldest universities in the world. Since common people cannot, or should not, be familiar with the complexities of the story, then one should not worry about increasing financial misconduct, threats of social media to democracy, and corrupt leaders because these institutions are resolutely resilient to a few bad apples.

However, scandalous ethical decisions in higher education or designed political misinformation campaigns in the digital community should not be interpreted as random anecdotes. Since anecdotes imply random and unusual links, the interpreter can consider ethical lapses as average human experiences. Unfortunately, when ethics is left out of the broader conversation to protect institutions purposefully, the topic of ethics learning, applied ethics, ethical process-making, and ethical outputs is left unexplored. Whether it be a disruption of ethical practices in the professional workplace, among university students, or during social settings, there is always a demand for teaching ethics as part of undergraduate and professional education. Whether in the political arena or the professional fields of finance and technology, bad apples need to learn, practice, and be trained to understand ethics to rectify their shortcomings. During Facebook selling personal information to third parties who then sold it to corporations and political campaigns, *The Atlantic Monthly* reporter Irina Raicu wrote "Rethinking Ethics Training in Silicon Valley," exploring whether these ethical training seminars were sufficient in changing thinking and behavior in the workplace.[1] The assumption is that ethical training seminars for professional techies would prepare them to make more "thoughtful decisions" when confronted with ethical dilemmas that involve the company's products. Again, the primary reason to support employee ethical training seminars was to ensure that the company's products and services are not abused or misappropriated according to law or the corporate culture. If these ethical seminars do anything, they attempt to realign corporate values with the employee's personal values.

However, if ethics training, and not ethical moral education, would help technologists make proper and thoughtful decisions and ensure that they reflect upon their values and personal choices, we need to ask whether ethics can be taught and learned. Yuval Noah Harari, historian and author of *The New York Times* bestseller *Sapiens: A Brief History of Humankind* believes personal ethics can be enhanced and enriched by seeing the world through the eyes and voices of others.[2] To move beyond a hyperindividualistic culture, Harari thinks the individual must learn from stories and experiences of other subjects. By learning from other stories, according to Harari, we can appreciate alternative modes of living, thinking, and processing information to benefit the broader society. Stories can empower and reframe our thinking of other cultures and societies, forming our ethical understanding of the world.

Instead of thinking about ethics as a series of random anecdotal stories of poor choice-making, it might be helpful to frame ethics not as choosing between consequences, rewards, or pain—as stressed by Hume and Nietzsche—but as genuine participation in moral culture, in moral institutions with moral actors. Then, it might be productive to inquire how these systems challenge, support, or obstruct ethical behavior. For example, what may be described as a system of incentives in a corporation must align with examining the employee perceptions of appreciation, rewards, and promotion. Should we teach ethics only to explore a history of intellectuals grappling with morality, evil, and seeking meaning and not provide students with the tools they will need to recognize the personal moral identity with social and cultural structures? Suppose students can distinguish and articulate the differences between ethical value-based systems and utilitarian ethics versus secular humanist approaches to social justice. Does this prepare students to be competent in ethics? For some, the answer is an unambiguous yes; however, critics in the field of ethics are disconnected from a broader moral education or moral formation that originally served as a foundation for ethical thinking, reasoning, and application. Critics against integrating moral education in ethical classes argue that such classes are theological in nature, and they do not invite students to think critically because morality is rooted in religion. Again, the intellectual bias against moral ethics, theology, and religious studies arises again. Nevertheless, this polarized thinking of teaching and learning ethics undoubtedly contributes to an essentialized thinking, or nurturing, of bad apples. Suppose organizations want their individual employees to understand the nexus between personal and professional ethics. In that case, it will make rational sense to increase the attention to the context of ethical cognitive understanding with application to real life. Suppose ethics courses did not have the long-term objectives to be mindful, empathetic, self-aware, and self-critical; perhaps, there could be a greater appreciation of how a few bad apples can infect the barrel of apples.

CONTEMPORARY ETHICS ISSUES

Tradition has been an enormous subject of critical inquiry by scholars and theorists and an important starting point for examining ethics and fundamental sources. Scholars from history, sociology, anthropology, political science, economists, and philosophers attempt to seek a better understanding of processes and thought and social interactions within tradition. Scholars argue that tradition is a process that unfolds over time and is formed within specific challenges and circumstances that arise. German philosopher Hans-Georg Gadamer believed tradition is precisely that which allows us to bridge the past and the present. For him, tradition possessed a critical element of malleability, "tradition is not simply a permanent condition rather, we produce it ourselves since we understand it participates in it and the evolution of tradition, and hence further determinate ourselves."[3]

Modern-day philosopher Alasdair MacIntyre contests the scholarly concept that we have an ongoing role in the construction of tradition by asserting that a tradition—what is handed down—is inherited by new stewards of each generation. For MacIntyre, those living in the present are just as involved in a tradition as those historic figures imagined in the past. Tradition is not just something we inherit, as a matter of reception without thinking or with blind practice. Each of us is a living steward of the tradition, who has a distinct role rather than a sagacious role before embodying it. The process of constructing, reconstructing, reengineering, and forming a tradition is connected to questioning ideas, questioning the past thinkers who contributed distinct ideas for specific purposes to serve in the tradition. Challenging these ideas examines how we ought to live and what correct and incorrect practices are fundamental to the debates. However, one of the key problems is that different and diverse opinions are woven into any tradition; the daunting task is to discern relevant and critical ideas today.

Talal Asad's "discursive tradition," an anthropological theory of lived tradition, believes that discourses in the tradition seek to instruct practitioners about the correct form and the purpose of a given practice because it has precisely been established as a historical precedent. These discourses relate to our past and future and how the practice can be best secured and uncorrupted throughout history. Asad's focus on tradition moves from ideas from intellectuals to practices by practitioners. He argues that orthodoxy in any tradition is a relationship of power specifically where Muslims hold the power to regulate and simultaneously adjust correct practice in the Islamic tradition. On the one hand, traditions are the means by which orthodoxy or heterodoxy is developed because there is an ongoing negotiation with resistance and reasoning.[4]

Viewing tradition as resistance to power, constructing or deconstructing tradition, being dependent on earlier intellectuals who decided the intellectual terms of practices and beliefs, or whether individuals are part of a rigorous process of discernment of the past to make meaning for the present time—all these perspectives share some degree of problems for the Islamic tradition. It is one exercise to contest or reconfigure philosophical constructions of past Muslim intellectuals, but it is another to ignore that Islamic tradition is primarily built upon a revelation from the divine to a selected prophet to guide, correct, and direct humankind back to the divine. As far as interpretations of scriptures of scholars formed orthodox structures of thinking, philosophical systems of ideas, or juridical pronouncements are concerned, the process of debating with these ideas has been ongoing for fourteen centuries. But tampering or deconstructing revelations is impossible because of its link with the divine. Scholar of Islam William Chittick said, "The eye of imagination sees God as immanent. It recognizes God's signs and marks in all things. It perceives the universe as the theatre of divine significance, infused with intelligent and intelligible light. It finds God's names and attributes manifest everywhere in the world and the soul, and it describes God in the positive terms supplied by revelation and the natural realm."[5] Muslim scholars cannot compromise the crucial role of God in tradition, be it the perspective of examining the unfolding of tradition or the contestations of tradition; the divine is central to the tradition. The point of raising these issues with tradition is when discussing contemporary ethical issues in the

Muslim world there are fundamental sources that are not open for critique, such as the Qur'an, *hadith*, and the seerah. However, ways in which ethical questions were designed or answered and ethical problems were constructed are ongoing debates within the community of scholars.

There is ample analysis of Muslims living in an age of globalization, and Western concepts of secularization can be assumed to be transferred or implanted into Eastern cultures and civilizations. Talal Asad has pointed out that secularism and proponents of liberal democracies have ingrained rigid orthodoxy asserting truth claims that "builds on a particular conception of the world and of the problems generated by that world." There are plenty of works on the compatibility of Islam and modernity, the need to model Western experiences by ensuring religion is properly reformed for modern politics and economics, and, of course, whether Western Muslims will assimilate, accommodate, or completely integrate as Westerns thereby abandoning tradition. We know that modernization theories of religion argued that the growth of rational liberalism and scientific progress would make religion disappear, which was an entirely misjudgment of history. Then of course, there are tantamount problems with the rise of militancy, extremism, authoritarian states, the lure of radical ideologies, human rights violations, refugee and migration problems, climate change, unnerving appeal of political Islam or Islamism, Muslim feminist movements, growing disparity of wealth in a globalized world, or the issue of interfaith and civilizational dialogue—all are very critical topics, but despite these concerns, this section is not covering these areas, while they are very important subject areas in their own right.

In discussing ethical issues, I will build upon John Paul Lederach's concept of moral imagination of peacebuilding. He suggests that whenever we frame life's challenges, problems, and existing conflicts as dualistic polarities, we immediately reduce them and essentialize them.[6] We miss the broader galaxy of potential ideas. Lederach suggests that in each moment, the moral imagination can use creativity to think of multiple solutions and multiple realities, which is part of the greater whole. He recognizes how individuals can be lost in the quagmire of pessimism in conflict or daily disputes, and in this mentality, it is natural to see the reality and solutions in dualistic terms. In this duality, it is common to think there is only a singular linear path for a political solution, or a peace process must have the established guidelines and structure met before any meaningful agreement can be achieved. But, with constructive pessimism, according to Lederach, the most "significant weakness in sustaining genuine change is the lack of authentic engagement of the public sphere."[7] There is a significant imagination gap about engagement, peace processes, and an actual deficit of public authenticity. Lederach is speaking about the peacebuilding methodology in realpolitik and how the politics of representative leadership defines, and often limits, the parameters of peacebuilding and peace processes by the individuals chosen to represent their communities and the design and execution of the process.[8]

Starting with the moral imagination in addressing questions of ethics means thinking and acting on the basis that the unexpected, the invisible, and the unknown are possible. Moving beyond regimented dualities for initial inquiries, the creative act of discovery is in each human potential. Creative moral imagination is not just moving intellectually outside the box but requires living outside the box with creative solutions. Creative moral imagination is not the sole responsibility of elected leaders, representatives, community and religious leaders, or charismatic leaders, but of the local communities who must always feel they have an authentic voice to be heard, respected, and their presence is as important as other stakeholders. Even when communities live in fear and conflict, they can unveil the mystery of moral imagination to identify what is necessary for peacebuilding because we all have natural aesthetics ("being sharp in senses") to access profound human dilemmas with transformation imagination.

A CALL OF SERVICE

How do we think about issues with our heart and soul that truly encourage us to pick up what we might otherwise neglect? How we feel about one another and regard those we oppose in our struggle were concerns for Dr. Martin Luther King during the civil rights movement. Can faithful Christians stand against others who diametrically oppose justice without losing our integrity and dignity while respecting their human dignity? There are always tensions between the prophetic messages and the actual application, the abstract and the concrete. One of the most memorable moments in my life was spending a few days with Maulana Abdul Sattar and Bilquis Edhi in Karachi, Pakistan, following their day-to-day activities in orphanages, shelters and schools for street children, and hospitals. Often called the "Mother Teresa" of Pakistan, the Edhi family and Edhi Foundation consist of six thousand volunteers and are entirely funded by private donations. Their social services include healthcare, ambulance services, clinics and hospitals, identifying missing persons, ending human trafficking, supporting refugees and displaced persons, emergency educational services, and helping with unaccounted corpses for burial services. School teachers called Maulana Edhi Abbu (Father), and the students and children in orphanages referred to him as Nana (Grandfather); most people recall him as the "Rahmat ka firishtah" or Angel of Mercy. When I asked Maulana Edhi about his call to service to others, he said, "I do it for God, I want others to know this message. We are responsible to each other. People may not agree with me, but they realize that I am putting my whole self on the line and trying to reach everyone." Pressing him for clarification, I asked if he felt he was directly impacting those individuals who did not feel a responsibility for abandoned children. Maulana Edhi smiled, responding "some people feel they do not have to do anything because Maulana's foundation is taking care of it, but because they even thought about this work, the children, and spent even a moment thinking, caring about these children, that in itself is an important form of charity."

With Maulana Edhi and Bilquis Edhi I walked through an orphanage to see the beaming enthusiasm, love, and youthful energy that bounced in the room when the two of them walked in. Children paused their activities to touch the Edhis; in return, the two stopped to speak with the children, ask about their day and homework assignments, and wait to ask one of the children if she found her lost soccer ball. These two individuals were intimately involved in the children's lives and with the needs of the staff, teachers, ambulance drivers, medics, and cooks. Maulana Edhi always took the time to go into the kitchens of the orphanages and schools to check on the staff and the quality of the food being served. He used a spoon to taste the beef and chickpea dish (*daal*) suggesting humbly to the head cook, "it needs less salt and more cumin."

On this morning Bilquis Edhi had a meeting with teachers and staff of the school to discuss their teaching, classes, and student participation; address the details of the availability of pens, pencils, and notebooks; and identify which textbooks were not accessible to students. When one of the teachers privately asked for funds to pay for outstanding electricity bills, Bilquis told her someone would come to her home to resolve the problem. Another staff member was in tears because her son was killed in an unfortunate street accident. Bilquis stopped to hug and console her, letting her know that it was God's will to have him return this way and that the foundation would support her with the burial expenses. It was afterward that I learned that Bilquis had established an informal trauma healing center with the help of psychologist volunteers. The practice of self-compassion, positive relational support, and vital emotional support is not listed in any foundations' annual reports.

A call of service refers to the work done by young volunteers: students raising funds for their organization, visiting nursing homes, spending a few hours at the soup kitchen, or helping a neighbor with chores. The Edhis created an organization to engage themselves in a broken world and use their moral energy, or more accurately, a moral imperative, to heal their communities. Service presents an opportunity to be better connected with other community members, to listen and learn from those we never see in our daily lives because it aligns, or in most cases, realigns ourselves, our values, and our desire to be engaged. With the public interest in mind, the act of service forces us to reflect upon needs, capabilities, priorities, opportunities, directions, and possibilities. In service we ask ourselves: who is the self in relation to others? The call to service is about consistent engagement with others to situate our lives with those who need another person. Famous anti-war Jesuit priest, Christian pacifist, and peacemaker Daniel Berrigan called this the "geography of faith." He thinks we ask two questions: Who am I? Where am I? Berrigan believed that in any authentic journey, the soul will discipline itself with the encounters of various geographies; the soul disciplines will finally need to confront humility, stillness, and sensual perception.[9]

Much of this discussion within the peacebuilding field is relegated to civic duties, the inclusion of civil society organizations, and ways in which individuals identify pathways to participate in conflict reduction or prevention. However, there is another side to civic duties where there is a call to service from a moral imperative or an act of faithfulness to serve others, the desire to aid others because in supporting others one can grow deeper in piety, humility, obedience, character, and spiritual awareness. Service to others is a vehicle for the pious to illustrate their ultimate surrender to the divine: that suffering of others is their own suffering; the isolation and alienation of others is felt by and through this service, and the act of bringing relief is heard. The call of service is not just doing good for a reward in the hereafter, earning a reward to enter heaven; instead, the service is heaven in our time. This ethos was the essential teachings of Khwaja Moin ud-din Chishti, the famous saint buried in Ajmer, India, where millions of pilgrims (Hindus, Sikhs, Muslims, Christians, and no faith traditions) visit his shrine. Known as Sultan al-Hind (King of India), according to this spiritual master, service to others was the final message of religion; in the beginning, in the end, serving others was the sole purpose of our lives.

COMMITMENTS AND AFFIRMATIONS

I have spent many years—since 1995—working with college students on their studies and students engaged with their community service. I've seen students tutor younger students, share their time with older people, run summer camps, design educational programs in prisons, run a mobile clinic in urban areas, volunteer with legal aid for those who cannot afford lawyers, and raise funds for medical expenses or other expenses. As one student said at the University of California, Los Angeles, Tutorial Program, "I want to tutor these kids to show them that there is a better life for them; if they only study and do well in school, there are opportunities out there for them." Students of any age are filled with idealism, but underlying this idealism is a timeline of an opportunity before cynicism kicks in. "If they do not study now, get into the right schools and get a good job, then they will be lost in a world of crime and drugs," explains a student tutor. For years, I reflected upon this youthful commitment and affirmation of helping others despite the grim socio-economic realities facing most urban teenagers. For students who had never experienced urban poverty and were from affluent suburban neighborhoods, tutoring was their affirmation of doing good in the world, seeking friendships, and participating in another person's life. Over again, "I wanted to make a difference" was repeated as the source of their motivation.

A commitment to a person's development is not just an affirmation of that person but a declaration confirming a personal role in that person's life. But the issue is, do students naturally find these commitments and affirmations to less fortunate students? Are there shared values, ethical principles, feelings of guilt, and the desire to "make a difference" when the opportunity is in front of their eyes? As a student explained, "I go to the after-school program twice a week. I sit with kids having trouble with their schoolwork and teach them spelling and reading; plus, I try to connect with them because that is the first thing you need to do. If you don't, then you might as well forget it." I am intrigued by how this student reflected on how she will be effective with her students, how her concept of making a difference was driven by improving reading and spelling skills, and how she wanted to serve as a role model in their lives. Students like her consciously decide where to make an impact on a micro-individual level because tutoring others empowered her to express her values to improve the lives of others.

The combination of commitment and affirmation are essential traits in the peacebuilding ethics world; without them, we would not see civil society members actively changing their communities. Many peacebuilding theorists point to the importance of involvement and social empowerment of civil society members to participate in taking action to transform and mitigate violence. Abu-Nimer states, "Social empowerment and involvement through *ihsan* (virtues) and *khayr* (good) are also important paths to justice and peace in the Islamic tradition."[10] Ibrahim Kalin uses the context of Islamic theology by treating peace and violence in terms of doing good and preventing the presence of evil (*sharr*). Kalin believes that "war, conflict, violence, injustice and discord are related to the problem of evil," and it is the responsibility of human beings to do good and establish justice while preventing evil from occurring.[11] Of course, the Qur'an recognizes the capacity of human beings to do good in the face of adversity and evil and to change their conditions, as in Q: 13:11, "Surely Allah does not change the condition of a people until they change their own condition." Muslim scholars interpreted this as the imperative for people to empower themselves to change their condition by doing good and ensuring evil is not done.

Aside from these theological and social empowering theories in doing good and preventing evil on earth, the ethics of commitment and affirmation relate to the horizontal capacity, the ability to build and sustain relational spaces of constructive interaction across the lines of social divisions. Just as the students volunteering at schools as tutors, they generated creative processes, initiatives, and opportunities for a deeper structural pattern of social inequalities. These commitments and affirmations were expressions of not being inactive passive observers of these inequalities; instead, they held an ethical principle of helping those open to support. Commitments and affirmations contribute to social change: they alter relationships from those defined or inherited as distant and fearful toward those characterized by proactive engagement based on mutual respect, affection, and friendship. In peacebuilding, the term used to describe this situation is constructive change. With constructive engagement comes the potential creative critical change with new ideas, capacities, and visions to see new solutions.

VOLUNTEERING AND MENTORING

Matthew Fox's *Creativity: Where the Divine and the Human Meet* speaks about a "creation spirituality" that stresses the presence of the divine in all aspects of creation and life.[12] Fox believes the creative process is inherently a spiritual practice; as human beings are creative beings, creating expresses one's unique spirituality. Tied to the creative process is the understanding that the divine is not connected to a historical moment or to a historical figure, which, according to Fox, means creativity is not limited to modern notions of breaking unexplored boundaries. Instead, creativity is a transcendental state of connecting or forming a communion with the divine, a spiritual transformation. This creativity-divine nexus transcends the ego, all the limitations of beliefs and doctrines of rituals, and opens new meaning, purpose, and a journey of spiritual exploration. In light of a spiritual paradigm, this theological approach to volunteering and mentoring could reveal some more profound reflection on this engagement.

Why consider volunteering and mentoring in a discussion of contemporary ethical questions? Some in the field need to connect with mentors to foster growth, knowledge transfer, personal development, and existing networks. Using social systems as a ladder for betterment, mentors need to challenge mentees in a supportive way so they can step outside of their comfort zones. Mentors need to focus on sharing knowledge, networks, help develop goals and objectives, and instill a strong sense of trust and confidence. Volunteering as a mentor can make a real difference in personal growth and professional achievements.

Volunteering and mentoring are a meaningful two-way dialogue to inform and share information to assist one party in learning a new skill or understanding from another party. Within conflict zones, it requires the capacity to develop and live with a high degree of ambiguity. This is because we must accept the contradictory issues of perceptions versus the realness of lived experiences. I learned how their perceptions and meanings merge or diverge by directly volunteering time and mentoring others in conflict. Trying to make sense of a person's experience in a conflict consists of complex dimensions of changing perceptions, meanings, and their place in the conflict. Lederach speaks of suspending judgment while mentoring individuals not to be led down the road of dualities. It is not relinquishing opinions or the ability to assess the capacity of colleagues but avoiding social polarization or falling into the trap of historical and current relational patterns of repeated violence.[13]

In peacebuilding, identifying key spaces for volunteering and mentoring requires spaces where relationships are developed, and interaction takes place for constructive social change. Within these spaces, strategic issues and problems focus on multiple options with the greatest potential for creating a broad impact. Volunteering and mentoring are mechanisms for individuals and parties to consider beyond the moment of conflict or status quo and critically identify critical stakeholders who can support capacity and seek creative change. This may include horizontal or vertical integration of players supporting these efforts, such as unexplored networks, organizations, philanthropic groups, untapped individuals, unrecognized influencers, opinion leaders, and other groups to form a coalition. In this process, individuals must create and sustain a foundation capable of generating responsive change processes that act as a platform for ideas. Some argue that religious motivations for the ethics of volunteering and mentoring must contend with moral jeopardy. One wants to do good without losing the qualities of humility and humbleness.

Volunteering and mentoring individuals in or not in conflict zones consists of building a deep connection and permitting the individuals involved to be vulnerable—sharing fears, insecurities, aspirations, and personal stories of past failures, which leads to creative trust and intimacy. In 2014 and 2015, I was part of a peacebuilding program sponsored by the UN Development Programme based in Afghanistan and several international organizations for a two-week workshop for university men and women on the topic of "Building Peace and Resolving Conflict." The program was in western Afghanistan, in the historic city of Herat; participants consisted of Hazara, Kuchi, and Tajik ethnic groups. Since participants traveled from far distances and stayed in dormitories, they needed written permission from a variety of authorities: tribal elders, parents, grandparents, their local imams, and consent forms approved by other relatives. The intensive program had forty Afghan participants, three international facilitators, and six experts in peacebuilding, conflict mitigation, and youth engagement. To build trust within the group we spoke about active listening skills, respecting boundaries and guidelines, being open to difficult conversations, sharing personal stories, and the need to be authentic during this time. Some programs unfold to meet expectations about 65 percent of this time, but these engagements from 2014 to 2015 exceeded our expectations because of the participants' desire to engage and seek genuine mentorship.

While I participated as an expert instructor for the workshop, the mentorship during and after the project made me realize the importance of sharing to seek acceptance and connection to a broader community. However, this process of self-acceptance sought forgiveness, both from themselves and others, and the vulnerabilities they shared were attempting to shed off stigmas, shame, and guilt from the wounds of conflict. I began comprehending my mentoring role beyond my expertise and the content material of peacebuilding and conflict resolution workshops because students were more interested in a compassionate way of living, focusing on empathy and connection. Not in the UN Development Programme workshop materials were mentoring students in emotional resilience and building trust with others with the openness that failure comes with trust; uncertainty meant recognizing the imperfections in others and us; and walking in this world does not have to be a lonely path with lesions from conflict. Beyond this moment in time and space—with all the social, political, economic, and personal insecurities—there is an inner world that has yet to be explored with no walls or limits. I incorporated trips to a Sufi master's shrine of Khwaja Abdullah Ansari (c.1089–1083), locally known as Pir-i Herat, who wrote poetry, was regarded as one of the most revered Sufi teachers, and whose devotional manuals are still studied today. Conflict and war do not permit an appreciation of the culture or your immediate surroundings; instead, in our conversations in the workshop, participants expressed a deep resentment of Afghanistan and its culture. But, for these students, becoming acquainted with local history, interacting with people who are these historical sites' custodians, and engaging with astonishing figures for the first time opened a new world for them to understand.

FORGIVENESS AND RESILIENCE

I think the field of peacebuilding should consult with scholars of theology, ethics, and philosophy on the topic of forgiveness and resilience.[14] It is neither a formula nor a process that can be outlined in a project proposal. Any single government or nongovernment organization cannot even orchestrate forgiveness at the national, provincial, and local levels. The field of peacebuilding has plenty of works on reconciliation, restorative justice, truth commissions, transitional justice, and constructing memorials of peace. The issue is that what scholars and experts write about is not as simple as it appears. People wounded by war are weary of processes that claim to heal broken souls because there is no trust in anyone or any institution. This should be recognized before writing on the topic of truth and forgiveness rituals or commissions on national dialogues and reconciliation.

In discussing forgiveness and retribution, scholars of Islamic peacebuilding Abdul Aziz, Nathan Funk, and Ayse Kadayifci-Orellana state, "There is an articulated preference in Islam for nonviolence over violence, and for forgiveness (*musamaha*) over retribution."[15] In the process of healing wounds and painful memories of conflict, reconciliation processes usually serve as a platform to address the past while thinking of the future. As with other religious traditions, reconciliation, and healing are critical in Islamic peacebuilding. Using an arbitrator or mediator, parties will be engaged in reconciliation and forgiveness of pardoning another person (*afu*). The act of pardoning or *afu* is interconnected with the act of pursuing goodness (*ihsan*) on earth. From scripture and the life of the Prophet, forgiveness is of a higher value than maintaining hatred or vengeance, engaging in forgiveness when they are angry,[16] or being reminded in Q: 2:36–38 that the very concept that human life on earth started with an act of forgiveness by God. The Qur'an states in 42:40, "the recompense of an injury the like thereof: but whosoever forgives and thereby brings about a reestablishment of harmony, his reward is with God, and God loves not the wrongdoers." Sincere forgiveness is advocated as the preferred path to establish God's harmony on earth. Islamic principles of forgiveness demand the recognition of their own wrongdoing, repenting, and asking for forgiveness.

Within Muslim-majority and -minority communities, more attention must be paid to addressing forgiveness and its intricate nature of transformation. Understanding the varieties of forgiveness to move past grievances and toward reconciliation is only the beginning: navigating inner pain and negative emotions involves the right time and ripeness for people to reach this point; external pressures to get to this stage of forgiveness may only complicate the willingness and outcomes; depending on the severity of the pain, one never knows if it is possible to move forward; some do not care and while others want accountability, apologies, and public testimonies; and then, there are legal ramifications for the offender publicly agreeing to the crimes. One of the primary reasons I think ethics for forgiveness is needed is because of the lingering pain and trauma in Muslim-majority communities where there are no spaces to deal with wounds and enduring pain. While there are religious precedents on this topic, it does not mean that political, social, and cultural influences have repressed processes for forgiveness.

ISSUES WITH CIVIC ENGAGEMENT

Modernity, liberalism, and democracy are contested terms with various prisms to understand them. For example, modernity has multiple concepts, multilayered meanings, and social-political phenomena. Modernity is tied to European political history and sociological paradigms in the Weberian positivist perspective. Fundamental to this understanding are two critical aspects: the application of rationalization rooted in eighteenth-century European Enlightenment principles and secularization, which demands the clear separation of Church and state as expressed in a Western Christian context. It is important to recall that Max Weber[17] (d.1920) asserted that rationalization is uniquely Western and lacking in other parts of the world; however, just because rationalization is not visible does not mean there cannot be "imitation or emulation" by other societies. Weber believed that modern capitalism, tied to liberal systems, represents a rational mode of economic prosperity because of its dependence on calculable production and consumption processes. This rationalization extends into all aspects of life: arts, music, science, architecture, sports, religion, politics, and so on. Modernity in Europe is an ongoing historical rationalization process and continued sharp bifurcation between Church and state. Within modernity, there has been a flourishing evolution of diverse cultural, political, and social systems of democracy. In France, democratic secularism is encoded in laïcité rooted in the French Revolution, and there are several examples in Europe and beyond of monarchial parliamentary democracy, socialist democracies, and representative parliamentary democracies.

Numerous works explore ways to operate in modernity or postmodernity, where scholars examine divergent spaces in which the faith tradition of Islam has or does not have democratic principles and institutions embedded in it. Moreover, analysis of Muslim modernist intellectual attempts to reconcile the legal tradition of Islam with modernity is a crucial step toward the question of compatibility. Essential to the examination of modernity and liberal democratic principles is the way Western scholars have understood religion to be a problem and obstacle to human social advancement. In Hegelian terms, religion should be disjointed from modern life because it no longer plays a role in individuals' and societies' intellectual formation (Gestalt des Geistes). Wesley Wildman, a scholar of philosophy of religion, claimed that religion is irrelevant whenever societies become secular and modern.[18] He claimed that religion naturally retreats from intellectual endeavors because of its authoritative beliefs that cannot compete when economies thrive in secular democracies, which renders religion superfluous because it cannot engage meaningfully with democratic economies. The elimination of poverty empowers people not to submit to religious authoritarianism. Before

Wildman, Christian theologian Reinhold Niebuhr[19] distrusted the "inflexible authoritarianism of the Catholic religion," and a host of German, English, and French scholars believed that Jews could not adhere to citizenship of democratic principles because they abided "too closely to their laws which prevented their full allegiance to secular liberal principles."

If we fast forward to the middle of the twentieth century, much of the scholarship in the 1960s to 1980s assumed that secularization, modernity, and democracy go hand in hand. For any state to progress in the modern world, it needs to shed its historical baggage of religious traditions. Essentially, with more modernization comes more secularization—thus, the emphasis on sciences and "scientific progress" was an epistemological foundation in developing countries. However, renowned sociologist Peter Berger believes those assumptions were too readily accepted and admits that civil participation and engagement, such as the civil rights movement in the United States or the Anti-Apartheid Movement in South Africa, were inherently conceived of and implemented by religious communities.

Acknowledging the diverse roles of religious dynamics in civil politics has not only contested assumptions of secularism and ways in which democracy thrives, but scholars like Charles Taylor, Alasdair MacIntyre, and Robert Bellah also coined the term "post-secular society" to demonstrate the fact that religion has played an increasingly prominent role in the public sphere. These scholars, and others, point out how religion is shaping—in some cases, defining—the debate in public policy conversations on various issues like climate change, abortion, euthanasia, racism, social and economic inequalities, immigration, extreme bias in the judicial systems, and ethical issues relating to technology and science.

In examining the compatibility of Islam in these intellectual, cultural, and political milieus, we are reminded that there is a significant transformation of understanding of secularism and democracy, of biases and faulty assumptions of secular democracies and the place of religion. Throughout the history of Islam, faith, beliefs, and practices fueled a critical rational tradition and civilization to evolve, adapt, accommodate, and seek innovations for new research and develop societal questions. The faith tradition was not a hindrance but a crucial foundation for scientific, mathematical, and medical discoveries in the twelfth to fifteenth centuries. By the tenth century, it achieved diverse and divergent theology, philosophy, and jurisprudence schools and accepted mutually dependent but different Sunni and Shi'ite sects. Religion was the basis for multiple interpretations of political systems from North Africa to Southeast Asia. Concerning democracy and liberalism, modern reformers of the nineteenth to early twentieth century, such as Sir Syed Ahmed Khan, Jamal ad-Din Afghani, and Muhammad 'Abduh, utilized traditional concepts and institutions such as consensus (*'ijma*) of the community, expert reinterpretation of law (*ijtihad*), and accountability in the public welfare (*maslahah*). However, these modernist scholars set in motion a complex intellectual, legal, and religious question relating to divine sovereignty and human agency, Islamic life vis-à-vis political systems, and relying on the first generation of Muslims as a historical precedent for political language, political philosophy, and political-economic systems.

The 1979 Iranian Revolution dramatically shifted the minds of the role of religion for Western scholars of philosophy, religion, and democracy. Within the Islamic world, they ushered a moment of truth for secular and socialist Muslim intellectuals to acknowledge that religion is part of the fabric of political-social life and not distinctly separate. Muslim modernist scholars such as Rashid al-Ghannouchi, Tariq al-Bishri, and Maulana Mawdudi believed democracy was the platform to usher in an "Islamic democracy"—not precisely a theocratic state as manifested in Iran—rather a state with a class of professional bureaucratic religious intellectuals who would an Islamic "influence" within political, economic, cultural, and social institutions. Tunisian scholar and political reformer Al-Ghannouchi, in *Al-Huriat al-A'amah fi al-Dawlah el-Islamiah* ("Public Freedoms in the Islamic State"), stressed the consultation process (*shura*) among leaders and the people to be a fundamental pillar for the Islamic system. But exactly how this will be implemented in practice, on the ground, is a complex and unresolved question.

It is no coincidence that the rise of Islamist political parties (The Muslim Brotherhood, Jama'at i-Islami, Muhammadiya, Hamas, and Hezbollah) developed and continues to be rigorously debated among Muslim intelligentsia and grassroots movements. Following the liberation of Muslim-majority countries from imperialism and decades of nationalism, socialism, Arab Baathism, secularism, and ethno-sectarianism under authoritative military systems, Islamist political reformers emphasized democratic principles and representative parliaments as a means to bring change to politics and political systems to reflect their vision. For example, during the Arab Spring revolts of 2011 to 2014, the Islamist political parties first formed coalitions to insist on popular elections to bring down authoritarian regimes. Except for Turkey, the Islamist parties have not been able to rise and remain in elected positions. With Islamist parties failing to gain public support in

Egypt, Morrocco, Jordan, Tunisia, and Pakistan, and the growing phenomenon of democracy backsliding in Arab and in the wider Islamic world, one needs to question whether Islamist parties are representative of a popular democratic Islamic narrative or are they posing as an alternative voice to current systems of totalitarianism?

Thinking about civic engagement in democracy or other liberal democratic principles within an Islamic context, Islamist modernists argue that the Qur'an and the Prophet's living example can be read to be democratic. Building on this, they pressed others to see how the Prophet's life was based upon tolerant liberalism—one that predated the Enlightenment period of Western Europe. In addition to these arguments, they believed that successive dynasties had utilized elements of liberal democratic principles, such as consensus (*shura*), or argued that the Constitution of Medina was the first democratic constitution. That is to say that taken as a whole systems approach, well-established judicial systems, moral principles, and theological and philosophical inquiries were inherently tied to liberal principles of tolerance, argumentation, and acceptance of the other. Aside from the anachronous criticism, there was very little attention in Islamic texts on popular will and the prominence of individual rights over the collective, or vice versa. Historically, there were rigorous debates over public rights (*al-haqq al-'amm*) and the protection of the public order over private interests or entitlements. These debates were connected to owning personal property or ensuring mendicants were adequately certified to practice healing.

Not surprisingly, Islamist intellectuals are heavily criticized for believing that democracies would transform Islamic civilization into universalisms and deconstruct Islam. Liberal conceptions of human rights, individual rights, and the variety of freedoms allocated to the individual would pose harsh contradictions to predominant Muslim societies. Scholars like Saba Mahmood[20] argued that liberal democratic principles were born in specific political-economic cultural contexts that cannot be duplicated, imported, and re-enacted in Muslim countries. To think this way is to believe, naively, that political systems are like commercial goods. Instead, she insisted on exploring what resources exist for imagining and developing an ethical system of tolerance, dissent, diversity, and pluralism.

Within the Islamic world, intellectuals are struggling, contesting notions of Western liberal democracy and the vision of "Islamic democracy" by Islamist parties while attempting to identify real practical solutions to current systems of authoritarianism. For many, the issue is not to make Muslims liberal or reconstruct educational systems that mimic liberal principles at the expense of eliminating or diluting local cultural and religious beliefs. Nor is it involved in manufacturing "mini-liberal democratic" principalities[21] to ensure that the intellectual market will consume liberalism eventually. Nor does it include enlightening or indoctrinating the scholarly religious class (*'ulama*) to preach liberal principles in the mosques. Perhaps the answers are coming from unexpected Muslim and non-Muslim scholars from the West and East exchanging views on a new chapter on enlightenment and liberal democracy.

Within these conversations, we know many Muslim scholars intoxicated with protestations of Western epistemology, Western hegemony, and the postmodern power condition. As a result, these contrarian scholars are more consumed with the pitfalls of cultural relativism, "privileging others," Western universalism, fears of losing to a neo-imperialism, and are willfully fixated on only aspects of liberalism, such as human rights, and not the whole. The ghastly political realities of the Muslim world mandate scholars and intellectual debates to go beyond reactive thinking, pessimism, and nihilistic unpractical recommendations for their societies.

In thinking about civic engagement with liberal democratic principles in an Islamic context, we need to be reminded that the presence of God is not an abstract practice for Muslims, nor is it foreseeable that the divine will be diluted from personal or public spaces. This means if Muslim intellectuals, political theorists, *'ulama*, civil society, and private and public sectors can design a liberal democratic system, it must be fundamentally affixed firmly with Islam and the evolving structures of postmodernity and postsecularity. A severe intellectual discourse will not abandon or romanticize the past or expend energy in dismissing the merits of present Western models of liberal democracies or reforming the faith tradition to fit into an acceptable model. Creative synergies are needed to tap into an imagination that forges new thinking on the function and purpose of the (post) modern nation-state in Islamic societies. There needs to be a deliberate balance between the protection of individual rights, gender rights, checks within the state's power while allowing Muslim citizens to freely adhere to their religious convictions within the rule of law, elected representatives, independent judiciary, and resilient institutions with accountability that embraces pluralism and inclusiveness.

In a world of increasing policy needs to see the Islamic world in a securitized prism—shielding the West from radicalism and at the same time propping up local governments with ammunitions to "eradicate" the virus of terrorism—it is attractive to find "moderate" Muslim intellectuals to propel this project. What is needed is not for moderates or liberal Muslims to engage in an echo chamber or polemic exercises but rather an internal scrutiny of ideas and intellectual examination of citizenship and democracy in the Islamic world.

NOTES

1. Irina Raicu, "Rethinking Ethics Training in Silicon Valley," *The Atlantic Monthly*, May 16, 2017.
2. Yuval Noah Harari, *Sapiens: A Brief History of Humankind* (New York: Harper, 2015).
3. Hans-Georg Gadamer, *Truth and Method* (New York: Bloomsbury Academic, 1960).
4. Talal Asad, *Genealogies of Religion: Discipline and Reasons of Power in Christianity and Islam* (Baltimore, MD: Johns Hopkins University Press, 1993).
5. William Chittick, *Science of the Cosmos, Science of the Soul* (Albany: SUNY Press, 1995).
6. John Paul Lederach, *Moral Imagination: The Art of Building Peace* (New York: Oxford University Press, 2005).
7. Ibid., pg. 58.
8. Ibid., pg. 60.
9. Daniel Berrigan and Robert Coles, *Geography of Faith: Conversations Between Daniel Berrigan and Robert Coles* (Boston: Beacon Press 1971).
10. Mohammed Abu-Nimer, "Conflict Resolution in an Islamic Context: Some Conceptual Questions," *Peace and Change*, 1996, 21, no. 2: 22–40.
11. Ibrahim Kalin, "Islam and Peace: A Survey of the Sources of Peace in the Islamic Tradition," *Islamic Studies*, 2005, 44, no. 3: 327–362.
12. Matthew Fox, *Creativity: Where the Divine and the Human Meet* (New York: Penguin Putnam, 2000).
13. Lederach, pg. 37.
14. See Raymond Helmick and Rodney Peterson, *Forgiveness and Reconciliation: Religion, Public Policy, and Conflict Transformation* (Philadelphia, PA: Templeton Foundation, 2001); Walter Brueggemann, *The Prophetic Imagination* (Minneapolis, MD: Fortress, 2001).
15. A.A. Said, N.C. Funk, and A.S. Kadayifci, *Peace and Conflict Resolution in Islam: Precept and Practice* (Washington DC: University Press of America, 2001).
16. Qur'an 42:37.
17. Max Weber, *The Protestant Ethic and the Spirit of Capitalism* (London: Talcott Parsons, 1992).
18. W.J. Wildman, *Religious Philosophy as Multidisciplinary Comparative Inquiry: Envisioning a Future for the Philosophy of Religion* (Albany, NY: SUNY Press, 2010).
19. R. Niebuhr, *Man and Immoral Society: A Study in Ethics and Society* (New York: Westminster John Knox Press, 2010).
20. S. Mahmood, "Modern Power and the Reconfiguration of Religious Traditions," in *Stanford Electronic Humanities Review*, 1996, 5: 1.
21. Cheryl Bernard, "Moderate Islam Isn't Working," *National Interest*, December 2015.

Chapter Eleven

The Sacred, Memory, Music, and Peacebuilding

This chapter builds upon peacebuilding activities focusing on culture, social, and religious rituals. It is interested in exploring how memory relates to sacred rituals and music, and how sound inculcates and reinforces essential peacebuilding values. It begins with analyzing *Qawwali* poetry and performances in religious settings and how the singing praising the Prophet Muhammad build upon memory, bring social cohesion, transcend individuals toward the sacred, and ultimately, practice and live a peaceful life.

Qawwali, or the devotional music of Sufis of South Asia and Central Asia, originated in the Indian subcontinent in the eleventh century. Sufi poets, scholars, and spiritual masters would use reciting and singing poetry as a musical group to express their esoteric experiences and devotional love for the divine, the Prophet, and saints. The first *Qawwali* performance examined is by legendary Nusrat Fateh Ali Khan at the Data Ganj Bakhsh sufi shrine's *'urs* in Lahore; the second is a *Milad an-Nabi* celebration, the birthday of the Prophet, performed by the Sabri Brothers in Multan; and the third venue is a private home in Karachi on Shab-e Mi'raj, the Night of the Ascension, performed by Munshi Raziuddin. An analysis of a particular *Qawwali* genre praising Muhammad reveals how the music serves as a poetic text to memories of the individual and, more importantly, how the present community remembers the Prophet. *Qawwali* music is a conduit for the community of Sufi listeners to reconnect to the sacred time while at the same time creating space for themselves in the past and the present.

Qawwali songs dedicated to the Prophet Muhammad move beyond the written biographical texts because the songs are sung by a party of singers praising his life, achievements, supreme standing as a messenger, pietistic legacy, his graceful relationship with God and his followers, and his incomparable model for being God-conscious. The songs reflect a yearning to meet him, or, more accurately, to prepare for his presence to appear at the *mahfil sama'* or the sacred arena of musical devotion. There are numerous themes in these songs praising the Prophet; one overarching theme is the Prophet's dedication to teaching others to find peace, live peacefully with oneself and others, and end human suffering.

MEMORY OF THE PAST AND *QAWWALI*

Tapping into memory is central to *Qawwali* music because it builds upon how listeners understand themselves in relation to the past and the ultimate divine. In memory studies, some scholars assert that memory is essentially connected to the intellect because it is our capacity to retain what we sense as an activity. Some scholars believe that memory is entirely incumbent on the ability to intelligently retain information and our ability to learn new skills, build on habits and customs, and develop a discerning capability of what is correct and incorrect. The ability to recall a set of events as our own and to situate the meaning of those events in our lives involves more than just an accurate account of the past. *Qawwali* music, in its presentation, its cultural context, and poetry of transcendence, raises the question of whether Sufi devotional music contributes to the memory of the audience members, both in retention and in the ability to recall specific episodes of the past as sacred or profane. Can *Qawwali* music be a significant medium where the listener mediates between experience and remembering the past?[1]

The role of *Qawwali* music in supporting listeners in recalling events or identifying with events they view as their own intimate history is an unexplored area of study. I think it is crucial to understand how audience members view themselves in relation to the past and how *Qawwali* brings this identity to fruition. The way this self-understanding is transformed or enriched by *Qawwali* music is critical to the listener's memory. *Qawwali* music serves as a text to the past, which reveals a place in the past and simultaneously contributes to historical memory and a memory of histories.

A series of images may facilitate recalling the past; what is essential is the combined product and process of remembering. Remembering, bringing back what occurred, or reliving the past increases the ties of the self with the past, making the past a living memory. The active process of remembering, reliving the past, and recalling episodes of history where the individual sees oneself as integrally connected to it means that it is not a dead past. In a sense, the past is present, and the past is with the past. *Qawwali* music helps in reliving the past and connecting the person or community with encounters of the past to the present. *Qawwali* music keenly builds upon the powerful feelings to recall, retain, and identify with past events as if these memories are the listener's own. *Qawwali* music ties the individual with intimate moments of the sacred past as a medium of reminiscing and struggling with the search for the divine in all things. If one of the primary functions of *Qawwali* music is to bring the listener to a context where the divine mystery is touched, and one is immersed in a dialogue of illumination, then there is a clear nexus of song, memory, and experience.[2]

The true power of *Qawwali* is its ability to use the music medium to connect or reconnect with the listener's memory and how feelings are shared and expressed through this voyage. Some scholars insist that images of memory are the center of recalling, but one cannot dismiss how imagery remains associated with our basic feelings about this power to recall. The important component to our ability to remember with specific certain intimate forms, particularly in the cases of reminiscing and reliving, involves imagery and expressed emotion. If there were an absence of imagery in our reliving the past or recalling the events, then our feelings restored the way we understand ourselves at the time would be lost. Feelings need to be a part of how we relive, recall, and ultimately express our memories to ensure that the quality of the experience is fully appreciated. So, while memory does not fit into a proper memory image box, there is a complex interplay of images and emotions in the processes of remembering that is critical to the matrix of ideas connected to memory.

Remembering cannot be reduced or defined solely as representing one's past. If remembering a memory is the ability to recount history, some have argued that past events are already embedded in memory and are tied to the power to recall. The group of scholars who advocate this position are the causal theorists; in essence, the actual act of remembering is not entirely dependent on the power to recall events in the past; instead, the most crucial component in remembering the past are "traces" or "patterns" of any event that are encoded in the information being recalled.[3] Once any relevant traces or patterns are determined, a causal effect occurs to recall the past event. Studies on memory challenges fixed ideas of the present to the past. Past events do not create memories that individuals automatically assume are valid. Instead, some disagree that memory revives an existing notion of the past. Scholars of the phenomenology school of thought believe that memory is more than a process of recollection, and what is critical to remember is what we call "the past and present" and how we weave them together and demonstrate the two are integrated into our lives.[4] This group of scholars, also known as the phenomenologists, contest notions of a past that create memories that we assume are valid. They argue that we create a past that is either very favorable with memories of nostalgia or we create a vision of tragedies. Essentially, phenomenologists argue that memory and the act of remembering is not an accidental phenomenon. What we remember, or what we want to recall, is partially tied to our present context, or to be more exact, it is essential as to what we tolerate in the present moment as it relates to what we define in the past.

Qawwali music as a text to the past enables listeners not only to recollect but to use the present context to find the recollection's place in history. The music is an unfolding text written, or more precisely, sung, collectively by the singer, poet, and community of listeners. It builds upon memory while, at the same time, the music formulates memories and identities. *Qawwali* musicians and listeners participate in historical knowledge through the experience and analysis of spatial metaphors in the music. The sound and imagery from *Qawwali* inform and formulate how listeners learn about themselves and others. Ethnographic studies illustrate how sounds, worldviews, voices, and spaces are interconnected social experiences. *Qawwali* music has social and religious contexts and fundamentally creates a socialization process between the musicians and listeners.[5] The repetitious nature of *Qawwali* lyrics positions the musician and listener in a different concocted time and framework to see the past as a common construction.[6]

MUSIC OF PILGRIMS

The devotional music has a precise spiritual and temporal role for pilgrims at Sufi shrines, in private homes, and in non-religious secular settings. Spiritual music has the incredible elasticity to be used and appropriated in various settings, which has multipurpose functions connected to other social activities.[7] For some *Qawwali* listeners, the art of performance and its aesthetic presentation is the most important component; how a singer communicates and celebrates a moment through poetic music brings a sense of belonging to another place and time. Some enjoy *Qawwali* music in "non-religious" settings such as festivals, weddings, birthday parties, private parties, theatres, street fairs, and national cultural events. While the *Qawwali* lyrics may be the same in content, the context of a secular setting allows both performer and audience to interact on various levels of aesthetics, poetry, imagination, memory, and the art of being moved by sound. The context of *Qawwali* performer and audience ultimately determines how both actors present, interpret, and internalize music.[8]

For Sufi disciples at a shrine attending during the *'urs*, when *Qawwali* is performed regularly, the music is not entertainment; instead, it is understood to be devotional, deeply intimate, and critically important to the journey of spiritual nourishment. To classify *Qawwali* as devotional music means that both listeners and singers alike are in mutually dependent worship, a type of visionary worship where the music creates another imaginary space of interaction and being. Unlike the formal liturgical prayers in a mosque, *Qawwali* devotional music at Sufi shrines is a shared communal praxis of worship using music to seek out divine love.[9] The *Qawwali* poetry, when sung, strives to bring a spiritual experience that transcends the norms of daily living. The *Qawwali* singer is merely an instrument that attempts to use poetry as a device to kindle the flame of love and, for the most part, to intensify the longing for a mystical union.

In Sufi literature, defenders of *Qawwali* music are in an academic, legal, and intellectual battle to justify music in the Islamic tradition. In one respect, Chishti Sufi scholars were defending the place of Chishtiyya Sufism (*tasawwuf*) in the Islamic tradition. Subsequently, they needed to prove that music was not contrary to the Qur'an's principles or the Prophet Muhammad's teachings. Scholars highlighting the benefits of *sama'* (or *Qawwali*), like Nizam ad-Din Awliya, Fakhr ad-Din Zarradi, and Hamid ad-Din Nagauri, emphasize how intellectual knowledge can take several forms, and the spiritual knowledge earned from music is like "wings used for flight for meeting the divine."[10] These Sufi scholars, like many of their contemporaries, understood knowledge in hierarchical terms: cognitive knowledge, spiritual knowledge, intuitive knowledge, and sensory knowledge. Within the Sufi tradition, these various types of knowledge were not equal. Their argument was based on distinguishing the links between knowledge and spiritual enrichment and how these differences define the ability to access divine knowledge.

Since inner esoteric knowledge was highly promoted as part of the Sufi path, and those who attained the "proper knowledge" were to be respected in every possible way, *Qawwali* music was a legitimate activity to connect, remember, and ultimately access the divine. *Qawwali* music, as argued by

Sufi scholars, was tied to a grander practice of inner and outer discipline of Sufism, where Sufi mentored individual masters (shaykh or *pir*) who were preparing the lovers of God (*'ashiq*) for their destiny. It is an interactive group activity where the audience members are participants who engage in a dynamic dialogue between the seeker and the beloved. Proponents of the music in the past and today state unambiguously the way *Qawwali* praises the divine, the Prophets, and the friends of God and the way it serves to connect their fundamental inner longing to be with the divine and have divine presence be an authentic experience. To not satisfy that hunger would defeat the very purpose of existence and destroy our natural connection with the sacred.

If *Qawwali* is a transcendental experience and the construction of a spiritual, sacred identity, then, for pilgrims, it is where body, soul, society, and everything merge.[11] The consciousness of the spiritual seeker is integrated with the very poetry that attempts to reveal the divine's dreams, aspirations, and profound reverence.[12] *Qawwali* poetry not only details the specific conversations yearning for the moment of the encounter, but the entire performance of singing, chanting, and collective coalesced inspiration accentuates the deepest spiritual feelings.[13] Whether the specific *Qawwali* song is eulogizing the Prophet, his family, or the friends of God, the song takes the pilgrim on a journey that crosses through time to a specific moment, which some have described as non-spatial and non-identifiable. For example, according to pilgrims at Sufi festivals, the purpose of *Qawwali* songs dedicated to the praising of the Prophet Muhammad (*na'tiya*) is to go beyond general veneration of the Prophet and for the musicians to bring his precise presence to the arena to shower them with love, mercy, and acceptance.[14] This event is not an accidental event without reason;[15] pilgrims claiming to have seen a vision of the Prophet will vividly describe his characteristics and insist on smelling a unique fragrance incomparable to any other scent.[16] To these pilgrims who testify to the Prophet's presence, the music ceases, time is not quantifiable, and there is a merging of the memory and direct experience of the Prophet in one single time. Pilgrims witness the moment as a state (*hal*), while the Sufi masters will carefully listen to the details of the description for its authenticity.[17]

PERFORMING *QAWWALI*

Typically, during the annual saint's death festival (*'urs*), following the last evening prayer, *Qawwal* singers assemble to arouse the audience of pilgrims to musical devotion.[18] The shrine's primary spiritual and temporal authority, Sajjadanishin, will supervise *Qawwali* groups to their appropriate spaces for performance. Those *Qawwali* singers who are guests of the Sajjadanishin will have proper and formal introductions on the main stage (*sama' khana*). As patrons of the Sajjadanishin, the *Qawwali* musicians will have a stage with an acoustic sound system, a sophisticated lighting system, professional musical equipment set-up, an elegant rug, pillows for seating, and, occasionally, a colorful mural positioned behind the singers.[19] Sufi masters and Sajjadanishin will publicly demonstrate proper Sufi etiquette (*adab*) to the *Qawwali* singers by hugging and greeting the *Qawwali* members. Their respect for the musicians and their position within the Sufi order and as singers to the community of seekers is always publicly displayed. Once seated on stage and after the formal introductions, on one side of the leading *Qawwali* soloist is usually a music accompanist, typically a harmonium player; on the other side is the primary tenor vocalist; behind the *Qawwali* soloist are six to eight vocalists with *tabla*, *dholak* (double-ended drum), and *jhinka* (frame cymbals) players.[20] Across the stage, sitting directly across from the *Qawwali* soloist is either the Sajjadanishin, the disciples (*muridin*) of the Sajjadanishin, patrons of the shrine, or individuals who are personal friends of the singer. During *Qawwali* performances, there are several codes of *adab* where the soloist will follow a strategy of shaping his music and behavior to achieve a specific cliental satisfaction objective.[21] These *Qawwali* concerts are performer-audience interactive, and the performer is expected to develop a spiritual kinship with the audience.[22] In exchange, audience members emotionally or spiritually touched by the devotional music shower the Sajjadanishin and *Qawwal* singers with money, garlands of roses, personal jewelry, or sweets—this act is commonly called *nazarana*. This public demonstration of appreciation does not go unanswered; *Qawwali* singers reciprocate the *adab* by acknowledging the praise either with a smile or by raising their right upturned hand toward their foreheads to recognize their love. The public display of appreciation by audience members to the *Qawwali* musicians is not just for bringing the individual to an ecstatic moment. Still, it can be a deep appreciation of a lyric being sung with graceful melodious technique. Some audience members or pilgrims who are engrossed by the *Qawwali* music and give *nazarana* do so because the moment transcends to another time and place—either with the divine, with Prophets, with Muhammad's family, or with a Sufi saint—and this movement brings about an encounter of thankfulness.

Their hearts are moved to a point to demonstrate a display of liberation, that is, if one can liberate oneself from money and jewelry while at the same these attachments can be used to celebrate the ecstatic moment. For the *Qawwal* soloist, *nazarana* is more than just an appreciation of their devotional music; it is the right time to elevate the *adab* of thankfulness by singing a particular lyric or rag repetitively in various artistic and aesthetic styles. For instance, at the *'urs* of Data Ganj Bakhsh, the renowned Sufi saint known as al-Hujwiri, Nusrat Fateh Ali Khan's hallmark *Qawwali* singing style began slowly with tones of a quest; he gradually moved toward the tension of love, devotion, and the journey of the divine. In one performance of "Oh Last Prophet," Khan sings "there is none like you" repeatedly softly with a gradual inflection on the words "there," "is," "none," "like," and "you." Seeing that listeners are touched by his ability to bring out the inner dimensions of the song, Khan continues to play with these words by skipping the order: he now stresses "none" and "you," then backward "you" and "none." Finally, Khan ends the poetic dance with the last syllables of "you" and "none." After emphasizing the words "there is none like you" in three different musical styles, he continues to sing the rest of the lyrics:

> There is none like you.
> Your face reflects the holy Qur'an,
> The holy Qur'an is from your generosity,
> Oh Sayyid of the world, you are the mark of all compassion.
> There is none like you.[23]

Seeing that *nazarana* is unfolding with these dancing words as several members of the audience have reached an ecstatic state or *hal*, the great *Qawwali* master deliberately returns to the lyrics "there is none like you" to show his appreciation to the audience. The singer is visibly moved by the *nazarana* gestures and how his performance of this song has brought about an environment of numerous encounters. *Qawwali* singers, like Nusrat Fateh Ali Khan, Aziz Mian, Sabri Brothers, and many others, use the moment of *nazarana* to assess, evaluate, and determine how their *Qawwali* performance is being received and whether their music is moving hearts and souls.

Conversely, the social-economic status of *nazarana* giving is not limited to the spiritual lives of audience members or to the ability of the *Qawwal* singer to duplicate the *adab* of thankfulness; instead, *nazarana* giving is yet another arena for audience members to compete against each other publicly. As a listener gives *nazarana*, they raise the bar for others to show their appreciation of devotional music and to demonstrate their status as patrons of the musician. In some instances, audience members will shower the *Qawwal* singer and Sajjadanishin with *nazarana* money and garlands of flowers while pointing to the other competitors who have not come to the stage to donate. This is done by gesturing or purposely taunting them for being shamelessly thrifty.

Divisions of the temporal world are played out in *nazarana* giving fierce competition widens between listeners or Sufi disciples. While there are no rigid guidelines, the unspoken golden rule of the *nazarana* game is not to give anything less than the previous person; to do so is to appear unappreciative of the music and appear too attached to the material world.

Qawwali singers purposely exploit this *nazarana* drama by reinforcing certain lyrics or rags that each person enjoys and often singing specific lyrics with astute eye contact with the potential *nazarana* donor. Unfortunately, the drama of giving to the musicians includes certain individuals elevating themselves in public as the audience's most enthusiastic, appreciative, and eminent patrons. The *nazarana* giving is thus a reminder to others of class divisions, especially those who wish to project their wealth class status or patronage. In some cases, the spirit of the competition pushes individuals to act against the true essence of devotional music by using *nazarana* to humiliate and denigrate others who cannot withstand the competition of offering money. Unable to be a leading patron in the *nazarana* drama, the "defeated listeners" watch from their seats as the victors celebrate themselves with more in *nazarana* giving.

Whether in private homes or at Sufi *'urs* celebrations on the grounds of the shrines, it is expected to observe a handful of individuals who take it upon themselves to use the stage of giving to situate themselves as the sole patrons of the *Qawwali* performance. The *adab* at *Qawwali* concerts and the performance of poetical lyrics have several uniting messages that bring a cohesive message between the *Qawwali* group and audience members. As the devotional music redramatizes a perfect moment in time and the *Qawwal* singer attempts to take listeners to that sacred place and time, both the *Qawwali* singer and listeners are joined together in a mutually trusted journey. An experienced *Qawwali* singer cultivates a certain degree of spiritual tension in the music so that the listeners gradually and carefully unveil the discovery of the unknown. At the same time, listeners use the *Qawwali* music as a spiritual springboard to move closer to heightened spiritual awareness and contact with the sacred memory.[24]

For most *Qawwali* groups still establishing themselves, the *'urs* is the perfect opportunity to display their talents to mesmerize their captive audience.[25] For the unknown *Qawwali* groups, the *'urs* is the primary arena to gain popularity and enter the devotional music industry. As a novice musical group, they may have one *tabla* player and one harmonium player, who also serve as choir members. But without an elegant sound system, these novice *Qawwali* singers fiercely compete over the voices of other singers, who may be sitting just a few yards away. However, different branches of the same Sufi order may support some semi-established singers at the *'urs,* and very often, their spiritual leaders accompany them to these performances at the shrines. *Qawwali* performances last the entire evening up to the break of dawn when pilgrims prepare for another day of rituals. The annual *'urs* celebration of Data Ganj Baksh in Lahore, Pakistan, is a complex multifunctional event with a series of purposes for pilgrims, visitors, tourists, and Sufi organizers.[26] For pilgrims who wait the entire year for the *'urs,* or in some cases, an entire lifetime, traveling to the Data Ganj Baksh's shrine (*dargah*) is their opportunity to request Data sahib for spiritual blessings, guidance from him directly, and interact directly with the Sufi heirs of the shrine. The content of the supplications depends on the individual: some may ask for relief from suffering or a specific request, such as curing an illness, whereas some repetitively seek intercession on their behalf in the hereafter. These supplications vary from person to person and may entail everyday issues of stress, conflict, unemployment, marriage, passing exams, infertility, and a whole host of wishes.[27] Pilgrims perform their rituals as often as possible, and some of the wealthier pilgrims unfamiliar with particular Sufi rituals may hire a *khaddim* (servant of the shrine) as a personal spiritual guide for the festival.

Pilgrims view their spiritual guide as an intermediary to Data Ganj Baksh, who can guide them through the religious rituals properly and ensure that their requests are adequately communicated. A fascinating aspect of the *'urs* is how the non-ritualistic supplications are recited inside and outside the shrine; these are not systematized with a fixed recitation.[28] The *'urs* festival establishes an ideal community and allows pilgrims to leave their daily religious, class, caste, ethnic, tribal, and provincial differences behind. Pilgrims pray together in public, circulate together inside Data Ganj Baksh's shrine, drink rose water from the same bowl during *Qawwali* concerts, and listen and participate in the spiritual lectures circles (*halaqat*)—all of these rituals unify pilgrims while instilling an element of solidarity. For pilgrims, the *'urs* provides an alternative time to their daily lives, where they can enter a new community that is governed by principles of love and respect for their fellow human beings and, above all, come for spiritual renewal as prescribed by the spiritual teachings of Data Ganj Baksh.[29]

From the perspective of the *dargah* management, the *'urs* celebration is an annual demonstration to prove their competency to the pilgrims. By ensuring spiritual guidance and reaffirming a message of hope, forgiveness, reconciliation, and a life built on peace, the Sajjadanishin draw their religious legitimacy from claiming their direct lineage to Data Ganj Baksh. The government of Pakistan has jurisdiction over the mosque on the grounds of the shrine, and the imam is a government-appointed religious leader. At the same time, the Sajjadanishin of the Shrine are designated and selected by the internal mechanisms of the Sufi order. Often, there are tensions between the imam and Sajjadanishin's authority on the grounds of the shrine because those appointed by the government tend to be from a competitive school of thought, for example, the Deobandi Sunni sect, and not from Sufi Islam. Throughout the year, the Sajjadanishin are consumed with administrative and political business, but during the *'urs* they make a conscious effort to be more visible and active to pilgrims and visitors. They will lead the daily ritualistic prayers, assist in distributing food to pilgrims, supervise the main *Qawwali* performances, and be prominent in disseminating Sufi knowledge in terms of lectures. By providing social services to pilgrims and visitors and demonstrating efficient management of the *dargah*, the Sajjadanishin strengthened their moral authority by situating themselves at the center of all activities during the *'urs*. The Sajjadanishin's efforts in maintaining the *dargah*'s prestige consist of incorporating it into a larger social, political, and religious framework so that pilgrims perceive the working of the sacred outside the *dargah*. As the modern-day representatives of Data Ganj Baksh, the Sajjadanishin need to constantly increase resources for the shrine and distribute them to pilgrims as proof of their authority. As custodians of Data Ganj Baksh's Sufi message, the Sajjadanishin carefully uses the *'urs* festival as a mixed arena of spiritual, social, and political activities. One way the Sajjadanishin authority maintains this balancing act is to use *Qawwali* performances to reinforce their intermediary connection to the sacred holy and emphasize that the holy ground of the shrine serves as an ideal society for a diverse faithful community.

QAWWALI NAAT[30]

The order of *Qawwali* songs follows a basic order; after the opening hamd, a song dedicated to God, *Qawwali* songs move to songs praising the Prophet (*naat*), and then devotional songs dedicated to Ali ibn Abi Talib, Ali's family, and Sufi saints (*manqabats*).[31] Nusrat Fateh Ali Khan (d.1997) indisputably became the ambassador of *Qawwali* music to the world by the time he completed his tours to Japan in 1982 and France in 1983. Nusrat was the son of Ustad Fateh Ali Khan (d.1964), a leading *Qawwali* singer and instrumentalist in Punjab, Pakistan, and was trained in the classical khayal tradition—a major form of classical Hindustani music with extensive styles of calls and complex technical virtuosity. The family claims to have belonged to the *Qawwali*-Sufi tradition for six hundred years. As a master in the tradition, Nusrat magically used improvised solos during the *Qawwali* song to implement the sargam technique—where the singer uses syllables to pitches (solmization)—to the notes being sung to illustrate the emotional text of the song. The music would stop abruptly to establish the song's raga or tonal parameter, often beginning with soft tones, with a prelude of the *tabla*, harmonium, and rhythmic clapping hands.[32] Nusrat Fateh Ali Khan sang the following *Qawwali naat* at Data Ganj Baksh's *'urs*.

Oh Last Prophet
(Ya Khatam ar-Rasul)

Oh, the last Prophet from Mecca and Medini[33]
There is none like you.
There is none like you.
There is no throne in the world like yours, you are the one. You are the bright
   light of this group.
Oh last Prophet,
There is none like you.[34]
In a time of giving forgiveness to all
There is no comparison to the level of your forgiveness[35]
Oh Prophet of God, your sacrifices are remembered, and there are like none[36]
There is no one who is like you Oh, last Prophet,
There is none like you.
In this world and in the next world, your blessings are requested in both worlds,
   you are the designated Friend of God and King.[37]
Sayyid Mecca and Medini[38]

Oh last Prophet, Oh Beloved of God, There is none like you.
There is none like you.
Your face reflects the holy Qur'an, the holy Qur'an is from your generosity.
Oh Sayyid of the world, you are the singer of all compassion.
There is none like you.
No other Prophet was ever born with your beauty Greetings to you Sayyid
   Mecca, Medini from Arabia. All people take your name in grace.
And no one in your community is without you Prophet[39]
There is none like you.
Oh, Beloved of God, there is none like you. There is none like you.
You are the embodied light, and only you are the beloved of God.
God created you with eminent and all divine qualities; yours is none to others.
From the earliest prophet Adam to Jesus, oh Prophet, there is none like you.[40]
If my eyes were given but one generous encounter.
On the day of resurrection, it will be our blessing to have such an encounter.
If my eyes were given but one generous encounter.
If these eyes were showered with your blessings, then my entire being
would contain your visions;
Oh Quraishi, Laqbhi, Hashimi, and Mutalbi[41]
If my eyes were given but one generous encounter,
There is none like you
There is none like you
If my eyes were given but one generous encounter, Oh healer on the day of
   Resurrection,[42]
You are the only granter of marvelous love
There is none like you Prophet.
Oh Sir, this is your remarkable glory!
This is your exceptional glory oh Prophet that you reached the steps of heavens,
This remarkable glory was seen in your heavenly ascension[43]
There is none like you oh Prophet, Mecca and Medini
There is none like you!

Another famous musician from Pakistan, Munshi Raziuddin, performed the following *Qawwali naat* in a private home in Karachi on the night of Shab-e Mi'raj, the Night of the Ascension.[44] Ustad Munshi Raziuddin, who later passed away, and his eldest son Fareed Ayaz assumed group leadership, following the Delhi gharana tradition. The Delhi gharana was established by Ustad Tan Ras Khan (d.1872), the eminent teacher of the last Mughal emperor, Bahadur Shah Zafar. Ustad Munshi Raziuddin's lineage is with Amir Khusro (d.1325) and falls within the classical *Qawwali* music or *qawwal bachoon ka gharana* category.

Do Not Ask How I Became
(*Meri Baney Ki Baat Na Poucho*), by Munshi Raziuddin

Allah the Supreme is generous, and Muhammad is great,
It is the generosity of both of them that allows sinners to be forgiven Through Muhammad, the pearls of knowledge became known,
Through *shari'a*, we are servants, but in reality, God only knows best, Through Muhammad, we know godliness,
And, through God, the presence of Muhammad is known.[45]
If one seeks to understand what will be understood,
If one searches in places, where will one end up?
Do not ask how I became[46]
Do not ask how I became
I have become nothing.
Do not ask me; do not ask how I became.

Do not ask how I became on the journey of the Mi'raj[47]
Gabriel asked are you ready for the journey?
This was no journey like any other,
No other prophets have been invited to see the majestic kingdom
It was a journey with the mystical beauty of Buraq and all of God's angels,[48]
This journey was not like any other,
No other prophets have been invited to see the majestic kingdom
Oh please, Do not ask how I became!
It was a time without time, space without space.
A fragrance created for the messenger on his journey
He left this world for the journey, but he never left us,
The journey secured our beloved, this was the time he became.
But do not ask how I became!

Internationally distinguished *Qawwali* singers from Karachi, Pakistan, the Sabri Brothers popularized their art in the late 1960s and 1970s with Western audiences.[49] The Sabri Brothers originally consisted of Haji Ghulam Fareed Sabri (d.1994) and Haji Maqbool Ahmed Sabri; both brothers learned the art from their father Ustad Haji Inayat Sen Sabri in the Northern Indian classical form.[50] Born in Kalyana, Eastern Punjab of India, the family migrated to Karachi during the independence of Pakistan and India in 1947. As descendants of Mian Tansen (d.1589), one of the legendary musicians in the Mughal court of Akbar, the Sabri Brothers mastered their *Qawwali* art under the mentorship of leading *Qawwali* masters such as Ustad Ramzan Khan and Ustad Latafat Hussain Khan. In Multan, "*Ya Mustafa*" was sung during a *Milad an-Nabi* celebration or the birthday of the Prophet.

Oh Mustafa
(*Ya Mustafa*), by Sabri Brothers

I have fallen to the darkness of grief with great pain, Liberate me from these sins.
Oh, you are the luminous savior and the messenger of God. I am in grief and in pain.
Oh messenger of God, with this grief, I am nothing but helpless,
Please come and protect the distressed[51]
The destitute are calling on you, calling for your kindness to please their hearts,
I bear my soul to you, oh Mustafa,
The two known worlds even belong to you.[52]
You are the sole supporter of the destitute,
Sinking ships come to your shore to be rescued,
You are the blessed for the two worlds.
Whatever reputation I claim in this world is due to you,
Still, my heart is impatient and in pain without your presence.

You cannot be compared to either this world or the next,
For you, oh Mustafa, are known for giving us restless ones.
Oh, beloved of God, who else is there but you?
Everyone from Ahl al-Bayt removes all pain and struggles.
Ali belongs to you, Fatima is your daughter who relieves our aches.
You are the grandfather of Hassan and Hussein, whose names force endless tears.
You, Ali, Fatima, Hassan, and Hussain are the secret veils of the two worlds.
Oh, you are the luminous savior and the messenger of God,
Oh, beloved of God, who else is there but you?
With divine order, the sun rises and the sun sets,
The world is filled with sorrow, pain, and nothing but despair
We are told these are mere trials for us to overcome,
You are the sole supporter of the destitute,
Oh beloved of God, Oh Mustafa, rescue us.
Oh, Mustafa, save us.

PEACEBUILDING THROUGH *QAWWALI*

Qawwali as an artistic expression of devotion and, as a musical genre, contributes directly to healing relationships and peacemaking. Examining *Qawwali* music beyond poetry, performance, and aesthetics and how this art addresses inequality, social conflict, injustice, and violence opens the thinking about the role *Qawwali* mediates in inner and outer conflict. There is a distinction between peacemaking, peacebuilding, and conflict resolution in peacemaking and conflict studies. While some use these terms interchangeably without real attention to the detailed theoretical work and processes involved, there are apparent differences in these terms, depending on the stage of the conflict. For instance, conflict management consists of taking concrete action to keep a conflict from escalating further and ensuring a certain degree of control via negotiation, diplomacy, and institutional organizations. Conflict resolution involves parties seeking to change the paradigm of conflict by altering the behavior of actors and working toward a strategic relationship of mutual existence and tolerance. Peacebuilders are those actors who attempt to reframe the context of violence by viewing conflict as an opportunity to improve upon broken relationships and accentuate areas of commonalities and mutual interests.[53]

The combined areas of peacemaking and peacebuilding attempt to address a specific conflict and transform the relationships and institutions in the civil society sector.[54] The differences depend on whether there is an emphasis on structural issues, such as governmental policies, economic debt issues, educational deficiencies, or failed political institutions. Peacemaking, generally, transforms human lives and heals broken human relationships and communities through strategic dialogue. It is a relational approach to increase dialogue and facilitate interaction toward further mutual understanding and trust between conflicting groups.[55] Until recently, very little attention was given to arts-based processes in peacebuilding work and how the arts serve as an important arena for improving relations between conflicting parties. Some have argued that in post-conflict societies, the arts are a very useful tool to transition the inner and outer worlds to move forward in accountability, reconciliation, healing, and reintegrating the individual back into society.[56] Despite these excellent works in peacemaking and peacebuilding, these approaches are centered on societies either in active conflict or recovering from conflict. The question arises: how can the arts contribute toward peacebuilding in times of inactive or nascent conflict? More importantly, can the arts contribute to the inner peace and spiritual formation of members of society to prevent and mediate potential conflicts?

Qawwali music touches on many complex layers of memory of the Prophet and is an important tool for incorporating peacemaking skills. While *Qawwali* is directly for spiritual nourishment and awareness, the imagination of *Qawwali* music also captures an ethic of proper conduct and living peacefully in the world. *Qawwali* music details specific ways of peacemaking and resolving interpersonal conflict that are based on Muhammad's actions and thoughts. *Qawwali* music praising Muhammad highlights his spiritual uniqueness, but it explicitly uses his life as the primary model to engage others in a constructive and respectful dialogue.[57] Qualities such as mediating conflict between warring tribes, companions, families, and sworn enemies are not meant for listeners to admire but rather for them to embody these very qualities in their lives.[58] *Qawwali* lyrics emphasizing compassion and acceptance of the poor are peacemaking skills to underscore the problems of classism and a polarized society based on wealth. These techniques can assist others in conflict to secure or improve an existing situation.[59] Conflicts consist of both interpersonal disputes and communal conflicts, and lyrical references to Mecca, Medina, and Muhammad's night of heavenly ascension demonstrate a comprehensive approach to creating a secure environment and ensuring social well-being for all.

Qawwali music capitalizes on historical memory, Sufi experience, the performance-pilgrim relationship, and the power of poetic peacemaking to instill an inner and outer discipline of preventing and managing conflict by stressing peacemaking's dialogic and nonviolent elements. There is no doubt of the function of the spiritual dimensions of *Qawwali*; however, the music makes it clear that it is vitally important that these learned skills are practiced and applied to everyday life. These skills can be categorized as "preventative capacity or preparedness skills" for any of the stages of violence. For instance, the following lyrics recall the memory of the Prophet's model:

> Love all and hate none.
> Mere talk of peace will give you nothing.
> Mere talk of God and religion will not take you far at all.
> Bring out all of yourself, the true powers of your being
> and the complete illumination of yourself.
> Be immersed in peace and joy and spread it wherever you go and with
> Whomever you meet.[60]

These lyrics directly speak about recognizing everyone and drawing no distinctions between oneself and other human beings. The lyrics stress the need to move beyond talking about peace and immerse oneself in the practical daily living of peacemaking. It instructs the listener not to waste time talking about God and religious matters and criticizes the vast number of theologians and scholars who practice the art of discussion. Instead, *Qawwali* lyrics poignantly blame the intellectual dimensions of peace talks and the lack of practical action by scholars. Such lyrics protest intellectual escapism and the ability to isolate oneself from the practical work of peacebuilding. *Qawwali* lyrics commonly critique the lack of action by scholars and some high-profile Sufi scholars while at the same time pointing out the actual need to practice peacemaking by immersing oneself in the critical issues that concern safety and protection from conflict. For instance, the phrase "with whomever you meet" means to initiate encounters with strangers and to move beyond the familiar world. De-emphasizing ethnocentrism, tribalism, and isolation are valued skills in enhancing dialogue. There is no supercilious theological, legal, or Quranic citation to support the poet's ethical instruction, nor does it advocate religious relativism; instead, it is an expression of living peacefully with others.[61]

Qawwali peacemaking lyrics focus on the relational components of living, where one thinks of oneself as belonging to a community of pious believers on a quest to heal oneself and the world while accessing the divine. Pious listeners hear *Qawwali*'s earnest call to cooperative problem-solving processes. *Qawwali*, as an arts-based medium, serves to provide meaning for identity and meaning for a purpose to those who are victims of injustice, violence, and conflict zones. *Qawwali* lyrics stress to listeners not to be passive victims of their situations but rather to integrate the meaning of the music into their lives and resist the temptation of losing hope to injustice. The indifference of others does not reflect the true reality of being and it does not correlate to how you see your own space in this world. It directly instructs listeners to protest those who humiliate their understanding of Islam (or Sufi practices) and recognize the weakness and inner suffering of the critiques. Muslim critics who condemn Sufism or non-Muslims ridiculing the authenticity of the tradition fail to understand the holistic and spiritual dimension of their faith. The music reveals how critics are more concerned with "winning" you over to their side to establish themselves as superior beings.[62] The construction of a competitive worldview is nothing less than wasted energy to elevate insecure egos in the temporary world. *Qawwali* lyrics, particularly *naat* music praising Muhammad and manaqabats for Ali and Sufi saints, bring back listeners to their struggles and tribulations so that they can relate to them as role models to emulate.

Sabri Brothers' classic *Qawwal Tajdar-e Haram* ("King of the Holy Sanctuary") resonates with the deep hunger to encounter Prophet Muhammad in Medina by requesting his support to remove their grief and pain. For example, a section of the *naat* lyrics states:

Oh, King of the Holy Sanctuary
Please cast your magnificent presence over us, The unfortunate lonely ones,
There is truly no one else to help us, the unfortunate, lonely ones, We have come to your doorsteps in Medina, the radiant light of Medina.
Oh, King of the Holy Sanctuary.
Please cast your magnificent presence over us,
We will die here, in your presence reciting your names.
Let us go to Medina, Let us go to Medina to meet the holy King, The holy King who was persecuted but did not tremble,
The Chosen who wanted liberation from the oppressors,
Let us go to Medina, Let us go to Medina to meet the holy King, Here, there, everywhere is all about God.
Where no one is forgotten, where everyone is accepted,
You showed us to worship; everything about you is worship.
Where the pious come to love you,
Even the forgotten disabled come to love you,
Let us go to Medina,
Let us go to Medina to meet the holy King.[63]

Qawwali naat music emphasizes that interpersonal and communal relationships are not static but dynamic. The Prophet's tomb in Medina not only serves as space for the community of the pious to congregate for prayers, supplications, and seeking intermediary encounters, but the historical memory reminds the pious to practice piety and to remember the importance of community in the struggle of remaining faithful. The *Qawwali* song brings the listener to reflect on the fundamentals of peacemaking practices on a personal level, ponder how we often fall short in personal convictions of faith, and remember the delicate art of kindness to others. The devotional songs bring the listener to the sacred memory of the Prophet's life and submerge them into an intimate connection of the self with him. During this connection the participant is transcending from memory to witnessing the sacred existence of the holy in action.

In Tajdar-e Haram, the lyrics "Let Us go to Medina" (*Chalo Medina, Chalo*) repeatedly highlight the traveling leitmotif for the listener to remember that crossing time and space boundaries means being active in making peace with oneself and others in the temporal world, even those who have harmed or persecuted you. To a certain degree, it is a reconciliation with the enemy because it acknowledges those who criticized and attempted to destroy or subvert the discipline of being a Sufi. To meet the holy king, the traveler must be a practitioner of peacemaking; the true meaning of re-enacting the customs of the Prophet as a conduit to meeting the divine is directly linked to how you live in peace with others and how your journey on temporary earth is interconnected with the sacred. The *Qawwali* song "*Chalo Medina, Chalo*" should not be construed as a rapture for those seeking to escape their lives, or escapism; instead, it is a poetic peacemaking tapping into the spiritual imagination of spiritual aspirants reconnecting them to identify and socially engage with their communities by interacting with those who are marginalized, destitute, and invisible poor.

Qawwali music as an arts-based process is healing for the individual, especially reconciling with others who have caused pain or harm. It brings people together to reflect and act upon relational peacebuilding by assessing their current spiritual lives in relation to the spiritual quest to encounter, engage, and ultimately surrender their love to the Prophet. Its therapeutic role for people who suffer from violence, conflict, or interpersonal violence is embedded in the lyrics as it is the interactive dynamic between the musician, the community of listeners, and the memory of a previous community. *Qawwali* music takes the listener to a past memory where the sacred is shared and simultaneously offers an alternative vision for the future. *Qawwali* musicians mediate between worlds, where individuals are inspired to see themselves in another time and space, and, as a result, conflicts are placed in perspective for reconciliation. The music is more than a dialogue between the musician and the community of believers because it goes beyond trust-building and into the heart of faith-building or, more accurately, faith-understanding. As a component of a larger tradition with immense history, *Qawwali* music directly contributes to peacebuilding efforts, an inner reconciliation process tied with an outer process of correcting one's moral actions.

NOTES

1. These works have been helpful to me in understanding *Qawwali* music in this framework: Theodore Adorno, *Introduction to the Sociology of Music* (New York: Continuum, 1968); L.I. Al Faruqi, "Music, Musicians, and Muslim Law," *Asian Music*, 1985, 17: 13–36; Martin Stokes (ed.), *Ethnicity, Identity and Music: The Musical Construction of Place* (Oxford: Berg Press, 1994); J. Shepherd, *Music as a Social Text* (Cambridge: Polity Press, 1991).

2. Regula Qureshi, *Sufi Music in India and Pakistan: Sound, Context, and Meaning in Qawwali* (Cambridge: Cambridge University, 1987); Qureshi, "Muslim Devotional: Popular Religious Music and Muslim Identity under British, Indian, and Pakistani Hegemony," *Asian Music*, 1992, 24, no. 1: 111–21.

3. David Hume, *An Enquiry Concerning Human Understanding*, third edition (Oxford: Clarendon Press, 1975).

4. Jean-Paul Sartre, *Imagination; A Psychological Critique* (Ann Arbor: University of Michigan Press, 1962).

5. Martin Stokes, "Voices and Places: History, Repetition, and the Musical Imagination," *Journal of the Anthropological Institute*, 1995, 3: 673–91.

6. See Peter Etzkorn, "On Music, Social Structure and Sociology," *International Review of the Aesthetics and Sociology of Music*, 1974, 5, no. 1: 43–49; Harold Powers, "The Structure of Musical Meaning, A View From Banaras (A Metamodel for Milton)," *Perspectives of New Music*, 1977, 14, no. 2: 308–34.

7. Alan Merriam, *The Anthropology of Music* (Evanston: Northwestern University Press, 1964).

8. See Regula Qureshi, "Musical Sound and Contextual Input: A Performance Model for Musical Analysis," *Ethnomusicology*, 1987, 31, no. 1: 56–86.

9. This subject of the legality of music and applying it in devotional terms is a long controversial topic between legal scholars and Sufi scholars. See Amnon Shiloah, "Music and Religion in Islam," *Acta Musicologica*, 1997, 69, no. 2: 143–55; Amnon Shiloah, "The Role and Nature of Music in the Practice of the Sama,'" *International Musicological Society, Report of the Twelfth Congress*, 1977; Arthur Gribetz, "The Sama' Controversy: Sufi vs. Legalist," *Studia Islamica*, 1991, 74: 43–62; M.L.R. Choudhury, "Music in Islam," *Journal of the Asiatic Society*, 1957, 13, no. 2: 54–61.

10. Fakhr uddin Zarradi, *Rislat Usul as-Sama, Jhajjar*, in Bruce Lawrence, "Early Chishti Approach to Sama," *Islamic Society and Culture: Essays in Honour of Professor Aziz Ahmad, Manohar*, edited by M. Israel and N. K. Wagle (New Delhi: Manohar Publishers, 1983).

11. I interviewed one of Lahore's most prominent Sufi teachers, Hakim Muhammad Musa sahib, about *Qawwali* and Islam; he repeated this statement to emphasize the immense value of music and the individual in society.

12. Interview with Hakim Muhammad Musa sahib.

13. Sufi scholars repeatedly highlighted the difference between spiritual feelings and general emotions. In my interviews, Sufi scholars noted general emotions related to daily ordinary urges or needs, such as feeling the anticipation of a marriage or the emotions of losing a person in one's life. Spiritual feelings relate to the desires of the self to return to the creator.

14. In my interviews, pilgrims stated, "I cannot go to Medina al-Munawwar to see the holy Prophet, so I come to Data sahib's *'urs* to meet him." This appropriately expresses the Sufi disciple's inner desire to encounter the sacred.

15. Pilgrims frequently expressed that their visions of the Prophet did not make them delusional or mentally unfit; instead, it was a rational experience, given their intense desire to meet him.

16. Interviews with Sufi disciples at Data Ganj Baksh's *'urs* festival.

17. Interviews with Chishti Sufi disciples at Data Ganj Baksh's shrine and after Sabri Brothers' performance in Multan.

18. It needs to be clear that *Qawwali* music is not permissible by all Sufi orders, and these orders do not allow *Qawwali* music at their shrines. Chishti Sufi, obviously, permits *Qawwali* music, and at certain Chishti *dargahs*, *Qawwali* music is performed without regulation. However, other major Sufi orders, such as Suhrawardis, Naqshbandis, and Qadris, do not allow *Qawwali* music at their shrines.

19. For some of the more organized and professional *Qawwali* parties, managers and publicists will ensure that the *'urs* performance is appropriately recorded to market the live musical performance for a later date.

20. A *Qawwali* party can range from three to fifteen members, and the number of singers and instruments used depend upon the principal soloist. This person is commonly a disciple of the *Sajjadanishin* or a guest member of the Sufi Order.

21. For studies about Sufi practice and *adab*, see Ian Richard Netton, "The Breath of Felicity: Adab, Ahwal, Maqamat and Abu Najib al-Suhrawardi," in Leonard Lewisohn (ed.), *The Heritage of Sufism* (London: Khaniqahi Nimatullahi Publications, 1993); Javed Nurbakhsh, "The Rules and Manners of the Khanaqah," in *The Tavern of Ruin* (New York: Khaniqahi Nimatullahi Publications, 1975); and Miles Irving, "The Shrine of Baba Farid at Pakpattan," in *Notes on Punjab and Mughal India: Selections from the Journal of the Punjab Historical Society*, edited by Zulfiqar Ahmed (Lahore: Sang-e-Meel Publications, 1988), pg. 55.

22. Brian Silver, "The Adab of Musicians," in Barbara Metcalf (ed.), *Moral Conduct and Authority* (Berkeley: University of California Press, 1984), pp. 318–20.

23. The high-profile *Qawwali* performances at Sufi *'urs* festivals are not pressured to finish their performances rapidly. These lyrics were sung for twenty minutes. For the rest of the *Qawwali* song, see the end of the section.

24. Regular Qureshi, "Musical Sound and Contextual Input: A Performance Model for Musical Analysis," *Ethnomusicology* 1997, 31, 56–86.

25. At Baba Farid's shrine in Pakpattan, *Qawwali* music is performed around the clock except during formal liturgical prayers. There is a substantial distinction between *Qawwali* singers and Chishti shrine authorities in singling out those singers who are commercially driven versus those *Qawwali* musicians who sing for the love of tradition.

26. For more on *'urs* studies, see Christian Troll (ed.), *Muslim Shrines in India: Their Character, History, and Significance* (New Delhi: Oxford University Press, 1989); Jalaluddin Humai, *Tasawwuf dar Islam* (Tehran: Sazmani-Wira, 1983); P. Lewis, *Pirs, Shrines, and Pakistani Islam* (Rawalpindi: Christian Study Centre, 1985); Harald Einzmann, *Ziarat und Pir-e Muridi* (Stuttgart: Franz Steiner Verlag, 1988); Nile Green, *Indian Sufism Since the Seventeenth Century: Saints, Books*; and *Empires in the Muslim Deccan* (London: Routledge, 2006); and Nile Green, "Stories of Saints and Sultans: Remembering History at the Sufi Shrines of Aurangabad," *Modern Asian Studies*, 2004, 38, no. 2: 419–46.

27. See Ibn 'Ata Allah al-Iskandari, *The Key to Salvation: A Sufi Manual of Invocation*, translated by Mary Ann Koury-Danner (Portland: International Specialized Book Services, 1996).

28. The supplications recited are in the vernacular language, so it is common to hear a variety of languages used in the shrine's dialogue.

29. For more about pilgrims, see Victor Turner, "The Centre Out There: Pilgrim's Goal," *History of Religions*, 1973, 12: 191–230; Muhammad Din Kalim Qadiri, *Halaat wa Rifaat Data Ganj Bakhsh*; and Seyyed Hossein Nasr, *Sufi Essays*, second edition (Albany: SUNY Press, 1991).

30. All *Qawwali* songs translated are condensed versions of the entire song performed. These performances were in front of a live audience, and as usual, they differ from recorded and edited versions on the market.

31. For a good article on the varieties of *Qawwali* songs and the order of presentation, see Regula Qureshi, "Indo-Muslim Religious Music, an Overview," *Asian Music*, 1972, 3, no. 2: 15–22; and Adam Nayyar, *Origin and History of the Qawwali* (Islamabad: Lok Virsa Research Centre, 1988), http://www.osa.co.uk/qawwali_history.html.

32. See Lorraine Sakkata, "The Sacred and the Profane: Qawwali Represented in the Performances of Nusrat Fateh Ali Khan," *The World of Music*, 1994, 36, no. 3: 86–99; *Nusrat has Left the Building . . . But When?* directed by Farjad Nabi, matteela.com/Nusrat (1997);

for liner notes on *Qawwali* music songs by Nusrat Fateh Ali Khan, by Qamar-ul Huda, see *Nusrat! Live at Meany*, https://www.arabfilm.com/item_print.html?itemID=107; and *A Voice from Heaven*, directed by Giuseppe Asaro (1999).

33. The city of Mecca is where the Prophet Muhammad was born in 570, and in the year 621, the Prophet and his followers migrated to a northern city, Yathrib, now referred to as *Medina an-Nabi* ("The City of the Prophet") where his tomb lies. For poetic purposes, Medina is changed to Medini. This reference to these two cities illustrates his profound love for the people of the region and the place of his prophetic work.

34. "There is none like you" is referring to the Prophet's unique spiritual and temporal qualities compared to previous Prophets and messages. To see an excellent analysis, see Annemarie Schimmel's *And Muhammad is the Messenger: The Veneration of the Prophet in Islamic Piety*, especially chapter 3 (Chapel Hill: University of North Carolina Press, 1985).

35. *Rahmat* or forgiveness is not only one of God's ninety names in the Qur'an, but this *Qawwali* song refers to the forgiveness the Prophet displayed to those who denied his missionary work and persecuted him. For example, after the community of Taif attacked Muhammad, Gabriel asked what should be done to the people of Taif; Muhammad replied, "May mercy be given to them."

36. *Qurban* or sacrifices refers to the Prophet's struggle to have polytheists reflect on their beliefs to accept the universal God's oneness. In his twenty-three years as the final Prophet, he persevered through bitter resistance, humiliation, isolation, and assassination attempts, demonstrating his self-sacrifice.

37. The Quranic reference to a friend of God or *Wali-Allah* is one of the closest relationships designated by God, and in this song, it reflects the closeness of the Prophet to God in terms of human potential. Both worlds refer to our world and the world to come when all people are resurrected in front of God. See Qur'an 10:62: "Remember there is neither fear nor regret for the friends of God."

38. A Sayyid is a title for persons with a lineage from the Prophet's household.

39. This highlights the idea that Muslims exist because of the very life model of the Prophet Muhammad. The poem alludes to how Muslims try to model their lives by the example set by the Prophet.

40. Many *Qawwali* songs are dedicated to Muhammad and to other earlier prophets before him. In particular, *Mi'raj Qawwali* songs commonly portray Muhammad's unique place in Prophetic history and his spiritual perfection compared to previous prophets. See Muhyi al-din Ibn 'Arabi, *Risalat al-Anwar* (Cairo: Maktabat 'Alam al-Fikr, 1982); Rifa't Fawzi 'Abd al-Muttalib, *Ahadith al-Isra wa al-Mi'raj* (Cairo: Maktab al-Khaniji, 1980); Nadhir Azmah, *Mi'raj wa-Ramz al-Sufi* (Beirut: Dar al-Bahith, 1973); John Collins and Michael Fishbane (eds.), *Death, Ecstasy, and Other Worldly Journeys* (Albany: SUNY Press, 1995); 'Abd al-Karim ibn Hawazin al-Qushayri, *Kitab al-Mi'raj* (Cairo: Dar al-Kutub al Hadithah, 1964); and Brooke Olson Vuckovic, *Heavenly Journeys, Earthly Concerns: The Legacy of the Mi'raj in the Formation of Islam* (London: Routledge, 2005).

41. Names of the different tribes of the Prophet.

42. *Shifa'* or healer is another name attributed to the Prophet, whereby it is believed that on the day of resurrection, he will be the one to intercede and help the weak in front of God. Healer is commonly used in poetry and music to illustrate the Prophet as a spiritual doctor and a guide for those in despair.

43. The Prophet's heavenly ascension (*shab-e-mi'raj*) was an event that marked his unique calling by God so that the divine may dialogue with him, as well as show what lies in the

heavens. There, Muhammad met all the previous prophets and led the prayers with all the prophets behind him.

44. *Qawwali* singers are commonly hired for private parties, particularly religious holidays like *Shab-e Mi'raj*. Munshi Raziuddin is a prominent *Qawwali* singer and a descendant of eight generations of *Qawwali* masters. On this evening, almost all *Qawwali* were exclusively dedicated to *naat*, except for one *manqabat*.

45. The poetic interchange of "knowing godliness through Muhammad" and "through God, the presence of Muhammad is known" does not imply the annihilation of one into the other or that Muhammad is a divine being. Instead, yet another *Qawwali naat* lyric shows the intimacy of the Prophet's status with the divine while being a human agent. As a human being and messenger of God, the Prophet's ascension journey sealed the notion, at least for Sufis, of Muhammad's place in human and divine history.

46. "Do not ask how I became" is sung in the first person to bring the listener to the potential inner thoughts of Muhammad as the events unfolded to him. The use of the first person is common in many *Qawwali naat* songs to illustrate the intimacy between the listener and musician; in this song, the journey is a personal venture that needs to be shared.

47. *Shab-e Mi'raj* is celebrated on the evening of the twenty-sixth of Rajab, or the seventh month in the Islamic calendar. Also known as *Layla Isra wa al-Mir'aj*.

48. The term *buraq* refers to the unicorn-type animal that carried Muhammad from Mecca to the heavens on his ascension.

49. There is little work focusing on the history of the Sabri Brothers *Qawwali* music and its impact on faith, devotion, and the music-audience context. Two publications on the Sabri Brothers music are very good: Amatullah Armstrong Chishti, *The Lamp of Love: Journeying with the Sabri Brothers* (Karachi: Oxford University Press, 2006); and Muneera Haeri, *The Chishtis: A Living Light* (Karachi: Oxford University Press, 2000). To read discussions on Sabri Brothers music elsewhere, see Bruce Lawrence and Carl Ernst, *Sufi Martyrs of Love: The Chishti Order in South Asia and Beyond* (New York: Palgrave, 2002); George Ruckert, *Music in North India: Experiencing Music, Expressing Culture* (New York: Oxford University Press, 2003); Judy Lochhead and Joseph Auner (eds.), *Postmodern Music/Postmodern Thought: Studies in Contemporary Music and Culture* (London: Routledge, 2002); and Pir Zia Inayat Khan (ed.), *A Pearl in Wine: The Life, Music and Sufism of Hazrat Inayat Khan* (New Lebanon, NY: Omega Press, 2001).

50. Since the death of Ghulam Fareed Sabri (or "Bara Sabri sahib") in 1994, the Sabri Brothers *Qawwali* party is not one single group.

51. *Qawwali naat* lyrics portray humility through suffering and broken hearts. In songs such as these, people refer to themselves as destitute and poor because of their separation from Muhammad's presence. In some sections of the lyrics, the reference to the poor means those who suffer from intense poverty and economic distress, and the interchange of these words is not accidental.

52. The reference to "two worlds" is a common lyric in *Qawwali naat*. Notably, *Qawwali* musicians and Sufi poets refer to the existing world and the hereafter as another motif of moving back and forth in fluid terms, as if one is on a journey.

53. See Dudley Weeks, *The Eight Essential Steps to Conflict Resolution: Preserving Relationships at Work, at Home, and in the Community* (New York: Tarcher/Putnam, 1992).

54. Louise Diamond and John McDonald, *Multi-track Diplomacy: A Systems Approach to Peace*, third edition (West Hartford, CT: Kumarian Press, 1996); Dennis Sandole, "A Comprehensive Mapping of Conflict and Conflict Resolution Research: A Three Pillar Approach,"

Peace and Conflict Studies, 1998, 5, no. 2: 1–30; John Paul Lederach, *Preparing for Peace: Conflict Transformation Across Cultures* (Syracuse: Syracuse University Press, 1995).

55. John Paul Lederarch, *Building Peace: Sustainable Reconciliation in Divided Societies* (Washington, DC: US Institute of Peace, 1997); Johan Galtung, *Peace by Peaceful Means. Peace and Conflict, Development and Civilization* (London: Sage Publications, 1996); Ronald Fisher, "The Potential for Peacebuilding. Forging a Bridge from Peacekeeping to Peacebuilding," *Peace and Change*, 1993, 18, no. 2: 247–66.

56. Malvern Lumsden, "Breaking the Cycle of Violence: Three Zones of Social Reconstruction," in Ho Won Jeong (ed.), *The New Agenda for Peace Research* (Brookfield, VT: Ashgate, 1999).

57. I use the term "uniqueness" in conjunction with the Quranic reference to the Prophet as the "Seal of the Prophets" (*khatam an-anbiya'*) and the Sufi use of the "perfect man" (*insan al-kamil*).

58. To see works on modeling and memory, see Hashim Ma'ruf Hasani, *Sirat al-Mustafa, Nazrat Jadidah* (Beirut: Dar al-Qalam, 1975); Mahmoud Ayoub, *Redemptive Suffering in Islam: A Study of the Devotional Aspects of Ashura in Twelver Shi'ism* (The Hague: Mouton, 1978); Harald Motzki (ed.), *The Biography of Muhammad: The Issue of the Sources* (Leiden: Brill, 2000); Gregro Schoeler, *Charakter und Authentie der muslimischen Überlieferung über das Leben Muhammeds* (Berlin, 1996).

59. For articles on the arts and peacebuilding, see Craig Zelizer, "The Role of Artistic Processes in Peacebuilding in Bosnia-Herzegovina," *Peace & Conflict Studies*, 2003, 10, no. 2: 62–75; C. Slotoroff, "Drumming Technique for Assertiveness and Anger Management in the Short-term Psychiatric Setting for Adult and Adolescent Survivors of Trauma," *Music Therapy Perspectives*, 1994, 12, no. 2: 111–16; J.P. Sutton (ed.), *Music, Music Therapy and Trauma: International Perspectives* (Philadelphia, PA: Jessica Kingsley Publishers, 2002); John Crandall, "Music and Peace: Thoughts on Musician as Peacemaker," *Music Therapy*, 2002, 8, no. 1: 122–25.

60. Sabri Brothers *Qawwali* song "Meri Koi Nahin hai" ("There is no one else for me") can be accessed from *Greatest Hits of Sabri Brothers*, volumes 1–3 (Sirocco: United Kingdom, 1994).

61. For examples of literature emphasizing specific recovery methods from conflict, see Barbara Wheeler, "Reflections on the Importance of Music in Dealing With the Tragedies of September 11" (2002); and S. Krippner and T. M. McIntyre (eds.), *The Psychological Impact of War Trauma on Civilians: An International Perspective* (Westport, CT: Praeger, 2003).

62. Examples of definite criticism against the critiques, listen to Nusrat Fateh Ali Khan's *Mei Jana Jogi de Naal, Tum ek Gorarhdanda ho*, and *Kali Kali Zulfon ke Phande Na Dalo*, and Aziz Mian's *Jannat Mujhe Mile Na Mile* and *Hi Kam-Bakt Tu Ne Pe He Nahi*.

63. This is a brief translation of Sabri Brothers *Tajdar-e Haram*; one can listen to it on *Pyar ke Morr*, volume 1 (Oriental Star, 1993).

Conclusion

The concepts of peacebuilding and constructing a peace infrastructure have been painfully dichotomous: the role of government versus civil society members. Within the field of peacebuilding and conflict resolution, government approaches toward peacebuilding are naturally designed to be top-down. Here, government bodies are in charge of engineering the coordination of dialogues, leading the timeline of the ceasefires in conflict, seeking out the specific terms of the peace agreement, and ensuring there is no retribution during the reconciliation process. Critics state that government operating at the national level might lead to a disconnect between national-level interests and local needs and needs of diverse communities. When a peace infrastructure, such as in Libya or Afghanistan, is centered at the national level and those in charge of critical members of the national federal government, it is common for local-level actors to be disconnected or even unincluded from the national-level process.

Critics commonly state that national peacebuilding efforts by governments lack the necessary sincerity or commitment to the vested interests of local decision-makers. Of course, there is no contention that the national government's involvement in peacebuilding is required—at all levels—because they bring the legitimacy of political will, the wide variety of resources, government capacity, international interlocutors, and the state apparatus to enact peace. Similarly, Islamic peacebuilding efforts fall either in local civil society member activities or with a close connection with state activities. Muslim peacebuilders, religious peacebuilders, and Muslim faith-based organizations are critically engaged with problem solving and identifying sustainable solutions to conflict. However, there is still a need to increase skills to analyze and adequately identify core reasons for violent conflicts and formulate solutions to complex problems. They need more significant support and resources for mediation and negotiation efforts to facilitate change in their communities. Unfortunately, analytical tools for conflict prevention, mediation, transformation, program effectiveness, and monitoring of peacebuilding progress are rarely shared with counterparts in the field.

An area I found absent in my research and fieldwork is a focus on truth commissions and transitional justice among the works of Islamic peacebuilding. Truth commissions, transitional justice, and restorative justice dialogues and programming are standard in the UN process and Western approaches to conflict resolution. In seeking to rebuild societies in post-conflict societies with sustainable peace by establishing the rule of law, judicial and non-judicial mechanisms designed to address past injustices, Islamic peacebuilders have not moved adequately in this space. Whether there are cultural, tribal, or geopolitical reasons for not developing thorough systems of truth commissions or transitional justice, there is a vast Islamic literature on dealing with compensation to victims, seeking justice from oppressors, etc. Islamic peacebuilders will need to engineer institutions that support transitional justice that is tied to truth commissions, retributive and corrective justice, and prosecuting perpetrators of human rights violations. This transparent process will heal the community by revealing the truth about past crimes through public truth-gathering forums, providing victims with reparations, scrutinizing governmental failures or complicity, and recommending effective reconciliation programs. Transitional justice and truth commissions will be a step forward in addressing structural violence—that is, the entrenched socio-economic conditions that cause poverty, exclusion, inequality, and deep divisions in society. Truth commissions must comprehensively address civil and political rights violations but intrinsic economic, social, and political disparities. The transitional justice mechanisms, if properly designed, have the dual purpose of being backward-looking and forward-looking because they seek to illuminate, expose, and come to terms with a violent and repressive past and identify practical strategies to promote peace and public participation. The reality is that truth commissions and transitional justice initiatives are not driven by the bottom-up, by civil society organizations; instead, dedicated resources and institutions are needed at the national government level to drive it. Unfortunately, in Muslim-majority countries, most national governments do not have the moral courage or ethical fortitude to address their complicit association with past atrocities.

In October 1999, the UN General Assembly passed Resolution 53/243 declaring a culture of peace, defined as a set of values, attitudes, traditions, and modes of behavior and ways of

life based on respect for life, ending violence, and promoting nonviolence through education, dialogue, and cooperation. Islamic peacebuilders and faith-based organizations need to have a similar vision of their societies; mitigating violence in Muslim-majority communities needs to be cultivated, nourished, and reinforced with a culture of peace, seeding and cultivating a culture of peacemaking, in which the principles and values of peacebuilding are founded on Islamic principles of justice and are affirmed publicly and privately. A culture of peace consists of instilling the skills and attitudes needed to recognize and defuse potential conflicts on personal, interpersonal, communal, regional, national, and international levels. Scholars of Islam have pointed out the need to critically focus on fostering a culture of peace through education. Other scholars and Islamic peacebuilders believe that there should be an integrated Islamic peacebuilding approach within the larger enterprises of sustainable economic and social development and a transparent, representative political system. An integrated approach would bring together government and civil society stakeholders to create an innovative target plan to transform cultures, institutions, systems, and relationships to prevent or transform conflict.

An integrated Islamic peacebuilding approach would require the government, the private sector, academia, research centers, industry leaders, and civil society organizations to develop an engaging sophisticated system that provides support throughout the conflict and peacebuilding life cycle. With resoluteness, intrepidity, and firmness to a long-term commitment, leadership must share their common purpose to inspire collective action. An Islamic peacebuilding approach would require a network of leaders to align essential values, principles, and ethics to define goals with clarity and firm purpose. To move beyond the barriers of government and nongovernment biases and suspicion, these fundamental values will forge transparency, trust, and effective collaboration. The necessity of dynamic leadership to sustain collaboration, interests, and the influence of various factors ensures people want to stay in the network.

In this book, I pointed out that Islamic peacebuilding approaches and frameworks, especially those established in the Islamic contemplative tradition, are distinguished because of the emphasis on humility as a virtue.

Humility within the contemplative tradition is not to forget or abandon relationships with others or relinquish one's obligations to the community or family; instead, debates centered on how it was a process of self-actualization. Shaikh Zarruq argued that inner humility involves a commitment to working toward a higher self-realization. Islamic humility was not a preoccupation with being insignificant compared to something else or lowering the self from participating in society. It did not involve being passive from public participation, but it meant being part of a moral-ethical system that promoted a transcendental meaning. The Islamic contemplative ethics of virtue teaches the inner struggle to constantly strive to cultivate humility in every state, both with God and all human relationships. When these virtues of humility are cultivated and connected with the divine names, such as gratitude, compassion, forgiveness, love, and mercy, these qualities signify an important state of poverty and the need to be in front of God. These virtues are part of the understanding that humility demands a responsibility to seek a meaningful life (*uluw al-himma*) with transcendence toward the sacred as the goal. And, in this journey of transcendence, the individual needs to uphold, preserve, and protect sacredness; that is, the individual understands what God holds as sacred which means the individual must be committed to finding what is holy to preserve (*hifdh al-hurma*).

Building peace is a long-term process and commitment. Local civil society organization members depend heavily on funded projects; the donor-driven model is broken as it does not provide adequate space, time, and long-term thinking to sustain peace. It is critically important to re-examine new models of partnerships, and sustainability that is locally driven and implemented. My research and collaboration with Muslim peacebuilders has revealed that local partners need a solid analytical framework to create effective long-term program design. I learned a great deal from Muslim peacebuilders without shiny gadgets or expensive programs to monitor and evaluate their work. They manage peacebuilding, peace education, conflict resolution, and development organizations operating on a shoestring budget without advocates or audiences to appreciate or celebrate their achievements. Many never came across terms like "human security," "integrated peacebuilding," or "mainstreaming cross-sectoral issues" in their endeavors; however, they do understand how to transform relationships and structures in order to reduce suffering, injustice, and the potential of conflict.

Before Mary B. Anderson's 1999 book, *Do No Harm: How Aid Can Support Peace or War*, where she suggested that there be a Hippocratic Oath for development workers to ensure that no harm is done while pursuing and implementing development goals, the Islamic contemplative tradition sought out ways for the individual to seek and live a peaceful life. Anderson's work drew attention to the unintended consequences of humanitarian assistance, especially during complex political emergencies, and the need to create a responsible risk analysis before immersing into a local crisis. Local Muslim peacebuilders are acutely aware of the international donor system, typical for stand-alone one-time programming contracts, and short-term commitments to the local area before another region disrupts their attention.

This work demonstrated that Islamic peacebuilding significantly impacts Muslim-majority communities, faith-based organizations, and religious leaders who are mainstream peacebuilders. The fact that the larger peacebuilding and conflict resolution worldview understands religious peacebuilding primarily through Christian concepts and worldviews and believes that these practices can be universally applied exemplifies both the uneasiness of religion and contesting the role of religion in peacebuilding. Acknowledging that the very communities peacebuilding and development programs operate in still uphold religious and spiritual traditions could enhance their ability to gain trust and confidence and ultimately develop dynamic relationships and connections among civil society members. Along the same lines, acknowledging the diversity of religious practices and beliefs, including within the Islamic contemplative tradition, would deepen collaboration between the secular global donor and peacebuilding community. It would be wise, if not practical, to consider limiting the desire to enforce and indoctrinate Western neoliberal progressive values onto local Muslim civil society members, which would bring a deeper appreciation of the long-term relationship. The challenges we face in peacebuilding require practical solutions and compel practitioners, religious leaders, faith-based organizations, secular peacebuilding organizations, researchers, community leaders, and scholars to develop a critical mind toward a new, reimagined vision.

Epilogue

During the final stages of the manuscript, the world watched on October 7, 2023, as the Palestinian Hamas organization attacked Israeli citizens and forcibly took hostages. In retaliation, the Israeli government promised a punitive retaliation that would eventually eradicate any presence of Hamas as an organization. Since the Israeli invasion of Gaza, over 1.1 million Palestinians have fled southward toward the Rafah border with Egypt; Israel has ceased all flow of food and medical supplies and stopped water and fuel to the citizens of Gaza. There are an estimated eleven thousand dead Palestinian Gazans, and over half of them are children.

Binary fixed positions were already in place: either one was with the camp ultimately supporting Israel's right to security and retaliation against Hamas or with the camp supporting an independent Palestinian state that would end Israel's occupation of territories. Debate, dialogue, and discussion of the roots of the conflict were not appreciated or encouraged because the political climate disengaged rational discourse. Those who even engaged in diligent conversations needed to resolve the seven-and-a-half-decade Israeli-Palestinian conflict were called *jihad*-sympathizers, anti-Semitic, or advocates for radicalism. It was déjà vu of the post-9/11 America. Sides were demarcated: colleges, universities, and the private sector issued official announcements on not tolerating hate, anti-Semitic, and Islamophobia rhetoric and reminders that civil action would be taken against any individual or group violating the code of conduct of the organization. As binary fixed positions paralyzed the world, it could not even muster up state alliances to convince or deter the Israeli military's campaign of mass killing of civilians, which was not the answer to their security issues. Suffering upon suffering, death, destruction of lives, screaming mothers and children, more orphans were being documented by the hour, and visuals of infant corpses numbed us—but the world was just paralyzed.

War needs scrutiny and criticism, not cheerleading. The field of peacebuilding and conflict resolution advocates an engagement with groups and parties using terrorism as a tactic that is not soul-selling or cutting a deal with the devil. The challenge is to make the violent extremist movements debate, articulate flexibility in their demands, and reshape their violent tactics into reachable reforms while opening a political process to broader participation to address the deeper problems of society that underlie their grievances. The American lessons of the Global War on Terror demonstrated that the most powerful militaries working together in a coalition could not eviscerate terrorism in Afghanistan or Iraq; instead, their activities created new mutations and offshoots of violent extremist groups. A war against an idea and tactic is unwinnable. It is important to see terrorism as a phase in a conflict waged by a group with longstanding political, social, economic, and other types of grievances, and the state applies this term to designate a group's activities as outside the rule of law. Focusing exclusively on acts of terrorism limits the serious analysis and necessary understanding of the broader range of issues at work in any given conflict situation. Using a conflict resolution framework, one can think about the more comprehensive set of issues, actors, and behaviors involved, as well as the history of a conflict and the grievances that terrorism is tied to—grievances that need long-term political, social, cultural, and economic solutions.

The aim of engagement, therefore, is to ensure that the use of violence is in check, transforming their ends from destruction to participation and dialogue, and engagement with violent extremists is a means to open the space for limiting, moderating, and ultimately containing violence. However, in this case, there is the militant organization using terrorism tactics, and then there is a sovereign state utilizing its armed forces with disproportionate levels of violence against a civilian population for collective punishment to eradicate an existing militant group. This war in Gaza is causing an unimaginable amount of suffering to a civilian population that does not have a representative government body to protect their security and represent their survival interests. The Israeli and Palestinian leadership, including Hamas, will ultimately come to a moment when engagement is inevitable, so why not do it early and save all of those lives, including innocent civilian bystanders. There will be a day when each party will find their defunct souls to move themselves away from being prisoners of confrontation and inflicting violence upon the other to realizing that they must work with fundamental peacebuilding concepts of *when* and *how* to engage with each other.

Reflecting upon the Israel-Gaza war, both sides are in the conflict to win, and any attempts at a conciliatory policy toward engagement undermine the commitment to that effort. However, another causality exists in this battle to save face: the global community of nations' inability and impotence to deter, mitigate, reduce, and produce effective interventions for a ceasefire to permit humanitarian, medical, and sheltering assistance for the civilian population. We are witnessing a state as a legally responsible organization and as a member of the international community of nations, purposely directing the bombing of civilian communities, religious centers, schools, hospitals, journalists, media outlets, prisons, UN relief institutions, schools, philanthropic organization centers, and so on. The global community of nations, the European Union; the United States; the US Agency for International Development; the Department for International Development; the African Union; the North Atlantic Treaty Organization; the Organization of Islamic Conference; the Association of Southeast Asian Nations; the Organization for Security and Co-operation in Europe; Brazil, Russia, India, China, and South Africa; the Group of Twenty; and other reputable alliances have illustrated complete incompetence to exert influence to reduce the bombing of civilians, and these multilateral organizations, and others, will be historically evaluated as associated, complicit, and having a duplicitous role in the war. This war reveals the fault lines of commitment and power in the field of conflict resolution, and there needs to be a new model, a new reimagining of ways to resolve conflict and build peace in a fragmented, polarized, divisive world.

Glossary of Terms

capacity building: a process whereby people, organizations, and society as a whole are enabled to strengthen, create, improve, adapt, and maintain their abilities to manage their affairs through training, mentoring, networks, technology, infrastructure, and organizational structure.

civil society: collective term for nongovernmental, mostly nonprofit groups that help their society while working to advance their own or others' well-being. It may include educational, trade, labor, civic, charitable, religious, media, cultural, recreational, and advocacy groups.

conciliation: the process by which a third party or parties attempt to help disputants define the facts of a dispute and reach an agreement on the trade-offs needed to resolve it.

conflict: an inevitable aspect of human interaction, often understood when two or more individuals or groups pursue mutually incompatible goals. Conflicts can be waged violently or nonviolently.

conflict analysis: the systematic study of conflict; provides a structured inquiry into the causes and possible outcomes of a conflict to understand better how to address it.

conflict management: efforts to limit and contain conflicts, particularly violent ones, while building up the capacities of all parties involved to undertake peacebuilding.

conflict prevention: measures taken to keep disputes from escalating into violence or to limit the spread of violence if it occurs.

conflict resolution: efforts to address the underlying causes of a conflict by finding common interests and grander goals. These include fostering trust through reconciliation initiatives and strengthening institutions and processes through which the parties engage one another.

conflict transformation: emphasis on addressing structural roots of conflict by changing existing patterns of behavior and fostering a culture of nonviolent approaches.

dialogue: an exchange of ideas or conversation that seeks mutual understanding through the sharing of perspectives; requires mutual listening, but allows insight into another group's beliefs, feelings, interests, history, needs, and concerns.

evaluation: systematic collection and analysis of data on a project to understand, assess, and monitor the project's process and effect.

human rights: basic rights and freedoms to which all humans are entitled. Established by several international conventions and treatises, such as the UN Universal Declaration of Human Rights in 1948, rights include the right to life, liberty, education, equality before the law, association, belief, free speech, and religion.

jus ad bellum: Latin, justice to war; the set of criteria used before engaging in war or determining the factors to justify a war.

jus in bello: Latin, the law of war; setting the limits of acceptable wartime conduct.

just war theory: the belief that the use of force is acceptable only if it meets certain standards: right authority, cause, right intention, last resort, proportional means, and reasonable prospects of success.

mediation: a mode of negotiation in which a mutually acceptable third party helps the parties to a conflict find a solution they cannot find by themselves.

negotiation: communication and bargaining between parties seeking to arrive at a mutually accepted outcome on shared issues.

nonviolent action: action usually used by a group of people to persuade someone else to change their behavior or thinking. Examples are strikes, boycotts, marches, and hunger strikes.

peacebuilding: originally used in reference to post-conflict recovery efforts, now more broadly includes providing humanitarian relief, protecting human rights, ensuring security, fostering nonviolent modes of resolving conflicts, fostering reconciliation, providing economic reconstruction, resettling refugees or internally displaced persons, and providing trauma healing services.

peacemaking: activities to halt ongoing conflicts and bring hostile parties to an agreement or find common ground to suspend violent conflict.

problem solving workshop: an informal, usually confidential workshop that brings together adversaries to reevaluate their attitudes and think creatively about joint solutions.

reconciliation: the long-term process by which the parties to a violent conflict build trust, learn to live cooperatively, and create stable peace; may include judicial processes, dialogue, admissions of guilt, or truth commissions.

reframing: to view a problem from a new perspective to find ways to reduce tensions or break a deadlock. It is a process to redefine a situation or a conflict in a new way based on input from other people.

training: processes of helping practitioners acquire and improve skills to be more effective in their roles. Usually, within the context of a conflict, training may be a form of indirect third-party intervention; it tends to be short term and focuses on specific enhanced skills.

NON-ENGLISH TERMS

adl: justice (*adalah*); wisdom or acting justly.
afdal: meritorious or of high honor.
afu: forgiveness; one of the highest virtues to be followed.
ahkam: legal injunctions.
ahsan: the most grand, for example, divine power or beauty.
ahsan al-nizam: the best of all systems.
ahsan taqwim: the most beautiful (see Qur'an 95:4).
akhlaq: ethics or principles of ethics; the way a person lives according to the principles of ethics.
al-birr: the struggle of the human soul to do good and transcend its subliminal desires.
al-du'a huwa al 'ibada: the idea that supplicatory prayers should be considered as a type of worship.
al-fasad: corruption and the decline of goodness.
al-ghayah al-khayriyyah: the ultimate good.
al-jandar: gender.
al-jihad fi sabil Allah: literally, "in the struggle for God."
al-muhaddithun: scholars who are specialists in the sayings and customs of the Prophet.

al-'ulum al-naqliyyah: the transmitted religious sciences.
amal: the actions of an individual or group; service.
aman: giving safe conduct.
amanah: the responsibility that comes with trust.
aml-e-salih: good deeds; good actions of a person.
aqidah: basic creeds and doctrines of the faith.
aql: the use of reasoning and rational discourse.
asbab al-nuzul: the specific "occasion of the revelation"; the context of a revealed verse to the Prophet.
at-tasawwuf kulluhu adab: literally, "all of Sufism is about *adab* or etiquette."
ausul-ad-din: principles of religion.
da'irat al-wujud: the great chain of being.
dar al-sulh: the land of agreed peace.
da'wah: the sharing of faith via missionary activities.
dayah: traditional religious school in Indonesia.
dhimmi: legal status of non-Muslim minorities, especially members of the Jewish and Christian communities.
fada'il al-jihad: "the virtues of armed combat"; a genre of literature defending the use of violence.
fada'il al-sabr: literally, "the excellences or virtues of patience"; a genre of literature expanding on virtues of patience and nonviolence.
fadilah: practices of virtues.
faqr: spiritual poverty; the mystical notion of complete dependence on the divine.
fard 'ayni: legal concepts denoting individual obligations, for example, prayer, fasting, charity.
fard kifa'i: the legal concept of community obligations to support orphanages, hospitals, schools, etc.
fatwa: legal decision rendered by an Islamic legal scholar; a qualified jurist who can make decisions of a general religious nature.
fiqh: an area within Islamic law that deals with jurisprudence, directly dependent on the Qur'an and *sunnah*, and rulings evolved with jurist decisions.
fi sabil Allah: literally, "in the cause of God" or "in the path of God."
fitna: referring to schism, deep differences, and secessionist ideas that may cause anarchy or chaos.
fitrah: innate human nature, instinct, primordial nature, insight. Islamic theology argues that human beings are born with an innate knowledge of

tawhid (oneness of the divine) to use with other attributes, such as virtues and intelligence.
fujur: wickedness; debauchery.
fuqaha (**sing.** *faqih*): experts in Islamic jurisprudence.
habl min allah: God-to-human relations.
habl min al-nas: human-to-human relations.
hadd (**pl.** *hudud*): offenses and their punishments specifically defined in the Qur'an, for example, drinking of wine, theft, robbery, impropriety.
hadith: collected sayings of the Prophet Muhammad; the Prophet's sayings, actions, and tacit approvals. The collection of *hadith* is the second most important source for Islamic teachings, after the Qur'an.
hawa: individual passions; impulsiveness to satisfy egotistical desires.
hikmah: wisdom stemming from mastering philosophy, theology, mysticism, and the religious sciences.
hirabah: to become angry and enraged.
harb: war or enemy.
hifdh al-hurma: the idea of upholding sacredness, where the individual understands what God holds as sacred and is committed to finding what is holy to preserve.
hubb (*muhabbah*): pure love.
hudna: a truce or ceasefire, usually temporary, in conflict.
hudur al-qalb: within the Islamic contemplative tradition, an understanding that the spiritual seeker's heart needs to be completely present.
husn al-khidma: the call for service, or the perfecting of service to others.
ihsan: doing beautifully or making beautiful; benevolence. Faithful Muslims believe their deeds should be done in as if the divine is present.
ikhtilaf: agreement to allow differing opinions on any given subject.
'ilm: field of knowledge, research, developing and acquiring knowledge; usually associated with higher insight.
iman: faith or belief; creedal statements of belief are in the one divine, the angels, the revealed books, the prophets, and the hereafter, all fundamental to Islamic theology.
irjaf: to bring commotion to society by violence and chaos; see also *rajafa*, *rajafat al-ard rajafa*: to quake or tremble; *rajafat al-ard*: the shaking of the earth.
islah: reform.

istihsan: a particular juristic preference. Jurists may use this option to express their preference for a particular judgment in Islamic law over other possibilities.

Istihsan: one of the principles of legal thought underlying personal interpretation methods.

jahada: one who is striving or in the act of the effort.

jalal: the awe-inspiring majesty of the divine.

jamal: the beauty of the divine.

jihad: exerting efforts according to the essential ethical principles of Islamic teachings.

jihad al-'aql: the use of intellectual efforts to bring forth a higher understanding of a subject.

jizya: originally, a poll tax on non-Muslim minorities.

kalam: field of Islamic theology based on dialectical theology and rational investigation.

kalam al-awa'il: attributing or invoking the opinions and views of previous scholars.

kamal: perfection of the divine.

khalifat Allah fi'l-ard (*khilafah*): man as God's vice-regent on earth.

khayr: to do good acts.

khayr mahd: pure goodness.

khutbah: the sermon of a preacher.

kufr: ungrateful or covering of truth; a general term applied to unbelief or infidelity.

la dhanb lahu: one without sin; stated when someone has passed away.

ma'rifah: knowledge; insight into divine essence.

madhab: a school of jurisprudence. There are four schools of jurisprudence in Sunni Islam: Hanafi, Hanbali, Malaki, and Shafi'i. The majority of Shi'ite Muslims follow the Jafari school of law.

mahabbah: spiritual love encountered in divine majesty.

maklumats: official decrees, issued by military authorities in Indonesia.

ma siwa' Allah: all that is other than God; parsing the theological distinction between divine and nondivine.

maslaha: the common good, a key principal objective in *shari'a*.

masqasid al-shari'ah: the overall teachings and aims of Islamic law, as established by the classical jurists.

mihnah: a general reference to an inquisition.

mudarat: peaceful and calm manner in dealing with others.

mushahadat al-wajh: literally, "witnessing the divine face."
muezzin: person who recites the call for prayer.
mufassirin: Quranic commentators.
muhabat: love.
muhsin: one who does good deeds, which makes something appear beautiful.
mujahid (pl. *mujahidun*): literally, "one who exerts himself"; those who participate in *jihad*, as both an inward and outward struggle for the realization of religious goals.
munkar: something disliked, that which is clearly wrong and incorrect.
murjifun: to make a commotion toward someone else.
muruwwat: to act generously toward others.
musta'min: those who are providing safe shelter and protection to refugees or displaced persons.
nafs: the self or soul; has many interpretations, but usually accepted as the human self that lies between the spirit (*ruh*) and the body (*jism*); the element of the human being that needs constant attention and reform.
nufudh al-azma: the spiritual prescription for individuals to be resilient and persistent.
pencerahan akal: Indonesian for "empowering the mind," "being a critical thinker."
pesantren: modern Islamic boarding schools in Indonesia.
qanun: laws promulgated by Muslim sovereigns, for example, Persian Qajar rulers or Ottoman rulers.
qat' al-tariq: literally, "breaking the road"; Quranic reference to individuals who brutally murdered innocent travelers during the time of the Prophet.
Qawwali: devotional music attributed to the Sufi Islamic tradition.
qudrah: omnipotence.
rahiba: literally, "fear of God," associated with inner wisdom.
rahma: the mercy of the divine; compassion; spirit (*ruh*), referring to the divine breath blown into Adam's body to take human form. The part of the human body is not part of this world but connecting the human to the divine.
sabr: patience.
sadaqah: voluntary charity, a category within almsgiving.
sidq al-tawajuh: the importance of the Sufi spiritual seeker to have a sincere commitment to the mystical path.
salah: prescribed ritualistic prayers; also, a term for goodness.
salam: peace.
shahada: testimonial creed of a Muslim believer.

shahid: martyr; honorific title for not only those who pass away in a struggle but also those who die prematurely or die in terrible circumstances.
shahwa: human passions and desires.
sharr: the discourse on evil; theodicy.
shari'a: Islamic law.
shukr al-ni'ma: having a deep sense of gratitude and appreciation of gifts in life given by the divine.
shura: the process of consulting others or seeking advice from others.
sirat al-mustaqim: the right path.
sulh: peace, peacemaking, and reconciliation.
sulha: the process of reconciliation between conflicting parties.
sun': the creations of individuals; what man makes.
sunnah: the general customs of the Prophet Muhammad that Muslims incorporate into their lives.
tadarru': requesting humble petitions in supplications.
tafsir: commentary on the Qur'an.
tahkim: use of arbitration to resolve differences.
tajalli ad-dhat: literally, "God's essence being manifested to a spiritual aspirant."
tajdid: renewal or reformist efforts within religious thought.
takfir: in Islamic law, the act of calling other Muslims nonbelievers or apostates because of violations of the principles of faith.
tanzih: transcendence toward divine grace.
taqwa: consciousness of the divine in the moment.
tashbih: closeness of the divine to all creation.
taslim: surrendering the self to the will of the divine.
tawadu: Islamic theological concepts on piety.
tawhid: pure monotheism; the oneness of the divine.
ta'wil: inner meanings and interpretations of the Qur'an.
thawab: rewards or blessings to be received in the hereafter.
'ulama: trained religious scholars in the field of Islamic theology, law, philosophy, history, and related fields.
ulum al-awa'il: generally, the ancient wisdom and intellectual work of Greek philosophy.
ulum 'aqliyyah: the pursuit of intellect studies.
ulum naqliyyah: scholars heavily trained in the texts of Islam, who then transmit their knowledge based on this training.

uluw al-himma: a notion in Sufism that a person believes life has meaning with transcendence.

ummah: the community of believers; originally, all those who believed in a monotheistic tradition, but transformed by Muslim jurists to mean the larger Islamic community.

ummah wasatah: the middle community, referring to Quranic and *hadith* sources that a balanced and middle path is the best way.

uswah hasanah: the Prophet as the perfect example to follow.

waqi: formulating an opinion according to the appropriate context of a group.

wasatah: the process of mediation for conflicting parties.

yakeen: faith.

yawm al-mithaq: dignity of a human being.

zakat: obligatory alms for the poor, one of the five pillars of Islam.

zamil: a type of poetry.

zulm: oppression and clear injustice to a person, group, or society.

Bibliography

Abbas, Hassan. *Pakistan's Drift into Extremism: Allah, then Army, and America's War Terror* (Armonk, NY: M.E. Sharpe, 2004).
Abu-Nimer, Mohammed. *Non-violence and Peacebuilding in Islam* (Gainesville: University Press of Florida, 2003).
———. *Making Peace with Faith: The Challenge of Religion and Peacebuilding*. Edited with Michelle Garred (Lanham, MD: Rowman & Littlefield, 2018).
Adams, David. "Toward a Global Movement for a Culture of Peace." *Peace and Conflict: Journal of Peace Psychology*, 2000, 6(3): 259–66.
Afsaruddin, Asma. "Recovering the Early Semantic Purview of Jihad and Martyrdom: Challenging Statist-Military Perspectives," in Qamar-ul Huda (ed.), *Crescent and Dove: Peace and Conflict Resolution in Islam* (Washington, DC: USIP Press, 2010), pp. 39–51.
Ahearn, Steve. "Educational Planning for an Ecological Future," in Betty Reardon and E. Nordland (eds.), *Learning Peace: The Promise of Ecological and Cooperative Education* (Albany, NY: State University of New York Press, 1994).
Ahmad, Mumtaz, and Matthew Nelson. *Islamic Education in Bangladesh and Pakistan* (Seattle: National Bureau of Asian Research, 2010).
Akhtar, Shabbir. *The Final Imperative: An Islamic Theology of Liberation* (London: Pellew, 1991).
Alavi, Hamza. "Pakistan and Islam: Ethnicity and Ideology," in Fred Halliday and Hamza Alavi (eds.), *State and Ideology in the Middle East and Pakistan* (Monthly Review Press, 1991).
Ali, Saleem. *Islamic Education and Conflict* (New Delhi: Oxford University Press, 2009).
Allen, J.R. Amr, D.L. Byman, V. Felbab-Brown, et al. "Empowered Decentralization: A City-based strategy for rebuilding Libya." The Brookings Institution, Washington, DC. 2019.
Amnon, Shiloah. "The Role and Nature of Music in the Practice of the Sama." International Musicological Society, Report of the Twelfth Congress, Berkeley, 1977.
Andani, Khalil. "Review of What Is Islam? The Importance of Being Islamic." *Islam and Christian-Muslim Relations*, 2017, 28(1): 114–17.
Andrabi, Tahir, Jishnu Das, Asim Ijaz Khwaja, and Tristan Zajonc. "Madrassa Metrics: The Statistics and Rhetoric of Religious Enrollment in Pakistan." Unpublished paper. 2008.
Asad, Talal. *Genealogies of Religion: Discipline and Reasons of Power in Christianity and Islam* (Baltimore, MD: Johns Hopkins University Press, 1993).

Avruch, Kevin. *Culture and Conflict Resolution* (Washington, DC: US Institute of Peace Press, 1998).

Ayoub, Mahmoud. *Redemptive Suffering in Islam: A Study of the Devotional Aspects of Ashura in Twelver Shi'ism* (The Hague: Mouton, 1978).

Azmah, Nadhir. *Miraj wa-Ramz al-Sufi* (Beirut: Dar al-Bahith, 1973).

Bajoria, Jayshree. *Pakistan's New Generation of Terrorists* (New York: Council of Foreign Relations, 2010).

Ball, Nicole, and Tammy Halevy. "Making Peace Work: The Role of the International Developmental Community." Policy Essay 18, Overseas Development Council, Washington, DC, 1996.

Bassiouni, M. Cherif (ed.). *Libya: From Repression to Revolution: A Record of Armed Conflict and International Law Violations, 2011–2013* (Leiden: Martinus Nijhoff Publishers, 2013).

Bekoe, Dorina. *Implementing Peace Agreements: Lessons from Mozambique, Angola, and Liberia* (New York: Palgrave Macmillan, 2008).

Bennett, William. *The Book of Virtues: A Treasury of Great Moral Stories* (New York: Simon Schuster Press, 1993).

Berdal, Mats, and Achim Wennmann. *Ending Wars, Consolidating Peace: Economic Perspectives* (London: International Institute for Strategic Studies, 2010).

Bergen, Peter, and Swati Pandey. "The Madrassah Scapegoat." *Washington Quarterly*, 2006, 29(2): 117–25.

Berrigan, Daniel, and Robert Coles. *Geography of Faith: Conversations Between Daniel Berrigan and Robert Coles* (Boston: Beacon Press 1971).

Bigelow, Anna. "What Is Islam? A Celebration and Defense of Contradiction, Perplexity, and Paradox." *Marginalia*, August 2016, 24.

Black, Peter, Joseph Scimecca, and Kevin Avruch. *Conflict Resolution: Cross-Cultural Perspectives* (New York: Greenwood Press, 1991).

Bowers, C. A. *Education, Cultural Myths, and the Ecological Crisis* (Albany, NY: SUNY Press, 1993).

Boyden, Jo, and Paul Ryder. *The Provision of Education to Children Affected by Armed Conflict* (Oxford: Refugee Studies Centre, 1996).

Brocke-Utne, Beth. *Educating for Peace: A Feminist Perspective* (New York: Pergamon Press, 1985).

Brookfield, S. *Teaching for Critical Thinking: Tools and Techniques to Help Students Question Their Assumptions* (San Francisco, CA: Jossey-Bass, 2012).

Brown, J., M. D'Emidio-Caston, and Bonnie Benard. *Resilience Education* (Thousand Oaks, CA: Corwin Press, 2001).

Brueggemann, Walter. *The Prophetic Imagination* (Minneapolis, MN: Fortress, 2001).

Buckland, Peter. *Reshaping the Future: Education and Postconflict Reconstruction* (Washington, DC: World Bank, 2005).

Bukhari, Muhammad ibn Isma'il. *Sahih al-Bukhari*, nine volumes (Chicago: Kazi Publications, 1979).

Burki, Shahid Javed, and Craig Baxter. *Pakistan Under the Military: Eleven Years of Zia-ul Haq* (Boulder, CO: Westview, 1991).

Burstyn, Joan, et al. *Preventing Violence in Schools: A Challenge to American Democracy* (Mahwah, NJ: Lawrence Erlbaum Associates, 2001).

Burton, John. *Conflict: Resolution and Prevention* (New York: St. Martin's Press, 1990).

Cahen, Claude. "Notes sur l'historiographie dans la Communauté Musulmane Idéale," in *Revue des études Islamiques* 1977, 13: 81–88.
Candland, Christopher. "Religious Education and Violence in Pakistan," in Charles H. Kennedy and Cynthia Botteron (eds.), *Pakistan 2005* (Oxford: Oxford University Press, 2006), pp. 230–55.
Casella, Ronnie. *Being Down: Challenging Violence in Urban Schools* (New York: Teachers College Press, 2001).
Chishti, Amatullah Armstrong. *The Lamp of Love: Journeying with the Sabri Brothers* (Karachi: Oxford University Press, 2006).
Chittick, William. *Science of the Cosmos, Science of the Soul* (Albany: SUNY Press, 1995).
Chodkiewicz, Michael. "The Futuhat Makkiyya and Its Commentators: Some Unresolved Enigmas." The *Muhyiddin Ibn Arabi Society Journal*, n.d.
Choudhury, M. L. R. "Music in Islam." *Journal of the Asiatic Society*, 1957, 13(2): 54–61.
Cissna, Kenneth, and Rob Anderson. "Theorizing about Dialogic Moments: The Buber-Rogers Position and Postmodern Themes," in *Communication Theory*, 1998, 8: 63–104.
Clark, Lee Anna. "Assessment and Diagnosis of Personality Disorder: Perennial Issues and an Emerging Reconceptualization." *Annual Review of Psychology*, 2007, 58: 227–57.
Cohen, Elizabeth. *Designing Groupwork Strategies for the Heterogeneous Classroom*, second edition (New York: Teachers College Press, 1994).
Coleman, Peter, and Morton Deutsch. "Introducing Cooperation and Conflict Resolution in Schools: A Systems Approach," in D. Christie, R. Wagner, and David Winter (eds.), *Peace, Conflict, and Violence: Peace Psychology for the 21st Century* (Upper Saddle River, NJ: Prentice-Hall, 2001), pp. 223–39.
Collins, John, and Michael Fishbane (eds.). *Death, Ecstasy, and Other Worldly Journeys* (Albany: SUNY Press, 1995).
Cooke, David, and Christine Michie. "Refining the Construct of Psychopath: Towards a Hierarchical Model." *Psychological Assessment*, 2001, 13(2): 171–88.
Cornell, Vincent. *The Way of Abu Madyan* (Cambridge: The Islamic Texts Society, 1996).
———. *Realm of the Saint: Power and Authority in Moroccan Sufism* (Austin: University of Texas Press, 1998).
Cragg, Kenneth. "Taddabur al-Quran: Readings and Meaning," in A. H. Green (ed.), *In Quest of an Islamic Humanism* (Cairo, Egypt: University in Cairo Press, 1986), pg. 181–95.
Cramer, Christopher. "Trajectories of Accumulation through War and Peace," in R. Paris and T.G. Sisk (eds.), *The Dilemmas of Statebuilding: Confronting the Contradictions of Post-War Peace Operations* (London: Routledge, 2009), pp. 129–48.
Crandall, John. "Music and Peace: Thoughts on Musician as Peacemaker." *Music Therapy*, 2002, 8(1): 122–25.
Crelinsten, Ronald. *Counter-terrorism* (Cambridge: Polity Press, 2009).
Cremin, Peadar (ed.). *Education for Peace* (Educational Studies Association of Ireland, 1993).
Daftary, Farhad (ed.). *Intellectual Traditions of Islam* (London: I.B. Tauris, 2001).
Danner, Victor. *The Book of Wisdom* (Mahwah, NJ: Classics of Western Spirituality Paulist Press, 1978).
Dayton, B.W., and Louis Kreisberg (eds.). *Conflict Transformation and Peacebuilding: Moving from Violence to Sustainable Peace* (London: Routledge, 2009).
Diamond, Louise, and John McDonald. *Multi-track Diplomacy: A Systems Approach to Peace*, third edition (West Hartford, CT: Kumarian Press, 1996).
Donner, Fred. "The Sources of Islamic Conceptions of War," in John Kelsay and James Turner Johnson (eds.), *Just War and Jihad: Historical and Theoretical Perspectives on War and Peace in Western and Islamic Traditions* (New York: Greenwood Press, 1991).

Doostdar, Alireza. "Review of Shahab Ahmed, What Is Islam? The Importance of Being Islamic." *Shi'i Studies Review*, 2017, 1: 277–82.
Durkee, A. *The School of the Shadhdhuliyyah* (Malaysia: The Other Press, 2005).
Einzman, Harald. *Ziarat und Pir-e Muridi* (Stutgart: Franz Steiner Verlag, 1988).
Esack, Farid. *Quran, Liberation, & Pluralism: An Islamic Perspective of Interreligious Solidarity against Oppression* (Oxford: England: Oneworld Publications, 1997).
Etzkorn, Peter. "On Music, Social Structure and Sociology." *International Review of the Aesthetics and Sociology of Music*, 1974, 5(1): 43–49.
Fair, Christine. *The Madrassah Challenge: Militancy and Religious Education in Pakistan* (Washington, DC: US Institute of Peace Press, 2008).
Feldman, Noah. "An Extraordinary Scholar Redefined Islam." *Bloomberg Opinion*, September 20, 2015.
Firestone, Reuven. *Jihad: The Origin of Holy War in Islam* (New York: Oxford University Press, 1999).
Fisher, Ronald. "The Potential for Peacebuilding. Forging a Bridge from Peacekeeping to Peacebuilding." *Peace and Change*, 1993, 18(2): 247–66.
Fountain, Susan. *Peace Education in UNICEF*. United Nations Working Paper, June 1999.
Frankl, Viktor. *Man's Search of Meaning* (Boston: Beacon Press, 2006).
Gadamer, Hans-Georg. *Truth and Method* (New York: Bloomsbury Academic, 1960).
Galtung, Johan. *Peace by Peaceful Means. Peace and Conflict, Development and Civilization* (London: Sage Publications, 1996).
Gambetta, Diego, and Steffen Hertog. "Engineers of Jihad." University of Oxford Sociology Working Paper 2007–2010.
Gartner, Scott Sigmund, and Jacob Bercovitch. "Overcoming Obstacles to Peace: The Contribution of Mediation to Short-lived Conflict Settlements." *International Studies Quarterly*, 2006, 40(4): 819–40.
Geoffroy, E. (ed.). *Une voie soufie dans le monde: La Shadhiliyya* (Paris: Maisonneuve & Larose, 2005).
Graff, Corrine. "Poverty, Development and Violent Extremism in Weak States," in Susan Rice, Corrine Graff. and Carlos Pascual (eds.). *Confronting Poverty: Weak States and National Security* (Washington, DC: Brookings Institution Press, 2010), pp. 42–89.
Graham, William. *Beyond the Written Word in Early Islam: A Reconsideration of the Sources. with Special Reference to the Divine Saying or Hadith al-Qudsi* (The Hague: Mouton, 1977).
Gribetz, Arthur. "The Sama' Controversy: Sufi vs. Legalist." *Studia Islamica*, 1991, 74: 43–62.
Griffiths, A., and C. Barnes (eds.). *Powers of Persuasion: Incentives, Sanctions and Conditionality in Peacemaking* (London: Conciliation Resources, 2008), pp. 9–14.
Guyer, Paul, and Allen Wood (eds.). *The Cambridge Edition of the Works of Immanuel Kant in English Translation*, sixteen volumes (Cambridge: Cambridge University Press, 1992).
Haeri, Muneera. *The Chishtis: A Living Light* (Karachi: Oxford University Press, 2000).
Harbom, Lotta, and Peter Wallensteen. "Armed Conflicts, 1946–2009." *Journal of Peace Research*, 2010, 472(4): 501–9.
Hare, Robert. *Manual for the Revised Psychopathy Checklist*, second edition (Toronto, Canada: Multi-Health Systems, 2003).
Hare, Stephen. "The Paradox of Moral Humility." *American Philosophical Quarterly*, 1996, 33(2): 235–41.
Harfiya, Abdel Halecm, Oliver Ramsbotham, Saba Risaluddin, and Brian Wicker, eds. *The Crescent and the Cross: Muslim and Christian Approaches to War and Peace* (New York: St. Martin's Press, 1998).

Harris, Ian. "Types of Peace Education," in A. Raviv, L. Oppenheimer, and D. Bar-Tal (eds.), *How Children Understand War and Peace* (San Francisco: Jossey-Bass, 1999), pp. 299–318.

Hasani, Hashim Ma'ruf. *Sirat al-Mustafa, Nazrat Jadidah* (Beirut: Dar al-Qalam, 1975).

Hashimi, Arshi Saleem. "Use of Religion in Violent Conflicts by Authoritarian Regimes: Pakistan and Malaysia in Comparative Perspective." *Journal of South Asia and Middle Eastern Studies*, 2007, 30(4): 22–49.

Heater, David. *Peace through Education* (London: Falmer Press, 1984).

Helmick, Raymond, and Rodney Peterson. *Forgiveness and Reconciliation: Religion, Public Policy, and Conflict Transformation* (Philadelphia, PA: Templeton Foundation, 2001).

Hicks, David. "Understanding the Field," in David Hicks (ed.), *Education for Peace: Issues, Principles, and Practice in the Classroom* (London: Routledge, 1988), pp. 3–19.

Hirtenstein, Stephen. *Patterns of Contemplation* (Oxford: Anqa Publishing, 2021).

Hoewe, Jennifer, and Brian Bowe. "The Impact of Online Network Diversity on Familiarity and Engagement with Social Issues News on Facebook." *The Journal of Social Media in Society* 2018, 12(1): 309–47.

Huda, Qamar-ul et al. *Nusrat! Live at Meany, and A Voice from Heaven*, directed by Giuseppe Asaro (1999).

———. "Anatomy in the Quran," in *Encyclopedia of the Quran* (Leiden: Brill Publications, 2001).

———. *Striving toward Divine Union: Spiritual Exercises for the Suhrawardi Sufis* (London: Routledge Press, 2003).

——— (ed.). *Crescent and Dove: Peace and Conflict Resolution in Islam* (Washington, DC: US Institute of Peace Press, 2010).

———. *Islam mein qiyam aman aur hal-e tanaza't* (*Peacebuilding and Conflict resolution in Islam: A Textbook for Teachers and Students*), second edition (Islamabad: Peace Education Research Institute, 2014).

———. *A Peace Education Curriculum for the Ministry of Education* (Hashemite Kingdom of Jordan, 2014).

Humai, Jalaluddin. *Tasawwuf dar Islam* (Tehran: Sazmani-Wira, 1983).

Human Security Report Project. *Human Security Brief 2007* (Vancouver: Simon Fraser University, 2007), pg. 35.

Humphreys, Stephen. *Islamic History: A Framework for Inquiry* (Princeton: Princeton University Press, 1991).

Husin, Asna. "Islamic Peace Education: Changing Hearts and Minds," in Qamar-ul Huda (ed.), *Crescent and Dove: Peace and Conflict Resolution in Islam* (Washington, DC: US Institute of Peace Press, 2010), pp. 151–78.

Hussein, Zahid. *Frontline Pakistan: The Struggle with Militant Islam* (New York: Columbia University Press, 2007).

Hutchinson, Frank. "Young People's Hopes and Fears for the Future," in David Hicks and Richard Slaughter (eds.), *World Yearbook of Education: Futures Education* (London: Kogan Page, 1988), pp. 133–47.

Ibn 'Arabi, Muhyi al-din. *Risalat al-Anwar* (Cairo: Maktabat 'Alam al-Fikr, 1982).

Imran, Sayyid (ed.). *Sulami, Tasfir al-Sulami wa huwa haqa'iq al tafsir* (Beirut: Dar al-Kutub al-'Ilmiyya, 2001), 2: 212.

Imtiaz, Sameena. *Aman ki Janin Pehla Qadam in Urdu* (Islamabad: Aman Publishers, 2004, second edition 2010).

——— and Javaid William. *Living Together: Value Education Manual, Module 1* (Islamabad: PEAD, 2007).

International Crisis Group. "Pakistan: Madrasas, Extremism, and the Military." ICG Report 36. International Crisis Group, Brussels, 2002.
Irving, Miles. "The Shrine of Baba Farid at Pakpattan," in Zulfiqar Ahmed (ed.), *Notes on Punjab and Mughal India: Selections from the Journal of the Punjab Historical Society* (Lahore: Sang-e-Meel Publications, 1988), pg. 55.
al-Iskandari, Ibn 'Ata Allah. *The Key to Salvation: A Sufi Manual of Invocation*, translated by Mary Ann Koury-Danner (Portland: International Specialized Book Services, 1996).
Izutsu, Toshihiko. "Ethico-Religious Concepts in the Quran," in Bruce Lincoln, *Death, War, and Sacrifice* (Chicago: University of Chicago Press, 1991).
Jannafi, Ayatullah Ahmad. "Defense and Jihad in the Quran." *Al-Tawhid*, 1984: 39–54.
al-Jilani, 'Abd al-Qadir. *Ghunya* (Damascus: Maktabat al-Ilm al-Hadith, 2001).
Johnson, James Turner. *The Quest for Peace: Three Moral Traditions in Western Cultural History* (Princeton: Princeton University Press, 1987).
Juergensmeyer, Mark. *Terror in the Mind of God: The Global Rise of Religious Violence* (Berkeley: University of California Press, 2001).
Kalin, Ibrahim. "Islam and Peace: A Survey of the Sources of Peace in the Islamic Tradition." *Islamic Studies*, 2005, 44(3): 327–62.
Kapleau, Philip (ed.). *The Three Pillars of Zen: Teaching, Practice, and Enlightenment* (Milwaukee, WI: Anchor Press, 1989).
Kathir, Imad al-Din Ismail Ibn. *Tafsiral Qur'an al-Azim* (Riyadh: Dar al-Salaam, 2000).
Kelman, Herbert. "Interactive Problem-Solving: A Social-Psychological Approach to Conflict Resolution," in John Burton and Frank Dukes (eds.), *Conflict: Readings in Management and Resolution* (New York: St. Martin's Press, 1990).
Khalil, Atif. *Repentance and the Return to God: Tawba in Early Sufism* (Albany: SUNY Press, 2018).
———. "Sufism and Qur'anic Ethics," in Lloyd Ridgeon (ed.), *The Routledge Handbook on Sufism* (London: Routledge, 2021), pp. 159–71.
Khan, Zia Inayat (ed.). *A Pearl in Wine: The Life, Music and Sufism of Hazrat Inayat Khan* (New Lebanon, NY: Omega Press, 2001).
al-Kharkushi. *Tahdhib al-Asrar*, edited by Sayyid Muḥammad 'Alī (Beirut: Dar al-Kutub al-'Ilmiyya, 2006).
Khashim, Ali Fahmi. *Zarruq, The Sufi: A Guide in the Way and a Leader to the Truth: A Biographical and Critical Study of a Mystic from North Africa* (Outline Series of Books, 1976).
Khol, Herbert. *Growing Minds: On Becoming a Teacher* (New York: HarperCollins Publishers, 1984).
Kreuz, Joakim. "How and When Armed Conflicts End: Introducing the UCDP Conflict Termination Dataset." *Journal of Peace Research*, 2010, 47(2): 243–50.
Krippner, S., and T. M. McIntyre (eds.). *The Psychological Impact of War Trauma on Civilians: An International Perspective* (Westport, CT: Praeger, 2003).
Kugle, Scott. *Rebel Between Spirit and Law: Ahmad Zarruq, Sainthood, and Authority in Islam* (Bloomington: Indiana University Press, 2006).
Lawrence, Bruce, and Carl Ernst. *Sufi Martyrs of Love: The Chishti Order in South Asia and Beyond* (New York: Palgrave, 2002).
Lederach, John Paul. *Preparing for Peace: Conflict Transformation Across Cultures* (Syracuse: Syracuse University Press, 1995).
———. *Building Peace: Sustainable Reconciliation in Divided Societies* (Washington, DC: US Institute of Peace, 1997).
Lewis, P. *Pirs, Shrines, and Pakistani Islam* (Rawalpindi: Christian Study Centre, 1985).
Lincoln, Bruce. *Death, War, and Sacrifice* (Chicago: University of Chicago Press, 1991).

Lochhead, Judy, and Joseph Auner (eds.). *Postmodern Music/Postmodern Thought: Studies in Contemporary Music and Culture* (London: Routledge, 2002).
Lumsden, Malvern. "Breaking the Cycle of Violence: Three Zones of Social Reconstruction," in Ho Won Jeong (ed.), *The New Agenda for Peace Research* (Brookfield, VT: Ashgate, 1999).
Luttwak, Edward. "Give War a Chance." *Foreign Affairs*, 1999, 78(4): 36–44.
MacFarlane, Neil, and Yuen Foong Khong. *Human Security and the UN: A Critical History* (Indianapolis: Indiana University Press, 2006).
Mahmood, S. "Modern Power and the Reconfiguration of Religious Traditions." *Stanford Electronic Humanities Review*, 1996, 5: 1.
Mahmud, Abd al-Halim, and Mahmud b. Sharif (eds.). *Al-Risala al-Qushayri* (Damascus: Dar al-Farfur, 2002).
Malik, Jamal. "The Luminous Nurani: Charisma and Political Mobilization among the Barelwis in Pakistan," in Pnina Werbner (ed.), *Person, Myth and Society in South Asian Islam* (Social Analysis, 1990), pp. 22–43.
al-Makki, Abu Ṭalib. *Qūt al-Qulūb*, edited by Maḥmud Ibrahim Muḥammad al-Ridwani (Cairo: Dar al-Turath, 2005).
Marshall, Monty G., and Benjamin R. Cole. *State Fragility Index and Matrix* (Vienna, VA: Global Report, 2014).
Mason, Herbert, trans. *The Passion of Husain Ibn Mansur Hallaj*, four volumes (Princeton, NJ: Princeton University Press, 1982).
Massignon, Louis. *La Passion de Husa.vn Ibn Mansur Hallaj* (Paris: Paul Geuthner, 1922).
Metcalf, Barbara. *Islamic Revival in British India: Deoband 1860–1900* (Princeton: Princeton University Press, 1982).
Mian, Ali Altaf. "Shahab Ahmed's Contradictions: A Critical Engagement with What Is Islam?" *Der Islam*, 2020, 97(1): 233–96.
Mian, Aziz. "Jannat Mujhe Mile Na Mile and Hi Kam-Bakt Tu Ne Pe He Nahi." Songs published by EMI Records, Islamabad, 1999.
Mian, Zia, and Iftikhar Ahmad. *Making Enemies, Creating Conflict: Pakistan's Crises of State and Society* (Lahore: Mashal Books, 1997).
Minow, Martha. *Between Vengeance and Forgiveness: Facing History after Genocide and Mass Violence* (Boston: Beacon Press, 1998).
Motzki, Harald (ed.). *The Biography of Muhammad: The Issue of the Sources* (Leiden: Brill, 2000).
Abd al-Muttalib, Rifa't Fawzi. *Ahadith al-Isra wa al-Miraj* (Cairo: Maktab al-Khaniji, 1980).
Nasr, Seyyid Hossein. *Ideals and Realities of Islam* (London: Allen & Unwin, 1965).
Nasr, Vali. "Military Rule, Islamism and Democracy in Pakistan." *The Middle East Journal*, 2004, 58(2): 195–209.
National Commission on Terrorist Attacks Upon the United States. *The 9/11 Commission Report* (Washington, DC: 9/11 Commission, 2004).
Nayyar, Adam. *Origin and History of the Qawwali* (Islamabad: Lok Virsa Research Centre, 1988).
Nelson, Mathew J. "Muslims, Markets, and the Meaning of a 'Good' Education in Pakistan." *Asian Survey*, 2006, 46(5): 690–720.
Nemiah, John C. "The Psychodynamic Basis of Psychopathology," in Armand M. Nicholi, Jr. (ed.), *The Harvard Guide to Psychiatry* (Cambridge, MA: Harvard University Press, 1999), pp. 203–19.
Netton, Ian Richard. "The Breath of Felicity: Adab, Ahwal, Maqamat and Abu Najib al-Suhrawardi," in Leonard Lewisohn (ed.), *The Heritage of Sufism* (London: Khaniqahi Nimatullahi Publications, 1993), pp. 457–82.

Niebuhr, R. *Man and Immoral Society: A Study in Ethics and Society* (New York: Westminster John Knox Press, 2010).

Nurbakhsh, Javed. "The Rules and Manners of the Khanaqah," in *The Tavern of Ruin* (New York: Khaniqahi Nimatullahi Publications, 1975).

Nusrat Fateh Ali Khan's Mei Jana Jogi de Naal, Tum ek Gorarhdanda ho, Kali Kali Zulfon ke Phande Na Dalo songs with EMI Records and Oriental Star Agencies, Islamabad, 1990, 1995.

Orfali, Bilal, and Atif Khalil (eds.). *Mysticism and Ethics in Islam* (Beirut: American University of Beirut Press, 2022).

Padwick, Constance. *Muslim Devotions: A Study of Prayer-Manuals in Common* (Oxford: England: Oneworld Publications 1960).

Papagianni, Katia. "Mediation, Political Engagement, and Peacebuilding." *Global Governance*, 2010, 16(2): 243–63.

Peace Education Program project. *Kuricukulum Aqidah Akhlaq dalam Konteks Pendidikan Dami* (*Islamic Faith and Ethics Curriculum in the Context of Peace Education*), two volumes. Aceh, 2005.

Perroux, Jean-Louis Romanet. "Human Trafficking, Smuggling and Governance in Libya: Implications for Stability and Programming." USAID and NORC at the University of Chicago, May 2020.

Peters, F. E. *The Hajj: The Muslim Pilgrimage to Mecca and Holy Places* (Princeton: Princeton University Press, 1994).

Philipon, Alix. "Sunnis Against Sunnis. The Politicization of Doctrinal Fractures in Pakistan." *The Muslim World*, 2011, 101(1): 347–68.

Philippines Council of Islam and Democracy. *The Islamic Model for Peace Education* (Manila, 2009).

Pilisuk, Maryam. "The Hidden Structure of Contemporary Violence. Peace and Conflict." *Journal of Peace Psychology*, 1998, 4: 197–216.

Powers, Harold. "The Structure of Musical Meaning, A View from Banaras (A Metamodel for Milton)." *Perspectives of New Music*, 1977, 14(2): 308–34.

Prothrow-Stith, David. *Deadly Consequences* (New York: HarperCollins, 1991).

Pruitt, Dean, and Jeffrey Rubin. *Social Conflict: Escalation, Stalemate, and Settlement* (New York: McGraw-Hill, 1986).

Qadiri, Muhammad Din Kalim, Halaat wa Rifaat Data Ganj Bakhsh, and Seyyed Hossein Nasr. *Sufi Essays*, second edition (Albany: SUNY Press, 1991).

Qureshi, Regula. "Musical Sound and Contextual Input: A Performance Model for Musical Analysis." *Ethnomusicology*, 1987, 31(1): 56–86.

Al-Qurtubi, *Tafsir al-Qurtubi* (Beirut: Dar al-Kutub al-'Ilmiyya, 2004); Muhammad bin Jarir al-Tabari, *Jami' al-bayan 'an tafsir al-Qur'an* (Beirut: Dar al-Ma'rifa, 1992), 25:30–31.

al-Qushayri, 'Abd al-Karim ibn Hawazin. *Kitab al-Mi"raj* (Cairo: Dar al-Kutub al Hadithah, 1964).

Rahman, Fazlur. *Major Themes of the Qur'an* (Minneapolis: Bibliotheca Islamica 1989).

Rahman, Tariq. *Denizens of Alien Worlds: A Study of Education, Inequality, and Polarization in Pakistan* (New York: Oxford University Press, 2005).

———. "Reasons for Rage: Reflections on the Education System of Pakistan with Special Reference to English," in Robert M. Hathaway (ed.), *Education Reform in Pakistan: Building for a Future* (Washington, DC: Woodrow Wilson International Center for Scholars, 2005), pp. 87–106.

———. "The Madrassahs: The Potential for Violence in Pakistan." 2005.

Ramsbotham, Oliver. "The Analysis of Protracted Social Conflict: A Tribute to Edward Azar." *Review of International Studies*, 2005, 31(01): 109–11.
al-Razi, Fakhr al-Din. *al-Tafsir al-Kabir* (Beirut: Dar al-Kutub al-'Ilmiyya, 1990).
Reardon, Betty (ed.). *Educating for Global Responsibility: Teacher-Designed Curricula for Peace Education, K-12* (New York: Teachers College Press, 1988).
———. *Comprehensive Peace Education: Educating for Global Responsibility* (New York: Teachers College Press, 1988).
———. "Human Rights as Education for Peace," in G. J. Andreapoulos and R. P. Claude (eds.), *Human Rights Education for the Twenty-First Century* (Philadelphia: University of Pennsylvania Press, 1997), pp. 21–34.
Reetz, Dietrich. *Migrants, Mujahidin, Madrassa Students: The Diversity of Transnational Islam in Pakistan* (Seattle: The National Bureau of Asian Research, April 2009).
Reilly, Robert. *The Closing of the Muslim Mind: How Intellectual Suicide Created the Modern Islamist* (Intercollegiate Studies Institute, May 17, 2010).
Reinhart, Kevin. *Before Revelation: The Boundaries of Moral Thought* (Albany: SUNY Press, 1995).
Reno, W. "Bottom-Up Statebuilding?" in Charles Call with Vanessa Wyeth (eds.), *Building States to Build Peace* (Boulder: Lynne Reiner, 2008), pp. 143–62.
Richards, Norvin. "Is Humility a Virtue?" *American Philosophical Quarterly*, 1998, 25(3): 253–59.
Ritter, Hellmut. *The Ocean of the Soul: Men, the World and God in the Stories of Farid al-Din 'Attar*, translated by John O'Kane (Leiden: Brill, 2003).
Robinson, Alan, and Alan Smith. *Education for Mutual Understanding: Perceptions and Policy* (University of Ulster: Centre for the Study of Conflict, 1992).
Robinson, Francis. *Ulama of Farangi Mahall and Islamic Culture in South Asia* (London: Orient Longman, 2001).
Rogers, Carl. *Counseling and Psychotherapy: Newer Concepts in Practice* (New York: Houghton Mifflin. 1942).
Romberg, Thomas, and Thomas Carpenter (eds.). *An Integration of Research* (New York: Routledge Press, 1993).
Ruckert, George. *Music in North India: Experiencing Music, Expressing Culture* (New York: Oxford University Press, 2003).
Sabri Brothers. "Meri Koi Nahin hai" (There is no one else), *Greatest Hits of Sabri Brothers*, volumes 1 to 3 (Sirocco: United Kingdom, 1994).
Sageman, Marc. *Understanding Terror Networks* (Philadelphia: University of Pennsylvania Press, 2004).
Sakkata, Lorraine. "The Sacred and the Profane: Qawwali Represented in the Performances of Nusrat Fateh Ali Khan." *The World of Music*, 1994, 36(3): 86–99.
Salomon, Greg. "The Nature of Peace education: Not All Programs Are Created Equal," in G. Salomon and B. Nevo (eds.), *Peace Education: The Concepts, Principles, and Practices Worldwide* (Mahwah, NJ: Lawrence Erlbaum Associates, 2002).
Sandole, Dennis. "A Comprehensive Mapping of Conflict and Conflict Resolution Research: A Three Pillar Approach." *Peace and Conflict Studies*, 1998, 5(2): 1–30.
Sandy, Stephen. "Conflict Resolution in Schools." *Conflict Resolution Quarterly*, 2001, 19(2): 237–50.
Sanyaee Development Organization. *Peace Education Training Manual for Teachers*. Volume 1 (Kabul: Sanyaee Development Organization , 2000).

Sanyal, Usha. *Ahmed Riza Khan Barelwi: In the Path of the Prophet* (Oxford: Oneworld Publications, 2005).
Sartre, Jean-Paul. *Imagination; A Psychological Critique* (Ann Arbor: University of Michigan Press, 1962).
Satha-Anand, C. "The Nonviolent Crescent: Eight Theses on Muslim Nonviolent Actions," in Glenn D. Paige, Chaiway Satha-Anand, and Sarah Gilliatt (eds.), *Islam and Nonviolence* (Manoa, HI: Spark Matsunga Institute for Peace, 1986).
Schimmel, Annemarie. "Some Aspects of Mystical Prayer in Islam." *Die Welt des Islams*, 1952, 2(2): 112–25.
———. *Mystical Dimensions of Islam* (Chapel Hill: University of North Carolina Press, 1975).
Schoeler, Gregro. *Charakter und Authentie der muslimischen Überlieferung über das Leben Muhammeds* (Berlin, 1996).
Schubel, Vernon James. *Religious Performance in Contemporary Islam: Shi'i Devotional Rituals in South Asia* (Columbia: University of South Carolina, 1993).
Seanor, Douglas (ed.). *Hare and Critics: Essays on Moral Thinking* (Oxford: Clarendon Press, 1998).
Seitz, Klaus. *Education and Conflict: The Role of Education in the Creation, Prevention and Resolution of Societal Crises-Consequences for Development Cooperation* (Eschoborn: Deutsche Gesellschaft fur Technische Zusammenarbeit, 2004).
Sen, Amartya. *Identity and Violence: The Illusion of Destiny* (London: Penguin Books, 2006).
al-Shawkani, Muhammad b. *'Ali Fath al-Qadir* (Damascus: Dar Ibn Kathir, 1998).
Shelton, Dinah (ed.). *The Encyclopedia of Genocide and Crimes against Humanity* (Detroit: Macmillan Reference, 2004).
Siddique, Omer. *The Illumination on Abandoning Self-Direction, Al Tanwir fi Isqat al-Tadbir* (Sydney, Australia: Dhikr Publications, 2022).
Silver, Brian. "The Adab of Musicians," in Barbara Metcalf (ed.), *Moral Conduct and Authority* (Berkeley: University of California Press, 1984), pp. 318–20.
Slotoroff, C. "Drumming Technique for Assertiveness and Anger Management in the Short-term Psychiatric Setting for Adult and Adolescent Survivors of Trauma." *Music Therapy Perspectives*, 1994, 12(2): 111–16.
Smith, A., and A. Robinson. *Education for Mutual Understanding: Perceptions and Policy* (Coleraine: University of Ulster Centre for the Study of Conflict, 1992).
Smith, Alan, and Tony Vau. *Education, Conflict and International Development* (London: DFID, 2005).
Smith, R., and S. Deely. *Insider Mediators in Africa: Understanding the Contribution of Insider Mediators to the Peaceful Resolution of Conflicts in Africa. Summary Report of Phase 1* (Prangins: PeaceNexus Foundation, 2010).
Stedman, Stephen. "Spoiler Problems in Peace Processes." *International Security*, 1997, 22(2): 5–53.
Sterling, Stephen, and John Huckle. *Education for Sustainability* (London: Routledge Press, 2014).
Stern, Jessica. "Pakistan's Jihad Culture." *Foreign Affairs*, 2000, 79(6): 115–26.
Stokes, Martin. "Voices and Places: History, Repetition, and the Musical Imagination." *The Journal of the Royal Anthropological Institute*, 1995, 3: 673–91.
al-Suhrawardi, 'Abu Hafs 'Umar. *'Awarif al-Ma'rif* (Cairo: Maktabat al-Qahira, 1973).
Sulami, Tafsir al-Sulami wa huwa haqa'iq al-tafsir (ed.). *Sayyid Imran* (Beirut: Dar al-Kutub al-'Ilmiyya, 2001).

Sutton, J. P. (ed.). *Music, Music Therapy and Trauma: International Perspectives* (Philadelphia, PA: Jessica Kingsley Publishers, 2002).
Suzuki, Shunryu. *Zen Mind, Beginner's Mind* (New York: Weatherhill Press, 1979).
al-Ṭabarī, Abū Khalaf. *The Comfort of the Mystics: A Manual and Anthology of Early Sufism* (Salwat al-'Arifin), edited by Gerhard Böwering and Bilal Orfali (Leiden: Brill, 2013).
Teitel, Ruti G. *Transitional Justice* (Oxford: Oxford University Press, 2002).
Tellis, Ashley J. "Bad Company—Lashkar-e-Tayyiba and the Growing Ambition of Islamist Militancy in Pakistan." Carnegie Endowment for International Peace, Washington, DC, 2010.
Toft, Monica Duffy. *Securing the Peace: The Durable Settlement of Civil War* (Princeton: Princeton University Press, 2010), pg. 151.
Trauthig, Inga Kristina. "The Current Situation in Libya and Its Implications for the Terrorism Threat in Europe." Paper presented at the third conference of the European Counter Terrorism Centre Advisory Network on Terrorism and Propaganda. Europol's headquarters in The Hague, April 9–10, 2019.
Troll, Christian (ed.). *Muslim Shrines in India: Their Character, History, and Significance* (New Delhi: Oxford University Press, 1989).
Turner, Victor. "The Centre Out There: Pilgrim's Goal." *History of Religions*, 1973, 12: 191–230.
UN Development Programme. *Annual Report 2008 of the Bureau for Crisis Prevention and Recovery* (New York: UN Development Programme, 2009).
———. *Preventing and Reducing Armed Violence: What Works?* (New York: UN Development Programme and the Ministry of Foreign Affairs of Norway, 2010), pg. 16.
Verhagen, Frank. "The Earth Community School (ECS) Model of Secondary Education: Contributing to Sustainable Societies and Thriving Civilizations." *Social Alternatives: Peace Education for a New Century*, 2002, 21 (1): 17.
Vuckovic, Brooke Olson. *Heavenly Journeys, Earthly Concerns: The Legacy of the Miraj in the Formation of Islam* (London: Routledge, 2005).
Walter, B.F. "The Critical Barrier to Civil War Settlement." *International Organization*, 1997, 51(3): 335–64.
Waseem, Mohammed. "Dilemmas of Pride and Pain: Sectarian Conflict and Conflict transformation in Pakistan," Working Paper 48, University of Birmingham, 2010.
———. "Sectarian Conflict in Pakistan," in K.M. de Silva (ed.), *Conflict and Violence in South Asia: Bangladesh, India, Pakistan and Sri Lanka* (Kandy: International Ethnic Studies Centre, 2000).
Wasti, Hasan. "Hazrat Shaykh-ul Shayukh wa 'Awarif al-Ma'arif," in Shah Owais Sohrawardi (ed.), *Suhrawardi Silsila Risala*, volume 3 (Lahore: Sohrawardi Foundation, 1989), pp. 5–22.
Weber, Max. *The Protestant Ethic and the Spirit of Capitalism* (London: Unwin Hyman, 1992).
Weeks, Dudley. *The Eight Essential Steps to Conflict Resolution: Preserving Relationships at Work, at Home, and in the Community* (New York: Tarcher/Putnam, 1992).
Wehrey, Frederic, and A. Alrababa'h. "Rising out of Chaos: The Islamic State in Libya." Syria in Crisis. Carnegie Endowment for International Peace 5, 2015.
Wensinck, A. J. *Concordance et Indices de la Tradition Musulmane*, eight volumes (Leiden: Brill, 1936–1969).
Whitfield, T. *External Actors in Mediation: Dilemmas and Options for Mediators* (Geneva: Centre for Humanitarian Dialogue, 2010).
Whyte, John, *Interpreting Northern Ireland* (Oxford: Clarendon Press, 1991).

Wildman, W.J. *Religious Philosophy as Multidisciplinary Comparative Inquiry: Envisioning a Future for the Philosophy of Religion* (Albany, NY: SUNY Press, 2010).

Williams, K. *The Pure Intention: On Knowledge of the Unique Name* (Cambridge: The Islamic Texts Society, 2018).

Winthrop, Rebecca, and Corrine Graff. *Beyond Madrasas: Assessing the Links between Education and Militancy in Pakistan* (Washington, DC: Brookings Institution Press, 2010).

Yazaki, S. "Morality in Early Sufi Literature," in Lloyd Ridgeon (ed.), *The Cambridge Companion to Sufism* (Cambridge: Cambridge University Press, 2015), pp. 74–97.

Al-Zamakhshari, Al-Kashshaaf 'an Haqa'iq at-Tanzil. (Riyadh: Maktabat al-'Abikan, 1998).

Zaman, Muhammad Qasim. *The Ulama in Contemporary Islam: Custodians of Change* (Princeton: Princeton University Press, 2007).

———. "Sectarianism in Pakistan," in Ian Talbot (ed.), *The Deadly Embrace: Religion, Violence, and Politics in India and Pakistan, 1947–2002* (Karachi: Oxford University Press, 2007).

Zargar, Cyrus. *The Polished Mirror: Storytelling and the Pursuit of Virtue in Islamic Philosophy and Sufism* (London: Oneworld Academic, 2017).

Zarradi, Fakhr uddin. *Risalat Usul as-Sama, Jhajjar*, in Bruce Lawrence, "Early Chishti Approach to Sama," *Islamic Society and Culture: Essays in Honour of Professor Aziz Ahmad, Manohar*, edited by M. Israel and N. K. Wagle (New Delhi: Manohar Publishers, 1983).

Zelin, Aaron Y. "ICSR Insight: Up to 11,000 Foreign Fighters in Syria; Steep Rise among Western Europeans," International Centre for the Study of Radicalisation, "King's College London, December 17, 2013.

———. "The Others: Foreign Fighters in Libya." The Washington Institute for Near East Policy, 2018.

Zelizer, Craig. "The Role of Artistic Processes in Peacebuilding in Bosnia-Herzegovina." *Peace & Conflict Studies*, 2003, 10(2): 62–75.

Index

Abi Talib, Ali ibn, 259
Abu-Nimer, Mohammed, 119, 124, 237
Abduh, Muhammad, 244
Abdullah, Abdullah, 15
Abadi, Houda, 63
adab (proper moral conduct), 146–47, 254; *adab* theology, 148–49
Afghan Communist Party, 138
Afghan National Party, 138
Afghan Socialist Party, 138
Afghani, Jamal ad-din, 244
Afghanistan War Commission, 14
Ahl al-Bayt Institute for Islamic Thought, 172
Ahl-e Hadith, 82, 83, 84, 86, 93
Ahl-e Sunnat wa-l Jama'at (ASJ), 83–84
Ahmed, Akbar, 122
Akhund, Mullah Mohammad Hassan, 15
Akhundzada, Mawlawi Haibatullah, 15, 18
Al-Ghannouchi, Rashid, 244
All Parties Hurriyat Conference, 111
All-Pakistan Muhajir Students Organization, 80, 83
Allen, Chris, 5
Amman Message, 108
Amnesty International, 46
American Anthropological Association, 30
Amiri, Rina, 18
Anderson, Mary B., 276
Ansari, Khwaja Abdullah, 240
Anti-Apartheid Movement in South Africa, 243

Appleby, Scott, 103, 106
Asad, Talal, 49
Asia Foundation, 139, 140
Aurelius, Marcus, 40
Awliya, Shaykh Nizam ad-Din, 252
Ayaz, Fareed, 260
Azar, Edward, 81

Baathism, 244
Badri, Hedayatullah, 16
Baluchistan Liberation Army, 54
Bangladesh, 7, 85, 130, 209, 211–12
Bartoli, Andrea, 106
Barelwi, 82–87, 91, 93, 97n26, 217
Battar Brigade, 56
Bayat, Asef, 123
Beck, Ulrich, 46
Berrigan, Daniel, 235
Beydoun, Khaled, 5
Bhutto, Benazir, 91
al-Bishri, Tariq, 244
Boko Haram, 62
Bowe, Brian, 48
Brockman, John, 24
Brookfield, Stephen, 39
Brookings Institution Saban Center for Middle East Policy, 32
Brookings Project on US Policy Towards the Islamic World, 32; Brookings-Islamic World Project, 32
Bouley, Robert D., 29
Burton, John, 127

305

Carr, James, 5
China-Pakistan Economic Corridor (CPEC), 18
Chisht order (Chishtiyya), 23, 85, 105, 235, 252, 268n18; Chishti, Khwaja Moin ud-din, 23
Chittick, William, 231
Christian evangelicalism, 34; proselytizing Muslims, relations with Islam, 34
Community of Sant 'Egido, 118n1
conflict, 28, 35, 36, 46, 62, 78, 88–90, 115, 131, 137, 174, 196, 200, 240, 260, 280; conflict resolution process, 35, 45, 88, 91, 239, 273; evolving types of, 47, 52, 61–62, 73; identity-based, 80–82; mitigation, 28, 31, 38, 81, 88, 90, 91, 132–34, 141, 280; Muslim-majority countries, 86, 88, 89, 105, 115, 116, 136–38, 141, 142, 208, 209–11, 277; organizations or activities by NGOs, 38, 45, 90, 105, 128, 135, 137, 141, 142, 276, 277; prevention of, 68, 89–91, 117, 128, 133, 136, 140, 179–82; post-conflict, 28; researchers and the field of, 30, 48, 52, 62, 90, 124–27, 135, 136, 204, 281; resolution studies and training, 195–203, 204, 217, 218, 263; in religious texts, 69–73, 76, 78, 17; violent extremism, 52, 60–61, 67
cosmopolitanism, 47–48
countering violent extremism (CVE), 52; CVE strategies, 63–64; CVE, security sector, and law enforcement, 64; trust deficit between government and community, 64; neglect of female leaders, 64
Cole, Juan, 123
Coptic Orthodox Church, 20, 124
critical thinking, 38
cultural idealism, 36

Dars-e Nizami curriculum, 217, 218, 219, 221
al-Darqawi, 152
Data Ganj Bakhsh, al-Hujwiri, 248, 255
Deobandi, 14

Eastern Orthodox Churches, 124
El-Affendi, Abdelwahab, 32
Edhi, Maulana Abdul Sattar, 233, 234, 235

Edhi, Bilquis, 233, 234, 235
empathy, 40, 81, 133, 195, 218, 240
Esposito, John, 122
ethics, 221–29, 230–31; applied ethics, 8, 228; ethics of forgiveness and resilience, 240–42; ethical moral education, 227, 229; ethics training, 227, 228, 229
Evans, Craig A., 34

fasad, 73, 74, 170
Fondacaro, Steve, 30
forgiveness, 2, 104, 132, 152, 154, 174, 183n10, 211, 215, 221, 239, 240–41, 258, 259, 270n35, 276
Frankl, Viktor, 156
Frances, Diana, 27
Fisher, Helen, 23
Fox, Matthew, 237–38
Fuchs, Simon Wolfgang, 129
Funk, Nathan, 124, 127, 240

Gadamer, Hans-Georg, 230
Gaddafi, Muammar, 55
Galtung, John, 26
Geelani, Syed Ali Shah, 111–13
Geisler, Norman, 34
Ghana, 90
al-Ghazali, Abu Hamid Muhammad ibn Muhammad, 6, 73, 150, 153, 155, 170, 215
Global Terrorism Index, 53
Global War on Terror (2001–2021), 27, 52
Green, Nile, 123
Greenberg, Melanie, 35

hadith, 69, 135, 154–55, 157, 158, 171, 215, 217, 232. *See also Ahl-e Hadith*
hajj ritual, 78
Hanif, Din Mohammad, 16
Hare, Robert, 81
Harari, Yuval Noah, 229
Hamas, 9, 244, 279, 280
ul-Haq, Zia, 91
Haqqani Taliban faction, 14
Haqqani, Sirajuddin, 15
Haqqani, Khalil, 15
Harkat-ul-Jihad-al-Islami, 87
Hellenistic schools of philosophy, 40

Hinduism, 2, 15, 78, 85, 124, 235
Hindustani music, 255–69
Hizbul Momineen, 87
Hizbullah in Lebanon, 87
Hoewe, Jennifer, 48
Hoskins, Edward, 33
Houssney, George, 34
human free will, 73, 170
human error, 73, 170
Human Security Report Project, 8
Human Terrain Systems (HTS), 29
Humanity United (HU), 34; HU Peacebuilding Strategy, 35
Hussain, Rashad, 20

Ibn 'Arabi, Muhyiddin, 42, 72, 73, 150
identity, 67; cultural identity, 68–69; and violence, 67–71; individual, 68; global world, 68; moral identity, 229; reasoning and rational decision-making, 68; religious identity, 68–70
Ignatius of Loyola, 150
infanticide, 77
Imtiaz, Nadia, 110
Imtiaz, Sameena, 210, 223n12
Indonesia, 7, 130, 136, 171, 207, 209, 222n1
inner ethical systems, 68
Inter-Services Intelligence (ISI), 83, 85, 87
International Centre for the Study of Radicalisation (ICSR), 56
International Security Assistance Forces (ISAF), 29
International Sociological Association, 48–49
irfan, 41
Islam: Democracy in Islam, 244, 245; global Islam, 122–24; Islamic piety (*tawadu*), 71; Islamic theology, 69–71, 72–74, 75, 149, 168, 175, 237; Islamic reasoning, 68–69; Islamization policies, 79
Islamists, 67, 123, 244, 245
Islamism, 5, 33, 50, 51, 97n26, 232
Islamophobia, 5, 31, 48, 279
Islamic State in West Africa, 62
al-Iskandari, Ibn 'Ata Allah, 41

Jaish-e Muhammad, 86
Jamia al-Muntazir, 86

Jama'at-e Islami, 82, 83, 138
Jamia'at-e 'Ulama-e Islami, 85
Jamia'at-e Tulaba Jafria, 86
Jama'at Nusrat Al-Islam wa al-Muslimeen, 54–55
Jammu and Kashmir, 108–14; The Association of Parents of Disappeared Persons, 109; All Parties Hurriyat Conference, 111; civil society organizations, 108–14; human rights violations, 108–11; illegal detentions, 109–11; International Peoples' Tribunal on Human Rights and Justice in Indian-Administered Kashmir, 109, 111; Kashmir University in Srinagar, 110; OIC Kashmir Contact Group, 111–12; Tehreek-e Hurriyat party, 111
Judaism/Jewish, 124, 162, 163, 166, 167, 243
jihad, 34, 48, 51, 74–76, 83, 96n10, 96n12, 97n28, 207, 208, 279; non-jihadi Salafis, 50
Juergensmeyer, Mark, 80–81

Ka'ba, 78
Kakar, Palwasha, 139, 140
Kalin, Ibrahim, 237
Kalam Research Institute, 171
Kandahar Shura Council, 14
Karzai, Hamid, 15
Kashmir and Jammu, 83, 85–87, 91, 108–19
Kashmiri, Ilyas, 87
Kadayifci-Orellana, Ayse, 124, 127, 136, 240
khaddim, 257
Khan, Ustad Latafat Hussain, 261
Khan, Ustad Ramzan, 261
Khan, Nusrat Fateh Ali, 248, 255, 259
Khan, Ustad Fateh Ali, 259
Khan, Syed Ahmed, 244
Khalil, Atif, 150
khalifah, 73
Khoury, Amal, 125, 127
Kerry, John, 19
Kepel, Gilles, 33–34
Klaasen, John, 34

Lashkar-e Tayyaba (LeT), 86, 87, 92
Lederach, John Paul, 8, 232–34, 238

Lewis, Bernard, 31
Lutzer, Erwin W., 34

al-Makki, Abu Talib, 41
Mahmood, Saba, 245
Malik, Jamal, 127
Mandaville, Peter, 123
Maududi, Abu 'Ala, 33
Mazar-e-Sharif, 17
Alasdair MacIntyre, Alasdair, 230, 243
Mecca, 155, 215, 259, 260, 264, 271n48
mediation, 17, 88–90, 92–94, 105, 127, 198; training and skills, 93, 94, 218, 274; by religious mediators, 2, 103, 107, 174; Islamic concepts of, 4, 150, 162–63, 174, 180, 218
Medina, 264–67, 270n33; Constitution of Medina, 245
memory of the sacred, 248–51, 253; community, bringing social cohesion, 248, 249–51, 254; poetic, 250–52; role of intellect, 249–51
Mesler, Bill, 25
meso-level markers, 58
Mian, Aziz, 255
micro markers, 58
Mirziyoyev, Shavkat, 17
McFate, Montgomery, 30
moral actors, 229, 79, 103; authority, 258, 103; courage, 274; culture and institutions, 229; formation and character, 41, 42, 227, 229; imagination, 8, 233; imperative for healing, 236; principles, 245, 73, 105, 167; realists and romantics, 42; theology and philosophy, 148, 150, 151–52, 157–58. *See also adab*
Moosa, Ebrahim, 127
Muhajir Qaumi Mahaz (MQM), 80, 83
Muhammad, Prophet ibn Abdullah ibn Abd al-Muttalib ibn Hashim, 69, 72, 85, 95n3, 129, 161; praise songs (*na'tiya*), 248, 252, 255, 259–63, 265, 264, 266–67; peacebuilding, 214–15, 248, 264; spiritual model, 75, 147–48, 248, 266; celebration of life, 85, 255
Muttahida Qaumi Mahaz, 80
Mujahid, Zabiullah, 13

Muhammadiya party, 244
murid (Sufi disciple), 85, 105, 152, 254, 157, 176; disciples at shrine, 251–52, 256, 268n14, 269n20; practices, 147–48, 152, 155, 178; relationship with Sufi shaikh, 147–48; adhering to law (*shari'a*), 148–49, 157–58; spiritual journey, 1, 148, 152–54, 155, 157; using Sufi texts, 145, 157–58, 178
Musharraf, Pervez, 91
Muslim Brotherhood, 116
multiculturalism power, 46

Nagauri, Shaikh Hamid ad-Din, 252
National Counterterrorism Center, 53
Nalewa Mada network, Republic of Niger, 62
Naqshbandi order, 1, 23, 85, 105, 157
Nayed, Aref Ali, 156–60
nazarana, 254–56
Niebuhr, Reinhold, 243
Nozick, Robert, 151
Nurani, Shah Ahmad, 83
Nye, Joseph, 36

Office of International Religious Freedom (IRF), 20
Office of the Secretary, Religion and Global Affairs, 19
Omri, Maulvi Attallah, 16
Organisation for Economic Cooperation and Development (OECD), 27
Organization of Islamic Conference (OIC), 111, 281; OIC Kashmir Contact Group, 111
Oslo Taliban Meeting, 16

Parshall, Phil, 34
Pasban-e Islam, 87
peacebuilding: "Future of Peacebuilding Conference," 45; violent extremism (VE), 49
Perroux, Jean-Louis Romanet, 56–57
Philippine-Mindanao conflict, 90
piety, 51, 71, 74, 151, 153–54, 235, 266
pluralism, 8, 132, 133, 171, 189, 190, 199, 218, 246; challenges of, 161; imam training in, 132, 175, 180–81; interfaith

and intrafaith pluralism, 161–69, 171, 245; religious pluralism, 127, 171, 175, 176, 179, 280
Pompeo, Mike, 19
post-conflict, 17, 25, 28, 104, 112, 138, 180, 263; recovery and reconstruction, 26, 91–92, 274
preventing violent extremism (PVE), 60–62; civil society organizations and PVE, 64; community-led approaches to PVE in Morocco, 63; ex-foreign fighters of ISIS, 63; women-led programs, 62; youth-led programs, 63
proximate peacebuilders, 35
Provincial Reconstruction Teams (PRT), 29

Al-Qaeda in Islamic Maghreb (AQIM), 55
Qutb, Sayyed, 33
quadrivium, 40
Qur'an: Abraham (37:104–13), 78; care for infants, against infanticide (6:140; 81:8–9), 76, 77; conflict (17:33; 25:68), 75; corruption, (30:41), 73; disbelief (4:167), 74; does not change the condition of people (13:11), 237; exegesis, 217; glorifying God (24:1; 57:1), 72; not to kill (25:68; 6:140), 75, 77; number of prophets, 76; peace, peacebuilding (59:23), 70; struggle (29:6; 22:78), 74, 75; signs (2:164), 70; unity of the divine (4:167), 75; unjust killings (81:8–9), 77; vicegerency on earth (2:30; 33:72), 73; violence to preserve order (17:33; 25:68), 76; where soever you turn there is the face of God (2:115), 70; worship one God (12:40), 73

Rajmohan, Gandhi, 33
Ramadan, Tariq, 8, 122
Raziuddin, Munshi, 260–61, 271n44
Al-Razi, Fakhr al-Din, 153–55
Rawls, John, 5, 151
reconciliation, 1, 3, 4, 5, 8, 45, 62, 68, 105, 116, 125, 134, 136, 138, 141, 162, 219, 240, 258, 274; in peace agreements, 104, 240, 241, 262, 273, 274; interfaith relations, 167, 174, 183n10, 219; peacebuilding practices, 104, 106,
116, 131, 141, 163, 240–41, 263, 266, 267, 273; Afghanistan Reconciliation Committee, 131; Afghanistan Ministries of Religious Affairs and Reconciliation, 133; women in, 136–37, 138, 141
Reilly, Robert, 33
Report of the United Nations Working Group on Lessons Learned of the Peacebuilding Commission, 25
Roedel, Chad, 34
Roex, Ineke, 51
Roman Catholicism, 51, 124
Rousseau, Jean-Jacques, 42
Roy, Oliver, 122
Rumi, Jalal ud-din, 150, 155, 215; *Mathnawi-i ma'nawi*, 155
Rumsfeld, Donald, 32
Russian Orthodox Church, 20
Rustom, Mohammed, 153

Sabri Brothers Qawwal group, 248, 255, 261, 262–66; Haji Ghulam Fareed Sabri and Haji Maqbool Ahmed Sabri, 261; Ustad Haji Inayat Sen Sabri, 261
Sajjadanishin, 254, 258, 269n20
Salafism, 50; as a security threat to Europe, 51
Sahel region, 54
Said, Abdul Aziz, 124, 127
sama', sama' khana, 249, 252, 254
Schmid, Alex, 50
Schultz, Kathryn, 23
security sector reform (SSR), 28–29
Seligman, Martin, 23
Sen, Amartya, 67–69
shab-e mi'raj, 248, 260
Shadhili order, 6, 157
Shankar, Vendantam, 25
Sharif, Nawaz, 91
Shi'a 'Ulama scholars, 86–87, 129
Shi'ism (Jafari school), 86, 87, 93, 127, 129–30, 147, 217
Sikhism, 2, 235
Sipah-e Mohammed-e Pakistan, 86, 87
Sipah-e Sahaba, 84, 86, 92, 98n32
spiritual masters, 1, 6, 41–42, 145, 156–57, 248
social change, 237, 238; ethics of, 5

Socrates inquiry, 38–39
soft power, 36–37
Sri Lanka, 90, 106
Stanikzai, Sher Muhammad Abbas, 15
Stoicism, 40
suffering, 21, 68, 103, 149, 159, 191, 218, 235, 249, 271n51, 276, 279, 280; ego suffering, 159, 267; spiritual suffering, 257, 267, 271n51; understanding suffering of others, 218, 235
Sufism: Sufi orders, 80, 83, 105, 157, 268n18
al-Suhrawardi, Abu Hafs 'Umar, 41
al-din Suhrawardi, Shihab, 42
Sulaiman, Mohammed, 49
sunnah, 69, 82, 129, 157–58, 219

Taliban, 13; engagement with Taliban, 17; "globally thinking" Taliban, 16–19; Tareek-e Taliban Pakistan, 87
Tahrik-e-Nafaz-e Fiqu-e Jafrriya, 86
Tajdar-e Haram song and lyrics, 265–70
Tansen, Mian, 261
Tashkent Conference, 16, 18
tasawwuf, 1, 42, 146, 157, 252
tawhid, 74, 75, 96n13, 129; *tawhid* awareness, 75, 96n13
Taylor, Charles, 243
Tehreek-e Hurriyat Party, 111
Tibi, Bassam, 50
Tillerson, Rex, 19
Trans-Afghan-Uzbek Railway, 17

UCLA Incarcerated Youth Tutorial Program (IYTP), 236
UN Assistance Mission in Afghanistan, 20
UN Assistance Mission for Iraq, 20
UN Children's Fund, 22
UN Development Programme, 34, 36; UNDP Libya, 56–58; UNDP Sahel region of Africa, 58–59; The Bureau of Conflict Prevention and Recovery, 90
UN Foundation, 34
UN Investigative Team to Promote Accountability for Crimes Committed by ISIL, 20
UN Trust for Human Security, 28
United States Agency for International Aid (USAID), 13, 36, 52; USAID report, "Policy for Countering Violent Extremism through Development Assistance," 60; USAID report "The Development Response to Violent Extremism and Insurgency Policy," 61; USAID and US Department of State Report, "Joint Strategy on Countering Violent Extremism," 61; USAID "Somalia Youth Leadership Initiative," 61–62; USAID Office of Transition Initiatives, 62
United States Institute of Peace (USIP), 13, 34, 36
US Special Representative for Afghanistan. *See* West, Tom
Uppsala Conflict Data Project, 88, 89
Uzbek President Shavkat Mirziyoyev, 17
Uzbekistan-Afghanistan relations, 17

Vatican II, Second Vatican Council, 166–67, 169, 172, 176, 177
violence, 67–71; reasons for, 69; classical Islamic interpretations of, 69–70; reconciliation of, 68; sources for, 69; in Islamic theology, 70–75; justification for, 70–71, 73–78

Wafaq-e Shi'a Ulama-e Pakistan, 86
Weber, Max, 242
Welty, Emily, 125, 127
West, Tom: US Special Representative for Afghanistan, 14
Western peacebuilding organizations, 35
winning hearts and minds, 30–31
World Health Organization, 22
World Muslim Congress, 171
Wrongology, 23

Yaqoob, Mullah Mohammad, 15
Yazaki, Saeko, 152

zahir, 148
Zakir, Abdul Qayyum, 16
Zardari, Asif Ali, 91
Zargar, Cyrus, 152
Zarradi, Shaikh Fakhr ad-Din, 252
Zarruq, Sidi Shaykh Ahmad al-Baurnusi, 6, 150, 157–60, 276
Zelizer, Craig, 26–27

About the Author

Qamar-ul Huda is the Michael E. Paul Distinguished Visiting Professor of International Affairs at the US Naval Academy in Annapolis, Maryland. Previously, he served as an associate adjunct professor at Georgetown University's School of Government. Dr. Huda co-founded and was the Vice President of the Center for Global Policy, a nonpartisan think-tank focusing on US security and foreign policies. Dr. Huda served as a Senior Policy Advisor for the US Department of State Secretary's Office for Religion and Global Affairs, where he focused on engaging with civil society and religious communities and diplomacy with nongovernment organizations. The US State Department recruited Dr. Huda to be seconded as the first Director of the Department of Dialogue and Collaboration to Hedayah: The International Center of Excellence for Countering Violent Extremism based in Abu Dhabi, United Arab Emirates.

He worked for ten years at the US Institute of Peace headquarters in Washington, DC, a Congressional-funded national institute to reduce and prevent global conflict. Within the Department of Religion and Peacemaking, he served as a senior expert, researcher, and resident scholar of religion and global politics focused on conflict resolution, peacebuilding research, religious peacebuilding, and training for global civil society members. Dr. Huda supervised and managed the development of conflict resolution and mediation studies in schools in South Asia, Southeast Asia, and various parts of the Middle East. He served as a director of the countering violent extremism project at the US Institute of Peace, where he led a team to design, develop, and implement numerous online and in-person training courses for the US Institute of Peace's Academy of Conflict Analysis and Conflict Transformation.

At the US Naval Academy, Dr. Huda teaches courses on US diplomacy, conflict studies, conflict resolution, international peacebuilding, foreign policy, international relations, Afghanistan, Iran, South Asia, and politics of religion. He taught at University of California, Los Angeles; Boston College; Brandeis University; and the College of Holy Cross. Dr. Huda has published three books and six training manuals on conflict, mediation, and religious peacebuilding. He was a Fulbright scholar, a Social Science Research Council grant recipient, and was selected on the prestigious 500 Most Influential Muslims List from 2017 to 2024. He earned his doctorate in political history from the University of California, Los Angeles, and a Master of Arts degree from University of California, Los Angeles in Middle Eastern and Asian history. He received his Bachelor of Arts in international relations, philosophy, and religion from Colgate University.